The SUPREMES

Also by Mark Ribowsky

He's a Rebel: Phil Spector:
Rock & Roll's Legendary Producer

Don't Look Back:
Satchel Paige in the Shadows of the Game

A Complete History of the Negro Leagues:
1884–1955

Slick: The Silver and Black
Life of Al Davis

The SUPREMES

A Saga of Motown Dreams, Success, and Betrayal

MARK RIBOWSKY

DA CAPO PRESS
A Member of the Perseus Books Group

Copyright © 2009 by Mark Ribowsky

Designed by Pauline Brown
Set in 11.5 point Garamond by the Perseus Books Group

Library of Congress Cataloging-in-Publication Data
Ribowsky, Mark.
  The Supremes : the saga of Motown, dreams, success, and betrayal / Mark Ribowsky. — 1st ed.
    p. cm.
  Includes bibliographical references, discography, and index.
  ISBN 978-0-306-81586-7 (alk. paper)
  1. Supremes (Musical group) 2. Women singers—United States—Biography. I. Title.
  ML421.S86R53 2009
  782.421644092'2—dc22
  [B]

                                                              2008051422

Published by Da Capo Press
A Member of the Perseus Books Group
www.dacapopress.com

Da Capo Press books are available at special discounts for bulk purchases in the U.S. by corporations, institutions, and other organizations. For more information, please contact the Special Markets Department at the Perseus Books Group, 2300 Chestnut Street, Suite 200, Philadelphia, PA 19103, or call (800) 810-4145, ext. 5000, or e-mail special.markets@perseusbooks.com.

10 9 8 7 6 5 4 3 2 1

For my son Jake,
who makes me feel 15 again
when he tells me to
turn the music down.

Contents

Acknowledgments

An archeological expedition back through the layers of Motown history requires the help of people who can shine a light through tunnels darkened by time. This book owes its existence to many such noble souls who made the path vividly bright and easy to follow.

There could not have been a better tour guide than Shelly Berger, who, as manager of the Supremes during their peak years, provided key insights and keen perspective on the business of overseeing the top female act of the '60s. My heartfelt thanks to a real industry heavyweight who made it a lot easier for Berry Gordy to chase his dreams.

From inside the walls of the recording studio, equally invaluable were the overseers of the Supremes' craft and artistry. As an admittedly fanatical student of how the greatest music of our time was made and who helped to make it, I was blessed to be given the opportunity to sit at the figurative feet of arguably the greatest producer and songwriter of our time—Brian and Eddie Holland. Soaking up the glorious minutiae of their Supremes sessions was the seminar of a lifetime—one that they presented with humor, detail, and patience for the sometimes dumb questions I asked as a rank outsider.

The genius of that recording process was the organically collaborative effort underpinning it. As the years have lengthened, the contributions of the Motown house band—known retrospectively as the Funk Brothers—have grown from obscure to Zeusian. The pity is that a dwindling number of these artists are alive to receive the long-delayed huzzahs due them. Thus, it was with pure joy that I took up the opportunity to spend long and wonderful hours with Jack Ashford, whose championing of the Funk Brothers' role in those sessions was as spirited as the rhythm he kept with his tambourine and vibe riffs.

There is no greater rush for a rock devotee than to tap the memories of an actual Motown artist, much less one who is the sole surviving original member of the greatest male soul group of all time. My deepest appreciation goes to the Temptations' Otis Williams, a man of endless good cheer who's still kickin' it and getting younger every day.

Other Motown luminaries whose voices resonated in the '60s were kind enough to go on record again for these pages. Claudette Rogers, the still cute-as-a-button former wife and singing partner of Smokey Robinson in the Miracles, had to relive a lot of old pain and anxiety about Smokey's adulterous affair with Diana Ross, and did so with amazing grace and calm. The Marvelettes' Katherine Anderson, the Vandellas' Annette Beard and Rosalind Ashford, and the Velvelettes' Cal Street had to recount distressing memories of their groups being taunted by Ross and shoved aside by the rising Supremes, and did so with candid honesty, as they also did in behalf of the ominously troubled Florence Ballard. Representing the non-Motown universe, the Crystals' Dee Kennibrew, La La Brooks, and Barbara Alston painstakingly recalled a classic clash with Ross on a Dick Clark bus tour from hell. A nonvocalist, but one of the most wired-in of Motown muckety-mucks, songwriter and office gadfly Janie Bradford was a font of terrific anecdotes—and phone numbers; she was, in a word (and title of the legendary song she penned), "money." A multi-track thank you to all of these talented and empowered women for their aid.

A pivotal factor in Motown's success was how it tethered its records to the top-rated radio stations and disc jockeys. Thus, a particular thrill for me was shooting the breeze with one of Detroit's biggest deejays of the era, Robin Seymour, who provided uncompromising examples of how the game was played on both sides.

An absolutely essential component of this book was to find a close confidante of Florence Ballard herself; only she could channel the thoughts, secrets, and motivations she'd kept under wraps all her life. Many members of Ballard's large family have remained aloof from the media, and were never very close to her to begin with. However, it was my good fortune to come upon Flo's cousin Ray Gibson, with whom she was tighter than any blood relative other than her mother, Lurlee, and her sister, Maxine. Ray, too, was reluctant to share intimate and scaldingly painful memories, having been down that route before with insensitive, sensationalism-seeking media types. Yet once convinced that this project wanted neither dirt nor caricature but, rather, a balanced portrait of a real woman, he illuminated the dark shadow that has always been Florence Ballard, and for that I am profoundly grateful.

Being able to contact such critical, firsthand sources was a matter of knowing where to look. For guiding me to the right places, a shout-out goes to longtime Motown miners such as authors Tom Ingrassia, Randall Wilson, John Clemente, and Marc Taylor; concert promoter and rock and roll collector John Grecco; and producer Harry Weinger, the grand poobah of the exhaustive *Supremes 2000* compilation box-set (an informational gold mine in itself).

Digging into the very grooves of every Supremes hit, down to the cellular level of the Motown sound, was a labor of love perfectly suited to Allan Slutsky. An accomplished musician, conductor, and producer, this Funk Brother–by–extension—not just the guiding hand behind the magnificent movie retrospective *Standing in the Shadows of Motown* but also the author of the James Jamerson chronicle and songbook on which it was based—can probably tell Holland-Dozier-Holland a thing or two about their songs that even they don't know, and my sincere acknowledgment is extended for so enlightening these pages.

In the end, the book in your hands is a triumph not only for its author but also for a visionary who saw the need for it to be written and skillfully steered it to fruition: my agent Michael Dorr, president of the LitPub Ink literary agency.

Having benefited from this diverse cache of quality people, I can claim, with only a small stretch, to know something of how the Supremes' magic was made: by channeling the alchemy of many quality people. And anything that can make one feel like Holland-Dozier-Holland, no matter how slight, is a blessing.

There is a remarkably mordant scene in Martin Scorsese's dark-hearted 1983 comedy *King of Comedy* in which a perfectly demented Sandra Bernhard, as Masha the obsessed fan, has helped Rupert Pupkin kidnap Jerry Lewis's late-night TV host character, Jerry Langford. Meticulously mummifying Langford in a chair with masking tape, Masha, with a swelling sense of domination and horniness, coos, "Let's do something crazy tonight. Just get insane. I want to be crazy. I want to be nuts. I want some fun. I want to be black—I want to be a Supreme!" Then, violently tearing off a last piece of tape to seal Langford's mouth, she half-sneers, "I've never had this much fun before . . . good, old-fashioned, All-American fun."

The choice of the Supremes as the counterpoint of Masha's madness could not have been more inspired: For a white female baby boomer and '60s refugee, no image other than the divine Motown girl-group could better cross-breed the soul of a black woman and the fables of All-American innocence. Such is the abiding legacy that after more than forty years it still alloys Diana Ross, Mary Wilson, and Florence Ballard (whose bristled participation in and enforced heave-ho from the group at the height of its success pumps that legacy full of dramatic tension). When an act lives in the subconscious mind as the model of all that is righteous in a complicated and cruel world, we can safely call that act mythologic.

Two more things that can safely be said of the Supremes: They are the most important modern American music act after Elvis Presley, and this may well be the first real biography of them—that is, one written from the perspective of an outsider, with no personal investment in how events are told (unlike, for example, Mary Wilson's couplet of memoirs). One suspects the lack of serious literary attention has had something to do with the geology of female acts and gender-based assumptions of what is a "serious" subject matter. The female rockers who have been adjudged as such are few and far between—Janis Joplin, Tina Turner, Grace Slick, Patti Smith, Deborah Harry, then pretty much nobody—and have been dispensed with fleetingly. Meanwhile, books about Elvis, John Lennon (with and without the Beatles), Bob Dylan, Jim Morrison, and Jimi Hendrix proliferate year after year; what's more, Joplin, Turner, and Slick are hardly made of puppy dog's tails, all having renounced any claim of gender-based immunity in their work, codified by Joplin in "Piece of My Heart"—"I'm gonna show you, baby, that a woman can be tough."

So what of the Supremes, who peddled seemingly little-girl dreams with an image as wispy as gossamer? If it seems that we cannot possibly elevate them onto the same contextual historical stage as the other women, look a little more closely. In actuality, they were not that far from the Joplin model of defiant but breakable toughness: They wished they didn't have to be tough, and longed to be forever loyal, provided that guys didn't mess with their hearts. The themes of their songs—written, as only they could have been back then, by men—likewise spoke of their innards being broken into pieces. Love, Ross sang in one, was "like an itchin' in my heart, tearin' it all apart, and, baby, I can't scratch it." Joplin could have killed with a natural blues line like that. In another, having been kept hangin' on, she laid down just the right touch of sarcasm: "Set me free, why don't you babe. Get out of my life, why don't you babe." That was such a cool and universal flip-off line that the song it came from would eventually be covered by, among others, a female pop singer (Kim Wilde), a male hard-rock band (Vanilla Fudge), and a babehound (Rod Stewart).

The notion that a girl-group may not meet the level of importance necessary for a "serious" biography is, as with most sexist notions, plainly absurd. Forget about any hedge that the Supremes, who were nominated for three, didn't ever win a Grammy; you seemingly had to be Herb Alpert & the Tijuana Brass to win one of those in the '60s, while people like Phil Spector, Cream, and Sly Stone not only went without but were never even nominated. The latter-day make-good for being stiffed in the '60s—entry into the Rock and Roll Hall of Fame—came the Supremes' way in 1988, as the first girl-group to get in (to be followed by their old Motown stablemates Martha and the Vandellas in 1995, the Shirelles in 1996, and the Ronettes in 2007). Still, the old canards linger. When *Rolling Stone* compiled a "100 Greatest Artists of All-Time" list in 2004, the Supremes came in at a stinging No. 97, a diss that simply cannot be reconciled with their Hall of Fame status or with the fact that a similar list by the Hall's brahmins placed "Stop! In the Name of Love" and "You Can't Hurry Love" among the "Top 500 Songs That Shaped Rock."

In their time the Supremes rolled off twelve No. 1 singles on the Billboard Hot 100 chart, more than any other act in history except Elvis (thirty-eight), the Beatles (twenty), and Mariah Carey (also twenty). Ross-Wilson-Ballard had ten more that landed in the Top Ten, all of which have been jammed into endlessly repackaged Motown albums and have sold an estimated 20 million copies of recordings formatted in vinyl, 8-track and cassette tape, compact disc, DVD, and MP3—bringing in something like $100 million to the Motown bottom line. *A cautionary note:* These figures may or may not be reliable. Perhaps only Berry Gordy and a few of his most trusted accountants know what they truly are. And they aren't saying, not after fifty years of silence vows that explain why Motown was never granted an "official" gold or platinum record sanctioned by the Recording Industry Association of America (an outcome requiring that the RIAA have access to a record company's books) until Gordy finally relented in 1977—although the RIAA did sporadically send Gordy gold or platinum disks back in the day as a promotional sop. Not that Gordy gave a whit; he simply issued ersatz gold and platinum records for his acts. But if these estimates are right, the Supremes, who likely would have racked up four gold and two platinum records, can be considered the third most profitable act in pop music history in terms of album sales—again, save for the Beatles and Elvis, but ahead of even the Rolling Stones.

Those recordings are a musical lodestone—"Where Did Our Love Go," "Baby Love," "Come See About Me," "Stop! In the Name of Love," "You Can't Hurry Love," "Back in My Arms Again," "I Hear a Symphony," "My World Is Empty Without You," "Love Is Like an Itching in My Heart," "You Keep Me Hangin' On," "Love Is Here and Now You're Gone," "In and Out of Love," "Love Child," "I'm Gonna Make You Love Me," to name just a few—and the chain of those smash hits never got tiresome. Even the songs with similar themes, lyrics, backbeats, and hooks provided a fresh gift to the ears. Eventually, set against a more socially conscious subset, they plumbed inner-city indigence ("Love Child," "I'm Livin' in Shame"), making it possible for Diana Ross, all covered in chiffon and sequins, to wail convincingly about wearing a worn, torn dress that somebody threw out, being always second best, but vowing redemption.

The Supremes' tart three-minute melodramas, which from 1963 through 1967 blushed with Holland-Dozier-Holland's roiling arrangements and fetchingly clever lyrics, worked on the counterpoint of not being overly girly. The adolescent "yearning, burning" motif was burnished by a sweaty hybrid pop and R&B that was left to the instincts and devices of jazz cats whom Berry Gordy culled from the "black and tan" clubs along Hastings Avenue—the nuclear core of which was the rhythm section of pianist Earl Van Dyke's jazz band and grew to include James Jamerson on bass; Johnny Griffiths on piano; Benny Benjamin and Richard "Pistol" Allen on drums; Robert White, Eddie Willis, and Joe Messina on guitar; Eddie "Bongo" Brown on percussion; and Jack Ashford on vibe and tambourine. Pledging loyalty to Berry Gordy, they were paid well and noticed little by the outside world until four decades later when they were "discovered" and dubbed the "Funk Brothers" (taken from a long-ago inside joke by Benny Benjamin); their own legacy is Motown's very spinal cord, putting the lie to facile criticism that Gordy always shouldered for compromising soul appeal for sales appeal. (For confirmation of the rhythm-and-blues root of the Supremes' songs, take a listen to Lamont Dozier's slowed-down and grittified renditions of several of them on his 2004 CD *Reflections Of* on the Lightyear label.)

The Supremes' songs were buttressed by horns and at times strings, but the hub of it all was that peerless rhythm section, which both geographically and sonically fell between the more stately R&B strain coming out of Leiber and Stoller's studio sessions in New York and Phil Spector's distilled "Wall of Sound" R&B in L.A. Unfurled in Motown's cramped basement Studio A, the songs congealed into a winning formula. Across the spatial image of each song, the rhythm rocked and rumbled and the horns blew the top off while the vibes, bongo, and tambourine provided the accents. The *chink-a-chink* of a sharp, jabbing guitar lick kept in time with a pounding snare drum and a twitchy bass line. Sneaking through this great tide of rhythm, Diana Ross's little-girl trill took flight, never rushed, and was surprisingly versatile across the scale, yet always on the precipice of an emotional crack. Behind her, Wilson's sugary alto and Ballard's forceful tenor meshed in tandem, filling in the lower end of the scale. We recognize this casserole now as a magical formula; but back then, for hordes of teenage girls in particular, some probably very much like Sandra Bernhard's Masha, all anyone knew was that the songs poured like batter out of transistor radios. We couldn't wait for the newest pouring. It never took long.

The Supremes' breakneck ride was relatively brief in real time; in virtual time, it never ended. It began with three teenagers singing as a sister group for the band that would form the basis of The Temptations,

gelled in fresh-scrubbed girl-group primping, and finally went chic—
and wonderfully campy to anyone tuned into those signals—with the
pomp of flouncing gowns, gobs of mascara, and peek-a-boo-curl Sas-
soon wigs. Ross herself, of course, was the musky voice and E.T.-like
face of the trio: the supreme Supreme, the one with the "star quality,"
the lure and slink of the kitten, and the claw of the tigress. She was an
illogical and imponderable sex symbol: a quivering, writhing waif who
without the wigs and face paint appeared emaciated and vacant. Ah,
but then there was her mouth, large and open—"so inviting, so exciting," as a phrase in one of her songs would have it—and coy bedroom
eyes that put the come-hither into a line like "Come see about me."

The Diana Ross few knew outside of the Motown colony was on a fast
rise to the top from the first day she got to Motown; not incidentally,
that was also the first day she knew who she wanted to sleep with to
keep up the momentum. That, of course, turned out to be Berry
Gordy, but only after affairs with in-house tunesmiths Smokey Robinson and Brian Holland. In no time, Ross would climb beyond the
group onto the A-List as a solo act, record six more No. 1 songs, and
earn millions as well as top billing in two movies. She wears her
haught—and haute—to this day, more than two decades after *Billboard*
proclaimed her "Entertainer of the Century," with little dissent; in her
60s, she still hangs tough on the A-List, even though her most recent
CD, in 2007, rose no higher than No. 32.

     Ross in her Supremes' incarnation may have been devious, quietly
twisting the knife in the other Supremes while Gordy moved her up the
company ladder. Still, even as a pop diva of epic dimensions, Ross never
shook her identity as a Supreme, and has, in a way, been forced to bow
before it. Indeed, the power of that brand can be an awesome thing to
behold. Heavy as it is with sentimental value and immortal pop hooks,
one measure is, inevitably, the bottom line. The fact that the numbers
cited above dwarf Ross's solo sales explains why, after decades of resistance to such a thing, she re-upped as a Supreme for a proposed world
reunion tour in 2000, a beyond-lucrative project carrying a top-ticket
price of $200. However, in a splendidly ironic role reversal, it was Mary
Wilson and Cindy Birdsong who back-stabbed Ross; offered a fraction
of the $15 million reserved for Ross, the pair refused to recede into her
spotlight for a second time in their lives. Ross then tried to replace
them with two nominal Supremes of the '70s, but Supremes fans were
interested only in the original configuration of the group and the tour

was called off. Moral of the story: For all of Ross's glitz and mega-diva status, she wasn't the Supremes after all.

To be sure, Ross, ever since her inner diva took flight in the late '60s, has put forth a weird, un-Supreme-like vibe. It's not only the haught; it's the Supremes' sensible glamour turned into an excess of self-parody. Not for nothing is the protoplast of Diana Ross—bejeweled and bewitching, hair teased to the sky and emaciated loins furbished by the latest neon-lit Bob Mackie or Issey Miyake original—the beau ideal of female impersonators worldwide and of the gay and transgender fans who make up a heavy slice of Ross's audience. Among Supremes' fans, that Ross plays the diva role to the point of asking to be called "Miss Ross" or even "The Boss"—even if she does so with a wink—is cringeworthy. Not that this evolution was unexpected back at Motown; it was evident even as Ross played out the Supremes. Indeed, many among this loyal legion felt as abandoned as Wilson and Birdsong when Ross abandoned *them*, just as they blamed her for Flo Ballard's banishment, though Ross's passive role in that drama was no different than Wilson's, and she later generously footed some of Ballard's mounting debts; after Ballard's death in 1976 at age 32, which came after years of indeed "livin' in shame," destitute and back in the projects, Ross was met with catcalls by Supremes fans at the funeral.

Clearly, the Supremes' saga has produced a good many fables, a convenient, fallen dream girl in Diana Ross, and a heavy in Berry Gordy. These elements provided the grist for what is assumed to be the veiled story of the Supremes in Michael Bennett's smash 1981 Broadway musical and later movie *Dreamgirls*. The assumption is only partly right; that set piece is tenuously based on the Supremes, but Bennett was no fool, knowing such an implied association would give breath and a large profit margin to his work. In fact, the story he hatched is close enough to the truth to peg Ross's passive duplicity in the betrayal of Ballard, presumably for being too fat. But here the parallels come crashing down: The real Ballard certainly had her battles with the bulge, but the cause of her enforced exile had to do with internal, not external, factors, as she was the product of great personal tragedy. She also was never bedded by Gordy, as suggested in the Bennett revision. And, of course, she never had the last laugh on him—that would have been somewhat difficult given her early demise.

Still, it was indeed true that Ballard was nobody's lackey. The inside joke was that Ross would call Flo the "quiet one" during her on-stage patter. The reality was seen in her wan smile and sad eyes, hinting at not a "quiet one" but a seething soul, tortured by her past, by Ross's ascendance in a group Ballard had put together back in the projects, and by Gordy's overbearing rules that kept them psychologically dependent on him. Even as the Supremes became rich and lived in anything but shame on swanky Buena Vista Avenue, they needed Berry's approval to make withdrawals from their own bank accounts, a system that endured well into the '70s.

Ross, for one, may have been so stung by the uncomfortable reminders in *Dreamgirls* of her, well, compromised past that she slammed Bennett for "turn[ing] my life into a paperback novel." Her real gripe, however, may have been a lack of proper deference, since the producers—"good friends of mine," she noted—hadn't "passed it by me." Nor did she relent when the movie adaptation was released in late 2006 and was an enormous success. When the producers of the Academy Awards wanted her to sing the movie's Oscar-nominated song, she clearly relished telling them to stuff it. (By contrast, the ever-amenable Mary Wilson said she loved the musical.)

Some semblance of what was real and unreal about the Supremes could, through the years, be gleaned in various works, at best, though not in full, in Wilson's 1986 autobiography, the mandatorily titled *Dreamgirl: My Life as a Supreme*, which with good marketing sense sniped at Ross as early as page 1 and didn't let up for the remaining 248 pages. It outsold Ross's two more heralded but gratingly narcissistic and insultingly detail-free memoirs of 1993 and 2000 (yet a third arose in 2007). Ross, who can give as good as she gets, retaliated by skipping the Rock and Roll Hall of Fame ceremony in 1988 rather than share a stage with Wilson, who accepted the honor alongside one of Ballard's daughters.

To be sure, the best and most honest Supremes story could have been told by Flo Ballard. Instead, seeking the next best thing, one has had to wade through the muck and mucilage of "celebrity journalism" in place of actual journalism.

And their effect on the industry? We are talking cosmic. The Supremes, after all, took Gordy light-years beyond his original mission with Motown, which was an admirable one: to see to it that white power brokers wouldn't annex and profit from the talents of new black artists and songwriters. When the Supremes upped the ante considerably, Gordy's influence grew. His shop's stew of gospel-based R&B and white pop thrived even as the old order's pop music purveyors were drained of power. From 1964 to 1967, after which the girl-group thing was essentially over, even at Motown, Berry kept American pop music breathing with a girl-group. One that was so singular and, well, dreamlike, that Gordy didn't even bother to try keeping his other ace girl-groups, the Marvelettes and Martha and the Vandellas, in the loop. Instead, it was the male acts that benefited; the balls to the wall Supremes "sound" was easily reformatted in songs for Smokey Robinson, the Temptations, and the Four Tops. In 1966 alone, twenty-two Motown singles—an astounding 75 percent of all of its releases that year—made the charts. And while R&B purists came to prick Gordy for his post-1963 assembly line of "black bubblegum," those records formed the DNA of soul music in the '70s and beyond, spread at first by Motown expatriates like Holland-Dozier-Holland and Philly soul masters Gamble and Huff. In retrospect, Motown's real legacy—and thus the Supremes'—was something palpable in the '60s, and a prime example of music's most desirable word: "crossover."

Motown, an unstoppable force, shot the moon. With 100 No. 1 hit songs in the bank, today it is the most successful black-owned corporation in history, clocking in at around a half-trillion dollars in business at last glance. But while that makes for a heartwarming trope, it is also a fact that by 1965, Motown's ethnic agenda was just a front; behind the black singers, black sessionmen, and black dancers (before their heels were cooled for Gordy's real target audience, the supper-club bourgeoisie at venues like the Copacabana and the Las Vegas casinos), the business end of Motown was being run in the main by white showbiz lawyers and other assorted sharpies from L.A., where Gordy himself would move Motown's operations in the late '60s rather than stick it out in Detroit. There were, as well, whispers around the shop and along the meridians of the industry that the Mafia had partnered up with Gordy to get his records pressed and played on the radio and stacked in record stores.

Gordy's moral penury was a worse-kept secret. At the Motown shop, it was a given that he would pay his artists only just enough to keep them from staging an outright revolt, or bolting to other labels— an exodus he was unable to prevent later on with Ross, Lionel Richie, and Michael Jackson. Or with Holland-Dozier-Holland, who first walked, then waged years of courtroom warfare against Gordy seeking back royalties. For a long spell, Gordy was able to keep his star acts at bay by engendering a kind of Stockholm Syndrome. As his premier act, the Supremes bore the brunt of Gordy's head games—and Flo Ballard received the most vicious treatment of all, which peaked after Gordy tried to ease her out of the act and an exasperated Ballard spat out an impetuous threat to spill his "secrets." Unmoved, in 1967 he fired her and continued his psychological torture by allegedly conspiring to snuff her ill-fated solo career. Ballard took to the bottle even harder and grew increasingly desperate.

Gordy may have retroactively thought twice about her threat as it seems he discreetly eased her financial burden. But the effects of his public excommunication of Ballard are felt to this day. At the old Motown building on West Grand Boulevard, now a museum and shrine to the magic of the name, Cindy Birdsong is ever present in a slew of Supremes photos on the walls. Ballard, as if official Motown has applied an eraser to her memory, can be seen in a single tattered black-and-white shot, affixed unsteadily to the wall with a thumb tack. (Not that it matters; among Supremes courtiers Ballard has become venerated, even martyred.)

Gordy, meanwhile, who lived in monarchical splendor even as inner-city Detroit was decaying all around him, has personally reaped the whirlwind. In 1989 he cashed out of Motown for $50 million (a paltry sum at that, according to industry analysts who thought he could have done much better) and sold off half of his publishing interests—over 15,000 songs—for $132 million. Eight years later, in 1997, Holland-Dozier-Holland took a loan on their publishing rights for $60 million. Yet as much as Motown has been divided, subdivided, and ultimately absorbed by the gigantic corporate entities MCA, Polygram, and Universal, its past remains a timeless dawn, black America's own Camelot. Shuffling and reshuffling the same Motown oldies into one repackaged album after another have ensured a profit, no matter who the corporate parent might be. What to say of a conglomerate like Motown, which in its old age can license the re-release of every record it put out from 1959 through 1966, good, bad, or in between—the top of the line being the amazing six-volume, thirty-six-CD *Complete Motown Singles* remastered box-set series on Universal Music Group's custom retro label, Hip-O Select—and turn a nifty profit, despite a per-volume price of $119.99 and an Internet-only availability? Hip-O Select in fact also found success with four other Supremes remastered sets—one a previously unreleased 1965 show-tune album *There's a Place for Us*, and another a compilation of the group's post–Diana Ross '70s albums. This no doubt helps explain why most listeners would rather hear "You Can't Hurry Love" for the 800th time than, say, "Love Hangover" for the second time. (Though the best way to glean the raw force, gentle nuances, and delicate camp/fantasy balance of the group is by watching with a hard eye the 2006 DVD anthology *The Supremes: Reflections.*)

The challenge to a would-be biographer of the three original Supremes is not unlike what Holland-Dozier-Holland did inside Motown Studio A: Draw a line at that blessed point when it sounded right. Because there are three discrete orbits here, with loyalists accrued to each, one must hear out versions of the same events ranging from the truth to shadings of the truth to outright nontruths. In the matter of Florence Ballard in particular, everyone seems to have taken sides, sending vectors of conflicting claims shooting in every direction. Add to that the unenviable task of having to wade into the swamp of the celebrity journalists' renderings of the same events, along with those by countless others who came through the Supremes' glam/kitsch trough with a story to market. For example, is it possible that a latter-day Mary Wilson once performed an impromptu one-woman rendition of "Stop! In the Name of Love" for a cocaine dealer in order to score a gram or two, or that she could have snorted lines with Sammy Davis Jr. after greeting him at her dressing room door in the nude? These claims actually appeared in a real book produced by a major publisher and written by a former Supremes "go-fer," who was also briefly Wilson's manager turned professional drag queen. And while one's first impulse may be to toss off sensational grist like this—or perhaps, given the very subculture of outcasts that worships the Supremes for the strangest of reasons (remember Masha), such claims come with the territory—a complicating factor is that other claims in that book actually seem to be on solid ground.

The multiplicity of opinion about what is factual, of course, would be especially virulent if Ross and Wilson were ever to find themselves isolated in the same room and discussing events they shared. Consider that the closest they've gotten to that scenario was at the Motown 25th Anniversary TV special, when Ross grabbed the microphone from Wilson's hand and nearly stiff-armed her aside. So, while pains were taken to indeed hear out everyone in the forum, Ross and Wilson may actually be the world's worst sources about the Supremes—at least when what they say is filtered through their own prisms, which is just about all the time. The same goes for Berry Gordy. All of them have been cited through the years in their own and others' works, and the most trenchant of their recollections are noted in these pages as well. In the end, though, the line was drawn at what sounded right, aided and abetted by the rules of corroboration. A great deal of stock was also placed on my own informed opinion because, well, it's a habit by now.

Given these considerations, it's only fair to call this book an unauthorized biography, though this should not be construed as a license to contrive or dish. Much time was spent tracking down as many original sources as possible, a good many of whom had never been consulted for their knowledge of the Supremes and the Motown operation. Some voices may have gone uncovered, but not for a lack of effort to locate them. Sadly, as with any story nearly a half-century in the making, many in that category are no longer around—most grievously, nearly all of the Funk Brothers and, of course, Florence Ballard.

The very good news is that enough crucial voices came forward to justify my hope and intention that these pages will stand as an invaluable reference guide to and looking glass into the Kismet that glimmered when Motown ruled the whole world, and when the Supremes ruled Motown.

Prologue

May 19, 2007, at a diner in New York City.

Eddie Holland didn't look up from his bacon and eggs when asked: What is the Supremes' legacy?

The question surely would evoke chapter and verse from the mouthy member of the fabled Holland-Dozier-Holland team who composed and produced all but two of the Supremes' twelve No. 1 hits, and practically everything else they committed to vinyl from 1963 through 1967. Then, and now, Eddie Holland was the wordman, fashioning peppy, then darkly plaintive narratives from Lamont Dozier's conceptual keywords and his brother Brian Holland's always infectious melodies. Today, they are in their mid-sixties, still cool enough to get away with wearing jogging suits and lavender-tinted shades to business meetings, and the years have done nothing to eat the relish off Eddie Holland's tongue or pen.

Yet the question of the Supremes' legacy left Eddie oddly inert, with only the clinking of dishes—and, appropriately enough, Motown tunes playing through speakers over simmering burgers on a grill—to fill in the lull. Finally, he raised his head.

"I assume," he began, "they'll be regarded as a great vocal group."

A second lull, with discomfort, knowing he couldn't get by with just that brief throwaway remark.

"They were the greatest ever did it," he amended, before returning to his breakfast.

Was there a song he favored above all others?

"Nope. It was just music to me. Just songs that we did at the time. That's what I liked, it's what I felt. It's what we all felt. We never thought in terms of, this is going to be a No. 1. We just thought, this is going to be a hit record."

You'd think there'd be more to it than that, considering that the Supremes' potentiation of HDH's songs made both the act and the production team wealthy beyond words. Before hooking up with Ross, Wilson, and Ballard, HDH were good, reliable Motown song-meisters;

after, they existed in a kind of ether not quite of this earth. Anyone with knowledge of Motown knows their catalog includes a flow of hits roughly equal to that of the Supremes, though far fewer chart-toppers, by the likes of the Four Tops, Marvin Gaye, Martha and the Vandellas, and nearly every other headliner on the company payroll. However, HDH's eternal identification as a vestigial organ of the Supremes, while a matter of pride, is at the same time a sore spot.

As Eddie Holland put it, walking a fine line, "Yeah, we had something good going with them so we produced them—when we took the time to produce them. It wasn't like we hung around them, begging to produce them. Hell, they were the ones beggin' *us* to produce *them*."

Sensing a cue, the Holland brothers' manager, an enthusiastic woman named Shirley Washington, interjected: "Why, do you know that Holland-Dozier-Holland songs have been heard more than any other songs by any other writers in history? I got that from BMI [Broadcast Music, Inc.]."

"More than Lennon-McCartney songs?" somebody wondered.

"Did you hear me?" she said, sternly.

"If all we did was the Supremes," Eddie went on, "then why am I sitting here?" Here being a continent away from home so that HDH could collaborate on a scheduled 2008 Broadway musical version of the Oscar-nominated *The First Wives Club*, the 1996 Bette Midler-Diane Keaton-Goldie Hawn chick flick based on Olivia Goldsmith's novel of the same name. Who better to compose the score for such a vehicle than the ultimate chick-group overlords? Indeed, not only was it a coup that the show's producers landed the trio, it was a chance for HDH to be real-world, real-time relevant again after decades of dormancy, and to carve another landmark: their first venture composing for the Broadway stage. Only this kind of A-List project—which was announced as far back as 2005 and still not ready for the stage in mid-2008—could gauze over the age-old feuds between the Hollands and the ever-reclusive Dozier, who's lived on and off in Europe since the '70s and been heard from little. It even got them all in the same room, and speaking again, as long as it was just about music.

Perhaps all that helps to explain why going back in time and reliving the Supremes' experience made Eddie Holland chafe, though he and Brian had agreed to do this retrospective. Indeed, dissecting their work for the group comes easily and in great detail—once the focus is squarely on their production concepts and techniques. Not that the Hollands and Dozier can ever really distance themselves from the Supremes in any case, nor would they want to.

For example, on the table near Eddie Holland's bacon and eggs sat a copy of Hip-O Records' 2005 three-CD box-set compilation, *Heaven Must Have Sent You: The Holland/Dozier/Holland Story*. On the inside cover are two superimposed vintage Motown publicity photographs, circa 1965. One shows the guys in a set-up studio shot, Eddie in the middle, pencil in one hand, music sheet in the other, as Dozier and Brian check out the piece of paper; all three wear snappy open-necked shirts and casual sport jackets, and are grinning broadly. The other photo shows them and the Supremes lounging on the lawn in front of the West Grand Boulevard house—"Hitsville"—where all the great hits were cut. They're intermingled, the young Brian at the far left looking eerily like Smokey Robinson, next to Diana Ross and Mary Wilson, and Lamont and Eddie flanked on the right by Florence Ballard. Ross and Wilson are wearing designer casual skirt-and-top outfits, Ballard a white sundress. Naturally, Eddie is the one doing the talking. No one appears particularly happy, with only Wilson bearing anything close to a smile. Ross seems to be staring into the ground with something approaching a scowl.

When this weird, un-serendipitous vibe was pointed out to Eddie, a grin crept through the brush of his beard.

"Diana looks mad, don't she?" he said merrily.

"They probably took that picture after you had to teach her to sing one of those songs," Washington offered, hinting that perhaps Eddie'd had his hands full with Ross in the studio.

"Well, I'll put it this way," he said. "A Holland-Dozier-Holland song is difficult for a singer to sing. We did a lot of off-beats, sharps, flats. The singers sang away from the chorus and the melody at times. The colorization of sounds is different; the voice trails off on a sharp key to extend the effect. It took a lot of work, with me working with the vocalist. Diana, Levi [Stubbs], Martha, whoever it was, they couldn't just hear the song on a demo and then sing it—they had to *learn* it. Diana did that. Definitely. She took direction perfectly. Levi was tougher. But she listened. That's why the Supremes happened. She was interpreting Holland-Dozier-Holland's vision, what we heard. It wasn't what she wanted sometimes. But it had to go down our way."

⟨Cee⟩

When HDH stopped producing the Supremes, both groups were on top of the world; HDH was big enough to walk away from Berry Gordy and live to tell the tale, eventually walking all the way to the

Rock and Roll Hall of Fame in 1990, just two years after the Supremes were inducted. Now, unlike his more excitable older brother, the normally Buddha-like Brian Holland can't avoid looking back and getting misty about HDH's Supreme oeuvre.

"I've never told anyone this," he said the day before. "I was driving down Sunset Boulevard one day in the '80s when I heard 'I Hear a Symphony' on the radio. And it just got to me, Eddie's lyrics really. I pulled over to the side of the road and cried, man. Now, this was like twenty-five years after we recorded the song. And I hadn't had any emotional reaction to it before that. It took twenty-five years for it to sink in how good that song is."

His voice rose. "Listen to the lyrics! *Listen* to it. *Those tears that fill my eyes / I cry not for myself but for those who never felt the joy we felt.* Things were happening in our lives by then, Eddie's and mine, that began to creep into the songs. Those songs were supposed to be about simple things. And at the beginning, they were. It was 'baby this, baby that.' But when I hear something like 'Symphony,' man, there ain't nothing simple about it."

While he won't deliberate on it today, unconvincingly laughing it off, his not-so-secret affair in the early '60s with Ross was the talk of Motown, precipitating a ballistic outburst from the woman he was married to at the time. All these years later, it's clear the infatuation never really ended, even after the sex did. Apropos of nothing, he found himself saying, "Diana was . . . very pretty."

Then there was the ill-fated Supreme. Of Florence Ballard, Eddie Holland said: "There was a girl who needed a good psychiatrist. Because what she was really frightened of was her own demons. That's what killed her, tryin' to push those demons away. We all . . . somebody needed to be more attentive to her, to save her from herself."

But then, everybody at Motown, it seems, had demons of some kind. Fucked-up people roamed through the house on West Grand Boulevard, artists sniping at each other—and at Ross—all the time, producers sniping at the musicians or at Berry Gordy over money, including a fistfight between Berry and Marvin Gaye in Gordy's office. Or, artists would be sliding between the sheets with someone they shouldn't be—a code of conduct that applied to Gordy himself, who has been married three times and constantly at play during and in between. This was the underbelly of what Gordy wanted the world to believe was an isolated culture of young, happy, shiny people—the "Motown family." By 1967, even several million dollars a year in advances from Gordy couldn't satisfy HDH's notions of self-worth and creative control, and so they were outta there. The Supremes, however, thrived as the Motown gold standard, cutting two more No. 1's written and produced by lesser entities, though by then the Motown soul was drained.

The Holland brothers can easily look back upon decades of courtroom wrangling with Gordy—which in the end concluded almost entirely in Gordy's favor—and blithely slough it off as business, not personal. Eddie Holland can wax glorious about Gordy all day, in a way he cannot muster for the Supremes. Because that was about money, not art. By contrast, an uneasy look on his face appears in a trice when that hoary canard about Motown's lost soul is entered into the record. This one especially hurts, given the obvious syllogism for some that soul began losing ground there once HDH sent the Supremes' crossover success through the roof with their songs. What of the notion that those tunes weren't "black enough"? What of the cries of "sellout"?

Though betrayed by his fidgety unease, Eddie tried to be defiantly blasé about it, even taking the tack that it *wasn't* black in nature, as if the entire matter were too parochial to matter.

"We never wrote black music. We grew up on pop music. We didn't set out to write R&B for the Supremes. That's why it had such mass appeal."

Didn't Dozier's *Reflections Of* CD reveal the imbued R&B in, say, "My World Is Empty Without You"?

"You can take any song and make it R&B. Shit, I can take the 'Star-Spangled Banner' and make it R&B, if I care to. We didn't want to be just another bunch of black guys making music as a cause. We didn't want to put all our energies year after year into making music three people would listen to, that would never get beyond a black radio station and the jukebox in some dingy blues club on the edge of the docks. Then, too, we loved what the Drifters were doing—'There Goes My Baby' was our favorite song. It blew Brian and me away. But we knew we couldn't write like that. We did our thing. We wanted to make hits. We wanted every goddamn thing we wrote to be a hit!"

HDH's curse, of course, was that they did exactly that, too damn well with the Supremes to ever be mortal again, even in times of extended failure later on. For all of their assembled body of work, for all the eternal cool of "Heat Wave" or "How Sweet It Is (to Be Loved by You)," only the Supremes ever made Brian Holland bawl on the side of a road a quarter-century after the fact. Only the Supremes' string of hits took them, and Motown, to an other-worldly level, and may have saved Berry Gordy's empire from an early demise.

In this context, Eddie Holland's reticence about standing in the shadows of the Supremes forty years after blowing out of Motown is an indicator of how powerful this Supremes thing is within popular culture. And how it permeates so many levels. Even for the Hollands—especially for the Hollands—it's not just about the music.

"Yeah, " Brian Holland would find himself saying, as if involuntarily, the far-off look back in his eye, a good hour after he'd said it the first time, "Diana was very pretty."

one

THREE GIRLS
FROM THE
PROJECTS

As we look back through the funnel cloud of time, it is clear that the only common ground other than their legacy that the three Supremes ever really shared was a fifteen-block grid of southeastern Detroit framed by the massive Cadillac plant within the Hamtramck Street beltway to the north, Hastings and Woodward Avenues to the west, St. Aubin and Dequindre Streets to the east, and the wide expanse of Warren Avenue to the south. This teeming concrete landscape bore the name of the Brewster-Douglass housing development, one of the first of its kind built in the bowels of America's inner cities, a prototypical sprawl of apartment homes, gardens, parks, and parking lots, all visible from a distance only through a dusky curtain of smoke belched from the rooftop smoke stacks.

The Brewster-Douglass Homes—known otherwise as Brewster-Douglass, BD, or, in the most frequently used shorthand, "the projects"—were home to all three Supremes-to-be in the mid-'50s, when they were junior high school girls. But had they never been thrown together by Fate, they might not have spoken to each other for the rest of their lives. As it was, they barely knew one another beyond a timid wave and an inner thought of: Gee, I wonder what that girl's name is. Such was life in the projects, where the crush of so many people— 15,000 at its apogee—brought so much turnover that in this great bustle of nameless faces and faceless names, one's next-door neighbors could be total strangers.

Diana Ross, Mary Wilson, and Florence Ballard lived in separate divisions of the projects, which were like different cities. Which is why, as every few years one building or another has been blasted into rubble as part of some sort of city urban renewal plan, the overall identity of the projects has remained intact and seemingly immune to any real change, even as they have visibly decayed. These days, off to the southwest, the "new Detroit" is taking shape, most notably in the parabolic dome of Ford Field and the adjoining Comerica Park, and the glass palaces of the Renaissance Center down near the Detroit River. But if you tip a glance anywhere beyond these cosmetic bandages, the redbrick cadaver of the projects creeps into view; a closer look reveals the boarded windows and abandoned, scarified skeletal remains of other downtown buildings evoking bombed-out Beirut.

Brewster-Douglass was plagued by crime and corrosion even during the time the Supremes—and a few white families, including that of future comedienne Lily Tomlin—occupied the grounds. Conditions deteriorated even further in the late '60s, and ever since there have been around 500 arrests on the premises each year. Recent renovation attempts have been halting; in the early 2000s, the *Detroit News* ran a story headlined "Unsafe, Unsanitary Areas Rile Residents." It began:

> It's not just the sight of used condoms and needles or the smell of urine that leaves Bettie Washington breathless, it's the 13 flights of stairs she's forced to navigate when the elevators break down at the Brewster-Douglass housing project off Interstate 75, near Mack. . . . "They have to do something about me not needing to walk down these steps all the time," said the 55-year-old, who depends on a wooden cane to support a bad knee. "There's a lot of old people in here. Some of them can't come down.". . . [R]esidents complain about trash-filled stairwells, broken elevators and windows, fungus, clogged gutters and faulty furnaces.

It wasn't like that in the '50s, when an address at Brewster-Douglass could actually inspire a sliver of envy. This was a holdover from the founding mission of the projects, which were conceived as a refuge from urban rot. When ground was broken for the Brewster Homes in 1935, First Lady Eleanor Roosevelt came to sink the shovel and dedicate the first federally funded black public housing development in the country. Three years later, it opened with 703 units caved between two-storey rowhouses and one three-storey apartment building. In the early '50s, its success bred construction of six fourteen-story towers for 1,300 families, which were bundled into a subdivision named for the abolitionist slave and author Frederick Douglass; the resulting Brewster and Douglass Homes, now a huge piece of property, had some high-minded guidelines: Its dwellings were earmarked for "working poor," the euphemism given to the broods of mainly black auto-plant and other workers making at least $90 a week. Brewster-Douglass was not confused with Arcadia, but it more than suited the Motor-Town analog of the Harlem Renaissance.

And it stayed something of an oasis into the '50s, even when the wrecking ball came to the neighborhood to clear the way for the new Chrysler Freeway and other interstate arteries that erased the roguish charms of the neighborhood. Many of these had been jazz clubs— the "black and tans," drawing the new leisure-class blacks and music-minded whites from the northern sectors where whites, mainly Jewish and Eastern European immigrants, retreated when the mass movement of blacks from the South changed the face of Detroit seemingly over-night. A saunter down Hastings Street or a wind down the side streets around the projects could net you a night with homegrown musicians like John Lee Hooker, Big Maceo Merriweather, Bobo Jenkins, Baby Boy Warren, Calvin Frazier, Boogie Woogie Red, Detroit Piano Fats, and dozens of others. Within the Brewster-Douglass borders, on St. Antoine, was the Rosebud club. By the end of the '50s it, along with all too many others, was a mere echo entombed under the asphalt on-ramp of the Freeway.

It was this Detroit, the storied Detroit of John Lee Hooker, that begat Berry Gordy's Motown empire, and the Detroit that Gordy mined not only for talent but also for public relations gold. In the mid-'60s, when Gordy walked the narrow line between his black roots and his crossover ambitions, the Supremes presented the perfect vessel to pump both sides. This was still a couple of years before Gordy punched his ticket to the West Coast and all he left Detroit was alone; for now, the roots thing was still in the Motown playbook. So, as the Supremes swept into the top niche of American music, their own roots— Brewster-Douglass—became a useful metaphor. One day in 1965, a *Detroit* magazine photographer snapped them on their home turf, where they still lived with their families, at least until the homes Gordy had helped them purchase on upscale Buena Vista Avenue could close.

The pictures taken showed them off as the perfect ambassadorettes of Gordy's copyrighted "Sound of Young America," and though he in no way wished for anyone to expand that blurb to its natural state—the "Sound of Young *Black* America"—the subconscious pull of the ghetto backdrop for the Supremes couldn't have hurt Gordy's coveting of hip whites as well as his base black audience. There they were, then, in *très chic* mode—Ross in a very continental black-and-white suit with a mink collar, Wilson in a leopard-print dress and matching chapeau, Ballard in a suede skirt and jacket, all under fashionable, high-sheen wigs—merrily tripping down a sidewalk on a cold winter day. Behind them, the high-rise tenements loomed; to the left, the row houses squatted. In one photo, Ballard extends her right arm, her gloved hand holding a purse, in a high-sign to unseen neighbors. Just to the rear, a mother and her young son stare into the camera, looking bewildered.

All this was intended to strike a homey, poor-girls-make-good theme. And, looking back thirty years later, Wilson would recall: "We were heroes of the projects overnight. You were hearing, 'Hey, Mary lives there.' You walked by and they yelled, 'Hey, Mary, right on! Hey, Diane, hey Flo.' I think it was the best experience I ever had in my life. It was probably more exciting than our first million-seller." But it's arguable whether that was really the vibe that day in the projects. Look closely and you'll see that the gulf between the three haves and the have-nots is fairly striking; it is as if the smiling young women weren't celebrating their roots as much as their impending exodus from them. In fact, within the next year all had relocated to Buena Vista Avenue, taking their families with them. They were the lucky ones. It wasn't the sort of luck that would have seemed anywhere near likely when they had moved into Brewster-Douglass a decade before. But decades later, with homes on both coasts and private jets fueled to fly to Europe on her whim, Ross had injected into her stage act a bit of between-song patter centering on her exodus from the place.

"Whatever happened to Diana Ross from the Brewster projects in Detroit?" she would ask in her coy kitten voice. "Whatever happened to that girl?" Then, after a pause, instead of answering, she'd merely say, "Who?"

Mary Wilson, who was the first to get there, was the only Supreme who wasn't a native of Detroit. Born on March 6, 1944, in Greenville, Mississippi, she spent her infancy on the move; such was the drifter lifestyle of her father, Sam Wilson, who took her and her mother with him on work-seeking jaunts to St. Louis and Chicago. Her mother, Johnnie Mae, knew that Mary deserved better and, making a choice between her man and her daughter, sent the latter at age 3 to Detroit to live with Johnnie Mae's sister, I. V. Pippin, and her husband, John, who worked on the Chrysler assembly line. Johnnie Mae, meanwhile, returned to Greenville, leaving Sam to bounder on his own, though he came back periodically at first—enough so that Johnnie Mae delivered two more children, a son and another daughter.

Their older daughter, meanwhile, grew older in Detroit with the surname of Pippin, not Wilson, led to believe that her aunt I.V. was her mother, and vice versa. Then, in 1950, "Aunt" Johnnie Mae showed up for a summer visit and wound up staying. The young girl began to notice arguments and awkward silences among the three adults. A few months later, Johnnie Mae took her aside and broke the truth: She was her mother, and her real name was Mary Wilson. While Wilson had not had an ideal life with the Pippins, at times given frightful spankings and whippings, the news was devastating. "My whole world had been turned upside down," she wrote in her 1982 autobiography. "I'd trusted these people, and they had lied to me." Trying to make sense of it, she would wander the streets aimlessly, "crying my eyes out."

Wilson never completely accepted her birth mother, who moved in with the Pippins but created all sorts of psychodramas. She got pregnant and suffered a miscarriage; she also constantly argued with the Pippins over who was going to make the decisions in the young girl's life, and just who "owned" her. As reconstructed by Wilson, the arguments would usually go like this:

JOHNNIE MAE: I never said you could have Mary. I just said you could keep her until I was on my feet again.
JOHN: You know we had an agreement that Mary was ours. You promised that she was ours.
JOHNNIE MAE: No, I didn't!

The Pippins, in fact, remained the girl's guardian, given that Johnnie Mae wasn't there for long stretches, especially after she took a job as a live-in maid for a white family and was home only on weekends. But over the next three years, their home on Bassett Street filled to the brim when I.V. gave birth to two children of her own and Johnnie Mae sent for *her* two other children, whom she had left in the care of her mother back in Greenville. Only then did Mary Wilson meet her siblings. She also would meet her father again—initially, during visits to Greenville where Sam Wilson had finally returned, for good, having lost his leg in an industrial accident in the early '50s. In 1953, when Mary was 9, Johnnie Mae moved her kids from the Pippins' home and into a series of tiny apartment flats. For a time, she couldn't find work and lived on welfare. By 1956, though, she could prove that she had sufficient earnings to be approved for an apartment in one of the high-rise towers at Brewster-Douglass. Mary remembered the flight to the projects as a step up, akin to "moving into a Park Avenue skyscraper."

Brewster-Douglass was a microcosm of big-city life in the mid-'50s. The first real effects of the baby boom were reverberating through the projects, and kids swarmed like locusts over every square inch. Not incidentally, it was also the thick of the nascent era of rock and roll, fueled by the angst and restlessness of their generation. In a black environment like this one, the rhythms of Little Richard, Chuck Berry, and the doo-wop groups provided the soundtrack of everyday life. In the projects, it went wherever the kids went, on the roofs, in the stairwells, in the gymnasium of the Brewster recreation center where a generation before Joe Louis had learned to box. The dynamic of three- or four-part harmony was such that it was unthinkable to sing alone. You had to be in a group, or risk being ragged as a prima donna.

Like the two other not-yet Supremes, whom she barely knew as neighbors, Mary Wilson felt somewhat left out of a music milieu generally dominated by the guys. She, moreover, was just as smitten with white pop as with R&B, though it was impossible not to be ingrained with the sounds of the ghetto, sounds that resonated on both the black and white Detroit radio stations—many of which had progressive disc jockeys who were nobly unafraid to play hard-core "race records."

Wilson found she could sing early in life, and developed a quite-nice baritone, deep for a girl but with an overall sweetness to it. Her venue for vocalizing wasn't the nooks and crannies of Brewster-Douglass but the more formal school glee clubs. At Algers Elementary School, where she was sent in an early busing experiment, she was befriended by the daughter of one of Detroit's most precious musical commodities, the Reverend C. L. Franklin, a preacher known widely for his overheated sermons at the New Bethel Baptist Church that invariably ended in even more overheated singing from Franklin, the audience, and the choir that included his daughter Carolyn Franklin and her sisters Erma and Aretha. Wilson sometimes observed these fire-and-brimstone paroxysms up close, when the Pippins could find a place in the crowded pews at New Bethel. There, she would ingest the intoxicating power of performing, later recalling how nurses "in starched white uniforms" would fan and comfort hysterical worshipers who got "too happy" and nearly fainted.

Carolyn would invite Mary Wilson into her own gospel-style singing group, but only until one of the group members insulted Wilson's voice, incurring her wrath. Reviews like that led Wilson to doubt her talent. She continued singing in the glee club when she went to junior high school. But when a talent show arose she took the safe approach of lip-synching, donning a borrowed leather jacket and mouthing "I'm Not a Juvenile Delinquent" as the Frankie Lymon record was played through the PA system. What the hell, it was still live performing, and it got a rise from the audience. But as quickly as it took for the next girl to go on, she was brought down to earth.

That next girl was Wilson's vaguely recognizable Brewster neighbor, Florence Ballard, who made it abundantly clear she didn't need any stinkin' lip-synch, not with the thunder she could unleash from her vocal chords. Wilson would remark about how pretty Ballard seemed that night, "with her fair skin, auburn hair, long legs, and curvaceous figure," though in fact Ballard was not nearly as winsome a girl as Wilson, with her full lips and killer smile—not to mention that Wilson was shapely *and* thin.

"Blondie," as Ballard was called (with a hint of racial snark because of her caramel complexion), was a pistol. Not pretty in the classic sense—her nose a tad too bulbous, her eyes too squinty—she was nonetheless striking. At times, as when her lips were pouting, she could be unbelievably sexy; at other times, if she had put on a few pounds, she'd appear plain and frumpy. Taller than Wilson by several inches and big-boned by any measure, she was kittenish in the way she walked and would curl her legs under herself when sitting on the grass. But she was no girly-girl, to be sure. She was mouthy, even swaggering, yet engaging rather than off-putting; she seemed to like to argue, but was so funny with her comeback lines that the tiffs usually ended with everyone laughing. And when she was on a stage singing, she was completely at ease.

"Flo was an extremely self-aware person as a teenager," averred her younger cousin, Raymond ("Ray") Gibson. "Guys in the projects would say she had a great behind. I think they said it because Flo would make you believe she did, by how she walked, how she carried herself; she made you believe she was sexy, made you believe anything she wanted you to believe. When I was a kid, I saw her as an overwhelming personality. Most people who knew her did."

Ballard's voice was similarly convincing, not because it was perfect but because she had immense power in the upper ranges of the scale, meaning she could more than handle loud, gospel-style belting, she too being a devotee of C. L. Franklin's tent shows and record albums. Following Wilson on their junior high school talent show, she rocked the joint with a soulful blasting of "Ave Maria," nailing it and earning a standing ovation.

Watching from the wings, Wilson was blown away, and would recall that Ballard "looked like a movie star" in her white gown and with her command of the crowd. Afterward, they got to talking. Ballard, saying she'd heard Wilson sing with the glee club, commended her on her stage presence and casually suggested they should start a singing group. Wilson regarded it as idle chatter. A *girl* singing group, she thought. Who in the world would go for *that*?

But what Wilson didn't know was that Ballard wasn't only serious; she was merely one future degree of separation from making it happen. That, too, was very much like Flo.

Florence Glenda Ballard was born on June 30, 1943, the eighth of fourteen children. Her father, Jesse, had been swept into Detroit in the great migration, arriving from Rosette, Mississippi, in 1929 to work in the Chevrolet plant. His wife, Lurlee, soon joined him and they found a small home on MacDougald Street, raising, and trying to keep track of, all the children they would have. In the interim, other Ballard relatives and their families moved up from Mississippi, making for family picnics that could fill Grand Circus Park. When Jesse and Lurlee were done multiplying, the only sufficiently large and affordable quarters available were at Brewster-Douglass, in one of the roomier, two-storey, three-bedroom row houses, though the kids had to sleep two or three to a bed.

They were a tenaciously close-knit brood, the epoxy being the parents' strict—if in Jesse's case hypocritical—moral codes. For his part, Jesse followed his own code, which he usually found at the bottom of a gin glass. His after-work hours were spent on bar stools all around southeast Detroit, and Friday nights had a particular air of suspense.

That was Jesse's pay day, and when he'd get home the kids would be lined up waiting for allowances from whatever meager change was left in his pockets. *If* there was any left.

One Friday night, Flo watched from the window for Jesse, only to see him thrown like a sack of dirty laundry out of a car, out cold, one shoe missing, his pockets turned inside out. Flo, her sister Maxine, and Lurlee had to carry him inside the apartment, where he lay face-down on his bed for hours, drying out. Another time, Jesse was so loaded that he went to the bathroom and unwittingly used a five-dollar bill as toilet paper. One of the kids saw the bill floating in the bowl and eagerly pulled it out and cleaned it off, a stroke of good fortune beyond words.

The most remarkable thing about these scenes was that they happened so regularly; none of it seemed overly unusual. It was part of life with Jesse. In time, as Jesse became even more disjointed, Lurlee grew understandably concerned that his alcoholism might be handed down to his kids, making her even more vigilant about shielding them. However, grim reality had a way of intruding. With Jesse's money almost always whittled away to nothing, they often lived hand to mouth. Sometimes, the only way to get dinner on the table was to send Flo and Maxine down to the corner market to collect food, spoiled or otherwise, that had fallen on the sawdust floor during the day.

They also suffered unspeakable tragedies that severely tested their faith and family bonds. First, in the mid-'50s, the youngest Ballard, a 3-year-old named Roy, strayed from two of his sisters who were taking him to the movies and was struck and killed by a drunk driver. Lurlee—like all of them really, but most obviously in her case—never did recover, losing much of the strength that had become a buffer against Jesse's neglect. They would all hunker down in grief again in 1959 when Jesse himself, his anatomy eaten away by booze, contracted stomach cancer and quickly died.

Lurlee from then on began to gain an enormous amount of weight, smothering her losses with bombast and unlimited calories; yet her spirit remained undiminished. Whenever any of the kids told her their teacher had yelled at them, she'd march to the school in her tent-sized housecoat and scare the teacher into promises never to do it again.

Florence "Blondie" Ballard was clearly cut from the same mold. While she was scarred—more than most people would ever know—by the travails of the family and Jesse's predilection for addictive substances, she rarely let on about it; her surface identity as an aggressive and sassy young woman was intact, just as Lurlee's always was. Even so,

Flo could seamlessly slip into moody silence, her eyes haunted by something unspoken. Even swathed by the closeness of her family, she needed to get away, into the musky air of the street, or to take her bicycle from the storage room and ride to her cousin Raymond's home a few blocks away.

RAY GIBSON: There were just so many of them in that apartment. They'd all be up each other's butt. And Florence was in the middle in age; she was too old for the young ones and too young for the old ones—hell, one of her sisters is like ten years older. And I'm younger than Florence and I barely even know the older ones. I only really know two younger sisters, Pat and Lynne. I never had anything to do with the older ones; I stayed away from 'em, some of 'em I heard were bad news, and that was borne out through the years. So, yes, they were close, but I don't think Florence got a lot of helpful guidance from anyone at home. I think she felt she was the most mature of them all, and felt kind of suffocated there.

Florence would come over to my house and begin to sing for me. She would just break into song, because she loved to sing more than anything in the world. She'd sing Billie Holiday songs, pop songs, whatever her mood was. I remember her father used to play the guitar and that the family had these sing-alongs, but when Jesse got sick they stopped. But Florence had to sing. She taught me how to sing. Even when she was with the Supremes, she'd come over and want me to sing with her, so she could get the harmony down. I was Mary Wilson's stand-in, man.

I'll tell you something. Through the years, Florence used to send me stuff, Supremes stuff, things she'd acquired on tours and whatever. Pictures, albums, I even have a Wonder Bread wrapper with the Supremes' pictures on it. It was a promotion thing and she loved it—y'know, the *whitebread* Supremes. She laughed about that, and kept it; then she gave it to me. That was near the end of her life and she was moving around a lot, so she wanted me to hold on to these things. And who knows, she might have in some way seen the end coming, and she wanted someone to preserve all this memorabilia. She knew I would, and to this day I have them on my wall. I have one of her dresses—a white gown with mesh netting on the bottom. It came one day with a note that read: "To Raymond, a very sweet fellow, Florence." You don't think my eyes lit up when I read *that*?

I mean, it really affected me deeply that she trusted me enough to give these things to me and not to any of her brothers or sisters, or even her mother. Because I wasn't immediate family. So one day I asked one of her older sisters, I said, "If anything happens to me, what do you want me to do with this Supremes' memorabilia?" I assumed that the family would want it. I told her I'd put it in my will, so they would have it. And she told me, "We don't want that junk." *Junk!* That's what they thought of Florence's treasured belongings. To them, it was just junk. She said, "I guess we'll have to bury it with you, Raymond."

He didn't need to gild the meaning of the story: that in the projects, Florence Ballard felt like she belonged in the trash, too.

Diana Ross's world didn't intersect with Wilson's or Ballard's until 1958, when her family moved into the maw of Brewster-Douglass, and even then only tangentially at first. Nor was she known generally as Diana Ross. She was born in Detroit on March 26, 1944, with the somewhat less glamorous name Diane Ernestine Earle Ross. This would become an issue when Ross renamed herself, the assumption being that she was putting on airs. By way of defense, she would insist that while her parents had chosen "Diane," someone in the maternity ward screwed up and wrote "Diana" on the birth certificate. If that sounded like the spinning of yarn, she would duly note that her mother, Ernestine, had always informally called her Diana because both mother and daughter liked it better.

Ross didn't arrive in the projects until she was 18, a worldly traveler to some and a pretentious phony to others; and to still others, both. Yet however people viewed her, there was no question she was on a faster track out of the ghetto than most. Clearly, she had some advantages. Her father, Fred, was a tall, handsome, taciturn West Virginia native who had fought in World War II. He was strict and hard-focused, maintaining a career as an amateur boxer while providing well for a growing family by working two jobs, one seemingly forever at the

American Brass Company. He had a vise-like grip on every facet of his family's existence—eventually he and his wife, Ernestine, had three sons and three daughters, Diane or Diana the second-eldest after her sister Barbara. And yet he was distant, physically due to long work hours and emotionally due to his nature.

"To this day, I don't know him well," Ross said in 1993, a few years before he died. "Throughout my childhood, he stayed unreachable." In an earlier interview with Barbara Walters in 1978, this seemed implicitly obvious when she confessed, "I guess being a second child and always wanting attention, and whatever the reason is I'm in show business, I always wanted everybody to care about me. I've tried very hard. . . . It's like [I've cried out] 'Love me! Love me, please!'"

Not hearing that from Fred Ross, inevitably she turned to Ernestine, a sunny and forbearing woman who sometimes was sickly because of tuberculosis but would rather have died than lie in bed pitying herself. She was far more liberal-minded than Fred, allowing her children greater leeway to spend time on their own, out of the apartment house where they lived on St. Antoine Street. Following Barbara's lead, Diane could hardly sit still, acting and singing in school events and excelling in swimming, though she developed a major insecurity, believing her sister was better at all these pursuits, and that her parents loved "Bobbie" more than they did her.

The Ross kids were a smart and curious lot, always ahead of the game compared to their schoolmates. For most of Diane's formative years, the brood, among them her Aunt Bea, were never rich, but neither did they want for much. Fred was proud that no one could call the Rosses a hand-me-down family. Still, there was no confusing St. Antoine Street with the Riviera, or even Pontiac. One day, when Diane was around 8, two of her friends in the building were playing hide-and-seek when one of the kids forgot about the game and the other, who'd hidden in an abandoned refrigerator in the backyard, was found hours later dead of suffocation when the refrigerator was pried open. Another time, Diane came home in tears and bloodied after being accosted on the street by a white gang, one of whom called her a "nigger" and punched her in the nose. That incident, she has claimed, turned her from pig-tailed wimp to tomboy, "skinny but wiry and strong," and the "protector of the family."

For that metamorphosis, she credited not Fred but Ernestine for telling her to stand up for herself and "fight for all you've got . . . and above all, to *win*." She began to assume a tough-guy demeanor and to get into tussles with other kids. In the personality transformation, she also became bossy, sarcastic, ornery, such that most of her schoolmates took to avoiding her; few took her side when she got into a call-out with some other girl. To be sure, though, Diane Ross made for an odd bully; most around her could see she had less confidence in her fighting than in her high-and-mighty attitude, thus explaining why she would usually back down from a fight she herself had picked.

It was as if she knew she wouldn't make a credible victim, not with her family's status; as if she knew her bravado was a front. There was the time she got into a spat in the kitchen with Bobbie, who was so exasperated by her sister's shrill whining that she picked up a can of Ajax and shook some of the white powder in Diane's face. Seeing their mother enter the room, Diane on cue broke into tears trying to gain sympathy from Ernestine, who instead laughed at the sight of her white-faced daughter. If that was a mite deflating to Diane, she knew she could usually get her way with that kind of histrionics. It was such an easy part, and she played it well.

Periodically, to get the kids off the baking streets in summer, Fred and Ernestine would send them to visit relatives in Bessemer, Alabama— not a vacation spot many blacks would have chosen. Riding southward, the Greyhound bus Ross was on would stop in Cincinnati and the blacks herded to the back seats; from then on, they could use only the bathrooms and fountains labeled "Colored." To the young, naive Ross, these were long, strange trips indeed; but the Ross family had also experienced the violence of racism firsthand, when a female cousin was found dead, her car wrecked, on a back road en route to Atlanta. Though the cops called it an accident, Ross would write, "To this day, we all believe [she] was murdered by the Ku Klux Klan."

In the mid-'60s, her younger brother, Arthur, whom the family called "T-Boy," was involved in a dispute in a convenience store while in Bessemer. When the cops were called, one of them came in shooting before asking questions, and winged T-Boy's ear before hauling him in. Ross by then was a star, and had to pull strings from afar to get him released.

Ross, then, had seen enough of life to have filed away some useful information as she grew into an attractive teenager. She'd morphed from a stick figurine into a pretty, and wily, young woman; still a rail, as were all the Rosses, but with beckoning lips, an oversized mouth that when she smiled spread halfway around her face, high cheekbones, and padding in all the right places. And her eyes. They were globular, the whites a vast sea encircling dark pupils that projected slightly outward. With her eyelashes painted, "striking" wasn't the word for her. She was weirdly sexy. Indeed, if the girls were wary of her, the boys kept no such distance. Almost all who encountered her in school fell hard, even if most were too intimidated to hit on her. For her part, she kept a distance, leading more than one young man to wonder what they'd have to do to get Diane Ross to pay attention to them. Which, of course, only added to her allure.

The answer to that question wouldn't come for a while, because she was still a bit of a prude in her mid-teens, unaware of her own budding charms. Yet, even if passively, she was making acquaintances who would bear future implications. As it happened, these were usually boys who had at least a modicum of musical talent. Even in elementary school, two such boys had been smitten with her, close friends named Melvin Franklin and Richard Street. Both were painfully shy, as was Diane then, and they all found singing a release. Then, when she was 12 and the Rosses moved to an apartment house on Belmont Street, she met a girl her age whose family lived on the block, Sharon Burstyn. Sharon had an uncle, a singer, who lived with them, and when Diane slept over, the two girls would hear him warbling downstairs 'round a piano with some buddies he'd formed a group with, first called the Chimes, then the Matadors.

He was surely a revelation for any young girl: light-skinned, blue-eyed, lean, and affable, and his voice was high-pitched and honey-dripped, nearly a falsetto, smooth and sensual. If you had to describe its effect, you could have called it smoky. In fact, *he* was being called that—not William or Bill Robinson, which was his name, but Smokey. Amazingly, the moniker wasn't for his voice but because as a kid he'd had blond hair, just like Flo Ballard, and blue eyes, and his uncle nicknamed him "Smokey Joe" so that, he explained, the kid wouldn't forget he was black. It was simply a quirk of Fate that it happened to be the perfect trope for his vocal persona, and even at just 17, he wore the single-name moniker as his persona.

Smokey had ambition and then some, and the talent and ideas to drive it. He'd cobbled together a girl-group, the Matadorettes, around his girlfriend Claudette Rogers, whose cousin Bobby was in the Matadors. It was all very close-knit, like a big family, which at once appealed to the impressionable Diane Ross. Right away, she became smitten with Uncle Smokey, both in the carnal sense, though she was still a committed virgin, and because he seemed to hone and stoke her own ambition. Around him, she loosened up, even getting bold. And he found his eye wandering in her direction.

Smokey Robinson has, for five decades, been circumspectly coy about the simpatico between them, recalling the young Diana Ross as "shy . . . but always persistent. If we were practicing in the basement, she'd be listening on the staircase. If we were in the living room, she'd be on the front porch. She was a fan, a music lover, and sometimes [she'd] sing. . . . 'I love singing,' Diane couldn't deny, 'but I'm not good enough to be a real singer.'. . . I always noticed her 'cause she was pretty and perky, pushing herself to do better."

The problem, as she freely admitted, was that she couldn't loosen up enough to sing for people without getting the vapors. Thus, she did terribly in music classes. As for ambition, that was another matter. One of her old music teachers recalls a junior high production of *Hansel and Gretel* in which Diane was supposed to hold a flashlight in front of her but instead made sure to shine it on her own face. Even if this tale is apocryphal, it fits into a long argosy of similar occurrences, stretching as far back as her gawky, pigtail days, foretelling her can't-miss future as a star.

At 15, however, all she had were dreams and a new address since Fred had moved his now-complete family to one of the Brewster-Douglass high-rise apartment houses. Diane, ever independent, chose not to stray from the crowd she ran in on Belmont Avenue and kept attending her old junior high, riding a city bus to the old neighborhood. Thus, in the projects, she was just another fleeting face to Mary Wilson and Florence Ballard, who all passed by one another going about their own business. Moreover, what was known on a surface level about the Rosses around the Brewster-Douglass byways made Diane a candidate for ostracism. This was based solely on appearances, on the fact that they seemed somehow better off than most there; in lieu of actually knowing or even speaking with them, neighbors put the onus on the Rosses for being distant. That family was just so *perfect*, went the put-down; no wonder they were so snotty.

The acrid irony underlying this impression was that the Rosses weren't perfect but merely, more or less, a normal and functioning family. Unlike Wilson and Ballard, and so many others, Diane Ross experienced no family rifts, no four-to-a-bed overcrowding, no long-suffering mother—and, most significant of all, no abandoning or alcoholic father. Fred Ross, always a stickler for education, was himself taking night classes in business at nearby Wayne State College, somehow squeezing enough time in between his multiple jobs. Yet rather than being admired for such self-attainment, out of envy the Rosses were perceived as "not one of us." Accordingly, Diane's contentious manner had to mean she was lording it over everybody else—though, to be sure, those who met Ernestine found nothing to dislike and had to alter their assumptions.

While the same could not be said of her daughter Diane, the rapidly maturing teenager carried forth on her own terms, toeing the line set by Fred Ross as an honor student. As of the spring of 1959 she, Mary Wilson, and Florence Ballard were still on separate paths, with no reason to believe they would ever cross. But Fate had other ideas.

two

MOTHS
TO THE
FLAME

D own on the corner of John R and Canfield, the plum-red brick
walls and dirty white arches of St. Josaphat's Church can still be
seen for hundreds of yards away, albeit in the creeping shadows of
downtown Detroit's new glassine palaces. Indeed, the stately old
church, still foursquare and as unyielding as a rusty old bolt, may
be the most identifiable vestige of the old, now dismantled, Detroit, its
stubborn refusal to go down a bold refrain of what once was. In its salad
days, by its location St. Josaphat's was part of the rhythm and blues of the
east side, a gateway to the seductions of John R and Canfield—and, to
the parish, a refuge, with priests on duty around the clock to catch a stray
soul or two after a particularly memorable night.

Not incidentally, the shortest walk from the front door took one to
the biggest seduction on the block, the Flame Show Bar at 4664 John R
Street. Its name could not have been more perfectly applied. The Flame
Show was beyond hot. At around 10 on a Saturday night, the joint was
jumping, stinking of sweat, stogies, cheap beer, and cheaper perfume. It
wasn't merely crowded, it was Siamese-twin close, felicitously, joining
blacks at the shoulder with a fair number of whites still extant on the
east side or on loan from the better neighborhoods. The fire marshals
didn't try to enforce the capacity limit of 200 seats, allowing a great fuse
of bumping and grinding when an act came on to sing or play jazz and
the blues with the Maurice King combo, the Wolverines.

The exterior of the Flame Show quickened the pulse. The front door,
angled catty-corner at the crux of the two streets, was recessed beneath
a giant semicircular marquee with wooden letters spelling "FLAME,"

each letter illuminated by dozens of neon lightbulbs. Acts were bill-boarded on three tiers of wraparound ribbons, and "FLAME SHOW BAR" emblazoned the entire white wall on each side. The best sign, though, was outside the lobby—"NO DOOR CHARGE."

At any given time, the acts could be T-Bone Walker, Billie Holiday, Wynonie Harris, Sarah Vaughn, hometown sons like John Lee Hooker, Jackie Wilson, Hank Ballard and the Midnighters, Little Willie John, or anyone who'd passed muster with the also aptly named King, who in his spangled turquoise tux was nearly royalty among the clubbing crowds. Having once led an all-girl touring jazz band some years before that had comprised whites, blacks, Mexicans, Chinese, and Native Americans, King wasn't just a bandleader; he and the band seemingly could make anyone into a crowd-pleaser with a few well-turned moves. He'd done just that with no less than Johnny Ray, the white crooner whom King let live with him during his tutorial, whereupon Ray had a brief but explosive run as a '50s record heartthrob.

With lines always stretched down John R, patrons realized the pre-ferred way of entry was to flash some green, not just for the doorman but inside, where the hustles went on nonstop, most heatedly along the 100-foot-long bar that snaked around two mirrored walls. As Thomas "Beans" Bowles, a horn player in the band, noted, "If you had enough money, you could get anything at the Flame"—and by that he meant *anything*, whether it be booze, reefer, women, and possibly a hot watch or ring.

But then, such bartering rituals were played out all around down-town, in the roughly sixty-block corridor that included Black Bottom—so named not for a racial component but because the soil tilled by its French settlers was so dark and fertile, yet centuries later no less suitable for the asphalt-paved streets—and the more bucolic-sounding Paradise Valley (a grid more recently named for the Asian paradise trees that lined its thoroughfares). Both metaphors, opposite yet in tune, had be-come quasi-official euphemisms for the inner-city experience, a tacit suspension of hard reality eased into wistful plausibility by the bounds of music and community.

One went with the other, gravy to the mashed potatoes, and the plate was especially full in the late '50s. The clubs were everywhere, clumped thickly along the motherlode of Hastings Street running straight down the heart of the Valley and bleeding onto side streets like Brush and Adams and Beacon, from the Ford assembly plant to the north down to Atwater Street hard by the docks of the Detroit River. As on John R, where the Flame Show formed a nexus with the Chesterfield Lounge, the Garfield Lounge, and the Frolic Show Bar, the clubs sat tooth-by-jowl with hotels, flophouses, rib shacks, barber shops, and pool joints, while in the street the hustle continued between the money-spenders and the money-grabbers.

Unlike in other big towns, where the club scene was supplemental to the industry that made rhythm-and-blues records, there *was* no such industry; it was a decentralized, small-time series of mom-and-pop operations run out of back rooms such as in Joe Von Batten's record shop at 3530 Hastings. But the deals were usually made at the clubs, by hustlers who fancied themselves, among other things, music entrepreneurs. Their offices were their bar stools, and if they could walk out with a signed contract with a singer, they might get a record pressed and out on the street by the next week; if the sales brought in a few bucks, there was money to be made.

But this wasn't Motown; it was Notown. There was a paucity of appreciable record labels in Detroit, so getting a nationally distributed record required shopping around a singer—or a songwriter or a new song—out of town, to established record labels in Chicago, New York, or L.A. That was a privilege only a select few had, and a few of that few could be found at the Flame Show—another reason why hustlers lined up at the bar sucking on Camels and draining malt liquor while hoping to cross paths with someone in the "in" crowd. Someone like, say, Al Green, the manager of the Flame Show who on the side managed Johnny Ray, Della Reese, LaVern Baker, and Jackie Wilson.

In the horde of wannabes at the bar, there were two hustlers who didn't yet know each other but would in time become bound in a way they could not possibly have dreamed.

By the late '50s, one of them, Berry Gordy, had actually made strides toward that end, giant strides indeed. And yet it wasn't Gordy who would first enter the sphere of the three girls from the projects. It was the other barfly, a guy every bit as smooth as Berry Gordy—and far better tailored and coiffed—but whose only real talent, it seemed, was his rap. This was Milton Jenkins.

Maxine Ballard Jenkins has a picture of Milt Jenkins taken in 1959 at the Flame Show Bar—possibly, if also ironically, by none other than Berry's sister Gwen, who, with another sister, Anna Gordy, operated the photo concession at the club. The shot captures what appears to be a carefree man in his early 30s posed in a wood-paneled corner, a curious fist-sized hole in the wall over his left shoulder. He wears a white sharkskin suit, its waist-length jacket cinched along his middle by a belt buckled on his right hip, and a white ascot sitting atop his open-neck collar. The jacket is burnished with three rows of two darker buttons from nipple to navel. Standing casually, and with maximum cool, his left leg forward and bent slightly at the knee, he wears black buckle-up shoes and his left hand is perched lightly on his thigh, a huge pinkie ring just under a cuff fastened by an ace-of-spades cuff link. His face is handsome, with a high forehead under bushy hair, a mole on his right cheek, a pencil mustache, and a smile so broad that his eyes squint. He appears to be no more than 130 pounds, pinkie ring included.

Little wonder that everyone knew when Milt was on the prowl. And as if he needed any more of a calling card than his appearance, he'd always make sure he was seen with a cast on his left arm, though no one ever knew why.

"I never knew if he hurt his arm in a fight with somebody or what, because he never did tell us what happened," recalls Otis Williams with a laugh. Williams, then a Detroit teenager with a doo-wop unit called Otis Williams and the Siberians, would intersect briefly with Jenkins later in 1959 when the group reformed as Otis Williams and the El Domingoes—the root of the future Temptations—and was managed by the enigmatic cat with the sling.

"We'd ask him all the time, we'd say, 'Milton, you all right? What's the story?' He'd just fluff it off, change the subject, and say, 'Yeah, I'm all right, man. Don't worry 'bout it, I'm gonna get y'all a big record deal!' So after a while, we just left it alone. We figured he was embarrassed to talk about it because he'd gotten into it with one of his girls who busted him up."

The truth was less colorful: He'd been involved in a car accident and broken his arm. But because he was afraid of doctors, he'd fashioned a sling and waited for it to heal, which it never seemed to. But then, Milt liked courting mystery—the biggest being how a guy with no job anyone knew of could afford threads like that and a fire-engine-red Cadillac convertible. Those wheels were his prized possession, his real calling card. He would keep it parked outside the Flame Show—he always seemed to get a perfect spot—and when he'd get out he'd have one or more gorgeous women on his arm and other gorgeous women would crowd around the car for a better look, some leaving pieces of paper with their phone numbers on the windshield. Once inside the club, Milt would go around shaking hands, talking big, and running long bar tabs.

How he was able to afford this lifestyle was never spoken of, even when he was among intimates. Even decades later, Mary Wilson was

writing in her memoirs of Jenkins's "secret life." "We never knew exactly where Milton's investment capital came from—he never had a
nine-to-five job, and he never volunteered any information. Of course,
to the streetwise, the answer was probably obvious. Because we were
so young . . . we didn't really think too much about it." It was good
enough to think of him, she wrote, as "one of the most interesting
people any of us had ever met."

Neither did Otis Williams blow the whistle on Jenkins in his
Temptations memoir. But he had no hesitation responding to a question about how Jenkins made his stack.

"Milton," he said, "was a pimp, a playboy pimp. A lot of them guys
back then were. They wanted to be a manager, but they needed bread
to do that, so they made it any way they could. Drugs, women, running numbers, whatever. They lived in seedy places where they could
ply those trades. Milton lived in a flophouse across the street from the
Flame Show Bar. That was his seat of power."

And from where he tried to score business as a manager. Working
the music crowd, he had accrued some pull. He could secure a rehearsal
hall or a studio, or book a gig; but though he would periodically em-
bark on trips to New York trying to score recording deals for his acts, so
far he'd come up empty. Still, he'd done well in Detroit for a guy who'd
gotten there only a year or so before.

Born in Birmingham, Alabama, Jenkins saw no possibilities for advancement in that city and emigrated to Cleveland in 1957. Looking
for acts to manage, he was in the audience one night for a show at the
Majestic Hotel where a five-man vocal group appeared, splitting the bill
with a contortionist named Caldonia Young. The former, known as the
Cavaliers, had three teenagers no older than 17 who, coincidentally,
had also come north from Birmingham. They were Eddie Kendricks,
Paul Williams, and Kel Osborne. Having formed the group back home,
they added another singer, Willy Waller, in Cleveland, subsequently
adding two more, Fred Fluellen and Paul Hayes. Jenkins took an immediate liking to the group and, after introducing himself backstage, they
acceded to his big talk of managing them.

The Cavaliers fused tight and intricate harmonies, but rather than
just stand there (as was the rule for such acts of the day), they added
nifty, finely choreographed dance steps. Jenkins wove in more material,
including high-toned Mills Brothers songs. He then chose a different
name for them, commensurate with their high-hat style—the Primes.

But the Primes never got prime. Certainly not in Cleveland,
prompting Jenkins to give it a shot in more-happening Detroit, where

he moved with the core trio of Primes late in 1958. But Motown was another no-town for them, and Jenkins had a brainstorm: creating a girl-group to back up, and sex up, the Primes, along the lines of Ike Turner's Ikettes and Ray Charles's Raelettes. No question Milton knew where to find girls—but girls who could actually look good and sing, that was a challenge. One thing he knew was that there were tons of girls who lived at that big housing project, Brewster something, who might fit the bill.

And so it was that, one hot afternoon in mid-June, 1959, Milt Jenkins, taking along his Primes to help make his case, jumped into his Cadillac, put the top down, and headed for Brewster-Douglass.

Diana Ross and Mary Wilson—allegorically, given their personal differences decades after the Supremes' demise—recall the origin of the Primettes in accounts that differ in nearly every detail. Wilson's is that Milt Jenkins found Florence Ballard on that fateful foray into the projects and that Flo then made good on her vow, just days before, to start a group with Mary; the two of them, Wilson recalled, had nothing to do with Diane Ross's entry.

Ross, for her part, insisted in 2007 that she remembers those days "like it was yesterday," but apparently too many yesterdays had passed even fourteen years earlier to recall anything much about Jenkins in her autobiography. She relegated Jenkins to just one page of the 275-page book, noting that he, Kendricks, Williams, and Kel Osborne—the first two of whom would of course find fame and fortune in the Temptations—happened to show up at her door, not explaining how they knew of her. Further, she said that she, Ballard, Wilson, and a fourth girl, Betty McGlown (whose name she misspelled as "McGlowan"), were already performing together at "church socials and the like." As an aside, she recalled that Jenkins was dating one of Flo's older sisters.

In fact, that sister, Maxine Ballard, would meet Jenkins during his Cadillac run to the projects—and wind up as Jenkins's wife until his death in 1973. And some of her own recollections are helpful in resolving a few of the differences between the Ross and Wilson tales. At the time, she was 16, married to a Marine who was stationed overseas—and clearly susceptible to the attentions of a dude like Milt Jenkins. As she recalled, "I had not seen my husband for months. We had no children and, truthfully, had not been together sexually for a very long time."

On that day, Milt, his arm in the ever-present cast, was clad in a knee-length white leather coat, black boots, and crisp black slacks. Williams, Kendricks, and Osborne also looked buttery in their linen pants, short-sleeved print shirts, and snap-brim hats. But it was solely Jenkins for whom Maxine had eyes. As for the "tall and handsome" Milt, "his eyes were busy undressing me." So aroused did she become that she confessed she nearly had an orgasm right then and there. Jenkins, she attested, "awakened me from a deep sleep. I thought I was a grown woman, but he made me feel like a young girl eagerly awaiting her wedding night."

He no doubt knew the effect he was having on her. But he was there for a reason, and he asked her, "Are you interested in singing?"

Barely able to speak, she replied, "No. Why?"

As he explained about the Primes and Primettes, Flo didn't know if the whole thing was some sort of con, but the guys in the car seemed down to earth and made small talk with her. And she was duly impressed that they had a singing group, and more than a little intrigued that they were looking for a singer, especially when Maxine, trying to keep Jenkins around longer, told him, "My sister sings."

At that, Flo jumped in. "I'll sing in your group, mister."

Maxine, always protective of Flo, told her, "Flo, you ain't doin' nothing until we go ask Mom and Dad."

Jenkins waited in the car while she and Flo went inside and told Jesse and Lurlee of the opportunity for Flo. Predictably, neither was excited about it. "Daddy wanted no part of the whole music thing," Maxine confirmed. "He said we were too young."

Jesse, though, was not calling the shots for the clan. He was very sick, and had not long to live. It was up to Lurlee, and she didn't cast the notion away. Instead, wanting to hear what this Jenkins character had to say, she went outside with Flo and Maxine and heard out his rap. He was smooth, all right; of that she had no doubt. Maybe a little too smooth.

"If you're a manager," she sniffed, "show me papers or something, or else you ain't getting nowhere near my daughters."

Lurlee perceived that Milt had designs on both Flo and Maxine. And it worried her that if she allowed him to have dibs on Flo, Maxine might enter into an adulterous fling with him. As it turned out, she had reason to worry. Still, how could she crush Flo's dreams of singing? As long as she had assurances that he was on the level, she'd go along with it. Milt obliged her. He left, soon to return with a sheaf of papers, including publicity photos of and newspaper ads billing the Primes.

Lurlee looked them over and made her decision. "You have something for me to sign?" she asked.

He whipped out a contract that required both Flo's signature and her own, since Flo was a minor. This document, in effect, granted Jenkins legal guardianship during the time she would be in his custody.

Milt left the projects that day feeling pleased. He now had a young singer under his thumb, and her hot sister soon to be in his bed. Driving back downtown, he sat a little higher in his soft leather seat. It had been a good day.

Because Florence told him she knew other singers her age, Jenkins left it to her to bring one around to his place later that week. That was when, according to Wilson, Flo ran up to her in school and gushed to her all about being in this new group called the Primettes, which needed another girl—"That's you!" Flo told her.

When Flo told her about going to Milt Jenkins's place to sing for him, Mary was game. But she, too, needed permission. That night she told her mother about the offer, her words spouting so quickly that Johnnie Mae didn't quite get the group's name.

"The Primates?" she said, looking pained.

"Prim-*ettes*."

Johnnie Mae, as warily as Lurlee Ballard—but seeing the look in her daughter's eyes when she said that this could be "the chance of a lifetime"—agreed that she could at least go and audition for Milton Jenkins.

A couple of days later, Mary and Flo set out on foot after school for the other side of the tracks, treading through the red-light streets of Paradise Valley looking for the address Milt had given Flo. It turned out to be a transient hotel across the street from the Flame Show Bar. The two wide-eyed girls were thankful for the late daylight, but had to ascend a dark stairway; as they went up, they gripped each other's hand tightly, not knowing who or what was lurking in the shadows. Arriving at Jenkins's room, they knocked and Milt opened the door to a large, furnished flat he shared with the Primes. Clothes and food wrappers littered the floor, lampshades were askew, the air reeked of God knows what. Bur Milt and his crew were again nattily dressed and courtly in manner. As the Primes ran through some songs, Flo and Mary sat down at a table at which there were two other girls. One of them was a tall, attractive, slightly older girl, around 17. She said her name was Betty McGlown, that she was Paul Williams's girlfriend, and that he'd asked her to be in the Primettes.

The other girl, with her pipe-cleaner limbs and bulging eyes, they knew from the projects.

"Hi, Diane," Mary said.

"Oh, hi," Diane Ross responded. "Do you girls sing, too?"

Mary and Flo blanched, arching their eyebrows at each other. They could have been thinking the exact same thing: "Does *she* sing?"

For her part, Ross seems not to remember anything of this interlude. It's absent in her memoirs, in which her only citation of the Primettes' mentor is that "[i]t was Milton Jenkins who really got us started when he brought around this group of guys from Alabama to meet us girls" before he "started managing us too." The gaps were large, and, once filled in, the story is far more fascinating than Ross and Wilson seemed to have realized, since it bespeaks young Diana Ross's passive means of getting ahead, sometimes despite herself. Consider that even as a complete unknown in the larger sense she had a name on the local teenage talent show circuit, an indication of how closely intertwined was the community of acts performing in East Detroit.

For instance, there was Otis Williams's act. A few years older than the Primettes, and worldly by their standards, Williams had actually recorded with some minor success. His first group, the Siberians, cut two sides for Detroit deejay Bristol Bryant's label, "Pecos Kid" and "All My Life," before re-forming as the El Domingoes. One would think he'd have been far beyond Diane Ross's realm of experience in 1959, but many of the kid-groups ran in the same circles and performed on the same talent shows as the adult ones, and on that circuit were the two former schoolmates of Ross, Melvin Franklin and Richard Street, who had maintained their friendship with Ross.

"Even back then," says Williams, "running with Melvin and Richard, I'd hear about Diane Ross. It was Diane Ross this, Diane Ross that. I'd think, Jesus, this girl must be something special."

Milt Jenkins, of course, lived by that grapevine. Thus, when he began his search for a girl singing group, the vine also led to Ross's apartment in the projects, where he worked his rap for Ernestine. Fortunately, Fred Ross wasn't home at the time, leaving Ernestine to hear him out. Surprisingly, she was impressed by his snazzy clothes and refined manners, as well as his notion, logically rooted, that by rehearsing and participating in a positive group endeavor, Diane would actually be safer with him than on the streets. Clean-cut Paul Williams clinched the deal by promising Ernestine that her daughter would be back home "before the street lights went on." She and Diane signed Milton's personal-services contract—and when Fred found out, he was perturbed, fearing aloud that this wistful musical excursion would derail Diane's education. In the end, though, he bowed to Ernestine's

wishes—surely a red-letter day for Diane Ross, who for once had reason
to think her father believed in her.

Up in Milton's room, the three girls sang together for the first time, with
historical trivia-question-to-be Betty McGlown, who, poised and confident, seemed almost a grand dame, though she did not have much of a
voice. Told to "sing anything," the foursome stood looking at one another before Flo took the lead and broke into the Ray Charles song
"Night Time Is the Right Time," whereupon the others awkwardly followed. Ballard, by dint of having the loudest—and highest-pitched, thus
"girliest"—voice, seemed to have established herself right away, by default, as the group leader and lead vocalist—not that the other girls had
any objection, agreeing that she was the best singer. Ballard took to the
role easily; anytime Milton asked the still somewhat overwhelmed Wilson a question, Flo would intercede and answer for her, to Mary's relief.

The Primes suggested they do Hank Ballard's "The Twist," and again
Flo took the lead without dissent, with Paul Williams tutoring them on a
few rudimentary steps. Then they did the Drifters' "There Goes My
Baby," with Ross on lead at Milt's request. Rough-hewn and squeaky
though they were, with Jenkins telling Ross not to sing so nasally, their
voices and personalities meshed; they were engaging, even endearing.

Milton was pleased. Later that day he made tracks for Brewster-
Douglass, a route he could traverse in his sleep by now, to obtain Johnnie Mae Wilson's marker—literally, as she could not read or write. She
reluctantly signed, as had Lurlee Ballard and Ernestine Ross, and now
the deal was done.

And so one of the most gender-empowering girl-groups in history was
triggered by a man who had women work on their backs so that he
could make a living. Ross, Wilson, and Ballard, however, were too
young to know something like this—if indeed they ever realized it—
and simply went along, operating on the idealized notion that Milt
Jenkins was the "most interesting" man they had ever known.

As the three girls walked back together to the projects after singing
together for the first time, they were giddy. Whatever Milt Jenkins was,
they were sure he was going to make them stars. And get them out of
the projects.

three

NOTOWN
TO
MOTOWN

The summer of '59 was the sixth hottest on record in Detroit until then, the temperatures causing tar bubbles that burst on the newly constructed Chrysler Freeway. On John R Street, Milton Jenkins switched to short sleeves, allowing his mangled arm some air in its sling. Leaving his sweltering flat, he found a rehearsal hall on 12th Street for the Primes and the Primettes, who often practiced songs and steps in adjoining rooms at the same time. Late that summer, the El Domingoes, having hooked up with Jenkins, joined the cacophony.

"I look back at those days and I say, *damn*, how's that for history?" remarked Otis Williams. "There in one room you had what was gonna be the Supremes and in another the Temptations. You'd take a break and go to the water fountain and you'd hear Diana Ross and Eddie Kendricks from opposite ends of the floor. It was like a duet, 'cause you'd hear their voices together, which wouldn't happen on record for another ten years, when we and the Supremes did 'I'm Gonna Make You Love Me.' Too bad someone didn't make some tapes from those rehearsals. Imagine what them suckers would be worth today."

True to their word, Jenkins or Paul Williams dutifully drove Ross, Wilson, and Ballard back home to the projects before sunset, sometimes as often as four days a week. Milton also had one of his girlfriends chaperone them to their early gigs at talent shows around town. She would also take the girls shopping, at Milton's expense, leading them to believe they'd be outfitted in glittery gowns. Instead, because he wanted to keep them firmly in a teenage niche, they came out looking like a pep squad, in virginal white blouses—sometimes with a big "P" across each one's chest—and pleated skirts; chic heels were eschewed for sneakers and bobby sox. This was an obvious influence of Frankie Lymon and the Teenagers, and while all the Primettes hated the look, Wilson, Ballard, and McGlown at least grinned and bore it in early promotion photographs. But Ross, who considered herself knowing in matters of fashion and style, is seen in those pictures looking genuinely pained.

Ross was still not sure enough of herself to do anything but defer to Ballard as the group's leader. Flo did nothing to dispel the notion, though she had less interest in the fashion issues than in her booming lead vocals. Itching to get before audiences, she nudged Jenkins to book them all throughout the summer. "Mr. Milton," she'd tell him, "we're ready." He agreed, and while it's not known what their first gig was, Wilson thought it was in a union hall. Milton, though, didn't settle for the talent show–lodge–church social circuit, intermingling those venues with bookings at the hard-core clubs, which took the Primettes despite the fact they were legally underage.

That was a common practice in those days; many teenage groups—male and female—regularly appeared in the clubs, with a wink-and-nod by the cops and city politicians likely paid off to look the other way. Sometimes they couldn't. For example, although the Primettes played gigs at the Roostertail and the Twenty Grand Club without incident, another gig at the Gold Coast turned ugly when a brawl erupted in the audience, sending chairs and drinks flying. With the club's liquor license at peril, the owner politely advised Jenkins it would be best if the Primettes didn't return.

Such exposure to the grimier side of life made the girls feel older, wiser, worldly. Indeed, Wilson spoke of audience rumbles not as scary but as "added entertainment," though Jenkins judiciously omitted reporting them to the girls' parents in his review of each show. Still fairly saccharine in sound and style, the group was quickly maturing under these trials by fire. Interestingly, though Milton's plan had been to pair the Primettes on stage with the Primes, it seems that never happened, as Jenkins found the girls more in demand than the guys.

In time, they'd forego the cheerleader garb for that of sophisticated ladies, their clothing chosen now by the precocious Ross. They'd be quite a sight, radical for an era when teen girl acts—and there weren't many of them—could have gone from the stage to the prom. The Primettes' sense of style—dictated by Ross as the imagined ingénue—

had them covered in orange and yellow waist-cinching gowns flared at the knee and dyed-orange peau de soie pumps (actually cheap heels bought in the bargain basement of Hudson's department store).

Also unusual was the fact that they had their own guitar player. That came about when the group, hanging out at Jenkins's hotel, saw a teenager milling about the crowd, a guitar case slung over his back. The kid, Marvin Tarplin, was understandably accommodating when the four pretty girls showered him with attention and asked if he'd be their accompanist. Jenkins had no objections, as it would add another male presence who could travel with them, leaving him more time to travel with the Primes. And Tarplin not only juiced up the act with some cool acoustic riffs, he did the arranging and taught the girls the harmonies on new songs. No longer did they need to wait on the Primes to do that.

Jenkins's most important contribution was to have Diane sing some of the leads, usually when a softer, more vulnerable vocal was called for. On those, she'd pour it on thick, trying to be a torch singer like Billie Holiday—but often coming across more like Moms Mabley, her eyes bulging and her jaws grinding as she mugged for the crowd, sometimes causing people to snicker at her. Wilson describes the early Ross vocal intonation as "a whiny little sound"; sometimes, she and Flo would look at each other while Diane was singing and have to fight hard to keep from giggling themselves.

For Flo, there was nothing even faintly amusing about the decision to give any of her leads to Ross. Nor did she hide her contempt from Ross. Years later she recalled, unapologetically, that during the Primettes' run she told Diane right out, "You ain't a lead singer." Ross might actually have agreed at the beginning, but she took Ballard's disses personally, and as a challenge. Reflexively, she would spring back with, "Well, what makes you think *you* are? Just 'cause everybody says so?" Flo would laugh at the irrationality of that statement, but she ended those debates with a firm, and convincing, threat. "Stop messing with me," she'd say, making the point by standing toe to toe with the shorter Diane and intimidating her.

Ross, typically, would back off, but she did not surrender. On the contrary, she wanted badly to spite Flo by going around her, always a safer and more effective way to get back at somebody. That meant sidling up to Jenkins to coquettishly thank him for believing in her. As with most men, teenage or older, he felt there was something about Ross that made her thoughts and opinions—especially those about herself—seem so convincing. And if Flo gnashed her teeth each time Diane sang a lead, the competition may well have made her work harder and get better as well.

Says Otis Williams:

> I remember watching them do Ray Charles's "Night and Day." Diane had the lead and she was okay. But when it came time for Flo to come in with the Margie Hendricks part—the *da-haaaaay*—she just made the place melt. People would stand up and get all crazy. They'd be shouting, "Sing that song, girl!" Flo could really upset the house, and she knew she could steal a song from Diane like that.
>
> With Flo, singing was a righteous thing. It wasn't that way for Diane. For her, it was more of a way of accomplishing things, to get attention. See, she knew what she had to do to sound commercial, whereas Flo would just sing and blow the doors off. That was why she never could accept Diane's emergence. 'Cause she didn't understand it. That it's more than who can sing better.

Ross, of course, seeing her ambition fed even with a still shrill and adenoidal voice, understood perfectly. Clearly, she knew where she was going to.

That the Primettes considered money an afterthought was fortunate, since their income that summer was nil, Milton Jenkins having advised them that he'd had to requisition whatever was due them to cover unnamed expenses. More problematic for the group, in any case, were the exigencies of life, real life. In the fall, school interrupted the showbiz fantasia and all of their parents—having gnashed *their* teeth all summer about the late nights and their underage daughters spending time in nightclubs—were adamant that the singing was not going to interfere with school.

Ross, Wilson, and Ballard began high school that fall, choosing which one they wanted to attend. Making no compact to remain yoked for the sake of the group, they began in different schools, Wilson at Commerce, Ballard at Northeastern, Ross at Cass Technical. For Diane, this was a coup, aided by Fred Ross's status as a Cass alumnae, and a proud one, as it was similar to a prep school. Wilson would describe Cass as "elite" and "a snob school," and that given the choice to go there herself she had declined. Diane's enrollment reinforced the notion around the projects that the Ross family looked down their noses at those not similarly disposed. But if Diane was up where she belonged, she was brought down when she petitioned for membership in a Cass sorority, only to be rejected because she was from the projects.

Ross did make an effort to keep the Primettes' sorority going, mainly by dropping by Wilson's apartment and acting out a sisterly ritual designing more outfits for the group, or just going to the movies. Absent from these excursions was Florence, though Mary had grown very close to her and switched from Commerce to Northeastern that freshman term—in part, to be near Ballard. If Ross had in mind drawing closer with Wilson to exercise leverage over Ballard, Mary may have been hip to the game. In a sense, as would become even more apparent in the future, Mary was—perhaps subconsciously at first—positioning herself as the cipher, the neutral buffer between the polar ends of Ross and Ballard to keep them from splintering.

Part of that objective, as well, was the influence of Betty McGlown, who because she was 17 could pull rank, and when she did it was usually to defuse a rant from Ross before it got out of hand. When Betty got in her face, Ross fell silent, a relief to everybody. McGlown, though, wanted no real role in the group. She had none of the ambition of the three core Primettes and did little but waft along as a favor to Williams, craving no glory. Even though she was egged on by Jenkins and even by the girls to sing an occasional lead, she had no stomach for it. And now, entering her sophomore year of high school on the west side of town, she had almost no contact with the other three.

Ross, for her part, spent only as much time bonding with Wilson as her increasingly busy life permitted. She took a night job at J. L. Hudson's department store on Woodward Avenue, busing tables in the cafeteria. (It's been speculated, though never confirmed, that Ross was the first black employee of Hudson's to work outside the kitchen. If so, she has never mentioned this herself.) At Cass, she took extra classes in dress design, hoping to craft stage costumes she would wear, not only with the act but on her own, as a chanteuse who would have the spotlight all to herself.

But those plans hit a snag that spring when, after they'd been booked into another round of talent shows and the like, Milton Jenkins was suddenly out of commission, laid up in Henry Ford Hospital, finally done in by his reluctance to have his injured arm treated properly. While no one seemed to know for sure the extent of the problem since Milton refused guests rather than let anyone see him helpless, Maxine Ballard, whom he had begun dating steadily, said that the arm had become infected, then gangrenous. When he could no longer ignore the debilitating pain he finally agreed to go in, and it was almost too late. Not only was he close to having the arm amputated, Maxine said, "he was fighting for his life" when he went under the knife, then lay on his back under heavy sedation hooked to IV tubes for days after.

He pulled through, but came home with fifteen pounds eaten from his already spare frame and was bedridden for weeks, allowing only Maxine to tend to him. As it happened, by then the Primes had moved out of his room, and out of his purview. They, too, had stagnated over the fall and winter, leading a homesick Eddie Kendricks to move back to Birmingham and Kel Osborne to pack up for California to make it as a solo act. As well, Otis Williams and his El Domingoes had had it with Jenkins's failure to do much for them and dumped him in absentia. They hooked up with another manager, Johnnie Mae Matthews, a former R&B singer who—most rarely for a woman, black or white, even today—had formed her own label, Northern Records, and managed and produced other acts. (In future years Matthews would be dubbed "Godmother of Detroit Soul.") She renamed the group Otis Williams and the Distants and cut two sides on them for Northern.

"Something happened and we left Milton," Williams recalls, still unaware of the circumstances of Jenkins's absence. "I think we really just outgrew him. He was operating in smaller circles than we thought we should be in. It was hard for Milton to take care of us and take care of all his ladies at the same time. Being a manager is a full-time job but so is being a pimp. Something had to give, and it was probably Milton."

(Taking the inbreeding of Detroit's nascent singing groups a step further, the Distants now took in Melvin Franklin and Richard Street—who themselves had come through a lineage of note, Franklin fresh from a group called the Voice Masters, two of whose members were teenagers named David Ruffin and Lamont Dozier; Street's stepping stone was a group with a brother and sister, Theodore and Barbara Martin, the latter of whom would shortly make her own jump in rank. What's more, Matthews's studio sessions with the Distants included some familiar names: guitarist Eddie Willis, saxophonist Eli Fontaine, drummer Uriel Jones, and pianist Richard "Popcorn" Wylie, who brought in a bass player he'd formed a combo with in high school—

James Jamerson. He also brought in a backup group, the Mohawks, one of whose singers was named Norman Whitfield. Everyone in that bunch—as well as the sundered Eddie Kendricks and Paul Williams—would find a far greater calling, and in short order.)

Jenkins, as he gradually recovered, didn't try to reconnect with the remains of the Primes, who were now down to one: Williams. He fell into an ennui of depression that could only be buoyed by the doting Maxine, who didn't cast him aside even as he hit rock bottom and gave up on his acts—really just the Primettes by that point. Too proud, humiliated by his fall, and too weak to carry on the grind of rehearsals and bookings, he never bothered to hold the Primettes to their contracts, a decision he would come to rue in time. For now, he turned his attentions from the rigors of music and prostitution to living a semblance of family life with Maxine, whom he would marry in 1961 after she obtained a divorce from her serviceman husband. As he looked for honest work, so did the Primettes.

With a touch of symmetry, Flo turned over the affairs of the group to a guy *she* was dating, Jesse Greer. This was a stretch since Greer was just out of high school and with a fledgling vocal group himself, the Peppermints, but they had played the Flame Show Bar and the Twenty Grand, and he was thinking big. Unfortunately, he lacked Jenkins's glib bluster and connections. After rehearsing the girls at the Brewster Center, he got them more of the usual talent shows and sock hops that the girls assumed they'd outgrown. Another was a fashion show in a beauty parlor called the House of Beauty, the owners of which ran an eponymous record label out of the back room.

These cut-rate gigs were memorable only for the chance they gave the girls to intermingle with boy singers backstage, where pubescent hormones and cheap liquor ran wild. Wilson would relate interludes of "sipping cheap wine," "making out," and "get[ting] down." Flo, in fact, carried her own experimentation far enough to break up with Greer, who of course bore her father's first name and was, she decided now, "too nice" for her tastes. Apparently, in matters of men and sex, her taste was bad boys.

Coming of age and rounding into desirable young women, the Primettes were already heartbreakers. When the Distants would intersect with them on the talent show circuit, Richard Street would trail Ross around like a heartsick lapdog—only to see her treat him as one, nearly literally with a pat on the head and a few words of empty chitchat. It was as if Ross herself had to choose a *swain*, who usually turned out to be an older guy with some pull in the music game; anyone beneath that, no matter how handsome or chivalrous, she wrote off. This may explain why, according to Mary, Diane seemingly "had eyes for everyone but Richard." Wilson, on the other hand, acted on hormonal impulse, coupling with Melvin Franklin during some of those backstage group gropes, though the most serious pairing was Flo and Otis Williams.

"We had," Williams confided, "an instant affection for each other. Flo was a few years younger than me, which could've been trouble, you know, for me. But I couldn't help but spend time with her. Flo had a lot of sexual energy, but she had to really trust you first. We spent a lot of time talking about life before we ever did stuff. It was more than sex; we loved and respected each other."

The most significant change during the early months of 1960 was in Diane Ross. Her confidence, tempered after being rejected by the Cass High School sorority, got a lift when they reconsidered and accepted her after all. The reversal came after she had refused to take no for an answer and threw herself into a plethora of school activities to impress them. It wasn't so much that she got them to like her much better; they may even have been the same as when, originally, as Wilson observed, "she brought out the worst in those girls." Rather, she simply overwhelmed them with her obvious qualifications and tenacious resolve, or else they were just tired of her bugging them.

That attitude was no different when it came to the Primettes. In all group matters, Wilson ventured, Ross "was certain that she knew everything, and no matter what everyone else did . . . Diane would comment on it." She almost always got her way. On fashion and cosmetic issues, her word was inviolate.

"Personal style," she would tell Mary and Flo, sounding *très* sophisticated, "is a real important expression of self."

"Self," evidently, was far more important to Ross than to her three mates. While throwing her weight (as sparse as it was) around was a constant with the Primettes, Wilson noted that Ross "didn't seem to mind being away from us" as she went about polishing and refining her own rising star by taking weekend modeling classes. Years later, after Ross had proven her lone-wolf priorities beyond all doubt, she offered some rationalizations, writing in her autobiography *Secrets of a Sparrow:*

"Mary, Florence, and I were not true sisters. [We] started out as three strangers who were randomly placed together. . . . When difficulties arose, we did not have the kind of bond that automatically exists among family members."

If Ross's plans, even in 1960, wandered beyond Mary Wilson and Florence Ballard, the latter was still somewhat blinkered—assuming, naively to be sure, that she was inveterately the Primettes' fulcrum. Her sassiness could always convey the image for outsiders. But she may not have noticed that Ross had curried Wilson for leverage; accordingly, the course they were following was being laid down by the girl Flo believed couldn't sing her way out of a paper bag.

But then Flo herself was providing a vacuum for Diane to fill. Falling behind in her final grades, she was ordered by Lurlee to quit the Primettes when school let out that spring. It took an impassioned plea from Diane and Mary for Lurlee to allow Flo to return after several days. Just in time, it turned out, for the Primettes to enjoy their first big break.

Cee

In late June, they decided to enter the talent competition at the Detroit/Windsor International Freedom Festival, an annual jamboree that began the summer before to celebrate in early July both the American and the Canadian Independence Day, with events on both sides of the Detroit River culminating in a gigantic fireworks display. One event, the talent show, sponsored by some of the area's radio stations, offered a venue for local amateur singers and bands to compete for a top prize of $15 and a bit of local publicity.

While technically a professional act, the Primettes qualified because they'd never been paid a thin dime by Milton Jenkins. As putative amateurs, the girls again needed parental permission to get a spot on the show, seemingly a formality for a harmless gig in an All-American, apple-pie environment a far cry from the smoke-filled nightclubs. At least that's what Johnnie Mae Wilson and Lurleee Ballard believed when they quickly signed the forms. Fred Ross was not so easily persuaded. When Diane presented him with the papers, he took the opportunity to make a stand, explaining calmly that the year-long singing excursion had gone far enough, and that any further indulgence for Diane would ruin her education. It was a rather strange case to be making, with Diane having just graduated tenth grade with honors. But Fred could see long-term implications in his daughter's obsession with performing. Unless he drew a line here, he knew, she'd never get a college education. Her entire demeanor, the way her eyes burned hot when she spoke of being a star, said it all. He didn't begrudge her, or her talent—but from where he sat, enough was enough.

The argument, which Ernestine was helpless to mediate, broke the fragile *detente* between Fred and Diane, inevitably recharging the psychological friction caused by his distance and her angst about feeling like the second-best daughter.

"What do I have to do to please you?" she screamed at him melodramatically according to one account, though this is another subplot absent from her memoirs.

The stalemate went on for several days, during which Mary and Flo kept begging Fred to reconsider. When he held his ground, Diane nearly imploded, in her frustration returning to an old habit of biting her fingernails to the nub. At her wit's end, she whispered to Mary and Flo that she might do something she'd never done before—defy Fred, by sneaking to the festival. One way or another, Diane wouldn't miss this big chance. "Nothing was going to stop her from going," Wilson would recall.

But Fred again blinked, saying later that he caved only because he was fed up with all of the "moaning and groaning" about it every day around the house. In truth, he almost always gave in to his children, especially, as Florence once remarked, if Diane "turned on the tears." If she played the drama queen with her father, it was for a purpose, and all too obvious. Watching her get her way about the show, Mary and Flo were naturally relieved, but a little embarrassed for him. Fred, Flo would recall, was hardly the unfeeling "daddy dearest" Diane sometimes made him out to be, and in fact a "softie." Indeed, both she and Mary envied her. As Flo noted, "At least she *had* a father."

Fred's capitulation is, in historical terms, a major event in the story of the Supremes. Because the Detroit/Windsor show was the first stage they mounted that really mattered—not that the show itself was anything special, with its day-long procession of acts that careened from singers to belly dancers to ventriloquists (one of whom achieved a measure of fame as a '60s television curio, Willie Tyler and his dummy Lester, who happened to be a classmate of Wilson and Ballard at Northeastern High). In this chaotic dog-and-pony show, the Primettes got most of the buzz. Standing in yellow chiffon dresses on another scorching day before an audience of 500 people scarfing down hot dogs and cotton candy, they proved that Milton Jenkins's intuition had been correct.

They weren't the best vocal group in the world, perhaps not even in the contest, but their voices and phrasing were tight and exuberant, swathed by Marvin Tarplin's amplified guitar licks. Their moves were yet a bit stiff and knock-kneed, but with the core trio having caught up with Betty McGlown in feminine curves, they were undeniably sexy.

Wilson would recall that when they did "Night Time Is the Right Time" during their standard five-song set, Flo's singing on the wild bass line was so intense that the crowd was "totally amazed." Then, when Diane pealed a fluttery, high-pitched counterpoint, "the whole place just went crazy." From that moment on, it could be said that the two polar, and nuclear, forces of the group—Ross and Ballard—were established, to the benefit of the group, but also that the two performers had embarked on a collision course.

On that day, though, they all were winners, and richer for it by $15—at least for a little while. As self-appointed group "treasurer," Mary stuck the cash in her pocket; later, after they changed clothes and went on some of the rides at the amusement park, she went to divvy it up but found her pocket empty. When she told the girls the money was gone, apparently taken by a pickpocket, Diane accused her of lying so she could keep the money for herself. Even at the time, it didn't seem the best of omens that the first payday they ever had, they still got nothing.

But it was Florence who committed a far more grievous sin after the show—or at least it could have been a sin had a decision she made stood. Assuming she was group leader, an enormously tall black man with a very deep voice approached her and introduced himself as Robert Bateman of the Motown company. At the time, Flo had strayed from the other Primettes, whom Bateman praised for their performance. Handing her a card with a phone number on it, he told Flo to call to set up a day and time for the group to come in and audition for his boss, Berry Gordy.

That name resonated with Flo as it did with everyone else on the Detroit music scene, but not completely favorably. Word on the street was that while Gordy's year-old Motown shop was happening, he had bled a lot of young, naive acts dry when the royalties were supposed to be paid—not that this was an uncommon occurrence in the music industry in general.

"Berry Gordy?" she repeated. "Ain't he the guy who cheats his artists?"

Bateman, who no doubt had heard this before, didn't flinch or withdraw the invitation. "This could be the biggest thing that ever happens to you," he said, his deep voice almost grim. "Don't blow it."

Flo, of course, always took such lecturing as an insult. Rather than hurry over to the other girls to tell them of the Motown entreaty, she narrowed her eyes at Robert Bateman as he walked away and then, believing she knew best, said nothing about it to the others. Indeed, Wilson has maintained stoutly that no one from Motown or any other record company spoke with anyone in the group that day. Bateman himself, however, contradicts that, saying he surely approached Florence Ballard.

"Yeah, I discovered them at that festival, I loved 'em when I heard 'em," he says. "I was the guy who brought them to Motown." But Bateman's own memory is a bit fuzzy in that he swears the meeting somehow happened *after* the Primettes had already been to see Gordy, plainly a chronology that makes no sense since, in that case, he could neither have discovered them nor brought them in.

In fact, he *didn't* bring them in. That came about only after Diane Ross reckoned it was high time to get the group signed to a recording contract, knowing exactly the man to broker that deal—the lean, pale-skinned singer she'd found so beguiling when she watched him rehearse with his group, back when Smokey Robinson was a nobody. Now, only two years later, he was a nobody no longer, and that *really* beguiled her, considering that in the interim Smokey's group—renamed the Miracles—had become the most recognizable signature voice of Berry Gordy's original label and up to then the only jewel in his crown, Tamla Records.

Still in its incubation stage, the label and its parent company, Motown Inc., had no national pull and Gordy had to lease out many of its records to other, bigger labels, including some by the Miracles. But Gordy had accumulated a raft of chits by writing for Jackie Wilson, and by calling them in he was able to get enough airplay on the Detroit radio stations to score the Miracles regional hits, as well as to parlay a family loan and some fleeting royalties into establishing a headquarters/studio in a rundown two-story row house on West Grand Boulevard. With characteristic bravado, he slapped a sign over its bay-windowed fresco front landing that read "Hitsville, U.S.A."

That was a prophesy that had a long way to go before it could be fulfilled. But Gordy had nerve, and he had a concept of black capitalism far more fantastical than his concept of music. He couldn't have known he was fated, like the Supremes, for unspeakable success, or that he was on the cusp of a social and historical context for his lofty dreams. All he knew was that he had his seedlings, in his label and in

Smokey Robinson. Meanwhile, Smokey himself, though *he* couldn't know it, was the piper of the next new thing—when pop would meet R&B and modify "race music" as never before, running clever lyrical and melodic hooks into venerable rhythm-and-blues grit. These were the *grooves*, as the cats on the street said, that would give Gordy's new paradigm of black self-reliance a virtual soundtrack.

For Diane Ross, then, it was suddenly a good idea to want to drop in on her old friend Smokey. With none of Florence Ballard's compunctions or principles, she seemed to already know that her future was tethered to the guy with the shady reputation who ran Motown.

four

BERRY

B erry Gordy ran on the same streets and alleys of Paradise Valley as Milt Jenkins, pursuing the same elusive success with women and music. But until the late '50s his luck with each ran sour. Unlike Jenkins, Gordy was not a high roller; he had no Cadillac parked outside the Flame Show Bar, no fly threads, no bling, no pretty face. He stood a good half-foot shorter than Jenkins, around five-six on a good day, and usually looked a bit scraggly. But he was always a player, or at least could convince the crowd he was. That he could do a convincing imitation of a high roller, however, was a factor of his birth into a rich and very helpful family.

Born, aptly, on Thanksgiving day, November 28, 1929, as Berry Gordy III, he was the second youngest of seven children, most of the rest of whom he watched grow rich and fat while for him life remained a constant struggle. His lot was, understandably, a source of embarrassment within the family, seeing as how he was the namesake of its patriarch, Berry Gordy Jr., who was such a respected and approachable grand duke that no one knew him as Berry Jr., only as "Pops." His son, Berry III, in turn, requisitioned the "Jr." for himself, chucking the more formal and pretentious honorific of a third-generation Berry.

Pops Gordy, though, was a tough act to follow. A self-made man from square one, he had arrived in the great black migration from his native Alabama in the '20s. He did his grunt work on the Ford assembly line, saved and invested his money wisely, and by the '40s had opened a market in a relatively upscale West Detroit neighborhood, calling it, tellingly, the Booker T. Washington Grocery Store.

The Gordy matriarch, Bertha, kept herself busy broadening her own horizons in academia. She studied retail management at Wayne State University and business at Michigan University, and after graduating from the Detroit Institute of Commerce she founded and became secretary-treasurer of the Friendship Mutual Life Insurance Company, whose mission was selling insurance policies to black families. Known and consulted regularly by white business and political leaders, Bertha was the classic example of what upper-class whites were talking about when they said some of their best friends were black.

The younger Berry Gordy never ran in crowds like that. He was a hard-boiled, unfocused teenager who got into so many brawls in and around school that Pops told him to save his fists for where they could help him—namely, prizefighting. In the city that produced the Brown Bomber, Brown Berry was no Joe Louis, either, but good enough to progress through the amateur Golden Gloves chain, first as a wiry 112-pounder, then a brawny 126-pound featherweight by the time he quit school in the eleventh grade to turn pro. This decision upset his parents and always haunted him, as he would become overly sensitive to the fact that he never fully learned how to read and write.

During his fight career, Gordy sparred with a slightly older Golden Gloves winner named Jackie Wilson, who wanted to sing for a living and soon would be fronting the R&B group Billy Ward and the Dominoes. Gordy would never have his glove raised as a Golden Glove winner, but he did ace eight of fourteen bouts. Fighting on the undercard of a few big boxing shows at the Detroit Olympia, he earned up to $500 a fight, and was trained by Eddie Futch, who would take Joe Frazier to the heavyweight title, and with whom he was nearly killed while driving back from a fight in Chicago. He also had fights in California, but if he had the hunger he never had the size to go much further.

When he hung up the gloves in the late '40s, he could have gone to work for Pops; instead, he enlisted in the Army, spent two years on bases in Arkansas and Michigan, then shipped out to Korea, all while earning a high school equivalency degree. Returning home in 1951, when he was 22, he married a 19-year-old girl named Thelma Louise Coleman, moved into an apartment, and fathered a son and two daughters. But he still couldn't find steady work. Usually his days were spent rolling sevens and craps in alleys. Somewhere along the line, he decided he could make it as a singer, then as a songwriter, and he began frequenting the clubs, making some early contacts with the music crowd. Talking the ever-optimistic Pops into lending him $700, he opened the 3-D Record Mart.

3-D, though, didn't survive beyond two years and went under in 1953. He then bit the bullet and went to work (as Pops had) in the Ford plant, fastening chrome strips and nailing upholstery to skeletal cars rolling down the assembly line. He continued to write songs and to spend time at the clubs—too much time, apparently, because in 1956 Thelma felt abandoned and hit him with divorce papers, alleging he was a hopeless philanderer who stayed out all night, had "refuse[d] to speak to her for long periods," had an "ungovernable temper," and had struck her "without any just cause or provocations." He didn't answer the suit, which Thelma soon dropped, but they separated in 1957; they would divorce two years later.

Berry kept looking for a break. And he got it without having to do anything except be the brother of two strong-willed, very together women, Gwen and Anna Gordy. They were typical (save for Berry Jr.) children of Pops Gordy, accomplished and beautiful women, and they, too, eyed the music scene, not as performers or writers but as would-be entrepreneurs. In 1957, they jointly purchased rights to the photo and cigarette concessions at the Flame Show Bar, putting two other of their brothers to work in the darkroom developing the pictures that Gwen and Anna had taken of merry-making patrons.

Berry must have thought he'd died and gone to heaven since, through them, he had an entree to the man he always wanted to meet— Al Green, who of course was managing, among his other acts, Berry's former sparring partner Jackie Wilson. Recalling this, the biggest break he ever got, Gordy duly noted his sisters' intervention in his memoir, but not without a strained attempt to justify their charity on his behalf. "Beautiful [and] glamorous, with business in their blood and love in their hearts," he wrote in *To Be Loved*, "they turned heads whenever they came through the room" and "[e]veryone adored them and seemed pleased to meet me, their brother, the songwriter."

In reality, at the time he could not claim a single songwriting credit, a single record, a single meaningful act in the business. But he did have his famous nerve, and charmed Green into extending an invitation to his office so he could hear his songs. When Gordy arrived, he found himself in the waiting room with another songwriter, Roquel Billy Davis, who wrote under the pseudonym Tyran Carlo. Neither had anything Green could use, but they became fast friends and song collaborators. A few weeks later, they returned to Green with a new composition, "Reet Petite," the title cribbed from the Louis Jordan song "Reet, Petite and Gone." Conceived by Gordy as a ballad, Davis changed it to an upbeat rattler, and while Gordy would call it "a so-so song," Green was sold.

At the time, Jackie Wilson had recently quit Billy Ward and the Dominoes for a solo career, and he and Green were seeking a song to cut as his first project for Decca Records' Brunswick label. That song became "Reet Petite," which, with Wilson's bombastic style and a big-band kick, went to No. 62 pop and peaked at 11 on the R&B charts, a handsome enough return to justify more work for the Gordy-Davis team. In the next two years they cranked out over a dozen, some of them bearing the name Gwen Gordy as co-writer—possibly Berry's way of paying her back for going to bat for him with Green, though a greater side benefit for Gwen was the romance she began with Davis. Four of these songs—"To Be Loved," "Lonely Teardrops," "That's Why I Love You So," and "I'll Be Satisfied"—charted, with "Teardrops" the best, a No. 7 pop hit.

Gordy now had a name, but little else that was positive. In fact, his life was a mess. At 27 he was broke, living apart from his young children, unable to afford housing. He'd moved in with another of his older sisters, Loucye, who had one of those amazing Gordy family résumés—having been the first civilian woman (and perhaps the first African-American) to be a property officer at the Michigan and Indiana Army Reserve base in Fort Wayne, Indiana. (She was also a successful businesswoman and the founder of and an instructor at the Brits and Spurs riding academy created expressly for black equestrians.) Unable to turn her little brother down, she opened her ritzy townhouse to Berry and, by extension, his clique of rag-tag music buddies, even permitting him to set up a makeshift studio in her basement, from which the din and cigar smoke billowed and stunk up the house.

It was only a matter of time before Loucye told him to move. Berry, whose pride was singed from having to mooch off his sisters (he even had to let Loucye pick up his child-support payments), quickly complied. That led him to his next destination—his sister Gwen's place.

By then, she too had moved deeper into the music business, forming a partnership with Davis in a label they called Anna Records, after her sister, who had invested in the enterprise. Mover and shaker that she was, Gwen had secured a national distribution deal with Chess Records, the Chicago R&B label. She lived in an apartment building that had become a kind of Gordy Arms, home as well to Berry Sr. and Bertha, two of whose sons ran the print shop and cleaning store on the ground floor.

The Gordy sisters were, like Gwen's mounts at the Brits, purebred show horses. Craving attention, they would step out on the town in feathered boas, satin gowns, and six-inch heels, to the long gazes of people on the street. If they were lucky, their brother Berry, with his raggedy clothing and hole-dimpled shoes, wouldn't be anywhere near them. And yet Berry was working on his own five-year plan that he figured couldn't be gauged right now but would take him far and beyond the for-show wealth of his family. That was why he wanted nothing to do with Anna Records. When Gwen and Billy invited him to be its president, he politely declined. It wasn't only that he felt guilty enough sponging off his sisters; it was that he saw Anna Records as the kind of small-time thing he wanted to sidestep. His vision, his drive, was suited to something *big*. He was, he told Gwen, going to own his own label and run his own empire, someday.

"Baby, we understand," she told him, trying not to sound patronizing about his pipe dream. "You've got to do what makes you happy."

There were hard lessons he'd already learned about the business. Writing hits for Jackie Wilson, for instance, meant nothing in terms of capital. Other than a $1,000 handout from Al Green early on, he and Davis had received nothing in royalties. Where did those dollars go? "Expenses," Green would say, mantra-like, "expenses." But at least they'd gotten something. Then, in late '58, Green, in New York on tour with Jackie Wilson, dropped dead of a heart attack, leaving the job of Wilson's manager to his young white assistant, Nat Tarnopol. Compared with Tarnopol, Green was a philanthropist; Nat would sooner have reached into an alligator's mouth than into his pocket, as Berry found out when he asked him if he could tack some Gordy-Davis songs on the B-sides of the Jackie Wilson records with their songs on the A-sides. Doing so would thus double the royalty. Nat wouldn't hear of it, and reacted obnoxiously.

"So, you guys want both sides, huh? Or what?" he said, in a veiled threat.

Feeling bold, if not wise, Berry said, "Or . . . we can't write for Jackie anymore."

"Jackie is a star. You need him—he doesn't need you."

With that, Tarnopol informed them that their work was no longer needed. Gordy then went straight to Jackie Wilson, but instead of loyalty from his old sparring mate whom he'd turned into a solo star, he got a spineless response.

"Berry, I love you and your family," Jackie said wanly, "but I can't go against Nat."

Gordy's only recourse was to call in contacts he'd made to pitch songs. One outlet was George Goldner, the racketeer-cum-music company owner who oversaw the New York R&B labels Gone and End, which put out records by Frankie Lymon and the Teenagers, Little Anthony and the Imperials, and the Chantels. Goldner had once, on a trip to Detroit, pressed a 100-dollar bill in Gordy's hand and winked, telling him it was for "future considerations." The future came sooner than they both expected.

Gordy also had cushioned the Wilson fall by lining up local singers to cut Jackie Wilson demos. One of those was the 17-year-old kid with the weirdly light skin who had become Diane Ross's object of desire and ambition back in the projects—Smokey Robinson, who had caught *his* break, without knowing it yet, when he brought his group the Matadors to audition for Nat Tarnopol late in 1957. Berry and Nat were still tight then, and Gordy was in Nat's office when the group—which now included Smokey's girlfriend, Claudette, replacing her brother who had gone into the Army—sang their songs. The ever-charming Tarnopol told them they were awful and to get the hell out. But Berry had heard something else, something endearing, and ran into the hall after them. He told them who he was and that he liked their stuff.

Smokey, who doted on music industry arcana, became excited. "Berry Gordy?!" You work for Jackie, right?" he gushed.

Gordy told the excitable boy to call him when he had a good, solid song he believed in. The call came within a week, sparking an Abbott and Costello routine.

"I got it," Smokey said.

"Got what?"

"Got a job."

"What's that?"

"Our first hit."

The song, a spinoff of the Silhouettes' enormous smash "Get a Job," was a tame knockoff that used the same "sha na na na" riff of the original; but the story it told of a guy trying to find work with comically bad results drew Gordy's attention. He quickly sold it to Goldner, who gave him the gig of producing it. Gordy and Smokey then cut it at United Studios using the same musicians Green used for cutting Jackie Wilson and Hank Ballard records: jazz pianist Joe Hunter's combo, who were regulars at a club called Little Sam's. Only weeks later Goldner had it out on End, but with a new group name, the Miracles, which Smokey thought up after Berry told him that "Matadors" sounded "a little jive." Gordy and Robinson picked up stacks of the records at the pressing plant and took copies around to the local radio stations, and though the disk tanked nationally it was a nice regional hit, as were three more Miracles records through the end of 1958.

The Smokey model was an indication of what Gordy was gradually building. Along with the Miracles, he was knitting a circle of similarly young, unproven but precocious talents. Another was 17-year-old Eddie Holland, who wanted to sing instead of going, as he was, to business school. He knocked on Gordy's door—actually Loucye's door—one day out of the blue and asked if he could sing for him. Because he sounded almost exactly like Jackie Wilson, Berry immediately put him to work—at no pay—cutting demos for Wilson.

Recalls Holland:

> I was sent there by this guy Homer Jones, who owned theaters in Michigan. When I met Berry, he didn't know me from Adam but he invited me in. That's how he is, he'll listen to anyone. He had a very charismatic personality, a different type of cat. He was confident. Yeah, he was living with his sister, but listen, he was not down and out. Hardly. I mean, he didn't *need* money. Because he was in New York like every week. Guys in the industry would be calling him all the time, telling him to come to New York and play his demos, and he'd take me with him; we'd be staying in hotels in New York. So *somebody* was payin' him!

Before long Eddie brought his younger bother Brian to meet Berry. Like Eddie, Brian was a baritone, but Berry took to him for his smarts, and for how well he absorbed Gordy's advice. With both brothers he cut a few sides, which he sold to the small Kudo label. That they went nowhere mattered not a whit to them.

"I didn't care about having hits, that's not what I was there for," Brian Holland says. "I just wanted to be around Berry Gordy. I'd be hanging around and he'd have me do things. Like one day he said, 'C'mon, Bri, let's get down to the studio. You be my engineer today.' I said, 'Berry, I never engineered a record.' He said, 'Just use your ears. Do what you hear.' Like it was as simple as that. But I engineered that day, and he kept on using me as an engineer, a singer, writer, whatever."

A laugh—"Of course, it didn't occur to me that he was doing this because he didn't want to pay a real engineer, singer, or writer. And he wasn't payin' me, neither. But what I was learnin' from him was priceless."

Other protégés came through, and stayed. These included a vocal group called the Satintones, a name associated most notably with bass singer Robert Bateman; Gordy's brother Robert, who recorded under the pseudonym Robert Kayli; soul singer Mable John, sister of R&B legend Little Willie John; and Raynoma Liles, a tiny young woman with platinum-dyed hair who sang in a duo with her sister Alice and had what Gordy thought was perfect pitch, ideal for use as a background singer. Soon he cobbled a loose, varying conglomeration called the Rayber Voices, after his and Liles's first names, to sing backups not just on his records but, at a $100 a session, on others' acts as well.

Notes Eddie Holland:

> One thing about Berry Gordy, he was totally unique. He was not cookie-cutter, man. He wanted to create a product totally unique, using the talents of others he sensed something in. Berry wasn't a genius, never came across like he thought he was. He was like us. Hell, we were *all* insecure. If we'd had to write in a certain style, we'd have been lost. But with Berry, he didn't *want* any one style. Didn't matter if it was R&B, rock, pop, whatever. You may not know this but Berry himself liked Doris Day music more than any soul music! He *loved* Doris Day music. So if he said to us, "Write what you feel," we knew it was no bullshit. That wasn't something you could have done working within the music establishment. Nobody in that crowd would ever have said, "Use your ears." They would've said, "Use *our* ears."

Most comforting to the inner circle, even amusing, was that a man a good decade older than they were could at times seem like a child. "Listen," Eddie Holland says, "Berry Gordy in his heart and mind was just a big kid. I think he wanted to be like us, rather than wanting us to be like him. If we had a better idea than him he'd say, 'Let's go with that.' We all learned to listen to everyone else, because among us, somebody was going to nail it just right, a guy, a girl, a kid, an older guy. Didn't matter who'd get the credit. We were doin' it for all of us."

In the end, he concludes, the secret of Motown's success was the community behind the music. Pre-Motown, Gordy's shop was heavily communal. Each record, demo or for real, was a group affair, with the Rayber Voices, whoever they happened to be at the moment, buzzing around like fleas. Without consciously going for one, Gordy found that his collective had created a "sound," in the smooth, balanced back-grounds characterized by Bateman's primordial bass and Liles's sonorous top end.

"I can remember that Berry started getting calls from record people all over the country," Eddie Holland says. "They'd come to town just because they had a new record and they wanted to play it for Berry, to see if it was any good. Berry might say, 'You know, man, that song can be a hit—but it needs another background dub.' And he'd suggest this backup group, the Rayber Voices, and then they'd get a paid gig out of it. He'd play those suckers."

Clee

Near the end of 1959, Gordy could finally stop depending on his sisters to support him financially. He was not materially richer, but after he'd become intimate with Raynoma, she bade him to move into the three-bedroom flat in which she lived with her 3-year-old son. By then, as with most women he met, she was in love.

That this happened so often with Gordy was more than coinci-dence. He had, to be sure, a remarkable ability to make women see in him only what he wanted them to. What Liles saw she described as "a latter-day Socrates" and "an inveterate philosopher" who would "spin beautiful, entrancing monologues about trust and sincerity and honor, all with a scholar's flair." Even the songs, she thought, were little para-bles of Berry Gordy himself, "embod[ying] a theme of honesty" under-lying, as she put it, the fact that "[l]iars were an abomination to Berry."

What she didn't see, apparently, was the hypocrisy underlying the fact that, for all his lofty ideals, Gordy could lie his ass off without qualm. To Liles, that simply meant he had a side that was "mysterious" and "untouchable," and nothing but "compelling." Splitting hairs fur-ther, she admitted that he often "avoid[ed] sticky personal problems or complaints," an indication, she maintains, that he was not a wimp but "a man who could see the leadership in others"—such as, well, her. Be-cause at those times when Socrates punted, he'd tell someone he didn't want to deal with, "Go and talk to Ray."

Meaning, perhaps, that Gordy's best talent was as a salesman rather than a decisionmaker. In fact, if Liles is right about one tale she tells, he was selling more than records. He was selling the same thing that Milt Jenkins was. According to the tale, he let word of it slip during a grumpy, unguarded moment.

"I've got to get out of this business," she remembers him saying when he stumbled in after a long night.

"What business?" she asked.

"I have a few girls," he went on. "Down on John R, but I've got to get out. I can't do what the motherfuckers down there do. They beat the women up, forcing them out on the street if they're sick or pregnant. Heartless sons of bitches." Saying he felt sorry for "my girls," he concluded, "I'm just not cut out for it."

Hearing this, Liles was torn between shock and amusement, the latter because if Berry did actually run in a subterranean world where procurers looked like Milt Jenkins, he surely must have been the world's least impressive and worst-dressed pimp. Or maybe just the world's worst pimp. How, for example, could he ply that trade and not even own a car? He may have fudged for a while by making sure he was seen tooling around town in a gold Cadillac—not letting on that the wheels were on loan from Nat Tarnopol. After they'd fallen out, though, Berry got around on city buses that took him over to John R. "What kind of a pimp was he," she remembered thinking, "taking the bus?"

The subject would not come up again, so it's anyone's guess as to whether and how long he continued in the flesh trades. But, in a believe-it-or-not plot twist, after this revelation Liles went out and turned a trick, without telling *him*—evidently to add a few bucks to the till. When she showed him the money, she wondered what she'd say if he asked where it came from. She needn't have worried; and if he suspected how, it seemingly didn't bother him.

"Wow, this is great!" was his excited reaction. "We sure can use it."

If indeed Berry Gordy was a common street pimp, it mattered not a whit to the hopelessly hooked Liles—yet another example of his irresistible good/bad-but-not-evil charm. Within a year, they married and, after first suffering a miscarriage, became parents of a son.

In late 1958, Gordy, looking ahead to a self-sustaining font of royalties from songs written under his aegis, formed a publishing company called Jobete, a conjunction of his three childrens' names. In this way he attempted to build, for now on a small scale, a model of the Brill Building power structure—an alliance of song publishers that so dominated the source material of American popular music that by the early '60s it had become a cartel, its uncrowned leader being Don Kirshner, whose stable of writers such as the Goffin-King and Mann-Weil teams churned out songs that were the mother's milk of the pop charts. Running in the canyons of Broadway as much as he did, Gordy soaked up the Brill mentality and method, marking time. Then, in early January 1959, he and Smokey Robinson were in his office and a royalty check for "Got a Job" came in the mail.

Opening the envelope with great anticipation, he pulled out a check for exactly $3.19. Both men nearly sank to the floor, and for Gordy it was all he could stand. For that year, he would claim on his tax return a salary of $27.20 a week and a bank account of $100; his net income was $4.85. His child-support payments to Thelma were sporadic at best, and when his son Berry IV had to be hospitalized with rheumatic fever, he could not pay the bills.

Smokey saw him staring at the check in disbelief. "You might as well start your own label," he told him. "You couldn't do any worse than this."

Jobete was the prelude for Tamla Records, a name that has led many people to think it had some kind of African connotation. Yet, in actuality, it derived from the anything-but-African 1957 Debbie Reynolds movie *Tammy and the Bachelor*, the name and title song of the flick he dug. Wanting to call the label Tammy, he found he couldn't because of copyright laws, and altered it to the inscrutable Tamla, not minding the racial speculation one bit.

Having his own label meant he would need to finance it. Doing the math, he figured he needed at least $800 to get it off the ground. At first, almost comically, he went to two banks for a loan, only to be shown the door for lack of any appreciable collateral. And so once again he beat a path to the family door. The pot of gold for him was the Gordy savings fund, known as Ber-Berry after Pops and Bertha. All of the children had for several years been contributing $10 a month for the purpose of investing in real estate. Now, he wanted them to invest in *him*.

Gathering the entire clan around their parents' dinner table, he proposed an $800 loan. Yet another sister, Esther, a prominent businesswoman married to a Michigan state legislator, pointedly brought up his many failures and wondered aloud how he'd pay the loan back. Loucye, a firsthand witness to his profligate lifestyle, demanded to know, "If you're so smart, why aren't you rich?"

Gwen and Anna, by rote, sided with him, and they prevailed on the family to proffer the loan. An agreement was signed on January 12, 1959, at the sweetheart interest rate of only $48, payable within two

years. Berry signed away his share of the fund—$113—and added a
handwritten addendum reiterating that any "future earnings" would be
covering the debt.

The first Tamla release went not to the Miracles but, rather, to a
young tenor he met in a record store, Marvin Johnson, who'd cut some
sides for the Kudo label and had written a song called "Come to Me"
that Gordy liked and polished up, earning a writer's credit. Then he
turned to cutting it. Johnson brought in some musicians from his previous studio sessions—who'd been assembled by Beans Bowles, the sax
player from Maurice King's house band at the Flame Show—and a vocal group called the Royal Holidays. Everybody, including of course the
Rayber Voices gang, crowded into Detroit's United Studios for the session, and in retrospect, there was much about it that had historical significance, as the raw material of the Motown sound was in that room.

The rhythm section was the most significant, led by the same funky
bass player who'd emerged in that early El Domingoes session, James
Jamerson, who played his upright bass according to the voices in his
head—and plucked all the strings, remarkably, with only his index finger, a digit he called "The Hook." The others were Eddie "Chank"
Willis and Joe Messina on guitars (the latter known for being the bandleader on a local TV show hosted by comedian Soupy Sales) and drummer Benny Benjamin, a baleful-looking cat with a pistol on his hip and
a wicked wit.

Gordy recalled that he did little that session other than allow the
band to "improvise off my little handwritten chord sheets." The product was an honest R&B track featuring yet another Jackie Wilson
soundalike (Gordy surely had the market cornered on this curious
copy-catting) and a mix bottomed out by Jamerson's spontaneously
edgy bass line and topped out by a mob of background voices and
Raynoma Liles's tambourine accents.

Gordy mixed the record for days, then released it with the catalog
entry Tamla 101. He would need to show strong local sales to get it
picked up by a national label for distribution, so he went to work as he
had with Smokey Robinson, hand-delivering copies of it to soul stations like WJLB and WCHB, and to disc jockeys like Bristol Bryant,
Frantic Ernie Durham, and Larry Dixon. But he didn't stop there; even
then, he knew he'd have to court the white jocks too, to get the
crossover that always made or broke any record. The go-to guy among
them was Robin Seymour of WKNR, who went on the air at the station in the late '40s and didn't go off until the early '70s.

ROBIN SEYMOUR: [Gordy] came to me a lot back then, and for years after, because I *had* no set playlist. You could do that back then, at least in Detroit. I mean, I would go from playing Mantovani to Smokey Robinson to Johnny Cash to Frank Sinatra. There were three big white jocks there—Jack the Bellboy, Bill Williams, and me—and we all did the same thing. We never needed to be told or begged to play the "race records," or as we called them, "*sepia* records." And I couldn't wait to get my hands on Berry Gordy's records because they were so damn good, they always got a buzz going.

I was good to Berry and he was good to me. All the record companies and the distributors were. I'll tell you one thing, my living room was filled up with gifts every Christmas. My kids used to love it. Now, I guess you can refer to that as payola. But it wasn't nutso money. It was tokens of friendship. Because, like I said, Berry never had to buy a favor, not in Detroit.

He was the man. There were a couple of huge song publishing guys from New York, Murray Deutsch and Lucy Karl, who came in one day. They knew me from industry functions and they called and asked me, "You know Berry Gordy?" They had heard about what he was doing in Detroit and they had a proposition for him, and asked me to set up a meeting. I told Berry and we met them at the Statler downtown, in their posh suite, and they pitched him a deal where they'd form a label with him. They said, "It'll be your label, Berry. We'll finance it and we'll split the publishing down the middle."

Well, Berry heard them out and we all walked to the elevator and he told them, most graciously, "Gentlemen, thank you very much, I'll think about it." Then, with just me on the ride down, he shook my hand and said, "Robin, I want to thank you for arranging this. But I'm not going to go into business with anybody else." When we said goodbye in the lobby—God, I remember this like it was yesterday—he looked me in the eye and said, "I'll never forget you, Robin."

And he never did. I always got first crack at a new Motown record. And in the early '60s I also became host of a TV show, *Swing Time*, a teenage rock and roll party thing, so he needed me, too, to get face time for the acts, and we did put all of them on.

But then there were the things no one knew about. For example I got a call from him in 1967, I believe, when he asked

me to come over to Motown because the Supremes were cutting a track for a Coca-Cola commercial and the director decided he wanted a spoken intro. He just asked me to wing it,
and I did a dumb Mr. Deejay thing, oozing something like
"Here are the swingin' Supremes for Coca-Cola!" It took about
eight seconds—and that eight seconds made me $47,000 in
royalties.

The interesting part of that gig was that I got to see up
close what a Supremes recording session must have been like,
even if in a scaled-down way. I was standing in the control
room with Berry after my bit was done—in one take, mind
you—and we were watching Diana singing, and they kept having to do it over and over because she couldn't get it right when
to start singing while listening to the music. Berry had to keep
telling her through the intercom, "Now! Now!" and she kept
screwing up, she couldn't follow anything. She couldn't get the
feel of it on her own. Even on a little thing like this, he had to
spoon-feed her. That was a real eye-opener. I could only imagine how much work she needed to sound the way she did on all
those great records.

Cee

When "Come to Me" broke out in Detroit, United Artists moved in
and leased it for national release. By April 1959 it was sitting at No. 6
on the R&B charts and at No. 30 on the pop charts. UA then bought
out Tamla's interest in Johnson and gave Gordy a $1,000 advance to
produce his future work; they also leased the record Gordy had released
as Tamla 102—Eddie Holland's "Merry Go Round," which, despite
going nowhere (unlike Marv Johnson's 1961 cover that hit No. 66 on
the charts), earned Holland a two-year contract with the label.

Offers began to pour in for Johnson to tour, with Gordy demanding his other acts be included on the shows. All of them piled into a
twenty-nine-seat Volkswagen van and set out on the first tour, which
had stops in Philadelphia for Johnson to do *American Bandstand* and in
New York at Carnegie Hall and, the big one, Harlem's famed Apollo
Theater, where Berry had been before with Jackie Wilson, but never as
an entrepreneur.

Royalties from "Come to Me" were pouring in, as were those from
the third Johnson single, "You've Got What It Takes," a flippant

New Orleans–style R&B tune that hit No. 10 and spent twenty-two weeks on the charts. As if dispensing gumdrops at a candy store, an imperious Gordy leased masters of six new songs in one shot to Chess Records, one being the Miracles' "Bad Girl." That cemented a gig at the Apollo Theater for Smokey and his group—at which they sang so poorly and danced so clumsily that the crowd jeered them and the Apollo's owner, Frank Schiffman, demanded Gordy repay the $750 he'd fronted them to travel to New York.

Berry talked Schiffman out of it, telling him he'd soon be begging to get the Miracles back. With the group busted in New York, he wired them more money. Indeed, his faith in Smokey was infinite. When a local label he'd leased some previous Miracles' records to insisted that it owned the group, Gordy procured vows from the local deejays to boycott the label if it didn't back down; it did, within two days.

Smokey would soon enjoy a dubious honor, courtesy of his mentor and patron. Late in 1959 Gordy branched out again with a sister label for Tamla. He called it Motown Records, appropriating and abridging the street-jive cognomen for the city of Detroit—"Motor Town." His plan was for the solo acts to be placed on Tamla; and the groups, on Motown. When he was ready to go with Motown product a year later, he test-pressed another version of the Miracles' "Bad Girl." There would be more pressings on the label in 1960, several by the Satintones, before Gordy was ready to go with a Motown release—the forgettable "I've Got a Notion"/"We Really Love Each Other" (Motown 1005) by Henry Lumpkin in early January 1961. Well before that signal benchmark moment, however, Gordy had realized the commercial kick of the name and broadened its role from label to overall company identity, incorporating the still piddling operation under the banner of Motown Recording Company, Inc.

With the birth of Gordy's new son in June 1959, the need for a new home for his family coincided with the need to find a home for his dream that Motown would become an empire. He could by then afford such a move by writing off any major expense as a liability against income. Even a year later, with Motown established, when Thelma sued him for back child support, he could declare assets of $32,600 against liabilities of $32,500, and thus claim he was still unable to afford the payments. He did, however, lend some valuable advice to his ex-wife when she started up a small R&B label that year, Thelma Records.

Still, as was his habit, Gordy was living large on all those "liabilities." One example was a $4,800 Cadillac he'd bought with a down payment of $1,300. But a much bigger one was the new digs where he and Raynoma relocated that spring—the future landmark of American music at 2648 West Grand Boulevard. Situated on the west end of Paradise Valley, it squatted midway down a relatively well-to-do block bordered by Henry Ford Hospital to the east and dotted with other small black-owned businesses—Sykes Hernia Control Service, Your Fair Lady Boutique and Wig Room, and right next door, Coles' Funeral Home. The house, a two-story, twice-foreclosed property that had been used most recently as a residence/photo studio, was purchased with $3,000 down and a $23,000 mortgage.

It needed a lot of work, but it suited Gordy's needs, personal and professional. Typically, it also became a reclamation project for the entire Gordy clan. In fact, well before it was anything close to a landmark, 2648 West Grand Boulevard was the new Gordy Arms. Members of the family were all over the place, many in official capacities. For example, Berry named Esther vice-president, though all that meant at the time was doing bookkeeping. Loucye came on to do billings, sales, and graphics, and to write liner notes for projected Motown albums. Both sisters were given upstairs offices next to Gordy's bedroom and an open den where Raynoma had put her piano. Berry's office was on the ground floor beside the reception area, and Raynoma had a smaller one down the hall.

The heart of Motown, however, was a dank, unfinished cavern that could be entered only through the rear of the house and down a flight of stairs. Used as a darkroom by the previous owner, it had a dirt floor and cracked cinder-block walls. The room may have struck most people as a good place for a septic tank, but Gordy from the start wondered what the acoustics would be like when he could get some session musicians in there.

It was that dingy basin—soon to be Motown Studio A—that Gordy built before anything else was renovated. Supervising its construction, he carried in the first piece of equipment himself—a rudimentary two-track recorder he bought from the deejay Bristol Bryant. Gordy would replace it with state-of-the-art equipment manned by brilliant music technology geeks, but Studio A—by intent—would forever remain a pit, never becoming modernized and retaining its ambiance as a grimy, sweaty, incorruptible geyser of live music.

Smokey Robinson, naturally, would own some of the earliest sessions, but the very first few dollars went toward cutting a song with

Barrett Strong, a Gordy pal who'd recorded for Anna Records. Berry had been noodling with a lyric but was stuck until he ran what he had past a young female songwriter, Janie Bradford, who met him when she was 14 and her older sister was dating Jackie Wilson; now 17, and having written a few songs with him, she had been hired on as Gordy's Motown receptionist.

He began singing, *"Your love give me such a thrill—"*

"But your love don't pay my bills," she rejoined.

Bradford contributed a few more similarly ticklish lyrical punchlines, and the song was done. Everyone who heard it agreed: Gordy had to get down to his new studio and lay it on vinyl, which he did with a rumbling bass, drum, and piano arrangement swelling a throaty, near-delirious vocal by Strong. Unsure of its potential, though, after its release on Tamla he chose to lease it to Anna Records, a bit of largesse for his sister having gone to bat for him. Both reaped the whirlwind when the record was issued in late August and sprinted onto the charts for a twenty-one-week residence, cresting at No. 23 pop and 2 R&B by the dawn of the new year, and the new decade.

The symbolism of the record's timing—the sound of Motown Inc. blaring from radio speakers just as pop music sought its next new thing—was matched only by the symbolism of its title, as the absolute perfect creed for the company:

"Money (That's What I Want)."

For the president of Motown Inc., that wasn't a wish anymore; it was a reflex, and an indisputable reality. And if, as Flo Ballard suspected, it came at the expense of his artists, such things as the fine print of contracts and clauses about artists' royalties paled next to whatever titanic forces were at work to forge together Diane Ernestine Earle Ross and Berry Gordy III.

five

PRIMING
THE
PUMP

L istening to Diane endlessly talk up Motown and Smokey Robinson caused even Flo to warm to the idea of auditioning for Berry Gordy, though she thought it best not to mention Robert Bateman lest the other girls not appreciate how she'd blown him off. Smokey was a better conduit, anyway, because of his pull, than some shadowy Motown underling. She dug Smokey, too, for sure, just as did every girl who ever saw or heard him. It never seemed to matter that he was now a married man, possibly because Claudette was so demur and nonterritorial, and for years she herself seemed not to know that she was too forgiving and trusting for her own good, especially when it came to Diane Ross.

In July 1960, though, the 16-year-old Ross wasn't quite old enough to seduce Smokey Robinson; but she was wily enough to use him toward the end of getting to Motown. Once again, she was aided by the serendipity that characterized her youth. In an amazing but true coincidence, the woman who owned and was renting to the Ross family their apartment at Brewster-Douglass, a Mrs. Wiggins, also owned a convenience store in the neighborhood, Two Sisters Unique—and recently had hired Smokey to work the counter, which helped him to make ends meet while waiting for a hit record.

That was all Diane needed to know. Sweeping in one day to greet the semi-famous Motown star, who looked anything but in his white apron—an image right out of "Got a Job"—she acted as if she'd run into a long-lost relative. "Smokey!" she burbled, "I've been hearing your records. I'm so proud of you." Then, in the next breath: "I have a group, too. Will you introduce us to Berry Gordy?"

Hit with this barrage, and barely remembering her from a year ago, he vacantly said, "Oh, you have a group?" Then when she clattered about the Primettes and about how she'd love for him to hear them, he tried to dismiss her nicely, telling her that he and the Miracles were going out on the road in a few days.

"Then we'll come over tomorrow night," she chirped, without a notion where she was inviting herself.

Having learned that Diane Ross was not a girl who could be dismissed easily, he could only give in, instructing her and her mates to come to Claudette's family house on Warren Court, where the Miracles did their rehearsing in the basement. The following evening they arrived with Marvin Tarplin in tow. Wanting to give Smokey the full aural and visual treatment, the girls wore matching white skirts and blouses, prompting Claudette, who was a few years older than the three core Primettes, to think of them as "quite the refined young ladies." Then they ran through three of their songs.

"I was impressed," she says. "Those girls could sing and they had a lot of energy. I could see Smokey was surprised. I think he probably thought before they started, How am I going to let them down? But then he felt that energy and knew they had possibilities."

It was possible, too, to get a read on each of them. "It was unusual for a group to have distinct personalities and voices like they did. It was like they represented a different side of young womanhood, and amplified that by having three different lead vocalists on the songs.

"At that point, I didn't feel there was any rivalry about it. They were equals, and wanted to appear that way. But at the same time, you could see Diane was . . . well, she had the most energy, was the most aggressive. Her attitude was there, as a go-getter. She had that determined quality. But it was still within the framework of the group.

"Diane was too young and immature to believe she could do something on her own. She needed the other girls for security and confidence. But that instinct, that ultimate goal, I imagine it was there, in the back of her head."

It was Flo whom Claudette thought was the most mature, both "charming and funny," and seemingly by default the leader. Wilson was, she says, "as she always was, and is. Very attractive. And she exuded class. So did the older girl [McGlown]. It's just that they all seemed to defer to Flo, and she spoke for them all. That girl had a great personality. Diane knew what she wanted to accomplish, but I think she knew it couldn't happen without Flo to lead the way."

Smokey's review of that performance, in his 1989 autobiography *Inside My Life*, was less than a rave, and was altered by memory. Confusing Betty McGlown with another girl who soon came into the Primettes, he wrote that they were "four foxes, sexy and stylishly dressed," but, "[f]act is, they looked better than they sang. They weren't bad, just not polished," and he admitted he was more taken with the cat on guitar, who was "a monster, the smoothest I'd ever heard" playing his "easy-wristed riffs."

Smokey, though his image was that of a sweetheart, had no reservations about coldly leveraging Tarplin away from the Primettes. "I think we can help each other," he told them, sweetly, explaining that the Miracles needed a guy like that to rehearse and tour with. If it was okay with them, he said, he'd like to "use him for a while."

Then, dropping the hammer, he promised that "[w]hen we get off the tour, I'll set up something for you with Berry. What do you say?"

What *could* they say? It was either a guitar player or Berry Gordy. So, a week later, Smokey and the Miracles were on a show with Jackie Wilson and Little Willie John, their singing keyed by Tarplin's easy wrist, performing far more harmoniously and effortlessly than they had at their disastrous Apollo gig. In Tarplin they'd found their missing link, one who would remain soldered to Smokey Robinson for the next four decades; in contrast, Tarplin would never again accompany the Primettes.

It was a large price to pay for a vague promise to "set up something" with Berry Gordy. But Smokey kept his word. In the late summer, Richard Morris, a Motown producer, called Jesse Greer and said he should have the girls come to 2648 West Grand Boulevard a few days later for an audition. Giddy about the invitation, the four of them met in front of the house with the "Hitsville U.S.A." sign. Ross and Wilson, a little jelly-legged, nervously hung back as Ballard and McGlown confidently strode across the weedy lawn, up the landing stairs, and through the door.

Once inside, they were met at the front desk by the co-author of "Money."

JANIE BRADFORD: Now, my mind may be playing tricks on me after all this time, but I remember it differently than the story about Diana being friends with Smokey and all that. That's the publicity story—just like that Diana discovered the

Jackson 5, which was a bunch of bull. See, what I think happened is that Eddie or Paul got them an audition. And then Smokey became involved with them later.

I also think I knew them before they came in. I never saw them performing, but I knew Milton Jenkins. Or rather, I knew of him. Because I got to know Paul and Eddie and Kel, and that whole crowd hung together. With the Primettes, though, Milton was very protective of them, and he was a guy you just naturally kept a distance from, you know, because you'd hear stories. So it had been a while since I'd even thought about them. Usually I had an idea which groups were coming in, there was word of mouth around Motown. Like, I knew Otis and Melvin had joined up with Eddie and Paul and formed the Elgins, and they were going to be coming in. But the Primettes, they were the furthest thing from my mind.

Mary Wilson recalled, conversely, that the Primettes were surprised to see Bradford, having lost track of her and unaware that she'd co-written a big hit song. They understood that another familiar face on the Motown lot boded well for them as part of the extended Detroit music family. However, if Bradford is incorrect about how they got there, she's right in saying the Primettes were still out of their league, as "just one of a million teenage groups that came on and thought they owned the world."

She laughs. "We were all just kids. We all thought we owned the world. But it really wasn't a big deal to be in a group. They came through that office, like lemmings, every day. Usually I had to be the one to tell them don't call us, we'll call you."

Confirming their appointment, she had them take a place in the waiting area; but this irritated Flo, who pontificated that in light of Motown's reputation on the street, "Mr. Berry Gordy is lucky we're even here." Mary and Diane, who were thrilled be there, ignored her. When a dashing-looking black man walked through the room and Bradford told them he was Barrett Strong, they squealed like the little girls they still were.

After a fifteen-minute wait, someone came and ushered the four girls into the studio, which with renovation was connected by a four-step stairway to the main floor.

Overlooking the studio was a glass-paneled control booth that had been converted from an old kitchen. The makeshift nature of the operation was evident from the dungeon-like atmospherics of the studio.

Tangled cables hung like cobwebs from the ceiling, and the walls had what looked like rodent holes through which peeked some sort of red matter, actually remnants of thick theater curtains that Gordy had used as soundproofing material.

The studio floor was unfinished; unsecured wooden planks wobbled when walked upon, and when one came up, the solution was to push it back into place with the stomp of a foot. The floor was also unpartitioned—unlike most studios, even ancient ones, which normally had drywalls or even panes of standing glass in order to separate musicians and isolate their instruments so as not to bleed into each others' microphones. In the entire room was only one very weathered amplifier the size of a small refrigerator, tucked into a nook abutting the stairs; during sessions, all the guitars and the bass would be plugged into the amp at the same time, inviting a blown fuse or even a fire, both of which had already happened. On the main floor adjoining the booth a bathroom was sometimes miked up and a track piped in through a speaker for use as an echo chamber, with someone at the door screaming "Don't flush!" while the music or vocals were playing.

It was every bit the "pit" that the session musicians called it, and must have been what Gordy was thinking of when he wrote in his memoirs of the early Motown formula of "rats, roaches, guts and love." For the Primettes, however, or at least most of them, it might as well have been Xanadu. Inside were Robert Bateman, who either didn't recall his brush with Flo or assumed they were there because of it, and Richard Morris. Moments later, bouncing in came the budding black Napoleon himself, wearing not rags but a dark suit. "That's Berry Gordy," Ross informed the girls.

He smiled pleasantly, and despite Wilson's recollection of him as "[not] exactly handsome" yet still a dominating figure, he didn't stay long. Appearing only minimally interested in the proceedings, and ducking in and out of the room, he must have been disconcerting to the girls as they ran through three of their standard songs—"Nighttime Is the Right Time," "There's Something on My Mind," and "There Goes My Baby." Knowing a valuable element was missing without Marvin Tarplin's guitar lines, they traded nuance for volume, singing loudly and with gospel flourishes. Ballard, Wilson, and Ross each did the lead in turn, and they all strained a bit, but the energy and interwoven harmonies jelled, and Gordy was moved to keep on returning, intrigued mainly by the scrawny girl with the big eyes. After she'd concluded "There Goes My Baby," he intoned from the booth through the intercom: "One more time, girls." During the encore, he murmured to Bateman, "That girl sings through her nose, but there's something about her."

Not enough "something," however, to overrule his instincts, which told him they weren't ready for his shop. Janie Bradford, who stood next to him in the control booth because Gordy frequently asked her opinion of prospective new acts, was even less impressed.

"They were all cute and clean-cut and all, but they sounded just so-so," she says. "They were just another teenage group to me, nothing spectacular the way the Temptations were when they came in. They had a cute little sound. I thought that Flo was the one who stood out. She had a very strong, very good voice, but it was nothing unusual in the commercial sense. I'll just say there was no Aretha Franklin among them."

Gordy, too, was cautious about girl-group acts, not having signed a single one yet. In fact, the only females on the Motown roster were Mable John (who doubled as his driver) and a new girl, 17-year-old Mary Wells, whom Bateman had found and Gordy signed up because she could also write songs, and who came in with one she'd originally intended for Jackie Wilson called "Bye Bye Baby." So while he had no reason to make the Primettes the third such act, he definitely saw them in terms of the future.

"I could tell what he was thinking," Bradford believes. "He liked them but he'd dealt with parents of young girls before, all the crap with the contracts, stage mothers, all that. He just wanted to put them on hold and wait for them to grow up a little and then come back when they were better."

Wanting to let them down easily, he first announced himself "very impressed" with their performance—making their hearts flutter and leading an exuberant Ross to ask, "Are you going to sign us now?" Stifling a laugh, he pointedly asked them their ages, not really caring what the specific numbers were, and then quickly told them, "I want you to come back when you finish school," barely finishing the sentence before he was halfway out the door.

The Primettes believed, correctly, that it was nothing but an excuse to be rid of them—no more than what Wilson later called a purely "business decision." And while they all felt as if they'd fallen through those loose floorboards, all of them "heartbroken," as Ross has recalled, here is where some truth must be sorted out. According to the unauthorized 1989 Diana Ross biography *Call Her Miss Ross* by J. Randy

Taraborrelli, Flo was so offended by Gordy's kiss-off that she finally revealed the conversation she'd had with Bateman at the Detroit/Windsor International Freedom Festival; angrily pointing a finger at him, she snapped, "But, hey! We won the contest. That guy there, he said to come down here [and] now you're telling us you don't want us? What kind of stuff is that?"

At that, Gordy was said to have strode over to Ballard and growled at her, "Get lost." Then, after the girls were shooed out, a livid Ross upbraided Ballard for keeping the secret, which Flo justified with an icy, condescending, "*I* decide for the Primettes."

The problem with this melodramatic account is that no part of it appears in the writings of Ross, Wilson, Gordy, or anyone else (Wilson, again, claims that no one from Motown approached any of the Primettes at the festival), nor in Bateman's memory pan. And while a *Miss Ross* endnote cites supporting, but unquoted, interviews with Ross and Ballard in the '70s, and with Janie Bradford, the latter becomes nearly apoplectic in smacking down all of it.

"Hell no! Nothing like that ever happened! They were just *teenagers*! Why would a grown man talk to a girl like that, tell her to get lost? People come up with bullshit stories like that all the time, 'cause it sounds good. But, come on, why would Flo get in anyone's face like that? Shit, Motown was the first recording company in Detroit. Kids would have done anything to get into Motown. And the fact that Berry invited them back, that speaks for itself. That was worth everything to those girls. Of course they were disappointed, but they knew they'd be welcomed back."

Indeed, it's improbable that following such histrionics they would have stuck around Motown—as they did, drinking in the vibes, making themselves known to the crew, and trying to fit in. As Bradford suggests, they construed Gordy's future invitation as proof that they'd someday soon be in.

For Ross, the emerging dynamic went a little further. Berry Gordy, she recalled coyly years after—using, tellingly, the first person—"had definitely not seen the last of me. In fact, it was quite clear to me that the relationship had only just begun."

Unlike Gordy, Robert Bateman and Richard Morris weren't prepared to wait on the Primettes. Scotching the "graduate first" hooey, they offered their services at once, angling for their own purposes to get the group. At the time, Gordy had not yet established the unwritten but implicit Motown code that enjoined anyone in the Motown "family" to spread their work around to other record companies in town—at least openly enough that Gordy could find out about it, in which case he might cut the offender out of the loop. In 1960, any of his underlings were free to make a few bucks outside the walls on West Grand Boulevard, and Bateman and Morris did so with the Primettes, shopping them around. Morris also displaced Jesse Greer as their manager, using his connections with the club owners to put the group into shows at the Graystone Ballroom and the Twenty Grand.

These were fairly big shows, too. The latter, for example, had them on a bill with the Falcons—whose song "You're So Fine," released on the local Flick label and subsequently picked up by United Artists, went Top Twenty in 1959—and a young rasp-throated, gospel-R&B singer, Wilson Pickett, soon to join the Falcons himself. Both the Falcons and Pickett recorded for and were managed by Bob West, a real mover who cut deals like it was second nature—many with Gordy, who had recently hired West's national record distribution company, B&H Music, to move Motown product to markets outside of Detroit. West also sold two Falcons sides to Anna Records. West is an overlooked but important R&B figure, having elevated to immortality not only Pickett but Falcons member Eddie Floyd—who happened to be West's nephew. (West himself had a cursed future; a few years later, he got into a tiff with Herman Griffin, the husband of Mary Wells, Motown's first female star, at which point Griffin pulled out a gun and shot West in the face, taking out one of his eyes. West recovered but quit the music business and moved to Las Vegas, where he lived until his death in 1983.)

And, of course, West was a way station for the immortal Supremes, who as the Primettes were pitched to him by Morris in the late summer of 1960. By then they had acquired some tentative studio recording experience, when Bateman began a small label with fellow Satintone Sonny Sanders called Son-Bert Records and put them to work doing background vocals on several songs by Gino Washington. West then signed them to his new LuPine Records label, which he created for the Falcons (not, as Mary Wilson has claimed, for the Primettes). West's interest, too, was to use them for background flavor, and he hired them for what would be a profusion of flop records, including a few that Pickett and Floyd would have preferred not to remember a decade later— Pickett's "Let Me Be Your Boy" and Floyd's "I'm Your Yo Yo Man," and other historical, obscurities such as Gene Martin's "Lonely Nights," James Velvet's "Bouquet of Flowers," Al Garner's "All I Need Is You," James Dee's "My Pride," and Don Revel's "The Return of Stagger Lee."

West also allowed Morris to cut some Primettes sides, which turned out to be two songs Morris had written, "Tears of Sorrow" and "Pretty Baby." Morris had already produced the instrumental track for the first of these at Motown, and for the vocals and the "Pretty Baby" track he brought the girls, two more female backup singers, and a band of seven musicians—including Benny Benjamin on drums and Marvin Tarplin on guitar—to West's Flick-Contour Studio on Forest Street in early September. The result was primitive pop fare, "Pretty Baby" with a fairly flat lead vocal by Wilson buoyed by Ballard's high-pitched hic-cupping, and "Tears" with a tepid Ross lead nearly buried by "bop shoo bop" choruses—something that may not have been accidental. Because Diane kept harping on how she wanted to sing the lead, picking argu-ments with Morris about it, Richie may have made her pay for it, in vanity, by mixing her vocals so low that it seemed as if Flo was actually singing lead.

West put both tracks out on the same record, LuPine 120, with "Tears of Sorrow" on the A-side and "Pretty Baby" on the flip. But it never moved and Wilson has her own theory why, mentioning in her memoir that just as Bob West's B&H Music had begun to distribute it the company became implicated in a local payola scandal. As a result, the record was stillborn. That may have been the case, but the primary reason is likely that the songs bit it. Wilson can't disagree, passing them off as "typical girl-group pop records" with "self-pitying lyrics about the boy who got away." But even with their quick death, having a record out—and, for a short time, hearing it played on the radio—was exhilarating.

It also, easily, might have ended right then and there. Not only be-cause West's influence was suddenly undercut, meaning that future LuPine records would be problematic, but also because reality began to slap down the reveries of fame.

First, only days later, Betty broke the news that she was getting married, a shocker given that she'd only recently broken up with Paul Williams. A bigger shock was that she said she was quitting the group. If this seemed to be cause and effect, the actual cause may instead have been that Betty simply had had enough of Diane Ross.

In the last hectic year, Ross had only become thornier toward all in-volved. Richard Morris, the newcomer, had already gotten embroiled with her, not just with her vocals. At the clubs where he'd book the Primettes, he took pains to keep them (and the owners) out of trouble, constantly reminding them not to mingle with the audience of mainly adult men. But Diane would defy him. At a Graystone Ballroom gig, she bounded from the stage in mid-song and began dancing with a man who had attracted her gaze. When Morris tried to pry them apart, she sneeringly told him, "Go fuck yourself, Richie."

Helpless, he had no choice but to turn to Betty, the only one in or around the group whom Diane feared. Seeing his hand signal, Betty came down from the stage, heatedly scolded Ross, and got her back on the stage. Often, McGlown had to set her straight when Ross wouldn't accept Morris's judgments on those vocals and demanded to sing lead.

There were Ross moments no one could control, however, more so after she used her earnings from her job at Hudson's to attend modeling school classes on Saturday mornings. She not only began strutting around like Coco Chanel but seemingly derived pleasure from making the group an adjunct to her fashionable self. For example, she'd agree that they would all wear matching outfits to a gig, then show up for it in a different, more chic outfit. She'd half-heartedly make the excuse that she'd "forgotten," but didn't seem to mind a bit that she had hung the other three out to dry—and that as the "standout" she'd naturally have to take most of the leads while they'd have to be the backing group. Several times, as well, she called in sick just before a rehearsal, angering Morris.

Wilson has opined that Ross's "stubbornness about certain things was almost childlike," but on further review her antics seem to have been measured for size, each a premeditated control game meant to send a message—and, at its core, a means to an end. And this was not something she made any great effort to disguise, as the observations of the formative Miss Ross by Claudette Rogers and Janie Bradford attest. Already, the difference between Ross and the rest was palpable: If Flo wasn't happy sharing leads and trading zingers with Diane, she was able to put the group first and smile—a code of conduct that for Mary Wilson was of course *de rigueur*, which is why she can freely admit that she'd always been content to merely "play on the team." Not so Ross.

"With hindsight," Wilson would say after decades of Ross tumult, "one can see that Diane had a plan."

For her part, McGlown had been counting the minutes until she could leave, neither desiring nor expecting a fairy-tale life beyond a husband and family. Indeed, seeing that Betty really didn't give a whit about the whole thing led Diane to her obeisance, not wanting to be the cause of her leaving, though in the end that may have been exactly the case. And even if it wasn't, even if Betty had simply decided it was time to live in the world of reality, she undoubtedly was relieved that she'd no longer have to play nanny to a brat.

And so, just like that, McGlown was gone, never to look back at or have a pang of regret about it. But this was only one concussion that buffeted the Primettes that fall. A more potentially devastating—and portentous—one remained, which would make McGlown's departure all but trivial.

six

SUPREME BEINGS

n November 1960, a whiff of optimism and epochal change was in the air, even the air around Paradise Valley. A young, new president had just been elected by a slim margin, with Detroit's heavily black and labor vote pushing Michigan's twenty electoral votes into John F. Kennedy's column. Over on West Grand Boulevard, meanwhile, another new-wave president, Berry Gordy Jr., had found his breakout song. Written by Smokey Robinson, it was the bridge between R&B and pop that Gordy was after, with Smokey's jocose confession about love and marriage—"My momma told me / You better shop around"— delivering the lyrical punch line.

The Miracles' "Shop Around" was a victory for Gordy's canine-like ears. Originally, he had released the tune on Tamla with, inexplicably, Claudette Robinson on lead. But Gordy, fretting that he'd produced it at too slow a tempo, called a disbelieving Robinson into the studio at 3 A.M. one night to re-cut it, with Smokey on lead. He then pulled the original and released the "Shop Around" redux, putting the entire clout of Motown, such as it was, behind it. This included a new nationwide distribution network that had replaced Bob West's tainted B&H company; for that, Gordy had hired a white outsider, Barney Ales, as head of promotions at a salary of $135 a week, or $90 more than Loucye Gordy was making as Motown's top-paid employee. While some around the shop frowned on Gordy going biracial with Motown so soon (he'd also tabbed a white public relations man, Al Abrams), reasoning that such a move would dilute the concept of self-sustaining black capitalism, Gordy contrarily believed that talented and gung-ho whites answering the black masters made the point even better. And, surely, Ales earned his pay, and then some, by lobbying and cajoling distributors into moving "Shop Around." At the turn of the new year, it hit the Top Forty in high gear, ran to No. 2 on the pop charts and No. 1 on the R&B charts, and became Motown's first million-selling record—at least as certified by Motown, Gordy again having blown off the RIAA and its gold records to keep his account books from the prying eyes of outsiders.

That record was the turning point. It was R&B and pop for a new, young generation and upgraded Motown's national image, both creatively and as a business nexus. It also made Smokey Robinson's bones—in 1961, he became Gordy's LBJ, vice-president of Motown Records, Inc., and Gordy's protégé in the control booth, entrusted to get off the ground the career of Mary Wells and other high-expectation Motown finds.

Around Detroit, it seemed folly to try and buck Motown's ambition. When Gwen Gordy realized that Anna Records could not compete with her brother for talent (not incidentally, she had also broken up with Billy Davis), she closed Anna and shunted its worthiest acts to Motown. After marrying a new beau, Gwen had given it a go with another label, called Tri-Phi, that she formed with her new husband, Harvey Fuqua, former lead singer of the R&B group the Moonglows. Within months, Tri-Phi was bought out by Berry, who took for Motown such artists as David Ruffin, Lamont Dozier (who had been recording under the pseudonym Lamont Anthony), the Spinners, Junior Walker, Johnny Bristol, and Fuqua himself as a producer and writer.

So, too, did he take in a 21-year-old, less-regarded singer, Marvin Pentz Gay Jr., who when he couldn't get singing gigs played sessions as a drummer. Gay had been in the Moonglows but was without a record contract until he caught the eye of Anna Gordy. When they began a romance, Gordy did her a favor and signed him as a session drummer. In 1961, Anna married him, meaning he had not one but *two* Motown brothers-in-law. Soon, using the name "Marvin Gaye," he was recording songs in Studio A that would pepper the charts. For Marvin Gaye, it was a case of Motown by marriage; for Berry Gordy, it was but one more example of luck and timing he now couldn't seem to avoid.

Flo Ballard also had reason to sashay a bit that fruitful autumn of 1960. Betty McGlown's exit aside, the Primettes were on a roll. With Ross and Wilson, Ballard had taken up a vigil most days after school to West Grand Boulevard, the object being to force-fit themselves into the Motown "family." Sometimes they even found their way into studio sessions to add some sweetening background vocals or hand-clapping, excited to no end by chores that were mundane around Motown.

"It was something we all did," recalls Janie Bradford. "If you were a warm body at Motown, you could be called in to clap hands or swell up a chorus. Basically, it was who the producers saw out in the hall. It was funny that those girls thought it was because of all their talent. But I'll give them this: They sure as hell made sure to be out there so they *would* be the ones called in."

That didn't apply only to the studio. The Motown crowd congregated for meals in a dining room where huge pots of chili, spaghetti, and hot dogs would be served up by Gordy's cook, a woman named Lilly Hart. It wouldn't take long for someone in the room to wave the girls in and include them in the repartee of dirty jokes and put-down one-liners—a milieu that was a natural fit for Flo, with her sarcasm and cocksure demeanor.

Feeling like part of the "in" crowd, Flo could now often be found making the scene at the clubs and talent shows around town. Shortly after Maxine had gotten divorced from her serviceman husband and married a recovered but still somewhat sickly Milton Jenkins, Flo attended a show at the Graystone Ballroom, escorted on the bus, at Lurlee's insistence, by her older brother Billy. There, she bumped into a boy she knew from Northeastern High School whom Maxine says was a popular basketball player and something of a hunk. After the show, Flo drifted outside to the parking lot, out of Billy's sight (reminiscent of when her little brother Roy had strayed from his sisters' view, with tragic consequences) and saw the boy in his car. When he opened the passenger side door and beckoned her in, she hedged for a moment, her instincts and the Ballard family ethos holding her back.

"Get in, Flo," he told her. "I'll drive you home."

It was late, Billy was nowhere to be seen, and she knew Lurlee would be furious if she got home after the time they'd agreed on. And so she got in, next to a boy she barely knew. Unclear is whether she willingly agreed to go for a ride and do some making out. In any case, after fifteen minutes on the road they wound up nowhere near Brewster-Douglass but instead on a side street in an isolated area. If there was consensual petting, it soon got out of hand. "I'm going to have sex with you," he spat, and began tearing at her clothes. She demanded, "Take me home right now!" When he didn't stop, she fought back, scratching at his face. He then reached under the seat and came up clutching a knife.

Pressing it to her throat, he ordered her into the back seat. Hurling himself on top of her, he tore off her panties and fondled her, slobbering all over her exposed skin. Terrified, she tried to somehow reason with him, revealing that for all her sass and assumed experience, he had her all wrong—"Please, no, I've never had sex. I'm a virgin."

But even if he believed her, there'd be no chivalry. Half-crazed, and apparently enjoying an act of cowardly conquest, he didn't stop until he'd raped her. Pulling up his pants, he left her in the back to dress herself as he started up the car. Only then did he drive her to the projects, saying not a word while she quietly sobbed. Opening the door for her, he was bizarrely cheerful.

"Why are you so upset?" he asked, seeming to consider the interlude a kind of acceptable young male sport.

Holding her ripped blouse at the neck with both hands, she ran into the apartment and blurted out the horrific details to Lurlee and Maxine, but was reluctant to report the crime or even to tell anyone outside the family. "Her feeling," said Maxine, was that "the boy was well known and she felt like no one would believe her."

It was not an uncommon reaction among rape victims, especially at that time and place. This was a period when such assaults went unreported in great numbers—and in the ghetto, according to Maxine, "young black girls were raped daily" and "sometimes [by men] in their own families." Women, and particularly girls violated by male teenagers carrying out rites of sexual passage, were expected to let it slide and move on.

Living within those cast-iron cultural and sexual strictures, Flo bore the shame silently; no authorities were ever notified. However, there was another option—ghetto justice, which could be meted out from family to family. And Maxine makes it clear that Flo was avenged, no surprise for a girl who had so many brothers, including one who took the blame for what had happened because he lost her in the crowd that bleak night.

A few days after, the rapist was beaten into a bloody pulp after school. No one who saw it ever ratted out his attackers.

Maxine says for the record that the Ballard family didn't know who they were. But, leaving little doubt, she adds: "We had an idea."

Flo didn't feel avenged. Sick to her stomach and petrified it would happen again, she refused to leave the apartment for two weeks. She missed so much school that she fell behind in her schoolwork. She also missed several Primettes rehearsals. Hearing not a word from her, Ross and Wilson would either call the apartment or knock on the door, only to have Lurlee answer and insist, skittishly and without explanation, that Flo didn't want to talk to or sing with them anymore.

Diane and Mary didn't know what to make of it. At this point, the group was teetering. Losing McGlown was annoying, but she was replaceable; losing Flo would be fatal. Confused and concerned, they were also resentful of her continued absence—for Diane, it was mostly the latter—and were relieved when Flo finally called Mary and said she needed to speak with them.

They met the next day at the Brewster recreation center, and Flo's appearance was shocking. She was gaunt, her color washed-out, her clothes unkempt; the glint in her eyes was glazed over in what Wilson recalled as a "faraway look that was frightening." Unsteadily, she began telling them what had happened the night she went to the Graystone.

"This had better be good," Diane said snarkily, not knowing how insensitive that remark would be once Flo relived the gruesome details, the knife being held to her throat, and how, she said, the unnamed guy had "hurt me." When she concluded, all three of them were in tears and Flo was wailing, "Why did he do it? I trusted him, I thought he was my friend. Why'd he do it?"

Diane and Mary were of course shaken by the revelations. Though they were too young to comprehend it all, Wilson, years later, told of a certain visceral reaction, the jolt of suddenly needing to make sense of life outside the fringe of a fairy tale and of finding the world "a darker, uglier place." While they tried to pull Flo back into their lighter, prettier dream by redirecting her thoughts on the group—something Flo, encouraged by Lurlee, agreed she needed to do as a kind of therapy— no one would ever fully bring her back from the dark place she'd been on that dreadful night.

In a sense, all of them lost some innocence along with her, Flo by far the most. Wilson would describe the post-rape Florence Ballard in her memoirs as "skeptical, cynical," and "afraid of everyone and everything." Ross, in hers, wrote that Ballard "was not easy. She had a strong personality, just like her voice. Everything about her was big. When she was happy, it was contagious. When she was unhappy, everybody around her felt miserable. She was terribly moody, constantly up and down. . . . We never knew if we did something to offend her and she wouldn't tell us. So she'd be in some dark mood, and then, miraculously and suddenly, it was over."

Most remarkable about Ross's disquisition about Flo, however, were her observations that Ballard "was hard to figure out," that "we could never really understand what drove her to her moods," and that "we were frustrated because we were none the wiser about what had caused the emotional roller-coaster. She was secretive about her feelings, so she was the only one everybody tried to appease."

Could Ross, blinkered by her years of separation from Ballard, have been so narcissistic that she actually *forgot* about Flo being attacked? Indeed, there is no mention of the rape in the Ross tome. How this could be even remotely possible is a mystery. Is it imaginable, for example, that she could have forgotten that she herself had been moved to tears and fear by Flo's rape? Alternatively, if Ross believed she was protecting Ballard's memory from shame, or her privacy, is it conceivable that she didn't know the incident had long been public knowledge?

Few others who knew Flo would have failed to understand, as time crept on, what so tormented her. Yet, for a few years the secret of that night would be kept so tenaciously that even some in the Ballard family circle had scant opportunity to know the details.

RAY GIBSON: My cousin always had that side of her, which became more pronounced during those quiet, introspective times when you left her alone. I didn't know why she would get so lost in herself as she got older—why would I? I was just a kid, so obviously Florence didn't tell me what had happened to her until years later. I mean, it took years before she could tell anybody, really, because she wasn't ready, and because she couldn't find anyone that she trusted enough. It just never got resolved the way it should have. She needed to address it early on, before it could fester. Because it just ate away at her, and I think she found out that all the fame in the world can't make something like that go away.

She just wasn't the same person after a while. She'd try to be the old Florence but it was like play-acting, know what I'm saying? She'd act how she thought Florence was supposed to act. But you could see she was suffering; her eyes, they never had that old sparkle. I don't blame Florence for not getting help. It was the attitude of the times. Women weren't supposed to have feelings about such things. Those attitudes changed when many women's lives were ruined—like Florence's. But I'll say this: Florence was also proud—too proud. She was stubborn; she thought she could get away from it. Just as long as she could sing, she felt everything would turn out all right. She was wrong. But by the time she realized it, she was too far gone.

Cee

From the near abyss of the winter, the Primettes were back in business by spring. They'd even found a foolproof way to defuse Diane's diva games. When she again came down with a last-minute "illness," Richard Morris hired her sister, and foil, Barbara Jean to fill in for her. *That* got her well in a hurry, and there'd be no relapse.

By then, too, they had replaced Betty McGlown—but only after Diane had vetoed Mary's candidate, a childhood friend named Jackie Burkes, who was in another singing group. Unwilling to take in someone who if a major disagreement arose would likely side with Mary, Diane made things so unpleasant for Jackie that she told Mary, "Forget it." Knowing what Burkes would have to put up with, Mary didn't try to change her mind. "Jackie," she would say, "would have been crazy to pursue it," given Ross's hostility and petty ways.

A more palatable choice for Diane was Barbara Martin, whose group with her brother Theodore and Ross's ever infatuated school chum Richard Street had split up, leaving her free. Cute and willowy, she'd graduated the previous spring from Northeastern High and the music teacher there suggested that Flo call her. She did, and Martin readily agreed to join. When they sang together a few days later, the chemistry seemed propitious, made so for Diane by the fact that Martin was the antithesis of the hectoring McGlown—and was actually intimidated by Diane herself. Moreover, she was a superior dancer who could tweak their wooden stage act.

After Martin was introduced to Richard Morris, he said he'd book a new round of gigs for them. Days passed, then weeks, with no word from Morris. Just as when Milton Jenkins went missing, no one seemed to know where he was, either, on the street or at Motown. As it turned out, his disappearance had a darker aspect, as Flo eventually found out when a friend who knew Richie, too, told her he was in jail—having been arrested for violating parole for a past, uncertain crime.

As little as the girls knew of Jenkins's shady doings, if he'd been busted for pimping, it wouldn't have shocked them the way Morris's incarceration did. And while his jail stay was brief, the Primettes wasted no time moving on. Understandably feeling as if they'd been put through the ringer by lower-case managers, and sick of being kept in the lurch after two years, they agreed that they would chuck any more Berry Gordy stand-ins and wannabes and cash in their precious chit for the real thing.

In late November, they went back to West Grand Boulevard, not to do hand-claps and nondescript backing vocals but to put it to Gordy. The message was that there had been enough fooling around, so sign us already.

In the time since their Motown audition, much had happened that would make Gordy more receptive to such a notion. It wasn't just that the group was a year older and had built a track record of sorts, even if it was mainly a failed single. More important, the girl-group genre had perked up again when a foursome from New Jersey, the Shirelles, went Top Forty in October 1960 with a sweet but suggestive song called "Tonight's the Night," recorded for a small independent label called Scepter; as the year ended, another Shirelles tune, the even more provocative "Will You Still Love Me Tomorrow," written by Donnie Kirshner's top tunesmiths, the husband and wife team of Carole King and Gerry Goffin, hit No. 1 on the pop chart in early '61—a first for a girl-group of the rock era.

Gordy, as an industry scion and student of the Kirshner exemplar, realized he needed to plant some pop seeds in his R&B crop. Robert Bateman, in fact, seemed to be his girl-group talent scout. Of course, he had seen the primal Primettes before anyone else who mattered. More recently, he'd witnessed a group from suburban Inkster, Michigan, perform in a high school talent contest, the prize for which was a Motown audition; even though they'd lost, Bateman went backstage and offered the group, which for some reason was called the Casingyettes, an audition, too. That could have meant appearing before anyone at 2648 West Grand Boulevard, but Bateman made sure Gordy heard them. Again, though, the latter couldn't commit, telling them to come back with an original song. (That would happen in early '61, when he'd sign them and call them the Marvelettes.) Gordy had also employed a distaff trio, the Andantes, as background vocalists—Raynoma Liles having quit singing late in 1960. (Their leader was a teen named Louvain Demps, who had been the first client of the Rayber Voices.)

Gordy would likely have called the Primettes back on his own. As it was, when he saw them again on the Motown lot, they didn't need to ask about a contract. Nor did he abide by, or seem to remember, his caveat about their needing to finish school before that could happen. Martin was already rid of school, and Ross and Wilson were only a few months away; and Ballard had chosen to drop out of school altogether, rather than run the risk of being left back—a decision about which Gordy was diffident now, but would hold over Flo's head like a machete later, when it served his purpose.

Noticing the girls in the reception area, he approached them with a big hug for Diane, Mary, and Flo, and another for the new girl. He then hustled them into Studio A, where he was supervising a Mary Wells vocal session. If it was meant as a signal that he had something in store for them, the girls picked up on it. Ross in particular. She had come in that day prepared to kill Gordy with kindness. She even had a pair of cuff links in her purse that she'd made for him in a school crafts class—with his initials inscribed on each. Finding an idle moment to hand them to him, she wasted no time in asking, with batted eyelashes, "Are you going to sign us today?"

"Didn't I tell you I would a year ago?" he said, avoiding a direct yes.

She stared at him with mock impatience.

"Welllll?" she demanded, drawing out the word playfully.

Gordy's cohorts could hardly believe it. Here was a sparring match of wits between the old boxer and a briny high school girl half his age, and he was the one covering up. He was able to keep the upper hand by informing them the contract papers had to be drawn up, and that would take a little time. In the meantime, he said, "Let's see what you can do."

The Primettes spent the next month and a half waiting on those papers. As semi-official Motown artists, they paid dues doing backup vocal work for Mary Wells on songs like "He Holds His Own," "You Lost the Sweetest Boy," and "Honey Boy"—all of which went unreleased— as well as for Mable John and Singin' Sammy Ward. Gordy even let the girls have studio time for themselves, during which they cut at least three singles.

The first was "I Want a Guy," written by Gordy, Brian Holland, and Freddie Gorman—the last a new Motown stringer who in another quirk of Detroit's inbred music community happened to be a mailman whose route included the Brewster-Douglass building Ross lived in. Diane heard him noodling the tune on a piano in the studio one day and pestered Gordy to let her group record it. Apparently, she asked very nicely because Berry himself produced it, with Diane on lead.

In retrospect, it's a wonder either of them survived the experience. Written as a perky ditty, it was murdered right off by Gordy with a bizarre deep organ sounding like something out of a Bela Lugosi movie that persisted with wild, inapt flourishes throughout the song. Ross completed the crime with a screechy twang, executing an odd, quivery glissando on the word "want." Both mentor and protégé, however, were quite satisfied with the work—Ross could even wax in *Secrets of a Sparrow* that "I vividly remember this session. It felt so important. With my eyes closed and my arms outstretched, I poured my heart into this song. When I listen to it now, I feel nostalgic; I can hear that teenage yearning in my voice."

Gordy must have heard the same thing. He penciled it in as their first release and, in its wake, approved more sessions for the group. Out of those came one more Gordy-written stinker, "The Boy That Got Away"—featuring Ross baying as if she'd inhaled helium and trying vainly to sound cool with a spoken "one-two, one-two-three" downbeat intro—and two others written and produced by Smokey Robinson, "Who's Lovin' You" and "After All." While the latter is intriguing because the lead vocal was split among all four girls—and, given this, the only record on which Martin's strong baritone can be clearly heard—all these tracks reveal less about the limitations of the group than those of Gordy and Robinson in getting a grip on the girl-group form. Not really knowing how to update pop and R&B the way they had in "Shop Around," they lost the buoyancy and effervescence that the Primettes had evinced when they performed on stage. What came out of the mixed tracks were more like two-chord demos that cribbed Chantels and Shirelles melodies and slapped them on top of the Gordy "sound," with its deep bottoms, crisply accented highs, and misty echoes. The missing element: imagination.

Gordy and Robinson agreed that they were rather lost in these efforts, and that the last two should not be released; they would remain unreleased until forty years later, when they appeared as historical curiosities on the five-disc *Supremes* box-set. Still, aside from Ross's troublesome nasal delivery—which was incidental to Gordy's opinion that her voice had an indefinable commercial kick—the Primettes were judged ready for their close-up. After the new year, Gordy got moving on the promised contracts, and on January 15, 1961, the girls were called in to sign them. All of them were accompanied by their mothers, even Barbara, who at 18 was of legal age; the others still needed parental consent for making Gordy their de facto guardian until they came of age. Again, Fred Ross had objected, on the usual grounds: that if Diane, now two months from her 17th birthday, went ahead with her singing, she would never go to college. And, this time, Ernestine was prepared to stand with him. Very skeptically, she agreed to come to 2648 West Grand Boulevard with her daughter, to meet Gordy face-to-face.

When they met, she wasn't impressed. Gordy was wearing a fluffy white Angora sweater—"Who's Mr. Fancy?" she said when he came into the room—and he seemed disinclined to say much as he turned over the contract business to Motown A&R* man Mickey Stevenson, who couldn't have been more than a couple years older than Diane, though he'd been in the music business since he was 9 years old, as a singer and behind-the-scenes mover. Eyeing Gordy mostly from a distance, Ernestine believed that the diminutive, baby-faced Gordy, too, was a young man. At least Milt Jenkins had some seasoning. Gordy, she kept telling Diane, was a "kid," a term she kept using even after being informed that he was in fact in his 30s. "How could this kid," she would ask, "be anyone's guardian?"

Seeing how wary all the mothers were, Gordy called in his sophisticated sister Esther to explain to them about the selectiveness of the Motown "family," how the men of Motown were Boy Scout–pure, and how the girls were all chaperoned on the road—often by some of the girls' mothers. Esther had the rap down to an art by now, having quelled many mothers' fears, but it was touch-and-go right to the end. Barbara's mother was, if anything, more recalcitrant than Ernestine, becoming haughty and, as Wilson recalled, "condescending in her attitude that her daughter was too good to be a singer." But under group pressure, intensified by the charged atmospherics of Motown, Ernestine Ross, Lurlee Ballard, Johnnie Mae Wilson, and Barbara's mother ultimately left their marker on each eye-glazing fourteen-page, double-spaced contract.

---

* This acronym is industry shorthand for "artists and repertoire," the functional meaning of which is the scouting and signing of talent, though Stevenson's purview was far greater, extending to producing, writing, green-lighting songs for release, and keeping musicians paid and loyal to Motown.

Technically, the deal was not with Motown but, rather, with Berry Gordy Enterprises and specifically Tamla Records, and was typical for such contracts of the era—which, if any young performers had run them by a lawyer, would quickly have set off alarm bells. Of course, it helped the industry panjandrums that this rarely if ever happened, the scent of fame trumping the notion of not signing. In this construct, the fine print, filled with numbing legalese, was a formality of interest only to the muckety-mucks. Of more compelling interest to prospective Motown acts and their elders was a simple proposition: Would Berry Gordy do wrong by his "family"? The answer, implicitly, was no. Still, not one among the three mothers felt sanguine about leaving their signature that day.

"They just didn't trust this little guy, Berry Gordy, not with our emotional development or with our money," Ross would recall.

Their gut feeling was well founded. As they would discover later, what they had signed was the abrogation of every conceivable right a human being has, except possibly the right to vote and to have a trial by jury. The decision on how, when, and how much to pay them rested solely with "The Company." They had no inherent right to question The Company draining such remuneration for unspecified "expenses" (Gordy having learned *that* trick from Al Green and Nat Tarnopol). In what may have seemed a trivial matter at the time, Motown retained 100 percent of all royalty rights to future commercial applications of songs in movies and commercials. And, though the Primettes probably didn't imagine this would ever pertain to them, Motown had the exclusive right to hire and/or fire any member of any group at any time for any cause.

As for those royalties, the terms were, again, standard: a 3 percent royalty to be split equally among the members—due on 90 percent of the retail price of each record sold (which was always at a discount on the market)—*less* taxes and "packaging costs." That broke down, in the market value of the times, to approximately two cents per record sold at seventy-five cents; the net earnings on a record that theoretically sold 1 million copies (and, again, that would have to be by Gordy's word, with no outside auditors to verify it) would work out to roughly $20,000, which when divvied by the current foursome would be $5,000 each. Gordy would pocket the rest—$730,000—*plus* whatever he deemed to cover expenses and costs.

Not that there weren't any operating costs, and quite legitimate ones, given the expense involved in paying musicians (who, unlike the singers, had a union that needed to be mollified), pressing plants, distributors, promoters, sundry middlemen, company salaries, studio equipment, and keeping the lights on at Motown. There was also, as has often been surmised but never proven, the possibility that Gordy greased the palms of a few Mafia types to ensure that production at the pressing plants and shipment of records down at the Black Bottom docks would continue undisturbed. And, of course, there were the emoluments for disc jockeys, such as their "Christmas presents."

In fact, as Gordy would soon learn when the flush of excitement and the initial rush of royalties for "Shop Around" subsided, his arrangements with distributors would keep the money coming only if Motown's hit parade proceeded unabated; otherwise his brethren around the country reserved the right to withhold monies from *him*. In his 1979 book *The Story of Motown*, Peter Benjaminson reported that Motown cleared only around $100,000 a year in profits from 1959 to 1962, most of which Gordy "immediately reinvested in the business, leaving himself with very little to operate on." Already, there were rumors on the street that Gordy had in desperation nurtured his alleged Mob ties to keep Motown solvent; that he had made "secret" deals with loan sharks and Mob bosses, pledging a handsome return of the company's future business. Such scuttlebutt, to his dismay and to the detriment of the company, only grew stronger, from whispers to open speculation in the media. To some onlookers, this explained Gordy's continued importation of white executives who soon came to dominate Motown's inner councils; to others, it explained his real motive in keeping his books away from the prying eyes of the RIAA.

Whatever the state of his books, by all appearances Berry Gordy was not hurting in 1961—especially considering the arrival of a fleet of glistening new Cadillac convertibles and the annexation of more property along West Grand Boulevard, several other townhomes having been purchased as an expansion of Motown office space. While Motown contracts were ironclad in their penury—Gordy prone to making self-serving and highly arrogant statements to the press such as "It's my money, I make the money," thus relegating his "family" to the status of mere courtiers—on a personal level he could be extraordinarily generous, when the spirit moved him, as when he reached deeply into his pocket for bonuses and handed out gifts to favored acts and toadies.

Still, even one of the most tended-to of Motown recipients would remain essentially in the dark. "To this day," Mary Wilson said in the early '80s, "I still don't know exactly how many millions of copies any of our records sold, though I still receive royalties."

Being a member in good standing of Berry Gordy's "family," then, required a strange compact. You were free, and even expected, to trill about his beneficence as a big brother figure. But if you had any designs on examining his account books, he'd be Big Brother—not only agent and manager for all of his acts but the accountant as well.

Yet for the Primettes, all of these considerations, the fuzzy math, the questionable ethics, were irrelevant on January 15, 1961. On that day, they fused into the fabric of Motown, their cache and identity instantly transformed. In fact, when the contracts were signed certifying Berry Gordy Jr. as their overlord, the group name typed in was not the Primettes. Gordy, as he had done with Smokey Robinson's Matadors, wanted a change to a classier, more market-friendly moniker. A few days before, he handed the task to his ubiquitous receptionist.

JANIE BRADFORD: I was good at that kind of thing. I had an ear for names. I named the Satintones, too. I thought that was the coolest, sexiest name ever; it was so, I don't know, *tactile*. You could "feel" it. Same with Supremes. That's a great color word; it makes you think of something grand and elegant. My hedge was that it didn't really tie in to girls. Girl-group names were always something with a feminine concept, something soft and girly—the Satintones actually would've been a fantastic girl-group name! I was fooling around with "Satinettes," but it was too close to the Satintones. They didn't need to be another "sister" group.

So rather than come up with one name, I just gave them everything I could think of, girly or not, whatever I thought would work for them. And I didn't want to get caught up in that "ette" thing. You literally could have used any word and put an "ette" on the end of it and it would be cute. Take a girly concept, flowers, spices, emotions. You could have "Passionettes," but that's too sexy. Or "Pamperettes," but how would that have looked when Pampers diapers came in? You could have cars, "Lincolnettes" or "Mercuryettes," or maybe just "Mercurettes," but the car thing was for guy-groups. You could try a commercial thing—"Chiclettes," like the gum; that would be perfect for a bunch of chicks, right? But that would be too contrived, too cute.

When I got around five names, I wrote them on little pieces of paper and put them in a hat. I did use one "ette" name, Jewelettes, even though it sounded too much like "Juliettes."

The others, to tell you the God's honest truth, I don't even remember. And when Florence came in, I handed her the hat and
said, "Pick one." The other girls weren't there, so it would really
be Flo's choice, and she was the one who naturally would have
made the decision, anyway. She had quite a bit of control then.
And she reached in and the first one she pulled out was
"Supremes." Of course, she could have said, "No way, I don't
like it." But she loved it. I think she liked that it wasn't the
most feminine name, because she didn't like the sweet and innocent kind of music. She said, "Girl, we are the *Supremes*!"

Although Flo might well have weeded through all the paper in
Bradford's hat until she got to "Supremes," it is interesting to play
"what-if" had whatever it was that guided Ballard's hand that day led
her to pick "Jewelettes"—or any of the other names that have become
so dwarfed by history's embrace of the Supremes that even Bradford
can't remember what they were, even though months later when she
found the scraps of paper in her desk drawer she had them framed as
prized memorabilia. The other four options, unearthed by Mary Wilson, were the Darleens, the Sweet Ps, the Melodees, and the Royal-
tones. Which begs some fair questions: Would Martin Scorcese's
moonstruck Masha in *The King of Comedy* ever have yearned to be a
Sweet P for just one night? And would the Darleens ever have been
chosen as the Muses for "I Hear a Symphony" or "Reflections"?

As with most things, Ross and Wilson have related differing versions of the rechristening, though their narratives (in Ross's case, two
whole sentences) do bisect with Flo Ballard making the final call. In the
Ross view, that occurred after Bradford had "handed [Flo] a list of what
she considered good names." Ballard, she said, "picked 'the Supremes'
because it was the only one that didn't have an 'ette' on the end"—Ross
evidently either having forgotten or never having known of the many
other options besides Jewelettes.

Wilson, for her part, omits Bradford altogether while injecting herself and Ross. "Flo was in charge of keeping a list of the names we'd collected," she wrote. "We were each pretty vocal about our favorite
choices, but Flo kept her opinions to herself." When Flo "read off her
list," she adds, "none of them really impressed any of us, but . . . after a
minute [Flo] said, 'I like this one—the Supremes.'"

These alternate takes again cause Bradford to bridle. "There are all
sorts of stories," she says with a deep sigh, "and I can understand the
girls not wanting to give credit to someone not in the group for pick-

ing the name that became so much a part of them. But. . . ." After a pause, she adds: "Look, I don't toot my own horn. But don't try to steal my thunder."

In truth, the only one whose opinion counted was Big Brother Berry. That he found "Supremes" more than acceptable was made evident by the fact that it was typed into the contract. And if Ross and Wilson weren't completely sold on the name, once the deal was finalized it began to grow on them. Wearing it like a sash, they treaded the halls of Motown with the impresa of a next new thing. To Gordy, and thus soon copied by everyone else, they were now identified not by name but as "the girls." Gordy, in his memoir, further gurgled that "[t]hey were the sweethearts of Hitsville" and that around the lot they were already something like icons; Wilson, he offered, "was probably the most popular with the guys," Ballard "sarcastic" and "kept us laughing all the time." But it was Ross who was Berry's "girl," possessed of "a drive in her that could not be denied. Nor could her appeal—which she used to full advantage."

That, to say the least, would become *molto* evident around Motown soon enough; but even before Gordy laid an amorous hand on Diane Ross, he couldn't get enough of her. Days after the signing, he made her his secretary, a function for which she was uniquely unqualified, as Ross has confirmed. "The truth is," she has said, "I wasn't his secretary. I couldn't even type or take shorthand."

Clearly it took Gordy's hand to wave "the girls'" first record into the pressing plant. Doing so for any Motown record was the result of an informal procedure that would become a regular Friday afternoon ritual, at which Gordy would assemble a dozen or so cronies and decide by vote which tracks made the cut. Naturally, whatever the vote, Gordy had the final say, and he had to overrule an emphatically negative verdict on "I Want a Guy." Flo Ballard had made it known that she hated it, and even his loyal adjutant Smokey Robinson turned thumbs down, primarily because of Ross's adenoidal vocal. But Gordy seemed to live in mortal fear of disappointing his secretary.

And so in early spring 1961, pop culture history arrived at an ennobling moment, one that at the time seemed to be significant of absolutely nothing. On March 9, "I Want a Guy," with a minor Gordy song called "Never Again" on the flip, was released as Tamla 54038, under the name "The Supremes."

Gordy threw his promotional machine behind the record and once more leaned on the deejays. And nearly everyone who heard it chose not to hear it again. With distributors unable to move it, jocks reluctant to play it, record stores refusing to stock it, and its sales negligible, "I Want a Guy" died a quick death.

Gordy took the failure in stride, figuring he could afford to wait for the girls to find their collective voice and niche. He just didn't know how long he'd need to wait. Or was it Diane Ross—his "girl"—whom he was really waiting on? Several months before he'd given contracts to the group, Gordy had been chatting with Mable John at Motown when he remarked, "I think I'm gonna sign that Diane Ross girl."

"What about the other girls?" she asked him.

"Oh yeah," he said, clearly as an afterthought. "Them, too."

John admonished him not to even think of breaking up a group of young girls; that, she warned, was asking for trouble.

"Would I do that?" he said as he walked away, leaving a laugh to echo after him.

seven

SMOKEY PLACES

ll through 1961, things kept falling into place at Motown, none
of which had much of an impact on the incipient Supremes.
This, despite Gordy's conscious efforts to get "his girls" some
traction. In fact, throughout the first three months of the year,
he put them frequently into Studio A, with Berry taking another crack at producing them on "Buttered Popcorn," a song he'd co-
written with Barney Ales, whom he'd bumped up to vice-president of
sales. For this one, he put Ballard instead of Ross on lead. Turned loose
over a gritty rhythm track—with piano riffs, appropriately, by Popcorn
Wylie—she busted a raw-throated vocal, serving up some unsubtle sexual cant with a hook about "liking it salty, gooey, and sticky," though
Ross, perhaps still smarting over ceding the lead, would later play
dumb in putting down the record, insisting she didn't even know who
wrote it and that "I'm still trying to figure out what it was about."

Gordy might have wished his name wasn't associated with it, since
he immediately shunned it. Ales, believing it was hit material, was set
to commit the Motown sales force to the record when it was released on
the Tamla label on July 21, backed with a ballad written and produced
by Smokey Robinson, "Who's Loving You," with Ross on lead. Ales was
even able to pull the first few copies of "Popcorn" off the market and
substitute a more sprightly version for sale. However, Berry grew distant from the record, then outright hostile about it. Ales tried to get
him on board, to no avail. After a raging argument between the two
men, Ales was directed to take the sales force elsewhere, rendering
"Popcorn" an unpopped kernel that got nowhere near the charts.

Ross may not have mourned its fate, possibly divining, or hoping, that its failure would be traced to the lead. And, as it turned out, for whatever reason, this was the last time a Flo-fronted Supremes song would ever be issued as a single.

Ales's redirection was well justified, and proved that Gordy could be admirably objective when it came to a record's hit potential, not withstanding his gaffe with "I Want a Guy." The context for his decision on "Popcorn" was that one of the most happening things at 2648 West Grand Boulevard during the first half of 1961 was the other girl-group Gordy had sent away months before to get some experience, the teenagers from Inkster with that strange name the Casingyettes (a wry inside joke by the girls acknowledging their limitations, as in "we can't sing yet"). When they returned, at Gordy's instruction, with an original song called "Please Mr. Postman," his ears perked up, and he sent them into the studio with Brian Holland and Robert Bateman. By then, it had many fathers; originally co-written by the group's Georgia Dobbins and a friend, at Motown it acquired no fewer than three more co-writers—Holland, Bateman, and real-life postman Freddie Gorman, all of whom earned royalties. At the session, when Benny Benjamin didn't show, Marvin Gaye played drums, laying down a spontaneous shuffle backbeat. And with Gladys Horton's lead vocal beseeching a mailman to "deliver the letter the sooner the better" and its catchy "Wait a minute, wait a minute" hook, it would catch the early wave of homesick blues as the Vietnam War escalated and girls pined for just such missives.

The Supremes—or, rather, one of them—earned an assist, too. Upon meeting the Marvelettes, as Gordy had renamed the Casingyettes, moments before they went in for their vocals, Ballard and Wilson sized up the new girls, not entirely favorably. "We were jealous of [them] encroaching on our territory," Wilson would recall. But an altruistic Flo, upon hearing their first takes, couldn't help but offer a few suggestions when the Marvelettes took five.

"Understand," says the Marvelettes' Katherine Anderson, "we'd never even been in a studio before. We'd only sang in choirs or glee clubs. It was our own song and we didn't know how to sing it."

Lead singer Gladys Horton adds: "Florence came over and said she had a few ideas that would make the song sound more loose and homey. We were all tight—petrified—and Florence was a sweetheart, and what she said was dead on."

That included having Horton draw out the word "postman" and having the group pepper the background with "oh yeahs." All these elements built Gordy his dream vehicle, not just any Cadillac but a fully operational crossover chart-topper. Released exactly a month after the abortive "Buttered Popcorn," fourteen weeks later it was sitting in the top slots of both the pop and R&B charts, clearing over a million records, at least according to Gordy.

In the wake of "Mr. Postman," distributors who had to be persuaded to take Motown product in the slump period following "Shop Around" now begged for it. In turn, Gordy had Ales drive a hard bargain: Distributors would get no Motown hot wax unless they paid every cent held back in the past for "expenses"—a most ironic and duplicitous demand, given how Gordy stiffed his own talent using the same dodge and promised to pay every cent that would be earned by future records.

And meanwhile, back on the Supremes front, there was mostly empty space. Not only had they been overtaken by the Marvelettes but they weren't even running second among the girls overall. In fact, Mary Wells had been the first individual singer to break out, when the song she'd penned, "Bye Bye Baby," hit No. 8 R&B and No. 45 pop late in 1960, followed in 1961 by "I Don't Want to Take a Chance," which hit No. 9 R&B and No. 33 pop. Smokey Robinson then wrote and produced "The One Who Really Loves You" for her, and it exploded to Nos. 2 and 8 (the first Top Ten pop song on the Motown label), kicking off a string of bright, bouncy collaborations between the two, with Wells's fey, feline voice a near-copy of Smokey's and the songs mirrors of his dreamy pop confections with the Miracles.

The Supremes did well by merely staying in the game, when the alternative might have meant withering apathy from Gordy. For this, they had Ross's gall to thank. At 17 and still working toward her high school graduation in January 1962, she had nonetheless won a reputation as an intolerable harpy among the women folk of Motown. Feigning friendliness for the sake of "family" comity while passing catty remarks about the female competition, she was especially competitive when the Marvelettes shot to the top of the charts. While the rest of the company, including Wilson and Ballard, delighted in their sudden success, Ross turned up her nose in disdain.

"Diane was so jealous, you could smell the jealousy," says Marvelette Katherine Anderson. "Florence and Mary were happy for us, so it wasn't like it was them against us. When we first met them, Florence took to us right away. And Mary was, well, Mary; she was always very nice. But Diane was standoffish. She felt we were a threat. And they were nobodies like us, but Diane felt like they were the first girl-group at Motown so they deserved to have the first hit. To her, the Marvelettes were like dirt, little ninnies from Inkster, and she was Miss Sophistication—and she was from the projects!"

"The thing I remember about her was what we called 'the look,' the 'Diane look.' She used to have this look on her face, like a scowl. Even when she was acting all buddy-buddy, she'd be scowling at you. Our attitude was, we don't really care whatever your problem was. We'd just laugh at her and walk away saying, 'Is she for real?'"

Ross's attitude would worsen. In the spring of 1962, when the Marvelettes were to go out on tour to promote their first album, one of the girls, Wanda Young, had to miss the tour because she was about to have a baby. Because their contract with promoters required that there be a full contingent of five Marvelettes on stage, the group proposed that the Supreme who had been so helpful to them be Young's stand-in. Flo Ballard agreed, and Gordy signed off on it.

As Ballard saw it, doing so was perfectly in keeping with the communal, all-for-one, one-for-all spirit of Motown, and of mutual benefit to both groups. "She went with us to help us out but also to experience life on the road on a big tour," said the Marvelettes' lead singer, Gladys Horton. But to Diane and, to a lesser degree, Mary, she was less D'Artagnan than Mata Hari. Ross kept the Motown crowd entertained for days with melodramatic diatribes when Flo came to Motown not for Supremes business but to rehearse with the Marvelettes.

"If she wants to be a Marvelette," she would say, "then she should be a goddamn Marvelette for all I care."

Mary, not given to such garish scenes, quietly brooded that Ballard was "our sister, not theirs," but, as always, she capitulated to decisions beyond her control after Flo explained that she had no disloyalty and no agenda. In fact, she had a hidden agenda, but that had nothing to do with group matters: She was sweet at the time on the Marvelettes' road manager Joe Schaffner, who was spending a lot of time with Katherine Anderson; Flo didn't mind a bit that she'd be making time for herself with Schaffner. In fact, when Esther Gordy Edwards, who would accompany them on the tour as a chaperone at her brother's request, forewarned the four actual Marvelettes that there'd be no time for fraternizing and they'd have to stay in their rooms and do their high school homework, Flo figured that being a dropout had a definite upside.

As for Ross's objections, Flo and her new temporary mates joked that Diane was so out of joint only because she hadn't been the one asked to sing on a major tour. Indeed, the loyalty issue would not be one Diane Ross reminded anyone else of down the road.

The Marvelettes-plus-one-Supreme tour, with stops in Washington, D.C., Philadelphia, and New York, went without a hitch, ending with the mandatory, and exhilarating, appearance at the Apollo Theater, where they shared the bill with the likes of Jerry Butler, the pre-Motown Gladys Knight and the Pips, Barbara George, and comedian George Kirby. Flo came out dressed like the other Marvelettes in a knee-length skirt and matching headband and twisted, jerked, and mashed-potatoed through the set as best she could.

"Flo did what we asked and Lord, that girl could sing. But it was obvious she wasn't that good a dancer. She had problems with the routines," Anderson says. "That was the difference between them and us. The Marvelettes were very high-energy and we were known for our dancing. The Supremes never really were dancers. They didn't have any moves, they just sort of stood there and swayed back and forth. They couldn't hold a candle to us."

A wry grin. "But they had something we didn't—they had, or Diane did, a hold on Berry. Even before they had a hit, they had Berry."

For Flo, the tour provided companionship she never found within her own group (though apparently not quite enough with Joe Schaffner, who would ultimately marry Katherine Anderson). Her kinship with Gladys Horton deepened; the two of them roomed together and sat beside each other for long hours on the bus rides, engaged in what for Ballard was highly personal conversation. When Gladys opened up about her rough childhood in a foster home, Flo was led to recount the rape. Recognizing how painful it was for her, Horton would keep the secret, not telling the other Marvelettes.

Horton is still proprietary about Ballard's revelations. "She told me about it, but I didn't learn a lot about her. Maybe because I was so young and I didn't realize the full extent of it, psychologically, when a girl becomes a woman. When you're young, things don't touch you as bad." But Horton did reflexively steer the conversation to other areas, such as when Flo abruptly switched her infatuation from Schaffner to a co-performer on the tour, the Pips' William Guest. "She'd ask, 'Gladys, was he looking at me?' Flo always had an eye for the sharpest guys."

Those sorts of schoolgirl crushes could temporarily divert Ballard from the scars of the rape, but Horton's silence aside, word of it still festered around Hitsville. Says Katherine Anderson: "The rumors got around. You know, there'd be whispers. It wasn't from Gladys, so I don't know where it came from. But there were very few secrets at Motown that all of us didn't know about sooner or later; that's how tight the community was. Maybe it was because it struck everybody that Florence was troubled. She was usually very, very quiet. Oh, she could have fun, get silly, and we had a lot of fun on that tour and on the Motown tours after that. But you could see that was a front. I could see something bothered her. Sometimes she'd get very emotional. There were things tearing her up inside."

Hard as it was to read Florence Ballard, though, "[i]t was easier to see one thing she felt: How much she disliked Diane. She wouldn't even try to defend her. When Diane went off on one of her crazy rants, she'd just roll her eyes, like, 'Uh-oh, here she goes again.'"

Cee

It wasn't group loyalty, then, that kept the Supremes in the mix. It was that the menfolk of Motown melted into puddles before Diane Ross. What's more, as if in a chemical recoil to Fred Ross's stifling moral codes, she was crossing sexual boundaries where she'd previously stopped short. All the Supremes were—most obviously so in the case of Barbara Martin, who in late 1961 got married and by early '62 was pregnant, portending the dilemma of how to fill a pregnancy leave by one of their own. Their virginity now a thing of the past, Ross, Wilson and Ballard could be found making the scene, usually independently, and pairing off with a revolving ring of men they barely knew. Recalling that haze of backroom parties and raging hormones, Wilson once coyly told of hooking up with a guy she could remember only by the white Dodge he drove, calling it a "lovemobile."

At one such party, attended by Mary and Diane, a punk called Silky began coming on too strong with Ross on the dance floor, clamping her against his body so tightly she couldn't pry herself away. Apparently this had been planned in advance to unnerve the haughty "princess" Diane. Mary, in on the gag, giggled as she watched Diane become more and more unsettled, until she wailed for help in cold fear. Only then did Mary play her part and intervene to "save" her.

That a staged act so inconsiderate in light of Flo's rape could be amusing to Mary was stunningly cruel. But it underscored the tenuous, razor's edge alliance of the three core Supremes, explaining why Ballard was already closer to a girl in a rival group than to anyone in hers. It might also explain why Ross could return the cruelty to Wilson in more subtle ways, such as constantly criticizing the prettier Mary for her tastes in clothing and makeup, as well as for her "skinny legs," an odd thing to say for a girl whose legs were no less skinny. When Mary, too, became engaged late in 1961, impetuously, to a childhood chum named Ronnie Hammers, Diane started sidling up to the young man in what Mary took to be flirting. When Wilson and Hammers decided to call off the engagement and broke up, Ross suddenly lost interest in him.

Around Motown the Supremes, who could sound blissfully cohesive in the studio, made people shake their heads about how divergent they were on a personal level. The Marvelettes were not the only ones who noticed how little Flo and Mary defended Diane when she created a spat between herself and other girls. Indeed, it seemed more than just for a hoot that Mary bided her time before coming to Diane's aid at that party; it was a message that she might not be as obedient as Diane assumed. That, in turn, likely made Ross even more apt to act in her own interests, and to get her own way.

Wilson, years later, echoed Gordy's descriptives of the individual Supremes.

They were, she wrote, "three completely different, insecure people," each gleaning from the other two character traits that she lacked—to wit, Flo's "earthiness, my nice guy demeanor, and Diane's aggressive charm," brightly concluding that "we accidentally discovered that these three separate, incomplete young girls combined to create one great woman."

While that was intended in the figurative sense, the postulation turned out to be all too true in the literal sense: Out of the mix of the three Supremes, there would be created only one great woman. The one for whom being great was an obsession.

Given her predatory impulses, daring, and thirst to slay a good challenge, it was natural that Ross would quickly have in her crosshairs a conquest that could help keep the Supremes—and Diane herself—lurching forward. In the long run, that target would of course be one Berry Gordy, but at 17 she knew well that the vast difference in their ages and experience made it all moot. Berry operated on a level far beyond hers. But if the same seemed to be the case with Gordy's top adjutant, Ross by habit had no compunction against taking aim at Smokey Robinson, her friend and courtier of favors. She began almost from the start to wiggle her way into Smokey's deep consciousness.

As it was, he had felt comfortable enough in his friendship with her to foot the bill—or "loan" her, as he has recalled it—for the cosmetology and modeling classes she was taking on weekends. But as she turned up her "aggressive charm," he apparently had in mind lessons of another kind for her. The kind for which he'd accrued a reputation around Motown—not his public incarnation as a doe-eyed romantic spinning lyrical mush about wanting "a lifetime of devotion" but the glandular, baby-faced Lothario wanting just ten minutes in a secluded nook.

Smokey, then, was a ripe target for any sweet young thing, and because there was no shortage of those around 2648 West Grand Boulevard, the exploits of "little Smokey"—and how he loved to "shop around" despite his storybook marriage to Claudette—generated tons of hushed "water fountain" gossip among the girls. The Supremes were typically curious about how accurate the stories were about his prodigious sexual appetite, and when he'd amble through the halls in his tight slacks all female eyes would steal a glance southward at the "goods." Flo actually seemed to be the most curious, detailing the inventive ways she would ravish him, but for her and Mary both, his "other" goods—his wedding ring—kept it a fantasy.

They assumed the same went for Diane. Not that she hadn't flirted with him in her cloying way, but she did that with all the Motown men, and always with Berry Gordy, harmlessly enough. But Ross also understood the ethos that drove those men, in which power was indeed an aphrodisiac as it was transfused into the plasma of Hitsville males by the biggest lecher of them all. Marvin Gaye once said of his boss to the writer David Ritz, "Berry was the horniest man in Detroit. He married black and fooled around with whites. You'd think he was working, but he might be freaking with some chick right up there in his office."

A similar Gaye quote, to J. Randy Taraborrelli, went: "Berry Gordy was leading the way, and he'd be up in his room freaking with whoever was in his life that night. He was the father figure. So why wouldn't all the 'children' follow suit?"

Yet there was a limit to Gordy's ways—Motown's female acts were off limits. Perhaps to prevent himself from going too far, Berry made it clear that his young girls were chattel in every sense, to be guarded, herded, and protected from men like himself, and not to be tarnished the way all other women in the world were wont to be. He went to extremes seeing to it that they were chaperoned on tours and shadowed by bodyguards who would menace any fans who got near them. The Motown circle of performers could turn only to themselves for company on the long, lonely road, initiating a slew of intra-company sexual canoodling through the years, most of which ended when the tours did.

Gordy liked to posture about those sorts of "incestuous" shenanigans, too, but with a presumed wink and nod, an artifice similar to his regular lectures to the "children" about the evils of, and fines for, gambling on the bus rides—then, when he would go along on a selected tour, he'd be in the back, betting thousands of dollars at a clip on endless rounds of hearts or five-card stud. But everyone could tell the difference when he ordered his lieutenants to keep their hands off the girls. About this, he was dead serious.

Diane Ross was not alone in her willingness to test Berry's First Commandment, but with a single-mindedness unmatched by any other Hitsville woman—or man—she broke ground that no other women, and few men, ever did. The magnetic attraction between the two of them was already palpable, though kept at bay by both. Again, if impure thoughts of hitting on a 17-year-old girl crossed his mind during the early Supremes history, his avuncular feelings for the Supremes as a whole submerged them.

Besides, as Marvin Gaye suggested, Gordy was up to his mustache with more experienced women, his marriage to Raynoma Liles doing nothing to prevent an affair he carried on with a woman named Margaret Norton—with whom he'd had sex on his *wedding night*, according to Robert Bateman. When Liles found out, she, too, had an affair, with the Satintones' Sonny Sanders. Soon after, she and Berry had it out, with harsh words and fists flying in the apartment they had moved to on Lawton Street in 1961 when Motown became overcrowded, right in front of a visiting, and startled, Smokey Robinson.

Things would get even worse, when a psychotic Liles stalked Norton in a parking lot and held a gun to her neck, before Smokey, who fortunately happened to be there again, collared Liles from behind and yelled to Margaret, "I've got her! Run!" Later, Raynoma sat in her car in front of Norton's home for hours, set on murder-suicide. But when Margaret didn't come out, she drove off—all the way to New York, Berry having agreed to be rid of her by letting her run the skeletal New York office of Motown Inc. There, she was subsequently arrested by the FBI for illegally holding back large numbers of Motown records earmarked for distributors and selling them directly to record stores—an early form of bootlegging. With Liles facing jail time, Gordy got her to sign away all her 50 percent stock interest in Motown in exchange for a $10,000 lump sum, $16,500 a year for ten years, $2,000 a year in child support, and a promise not to press charges. (None of these highly entertaining details made it into Gordy's memoirs, or Robinson's.) He would obtain a Mexican divorce and take up with Margaret openly, though refraining from marrying her, his eye ever wandering.

But if the busy—and no doubt exhausted—Gordy was out of range for Diane Ross in 1961, she and his loyal 21-year-old scion created in his image quickly bloomed from stablemates to bedmates, under the guise of working on "projects." What's more, rather than murkily "living in shame," Diane made sure it didn't stay a secret. One day late in '61, she flounced in with some shocking news for Mary and Flo.

"Guess what? I dated Mr. Smokey Robinson!" she crowed, as giddy as if she'd just hit the jackpot in a casino.

Mary and Flo were duly impressed, not least by her absolute lack of discretion about making it with a married man, but also by her flaunting of the Motown moral etiquette, flawed and hypocritical as it was. Seeing them with their mouths agape, and not really knowing what to say, Diane was radiant.

When Flo was finally able to blurt out, "This is gonna get back to Berry," Diane's smile was the only retort she needed: If she was to be the "it" girl, she wouldn't give a damn about her bad reputation, which might even make Gordy see her more as a woman than as a daughter figure. It's not clear when Berry did get wind of it, but with Ross boasting to everyone but the janitor about how Smokey would send her flowers on the morning-afters, their affair became the worst-kept nonsecret ever at Hitsville, at least until her future liaison with Gordy took off.

Not that Smokey would ever own up to it. Walking a verbal highwire and using every euphemism he could think of for "adultery," he wrote in his autobiography that "[w]e rehearsed together, we worked late. We developed an intimacy, genuine love, and respect. We enjoyed each other's company." Eventually, he noted, it got back to Claudette, who confronted him, with the colloquy going like this:

"Word is [that] you're really enjoying Diane's company."

"She's my friend."

"People say she's more."

"People say all kinds of shit. If the gossip's upsetting you—"

"It's upsetting me a lot."

"Would it make you feel better if I didn't see Diane so much?"

"It would."

"Then I'll cool it."

(Perhaps Smokey had a certain interlude in mind when he later wrote one of his most famous lyrics, for the Miracles' "Ooh Baby Baby": "Although she may be cute, she's just a substitute / Because you're the permanent one.")

Given Ross's pride and joy in her handiwork—knowing that any opprobrium by the Motown women would be undercut by their envy—she clearly relished the *schadenfreude* in humiliating Claudette, justifying her own immorality on the thin reed that she wasn't the other woman but the *only* woman keeping Smokey satisfied. In this, Ross wasn't the only Motown woman about whom Claudette Robinson was scorned for being so blind in the face of her husband's obvious philandering, though as the years wore on most everyone would pity her for her long-suffering gallantry—enduring no fewer than *eight* miscarriages, once after Smokey was ill and he, unbelievably, let her take over the role of lead singer for the Miracles on a long tour, despite being eight months pregnant. She stoically stuck out the marriage for twenty-seven years. Yet, today, dispassionately, she rejects any grudge or blame for how he repaid her blind loyalty.

CLAUDETTE ROGERS: That was so long ago. The whole Motown thing is like a past life. People still like to dredge up things that may have happened, but for me, it's like who cares? I look at it like this: Only Smokey and Diana could tell you what they did with each other. Because I don't know. I mean it. If they had an affair, I wasn't aware of it. There have been a lot of rumors, and when you hear something so many times, it might very well have been that way.

People do things in the dark, and if they ever want to share it in the light, I'll be listening. But all I know is that I asked Smokey, one time, if he was doing it with Diana, and his answer was no. And obviously, for me to stay married for all those years, I had to believe him or it wouldn't have gotten very far.

She has had a good guffaw over the years seeing herself alternately cast as a shrew and a wimp in various deliberations of this topic. One account had her slapping Ross's face; another, pushing Ross out of the way when she stood next to her trying to act congenial during Motown publicity photo shoots. Still another had her stabbing one of Smokey's tarts. By contrast, she was also said to have walked in on one such tryst, politely excusing herself, and walking back out.

> Oh, God, there are so many stories, so many rumors, and I treat the Smokey and Diana thing as one of them. What Smokey wrote in his book, that dialogue between us, if I said that, I don't remember. I always thought the reason he stopped recording them had nothing to do with me. It was because he wasn't producing any hits on them.
>
> Oh, I have no doubt she liked him—they all did. Many, many women today still do. If he and Diana took it further, so be it. But all you can do as a wife is trust your husband. And I never thought I had to shun Diana, either. We've been friends for a long time. When she lived in California, we were five blocks from each other and she would come over with her children. Our daughters played together, her nephew played with my son. What would be the point in not being friends? If that happened forty-five years ago, what would it mean at this point in my life to be upset with her, or him?
>
> Whatever happened, happened. It didn't make a dent in my life. Whatever it was, it's something they have to deal with, on their own, with their God.

While the liaison continued, Smokey took time from his work with Mary Wells to squeeze in sessions in late December 1961. For the floundering Supremes, this proved critical, as it came at a time when the group had kept active by taking more backup singing gigs, at the going rate of $2.50 each per session. One of those involved a song written and sung by Gordy's brother Robert Kayli, "Small Sad Sam"—a comic riff on the Jimmy Dean hit "Big Bad John," which became a minor hit late in '61. The only known Supremes date after "Buttered Popcorn" was on August 14 when Gordy cut low-grade fodder with the titles "(He's) Seventeen," "Save Me a Star," and "Heavenly Father"—with Mary singing lead on the first and Flo on the others, all probably intended as future B-sides.

The December session had a make-or-break feel to it. The girls would record a tune called "Your Heart Belongs to Me," which Smokey had composed to chip off the separation-anxiety theme that had driven the massively successful "Please Mr. Postman," but going a step further by placing the wayward boyfriend in Army boots overseas. For this schmaltzy cry of a lonely heart back home, Ross stepped up and over a funky bossa nova beat, pouring heavy vocal syrup about her "lover of mine, gone to a faraway land, serving your country"—and she did it convincingly, over some nicely turned backing harmonies by Wilson, Ballard, and Barbara Martin Richardson.

The cut passed muster with Gordy, who released it with "(He's) Seventeen" as the flip side on May 8, 1962. Gordy's support was evidenced by his decision to put out the disc on the Motown label, which had no viable acts save for Wells and the prodigal Eddie Holland; Eddie's United Artists run had ended in '61 and he was now back with Gordy, scoring a Top Forty hit in March 1962 with his song "Jamie."

This put the Supremes under the pressure of expectation, and the results were mixed. While "Your Heart" was no "Mr. Postman," ringing in at No. 95 pop, it did so under the handicap of being beaten onto the market by the Shirelles' "Soldier Boy," a thematic duplicate that tore up to No. 1 and all but obscured the subsequent Supremes song. Given this, the latter's showing was arguably satisfactory—and, as their first charting, inarguably a step up for the Supremes, proving they could play on the same field as the Marvelettes and Shirelles, if not as cleanup hitters.

That was good enough to convince Gordy to schedule more sessions for them, minus Smokey for now. Even so, they were hardly on the front burner. It would take until November 1962 for the next Supremes product to see daylight, as other more urgent girl-group doings played out at Motown. Most notable among these were the Marvelettes' three chart hits in 1962 alone—one a Top Ten, "Playboy." Another was the quick rise of a girl-group that had been named the Del-Phis, who were seemingly borrowing the Supremes' script, with lead singer Martha Reeves having made her entree at Motown as Mickey Stevenson's secretary; by late '62, she and her two groupmates were cutting songs in Studio A as Martha and the Vandellas for Gordy's third label, the eponymous Gordy Records. And the Andantes had begun to emerge progressively as the go-to girl-group for backup work, their piquant yet unobtrusive three-part harmonies like powdered sugar to be sprinkled into any tempo or mood.

The Supremes could surely gauge where they stood at the Hitsville Christmas party shortly after the "Your Heart Belongs to Me" session. Doling out goodies while dressed as Santa Claus, Gordy lavished on each Marvelette a diamond friendship ring. For the Supremes, he had transistor radios.

The chance that they'd hear themselves on radios such as those would become no more bankable over the next year, when they would face a serious convulsion. Even Diane's *chutzpah* could deliver only a short-lived and limited benefit, and in the end it took the Smokey card out of her hands. Still, hangers-on that they were, they would be able to glom a ride, albeit as outriders, on Berry Gordy's next big idea: taking Motown on the road.

eight

THE "OTHERS"

Now able to upgrade their old stage act repertoire with their new, original Motown songs, including a chart scraper, the Supremes continued to perform live around Paradise Valley, hitting the stage at some high-toned nightclubs such as the Chit-Chat Lounge and the Roostertail—though Mary Wilson exaggerates in her memoirs by saying they were "*the* live act in town." Gordy also began to occasionally send them on out-of-town weekend gigs, with one-nighters in Cincinnati, Cleveland, and Pittsburgh. For those, he had a burly Motown bodyguard and former boxing buddy named John O'Den drive them to each stop in one of Gordy's Cadillacs.

Berry was making all the bread from these appearances. Expense money was given to O'Den to disburse, sparingly. With no prior arrangement about how much the girls were due, O'Den took what each club owner or auditorium promoter handed him after the shows, jammed the cash in a satchel, and brought it back to Gordy, who took his own "manager's" cut. By early 1962, these extortions were performed in the name of the company's all-encompassing talent management agency administered by Esther Edwards, International Talent Management, Inc. ITMI's standard commission was 10 percent on all artist's earnings—a number that, unofficially, edged ever upward when the "expenses" kicked in; then, it could go as high as 50 percent, normally the case on those tours, with all of the travel expenses, promoter's fees, and under-the-table "schmearing" of club owners to give top billing to a Motown act.

The ITMI existed with the main intention of catering to the performers' individual needs; hence some rather cosmopolitan-sounding clauses were entered into the ITMI agreement each Motown employee was required to sign, outlining such perquisites as career and personal financial advice, as well as the escrow accounts in the name of each performer. Meaning at least theoretically that they owned plow shares of Hitsville's fortune, to be delivered to them when expenses were deducted. The real significance of ITMI, however, was that Gordy's loosely defined managerial role was now sanctioned, and inviolate: No performer could hire an outside manager or promotion agent or, God knows, an independent financial adviser.

Capitulation to these terms was quick and uncritical, though today Katherine Anderson, for one, says most Motown artists smelled something rotten on West Grand Boulevard. "We knew what that whole ITMI thing was about," she says, "that it was a terrible conflict of interest. I mean, Berry was supposed to be managing us, looking out for our interests—but at the same time he was finding ways not to pay us! Hell, he would dock us for records we made that were never released—by *his* decision. How is that *not* a conflict of interest? Today, a record company can't manage its talent; [acts] know they'll get a fair shake with a manager on the outside, unless of course the manager steals the money. But we didn't need any unscrupulous manager to steal our money. We had Berry Gordy to do that.

"But what did we know? We were all just kids. People talk about how inspired Berry was by young talent. Okay, sure. But there was another side, too: Could he have been able to take advantage of older, wiser people? You figure it out."

Gordy never had a qualm defending his practices as both necessary to the sustained health of Motown and munificent toward his flock, citing the legendarily tight-fisted ways of Colonel Tom Parker, Elvis Presley's flinty manager, who pocketed no less than 50 percent of Presley's earnings. Such a heavy tribute, he contended, was "worth it to Elvis," not to mention that such managerial imbalances were standard in the recording industry.

The Motown acts regarded their earnings as an afterthought, at least for now. With no accounting that anyone could find—such information being classified and access available only to Berry and Esther Gordy, to their accountants, and to Barney Ales—few of the performers ever made money on regular annual, biannual, or even quarterly intervals; usually, they'd be paid when Gordy felt generous. The rest of the time, they were told, those deductions for expenses made their earnings moot. On the road, performers were given all of $10 for their meals. *Everything* above and beyond that they should get receipts for, they were told—the inference being that they'd be reimbursed. Instead, Motown would use the receipts to justify deducting them as expenses. With this iron vise on his acts, Gordy could, with a straight face, inform people making scads of money for him that they were due nothing; and that since expenses actually outweighed profits, he could actually *dock* them. Not doing so, went the implication, proved how magnanimous he was.

These charades endured for years, during which time only the Gordy clan and selected Motown executives actually profited from the company's unfathomable success. It's open to question whether even Vice-President Smokey Robinson was paid anywhere near what his enormous value was to the shop as an incredibly versatile creative font. Because Smokey was a crooner by trade and an artist by sensibility, Gordy may have found him to be an easy mark, a guy who'd be grateful merely to live beyond what he had once believed was his lot in life. Like Smokey, Brian Holland and Mickey Stevenson were living comfortably now, mostly on Gordy's handouts, pacified by slowly growing bank accounts and lulled by the Motown "family" of communal advancement.

Only Robert Bateman seemed to think something was amiss. Having pocketed only small change after producing and writing cash cows like "Please Mr. Postman" and the follow-up "Playboy," he asked Gordy for some advance money, as Berry sometimes did with Smokey Robinson. Rebuffed, the lanky ex–Rayber Voices stalwart jumped ship.

Because other record companies were eager to recruit Motown people who might possess the magical nectar of hit-making, he wasn't out of work long—though, ironically, it was his connection not to Gordy but to Bob West's shop that was the stepping stone. Bateman, who had produced West's moneymaker the Falcons, used their current lead singer, the raw-boned Wilson Pickett, as leverage, introducing him to the R&B star Lloyd Price, who in turn was just starting up his own label, Double-L Records. In mid-1962, Price signed both and brought them to New York with Bateman as a staff writer. The first Pickett-Bateman collaboration, Pickett's first solo release, "If You Need Me," made No. 30 on the R&B charts, 64 on the pop charts, and was subsequently covered by Solomon Burke at Atlantic as well as by the Rolling Stones and Tom Jones. They'd also collaborate on two more middling hits, "It's Too Late" and "I'm Down to My Last Heartache," before Pickett began his legendary run with Atlantic Records, while Bateman remained a top hand in the New York studio scene for most of the decade.

Bateman's apostasy was something Gordy dreaded might become common. A bit madly, he began calling in his inner tier of writers and producers and asked whether they'd been contacted by outside labels. He'd stare into their faces, judging to his satisfaction whether they were telling the truth. The studio musicians got the same treatment, even though they worked on an entirely different basis, not on contract to Motown but as members of and paid according to the regulations of the musicians' union. Knowing he couldn't possibly keep top cats like Benny Benjamin and James Jamerson through intimidation—as it was, he'd lost Popcorn Wylie, who that same year signed on as a producer with the Detroit label Northern Soul—he began paying select session men inordinate sums from out of pocket, with the proviso that they record for no one else, stay on call to Motown (even if it meant they'd have to miss a gig at a local club), and agree to go out on tours with the Motown acts. And, soon, he and A&R head Mickey Stevenson would become even more obsessive about keeping the musicians intact and in line.

Rarely were the Motown artists treated to such emoluments. They had to fend for themselves as best they could. By example, Martha Reeves, who was making $2.50 a day as Stevenson's secretary—and had taken advantage of her power to book sessions and personnel in his name by booking her group, the Vandellas, to sing backup on Marvin Gaye's early hits—agreed to babysit for a new Motown arrival, a blind, 11-year-old prodigy known as Little Stevie Wonder. As for the Supremes, Diane Ross in 1962 was still doing pseudo-secretarial chores for Gordy, for the same $2.50 a day. Mary Wilson and Flo Ballard were working behind the counter at a record store where their own records were laid to rest in the bargain bin. The newlywed Barbara Martin Richardson, who became pregnant in early 1962, was the rare Motown performer with the luxury of being supported by a breadwinner.

Of them all, it shocked not a soul that Ross was the most uneasy with the life of struggling artistry. Still being driven back to the projects with Mary and Flo by Berry or one of his drivers after late sessions, they once were joined by Carolyn Gill, a member of another recent girl-group arrival, the Velvelettes. Gill, who lived in upscale northwest Detroit, remembers Ross staying in the car when the other two Supremes got out at Brewster-Douglass, so she could luxuriate in what for her was a fantasy trip.

"Diane would just sit and stare out the window at the nice homes when we'd get out of downtown Detroit," Gill says. "I was living with my aunt and uncle and they had a boat in their driveway. When Diane saw it, she exclaimed, 'Berry! Look at that boat! This girl is rich!' The truth was, I wasn't. We weren't. We just had more than they did in the projects. To Diane, there was just one line of separation. You were either rich or poor. And she always made it very clear she wanted no part of being poor."

In Ross's reasoning, being epoxied to Gordy's imprimatur was a reward in itself, an entitlement good for a few perks.

JANIE BRADFORD: I remember one Saturday, Diane and I were hanging around the studio, which was like the magnet, where everybody'd sort of congregate. And we were all alone, no one else was in the whole place. And Diane, out of the blue, said, "Janie, let's rent a car." I don't even think she knew how to drive. And there was no way we could pay for a car, anyway. I said, "With what?" and she didn't even think; she had a plan all thought out. "Here's what we'll do," she said. "We'll rent a car under Berry's name, on the Motown account, and by the time Berry gets the bill and yells at us, we'll have our paychecks and we'll give him the money back."

That's how her mind worked, making things happen, whatever the circumstances.

And, you know, something like that could easily get you fired at Motown. Berry had to approve *everything*, every expense, in advance. But Diane was fearless. It was obvious why. Of everyone, she was the only one there who knew she could handle Berry.

So we went and rented, oh God, I remember it so clearly, a yellow convertible.

And I drove us around the whole day, in and around Detroit. We probably put 200 miles on that car. We felt like such big shots. And sure enough, the bill came in and Berry started to huff and puff. But after he called Diane into his office, it took, like, two minutes for her to straighten it out.

I think we did pay the bill; but you know what, Berry may have said, oh, forget it and paid it himself. Nobody, and I mean nobody, could have gotten away with that—or *tried* it, or even *thought* about it—but Diane.

In similar fashion, one of Gordy's Cadillacs was requisitioned by the Supremes one day on the road. It happened when John O'Den acceded to the girls' begging to let them take turns at the wheel, though none of them had anything more than a learner's permit. The episode nearly turned disastrous when Barbara pulled away from the curb and in an instant collided with another car. Fortunately, it was just a fender bender, but the impact left the Caddy dented—and Richardson with a summons from a cop for a misdemeanor violation.

Fearing the wrath of Gordy, O'Den and the girls tried to keep it from him. John took the car to a body shop and had the dent sanded out, and he and Richardson went to traffic court the next day, having hatched a plan by which Barbara would pretend to be O'Den's wife so her permit wouldn't be revoked. Somehow, the judge bought it and they were excused, with John paying a nominal fine. But Gordy, who seemed to have spies all over, found out about the incident and was livid that O'Den, and the girls, could be so irresponsible. Confronting them all when they got back to Motown, Gordy asked who had been at the wheel, and when Mary spoke up and said it was Mr. O'Den, he growled, "You're lying! I know who was driving!" Frightened by his ire, she fled into the street in tears rather than face being fired.

She might have been, too, but for the ability her groupmate had for making squalls like this evaporate with a few beseeching words. Indeed, when Mary returned, she found Gordy pacified. After a brief lecture to the girls and O'Den about the evils of lying, he said no more about it. That led to yet another round of a now-well-worn question heard at Hitsville: Was there *anything* that Diane Ross couldn't talk Berry Gordy into and out of?

Only one thing, it seemed: making the Supremes into stars. In fact, the group's stagnation, which had become a matter of concern to Gordy and of derision to the more prominent acts, led Barbara Richardson to a momentous decision in early 1962. Ross, Wilson, and Ballard knew she would be taking a leave of absence to give birth; but she stunned them when she announced she wouldn't be coming back thereafter.

Mary and Flo tried to talk her into returning. But Diane—who now thought of Barbara as excess baggage, and had shown pointed contempt for her by not attending her wedding—merely shrugged, having already concluded that the group had a better chance of flourishing as a trinity. When Mary brought in a replacement candidate, a singer-dancer named Diane Watson, Diane was uninterested.

"Forget it," she harrumphed. "If the three of us can't make it as a trio, we won't make it at all."

Too weary to go to war with her, and no doubt cowed by her semi-mythic tendency to get her way, Wilson and Ballard acquiesced. For better or worse, from here on out they were going to be a threesome.

Gordy, for his part, didn't give a fig about the latest Supremes intramural exercises. However, even the most insignificant action could inspire a Gordy overreaction. Because Richardson had not bothered to come to him first before announcing her departure, she technically had violated Gordy's sovereignty in matters of hiring or releasing a performer; accordingly, she would not see one thin dime in royalties from past or future uses of Supremes records she had sung on, several of which were included on the first Supremes album in 1963. Thus was the fourth Supreme excommunicated from the Motown sacrarium. But because history had a way of repeating itself at Motown, in ways good and not, it portended a vague sense of unease around 2648 West Grand Boulevard. Too vague, surely, for the first Supreme to foretell that the very same fate would await her, further on down the road. As for Richardson, she didn't mind enough to fight Gordy for what she was due; she became a nurse and quietly melted into the loam of Detroit, rarely making mention of her brush with the cosmos.

To be sure, Gordy's gaze was trained far over the heads of any group as 1962 drew on. That summer, he was deep in the plenary phase of his most ambitious gambit yet—turning Motown into a virtual touring company. It had not taken Gordy long to hatch this idea as a logical outgrowth of the fragmented tours that had brought him such a handsome return. The chore was given to Esther Edwards to cobble the details. She immediately went to work studying the logistics of the Dick Clark "caravans" and grand-scale soul "revues" of the 1950s, which had been so pivotal in helping Jackie Wilson hone his act and sell the songs written by her brother. But her marching order was to keep control in the hands of the ITMI and not leave Motown at the mercies of outside bookers and promoters.

The first piece of business was to hire a tour manager. For that, Edwards plucked from out of Maurice King's orchestra at the Flame Show Bar the lanky baritone sax player Beans Bowles, who was given the unenviable task of hiring musicians who could take a two-month sabbatical from their local gigs to travel thousands of miles on a bus. True, just about all jazz and R&B cats had gone that route in their days, so many of them having ridden shotgun all over the South, East, and Midwest on the chitlin' circuit; but they'd not done so accompanying acts they didn't know a thing about. Even though the Gordys would be paying $300 a week, a handsome wage for the hep-cats of the era, Bowles could find no takers in King's combo. He had better luck when he ran the idea past Choker Campbell, a garrulous, barrel-chested, bespectacled sax man who'd been in the Lionel Hampton band and whose twelve-piece Show of Stars Band had been the house band for many of the '50s soul revues, at times graced by the legendary jazz pianist Big Joe Turner. The Show of Stars unit was considerably younger now, generally aware of the Motown sound and hungry for that kind of pay at a time when the hard-core R&B gigs were beginning to dry up. The Motortown Revue, as the 1962 tour would be called, had scored its first coup.

Even so, the biggest cog in the Revue machine was having one of those outside heavy hitters whom Gordy was wary of but realized he needed. He did make sure to go with a black promoter, figuring a brother in arms would be less inclined to skim, grift, or swindle him— that sort of thing, he reasoned, was *his* province, in underpaying his own stable of talent. The promoter in question was the savvy Henry Wynne, whose booking agency Supersonic Attractions had made its mark in the '50s convincing white theater owners to take his acts, most of whom were black. Wynne strung together a growing list of local promoters who were willing to advance Gordy (with a huge cut for Wynne) cold cash for the Miracles, Mary Wells, and the Marvelettes, thereby stoking a cash flow that could spill over to other Motown acts on the tour.

The Gordys likely would have been satisfied with a dozen or so shows along the Midwest-Northeast corridor, but Wynne pulled in deals all along the eastern seaboard, south of the Mason-Dixon Line, from border states Kentucky and Tennessee, down through the Carolinas and Georgia, Florida, and—most intriguingly and forebodingly— the Deep South grid of Alabama and Mississippi. The South in general was a two-sided coin. Save for the cosmopolitan markets of Nashville, Memphis, and New Orleans, Dixie was a largely untapped rock and roll market, lagging behind country-western and hillbilly music in the cradle of the Grand Ole Opry. In the Mississippi Delta, where the blues were born, in markets like Mobile and Birmingham, rhythm still hadn't caught up to the blues. Thus, millions of black teenagers had been neglected by the white radio stations; and they were too young and too disinclined in the new, emerging pop culture to indulge in the hoary blues and jazz of the chitlin' circuit.

Gordy, then, was excited by the idea of prospecting down South, but he knew that doing so would be wading into treacherous waters, sending young and sassy black men and women through the back roads of Jim Crow country, in no less than the ultimate symbol of black uppityness—a *bus*! Even in the planning stages, the prickly realities were daunting. Some shows in Dixie would see the races partitioned by police tape, and local police were no doubt eager to enforce the separation (necessitating that an act perform the same song twice, once to each side of the arena). This made a mockery of what Gordy was trying to accomplish with his crossover musical dreams. But in 1962 he was still going to have to take his dreams in small doses, and with much trepidation, considering the potentially catastrophic nature of the risks.

Indeed, any incident that would reflect badly on someone in his employ, or be rigged to do so, could have set the cause back years. Moreover, if any of the performers became a victim, he couldn't have faced himself. How to explain such a horror to a parent, since to begin with most of the parents hated the idea of sending their children into this region? As much as his black pop was a stimulus for, and a marker of, civil rights gains, and as much as Gordy wanted to be an emperor, he had no interest in being a martyr, Berry the Just, figuratively stoned to death for his cause and the greater one.

These considerations were implicit in Motown's music; by design, it was organically but not overtly black. Its themes were rigorously anti-racial. If covers of Little Richard and Fats Domino songs by bland white acts sounded absurd and alien in the '50s, covers of Motown fit snugly into the early '60s pop fold: The nascent Beatles, in the cellars of Liverpool and Hamburg, were among the first to do so, appropriating "Please Mr. Postman" in their act (though not half as well as, or with the hit quality of, the still-whiter rendition by the soft-pop band the Carpenters twelve years later, which retraced the trip to the top of the pop chart taken by the Marvelettes' original). This was why Gordy felt sanguine enough to dare try prying open the alligator jaws of the South. If Jim Crow was to be slain, it would have to be through the persuasive powers of the new crossover recipe of soul music.

With all this as prologue, on October 23, 1962, two rented buses rickety enough to make one wonder if it would survive the first right turn off West Grand Boulevard rolled up in front of 2648, each with a sign reading "Hitsville Motor City Tour" on its sides. Forty-five people carrying light luggage, suits bags, cosmetic cases, and other sundries clambered inside. Among them were eight Motown acts, twelve musicians, two chaperones, sundry roadies and bodyguards, and one emcee—comedian Bill Murray, known as Winehead Willie (and a distant cousin of Mary Wilson). Ready or otherwise, they would be spending the next fifty-six days in each other's close company, moving in and out of thirty-six cities on an excursion that would have room for only four days without a show, including one stretch that would burn through November 2 in Boston until December 4 in Pensacola without a single day off. There'd also be no less than a week of shows at the Apollo Theater.

Three of the seats on one creaky bus were reserved for the Supremes. But if Gordy had his druthers, they would have been waving goodbye to the tour-goers with him.

The girls naturally assumed they'd earned their place on the tour by having a hit, such as it was in the case of "Your Heart Belongs to Me," and were eager to pump themselves into a known commodity. Yet for weeks Gordy dithered, reluctant to make a decision, apparently wanting to shelter them from any harm. It was an odd concern for three tough chicks from the projects, and one he didn't share for the even younger and more obscure Vandellas. But Gordy was rarely rational about the Supremes—or, more centrally, Diane Ross. With his Freudian admixture of paternal and predatory impulses toward her, he couldn't help but worry about her welfare—as Ross would write in her memoirs, Gordy regarded her as a "baby deer." But, with the Smokey Robinson episode in mind, was it that he simply wanted other men—music men like him, the worst kind, he would have agreed—to keep their mitts off her? Knowing how well she could always make his eyebrows sweat, how many others might fall hard for his "Bambi" on the long road?

Whatever his reservations, in the end Gordy knew he stood no chance against Diane's dewy-eyed pleadings. Even Fred Ross was defanged by now, unable to stand in the way of a daughter of legal age. He, of course, loathed this tour thing that would leave these black people virtually naked against the perils of the South. And he now was forced to sit up at night waiting for her to get home; when she would walk in he told her she looked like a cheap hooker. But if Fred Ross, as she would write, "couldn't come to terms with [my] dressing up and wearing makeup" and ask through gritted teeth, "Why do you have all that black stuff around your eyes?" his biggest peeve was his abiding distaste for Motown's father figure. Fred, she said, putting it mildly, "wasn't sure he trusted Berry." Neither did Ernestine. Again, it was Esther Edwards who assured the both of them that, as the head chaperone of the girls on the tour, she would protect their honor from men who, she didn't need to add, were not unlike Berry Gordy Jr.

After giving in, Gordy gave the Supremes a fresh record to pimp, one from his own pen, "Let Me Go the Right Way," with which he would cast a soulful veneer around the group. The song was written with room in the lyric for Ross to show off a grittier, funkier texture to her voice, and Gordy took them into the studio on August 30, 1962. But Gordy couldn't produce it as deep soul; trying to strike a balance, Marvelette style, between offhand soul and vanilla pop, he came up with a sprightly dose of catnip set to a cha-cha beat and featuring some interesting chord changes, as Ross sang the lead in a lower, more mature pitch over a repeating "ba-doo" chorus by Wilson and Ballard. Unsatisfied, he kept mixing and remixing the tapes, by his own estimation over 100 times, which he insisted occurred over fourteen straight hours in the Motown control room, long after everyone else had left for the night.

In his autobiography Gordy insists that he stumbled out of the building after putting the song to bed, haggard, unshaven, and half-asleep—just in time to wave goodbye to the Motortown Revue as it pulled away on its maiden voyage. But, as with many of Gordy's recollections, this one is probably fanciful; in truth, the tour didn't commence until nearly two months after the Supremes' session, and when it did push off Gordy was bright-eyed and clear-throated, issuing to his troops a rousing pep talk.

It was quite an assemblage, too. By the time the big day came, virtually everyone on the Motown roster was on board—though the privileges of being a Motown vice-president were clear when Smokey and his Miracles left not on the bus but in their own car, one of five that accompanied the Revue; the others were used to tote the musicians' instruments and occasionally one of the other top-shelf acts like Mary Wells and the Marvelettes.

That triumvirate of Wells, the Miracles, and the Marvelettes—the only well-known acts on the tour—would be the headliners; their names always appeared high on the marquees in the biggest letters. For the rest of the crowd, it would be strictly potluck as to billing order; if any of them had a breakout hit along the way, they'd get on the marquees, too, and higher placements along with their pictures in newspaper ads and on the theater-lobby placards and cardboard, fight-show-style flyers posted by the promoters. Gordy also instituted the "crowd rule," by which an act pulling the most fevered audience response each night would get billing for the next show—the intention being to make everyone bust a gut on stage trying to top everyone else, but which also turned allies into enemies, sparking horrible arguments about who scored higher. Not that Gordy cared a whit about the personal consequences—in fact, he loved such acrimony, figuring it made the acts more intense on stage.

The historical curiosity of the first Motortown Revue was that when the bus shoved off, some of the company's biggest acts of all time were mere throw-ins, with little hope of attaining billing. In this bottom drawer were no less than Marvin Gaye and Little Stevie Wonder. Martha and the Vandellas, with no hit record for another year, went mainly to continue their work as Gaye's backup singers. At the Apollo gig, there would be a group half-composed of the remnants of Milton Jenkins's Primes—Eddie Kendricks and Paul Williams—who after the Primes' breakup joined the Distants' Otis Williams and Melvin Franklin to form the Elgins. Signed to Motown in '61 and renamed the Temptations, they had spun their wheels ever since; now, the group would be called to the Apollo shows just to back up Mary Wells.

And then there were Ross, Wilson, and Ballard, who, despite Gordy's attentions and affections—or because of them—had begun hearing that people around Motown were, with great pleasure, ragging them as the "No-Hit Supremes." Yet, even that insult wasn't as scalding as the indignities they faced on the tour, when, far from the marquees, the only place they could find the name "the Supremes" was on the flyers, in the smallest type, thrown in with the other nonentities under the collective heading "And Others." Another marker of also-ran status was that they were regularly chosen to open shows, flitting out on stage amid the clutter of people shuffling to their seats and conversations that didn't end when they began singing. This was the "graveyard" of slots, its only importance being to warm up the crowd for the "real" acts.

At the first show of the tour, October 26 at the Howard Theater in Washington, D.C., they may as well not have been there. They nervously ran through a stillborn rendition of the just-released "Let Me Go the Right Way," with Diane doing her bug-eyed mugging to almost no reaction before exiting—the who-cares acts being permitted no more than one song per show. As it happened, Gordy was in the back of the hall that night, making a surprise drop-in to check out the concert, and pronounced the Supremes a total failure—admittedly, with his song a big reason why.

Following them, the Vandellas by contrast riveted all in the house, and got everyone up and dancing. Indeed, when stacked up beside nearly every other act, the Supremes suffered, and even looked out of place. The Motortown Revue was a wild affair, a worthy throwback to the frenetic R&B traveling circuses of the '50s, and the precious, brittle quality and rather faint pulse of the three girls from the projects didn't seem to belong.

Part of this was Gordy's fault. On the surface, his selection of material for them was faulty, but the reason why was deeper than merely a matter of picking wrong. It was his unwillingness to let them get down and dirty, or try to. In live-music formats like this, the form and function of music were tethered to sex. It was Gordy who, glowingly, once explained that Smokey Robinson's immense appeal for swooning girls—and their mothers—had to do with how he figuratively "made love to the women" by singing while falling to his knees or lying on the floor, hips undulating. Of course, at *his* first gig, the disaster at the Apollo, Smokey had been a bust, too. But whereas Berry had approved of injecting Elvis-style sexual gymnastics into his act, he was so guilty about lusting for Diane Ross that such a transformation was unthinkable for the Supremes. The best tack for them, he determined for far too long, was to perform "like ladies."

Accordingly, since it was he who guided them, and with his investment in them so personal, Gordy was not about to let them wash out. He and Barney Ales moved the earth to get "Let Me Go the Right Way" played and sold, and though all that their work bought was another fleeting visit to the pop chart—No. 90 around Thanksgiving time—the song did hit No. 26 on the R&B chart. Whether this was the product of Ross's easy transition from bland to raw and emotive yearning, the mesh of Wilson's deep resonant wails, and Ballard's top-end, gospel-style flourishes, or just something as magical as James Jamerson's frisky bass licks, the showing was an affirmation that a genuine soul breathed beneath the frigid veneer and stiff moves of the Supremes.

They'd get better, too; more at ease at each show. But this was generally overlooked, obscured by the breakout acts. First were the Contours, a bump-and-grind, leather-lunged sextet with an old-school R&B sensibility—and a reputation as incorrigibly lecherous. They had recently cut a deliriously lewd, and loud, song called "Do You Love Me," which Gordy had written for the Temptations but produced on a whim with the Contours; in October, pimped by the tour, it caught fire and went No. 3 pop, 1 R&B. The rich also got richer, with Mary Wells's

"Two Lovers" and the Miracles' "You've Really Got a Hold on Me" both nestling in the pop Top Ten by the new year. The Marvelettes' third smash, "Beechwood 4-5789," co-written by Marvin Gaye, went Top Twenty.

It was Gaye who really was the Revue's cause célèbre. After an odd, and failed, album of Broadway show covers and jazz fare, his first R&B-flavored song, the autobiographical "Stubborn Kind of Fellow," crashed into the R&B Top Ten, fueled by word of mouth of his electrifying, blatantly lascivious performances, his groaning, cooing, and pelvic thrusts making Smokey's "lovemaking" seem subdued. Teenage girls, and their mothers, couldn't help but mob the handsome singer on stage and outside his dressing room—an irony considering that Gaye, unlike his brother-in-law who often thought with his fly, was actually shy about sex and dutifully monogamous to Anna Gordy Gaye.

Watching from the wings as audiences lost control when nearly everyone else performed, the Supremes reacted along the usual lines. While Mary and Flo were swept up in the shared sense of excitement, dancing in place and clapping to the music, Diane stood without motion or expression, envious of the others and frustrated that her group seemed not to belong on the same stage. And she simply detested their relegation to the "And Others" compartment.

"She was really offended by that," recalls Marvelette Katherine Anderson, "and she took it out on everyone else—mostly us. She'd give us that same sourpuss look, make little cutting remarks about our clothes—which were a lot better than theirs—things like that, which she had no right to do because they weren't exciting anybody on stage. But, to Diane, she wanted to be great so bad she convinced herself she was."

During the tour, Ross apparently believed it was her responsibility to be Gordy's eyes and ears. "Whatever Diane saw going on on the bus, she reported back to Berry," Anderson laughed. "If the guys were playing cards for money, or if a guy was making out with a girl, she'd call him from the next stop and blab it. I mean, come on. Who made her the keeper of our morality—this is *Diana Ross* we're talking about!"

Gordy evidently took such tattling from the road seriously. When he flew to greet the flock at periodic stops along the route, he'd sternly repeat the same lecture, particularly about the sexual hijinks, which of course did nothing to cool it. Despite the prying eyes of Ross, Esther

Edwards, and two other matrons, the Motortown Revue was a hormonal buffet. According to Mary Wilson, the wanderers "were pairing off before we'd crossed the Michigan state line." Gordy, she added, "could have saved his breath. We were too young and too excited to care about the consequences." Among the hottest pairings were Gladys Horton and Contour Hubert Johnson, and Wanda Young and Miracle Bobby Rogers. It's possible, too, that Ross snitched on her own groupmates, since Mary got into it with Eddie Kendricks, and Flo rekindled things with Otis Williams, though both men were married.

But Diane had her own impulses, trained on a now-extinguished flame. Throughout the trek, she was, wrote Wilson, "eyeing Smokey," perhaps seeking a way to circumvent Claudette. Several times, Diane, who always felt trapped with the chaff on the fetid bus, begged the Miracles to let her come with them in their car, complaining about having to ride with the "nobodies." Smokey, very much aware of his wife's presence, shooed Diane away.

Continually fretting, she was frequently in tears about the Supremes' unappreciated performances—and her spirits probably weren't lifted when Gordy, during one or another of his drop-ins, would board the bus en route to its next stop. Instead of easing into the seat she told people she was saving for him next to her, he'd amble to the back— "Harlem," as the grizzled musicians waggishly dubbed their "restricted" turf, as opposed to the front where the performers camped in "Broadway"—and become lost in the madness of escalating poker jackpots. Once, he dropped five grand to Choker Campbell, without blinking an eye. A man who could sneeze at five grand clearly had other things on his mind than sitting with Diane Ernestine Ross.

The Motortown Revue presented a strange yin-yang between discovery and disgust. As the autumn temperatures fell in the Northeast during the first leg of the tour, the bus heater sputtered and died. With the windows jammed shut, the collective stench of nauseating gas and exhaust fumes, junk food, endless cigar (and sometimes reefer) smoke from "Harlem," and forty-five humans unbathed for days on end became unbearable. And for the girls there was the added discomfort of having to keep on their beehive wigs and makeup, even in the middle of the night, Esther Gordy having decreed that the Motown ladies must always be kempt and "in character" in public.

The rigors of this cattle-call was too much for the Marvelettes'
Juanita Cowert, who suffered a nervous breakdown shortly after the tour
ended and was hospitalized, forcing her to quit the group. Tempers often
flared, in one instance precipitating a fistfight between several members
of the Temptations and Contours over the divided affections of a woman.
Little Stevie Wonder, who would choose the wee hours to practice his
harmonica, had to stop when people trying to sleep unceremoniously
threatened to stick the harmonica where the moon don't shine.

"I don't think any of us were prepared for the hardships," says the
Vandellas' Annette Beard. "Every few days we'd stay at some dive motel
and get to wash our clothes, shower, and stay in bed all day. Then Beans
or Esther would say, 'It's time to go,' and it was back on the treadmill.
You put a lot of people in that situation and things are gonna get edgy.
And Diane, I remember, never enjoyed herself. I think Diane was born
edgy. I mean, most of us tried to put aside the hardships. We were away
from home, singing every night, seeing different places. It was exciting.
We didn't need to be brought down by someone sitting there with a
long face."

Mary and Flo apparently felt the same. They kept a distance from
Ross, and when she'd get into one of her hissy fits with one of the other
girls, they'd slink low into their seats so they wouldn't have to take her
side, though Wilson in her autobiography makes a passive, halfway stab
at the notion that she and Ballard "would get caught in the middle" and
"admit—privately—who was right in a spat, and it wasn't always Diane.
But she was in our group, and solidarity was crucial, right or wrong."

However, solidarity on the tour looked like this: Wilson and Ballard each sitting with other people, and Ross sitting by herself, either
staring out the window at the Miracles in their car or staring bullets at
her foil Gladys Horton. The latter, a feisty girl of Virgin Island descent,
would stare back, leading onlookers to make wagers about how long it
would be before Horton pounced on Ross like a linebacker.

The Supremes, as with all but the top few acts, were salaried at $290 a
week for the tour, but owing to Gordy's typical economic tricks they ac-
tually were given no more than $10 a week by Beans Bowles. With the
Supremes unable to afford glitzy dresses of the kind the Marvelettes and
Mary Wells wore, Diane began to get sneaky trying to even the scales.
Sometimes, acting sincere, she would use her fashion-school back-

ground and counsel the other girls not to wear the dresses she knew they looked the best in.

Other times, it wasn't their clothing she envied as much as their on-stage moves. Devising a devious way to benefit from the Supremes' opening-act albatross, she would watch all the acts from the wings and take to Mary and Flo the "new" moves she thought of—generally the slickest moves she could cull from the other acts, which the Supremes couldn't do nearly as well. Gordy, recalling this artifice, bluntly told *Rolling Stone* in 1973 that Ross "stole everybody's act," and that the victims of the thievery—as Ross knew—would either look "ridiculous" coming out after them and doing the same moves or cede them altogether to the Supremes, and then need to "change their shows every day" to stay fresh. As a result, he said, "they all hated her guts."

This kind of byplay became more and more trivial as the itinerary moved from the relatively friendly geography of Boston, New Haven, and Buffalo and headed due south, a day later crossing the Rubicon of the Mason-Dixon Line. As halting and bitter as racial progress was throughout most of the South, few believed this phase of the journey would be without incident, or even calamity. Indeed, though no one knew it, not a soul would have been surprised to learn that the worst of last-ditch Jim Crow resistance was yet to come; still down that road, in Mississippi, were the murder of Medgar Evers in 1963 and of Michael Schwerner, Andrew Goodman, and James Chaney, whose bodies were dragged from the Bogue Chitto swamp a year later. As it was, the traces of real and brutal enough horrors were all around; later, when the bus would pass through Lynchburg, Mississippi, Martha Reeves once recalled, some among them recognized from the history books the infamous "Hanging Tree," on which hundreds of blacks perished. "There was not a leaf on it," she said, seeming to buttress the legend that no leaves had grown on it for twenty years.

Uneasy and tense as they eased down Tobacco Road, making stops for shows in Raleigh, Charleston, Augusta, and Savannah, there were the requisite obstacles Gordy had told them to expect, the crude "nigger" remarks, the restaurants that refused them service, the locked doors of the "white" service-station bathrooms. Such moments, however, could have an uplifting ending; in South Carolina, decamping at a motel on a brutally hot day, Diane, an accomplished swimmer and diver, got the idea to put on shorts and take a dip in the pool, wig and all. Following her lead, about a dozen Motown performers jumped in with her. They were happily splashing around, unaware that the all-white guests had clambered out of the pool rather than share it with "those niggers." Upon hearing that the savages were actually Motown stars, several actually returned and asked for autographs.

Things turned darker when on November 9 the tour hit the Deep South. In Birmingham, Martha Reeves, thinking she heard gunshots outside the bus, dove for cover between two seats. Others twitted her, insisting the noise must have been firecrackers. Then, when the bus parked at the National Guard Armory for the show—a landmark event, as it would be played to the first integrated audience in the city's history—the driver got out and noticed two holes in the "Motor Town Tour" sign on the side. Looking closely, he dug out two bullets.

There are several versions of this incident, which has become etched into Motown's legend, usually with a dollop of theatrical license. Some recall it happening as the troupe was leaving the bus, causing a stampede off. In Mary Wilson's take, it was during the time they were boarding after the show; when people heard what they thought was the sound of rocks hitting the side of the bus, Choker Campbell called out, "Them's bullets!"—touching off a mad scramble to get *on*—and Mary Wells, who had fallen on the bus steps, moaned, "I'm shot! I'm shot!" as she was nearly trampled. In any case, once they were all safely inside, Wilson said, "We flew out of Birmingham."

After one-nighters in Columbus, Atlanta, Mobile, and New Orleans, they rolled into Mississippi. In Jackson, where Medgar Evers lived and would be gunned down on his doorstep, Gordy's worst nightmare seemed to be playing out when after ten straight hours on the road the bus pulled into a gas station. As the riders piled off and made for the bathroom, the redneck owner of the station got in the way and drawled, "Y'all niggers better get out of here."

"Who you calling nigger?" barked Miracle Bobby Rogers.

At that, the owner went and got a double-barreled shotgun, sending the group running for their lives back to the bus. Who knows what might have happened next had not two cars carrying state troopers been cruising the highway and its occupants not seen the commotion and turned into the station. Of course, the presence of Mississippi cops didn't necessarily bode well for interloping blacks involved in disputes with the locals. And, even now, they were hardly ready to intervene on the outsiders' behalf. Rather, listening to the owner complain that "these niggers are trying to take over my station" and Rogers explain that they just wanted to use the can, the troopers just stood by, not knowing what to do.

As the minutes ticked by, Flo Ballard, a natural mediator, took the redneck aside and convinced him to let them at least use a hose and a bucket to relieve themselves, prehistoric style. One by one, according to Ballard in the book *Call Her Miss Ross*, "someone would do his business in the bucket, come back out, empty it behind the gas station in the woods and clean out the bucket for the next person using the hose. [It] made me wonder if I wanted to be a star after all." Finally, the cops decided that if they wouldn't act in the name of justice, they would in the name of peace. They escorted the visitors back onto the bus and the two police cars escorted it out of town, with all on board—and one man in Detroit—relieved in another sense: that they were all in one piece.

These tense moments seemed particularly unnerving for Ross. About the only ones who didn't seem frightened were some of the veteran musicians who had been down this road before in years past— every reason why many of them kept their own pistols close at hand whenever the bus broke down, which was often, and they would have been ready to use them if the shotgun-totin' pump boy pulled the trigger first. The irony was that, unlike most of the Motown artists, both Diane and Mary had visited the Deep South themselves, Diane on her summer trips to be with relatives in Bessemer, Alabama, while Mary, only months before, had traveled to Greenville, Mississippi, to be with her long-estranged father when John Wilson became gravely ill, then once again for his funeral. While they'd not encountered any problems, both Supremes were under no delusions about the South. Still, Diane, naively, was under the impression that because these black entertainers were a popular attraction in the South, they would somehow be accepted. Certainly, the benign swimming pool episode in South Carolina had reinforced that impression.

Now, frazzled by the bullet holes, white trash with shotguns, and endless "nigger" invective, she grew more withdrawn, even paranoid. Bobby Rogers recalled that she was "wide-eyed and scared shitless." All three Supremes, he went on, were "just waiting to see who was gonna get killed first."

"These damn whites in the South are *crazy*," Ballard would quote Ross as saying, and with a new sense of outrage. "What makes them think they're better than us?"

Given the hard slap of reality the tour engendered, it strains credulity that Ross apparently *forgot* the Motortown Revue in her memoirs, or thought it unworthy of mention. She does, briefly, cite the "sniper" incident, but misplaced the location as Macon, Georgia, and the tour as the 1964 Dick Clark Caravan of Stars. All too brief, as well, is her toss-off cerebration about the dark heart of racism, which she confined to all of two sentences: "In some Southern towns, you could just feel the bigotry in the air. You could slice it with a knife like stinking cheese," adding only the visceral detail that "[w]e had to squat beside the bus and pee in the bushes."

This omission is especially grievous since the Revue would see the Supremes on the sacred boards of the Apollo Theater during the tour's penultimate stop, for a week of shows starting December 7. Such a milestone is not unlike a ballplayer brushing off the first game he played at Yankee Stadium as piffling. In fact, that place in the sun was even more emotionally charged than it might normally have been, as it was shrouded by tragedy.

Early on the morning of November 20—Thanksgiving Day—in Greensville, South Carolina, Beans Bowles and a roadie named Eddie McFarland got into one of the cars and drove ahead of the company to do advance work at the next stop, in Tampa. Both men had been drinking at an all-night party at the motel and, soon after leaving, McFarland fell asleep at the wheel and the station wagon plowed head-on into a truck, shearing off the entire front end of the car. McFarland was killed instantly and Bowles, riding in the back seat, was trapped in the wreckage and when pulled out was barely alive, both of his legs and one of his arms mangled, a flute that he'd been holding pushed through his armpit and jutting from the back of his neck. (Amazingly, a satchel with $12,000 in cash, proceeds from the last show, was recovered in pristine condition.)

When the bus got to Tampa hours later, Esther Edwards was told of the accident and broke the news to the stunned company. Right up until the time of the show as people milled about, crying and shaking their heads, there was serious discussion between Berry and Esther about whether to cancel the remainder of the tour and just come home. Esther also conducted a brief inquisition about the party and who might have plied the two men with drinks, but let it slide. The tour would go on, with the participants spending a sad Thanksgiving far from home and suddenly little to be thankful for, other than that Bowles was alive and would pull through. (Gordy, in his memoirs, tells of keeping a bedside vigil for Eddie McFarland for days until he died—though McFarland had been decapitated in the horrific crash.)

The determining factor in the continuation of the Revue may well have been the Apollo gig. Indeed, Gordy, who had made plans to record and film one of the shows there for a live album and movie feature, was only days after the accident prepping the troops in Florida for the eleven-day marathon of shows at the Harlem showcase. That would be a real grind—there would be six shows *a day* over that week and a half, the first kicking off at noon each day and the last ending at 1 A.M. Displeased by the reports of partying, drinking, and waning enthusiasm on stage, Gordy minced no words: No more parties, no more clandestine carrying on, at the risk of being sent home. Horrified at seeing one of the Marvelettes chewing gum on stage at a recent show, he warned that there would be no similar sullying of Motown's "high-class" image.

Snaking back up north with stops in the Carolinas, Louisville, and Richmond, the tour took on a new sense of focus. On stage, the performers were tighter; only time-proven moves and prefabricated banter with the audience were permitted. It would be up to them to stay programmed and still emote a sense of wild, uninhibited glee. For Ross, Wilson, and Ballard, that equation was a tall order. They tried to hone their dance steps, tepid as they were, and to get more folksy and less perfunctory, but it never seemed to work quite right, not with the two minutes they had to do it in.

Not having been to New York before, when they arrived and checked in with the company at Harlem's Theresa Hotel, they seemed a tad overwhelmed. As much as Gordy had warned everyone about how rough Apollo audiences could be, they weren't ready for the rough treatment they got on the *street*. On opening day, when the bus rolled up to the theater and the troupe began lining up at the stage door, a guard greeted them by asking, "Who the hell are you black motherfuckers?" Annoyed passersby trying to get through the crowd of people on the street saw the "Motor Town" sign on the bus and hissed at the "Detroit niggers." Once inside, those who hadn't previously seen the place reeled at the grimy interior of the old theater. Rats scurried around, walls were peeling and covered with filth, the whole place smelled like a bus terminal bathroom. Some of the performers were assigned dressing rooms that required a five-story climb up a narrow staircase. Expecting a Taj Mahal of their heritage, they found a mausoleum, with few appreciating the romance of grime left behind by the likes of Louis Armstrong, Duke Ellington, and James Brown.

The first few days of shows, the Supremes were noticeably twitchy. And while the audience reaction was good, when they heard a few shouted raspberries it disrupted their timing and concentration. Gordy, taking in the shows peering through the curtain from backstage, was harsh in his judgment. Rather than words of encouragement, he was waiting for the girls when they came off stage, brow furrowed, putting them on notice: Do better or be pulled from the show.

Years later, Ross may have had those tender moments in mind when she deviated from her normal slavish praise of Gordy to aver that "Berry wasn't careful of people's feelings, and his domineering manner antagonized us." Gordy, she said, would either coldly ignore them or "come crashing backstage with a multitude of notes and corrections [and] we all resented the criticism because he was too hard on us. . . . It was like parents making you study. You might be getting better and smarter, but it was too punishing and you ended up hating them for it. That was how we all felt toward Berry."

Ross always took any such criticism hard, and personally. "It was all about Diane," Katherine Anderson says. "It was like sometimes she didn't know or care that there were two other girls in the group." A story has been told that after the Supremes' opening-night performance at the Apollo, Motown A&R man Mickey Stevenson overheard a conversation between Gordy and Ross. "They didn't like us—they didn't like *me*," Stevenson recalled Diane whining. And yet this take might be a bit shaded, or even contrived, given that the only historical visual record of the group onstage at the Apollo, the grainy images of Gordy's amateurish, two-camera-angle movie of the Motortown Revue on December 17, present the trio as sexy, calmly confident, and in fine throat. And also completely forgettable in all ways but historical.

They stepped breezily out, Wilson and Ballard from the left wing, Ross from the right, in matching beige dresses hemmed at the knee and wigs piled high, and they sounded pert and soulful, doing little that could pass for dancing but smoothly slinging their forearms in and out, snapping fingers to the beat. Diane, eyes popping and mouth contorting, was slinky and passably vixenish. When they were done, they bowed and quickly exited stage left, to polite if not quite the delirious applause most of the other acts received, particularly the Miracles and Marvin Gaye.

"It wasn't that they were bad, not at all," recalls Vandella Rosalind Ashford. "They just had a different approach, sweet, not tough but kind of understated, sexy elegance. The other girl acts at Motown weren't subtle like that, we just let it all go. We hit you across the face with our energy.

"The Supremes knew their limitations. They couldn't do that. Their energy was in their voices, their harmonies, their personalities.

That was their act. The problem with that, though, is that you need a good, strong song to go with it, and at that point they didn't have that. But they always had a great work ethic and great style. I admired them for that."

Pause. "But I thought we were better in what we did."

Mary Wilson's postdated (by twenty years) review of the epochal gig was an irksomely skimpy passage in her autobiography to the effect that "the Apollo was a tough venue" and that "[w]e won the crowd over from the first minute . . . and came off the stage thrilled to death—We had played the Apollo."

Gordy, meanwhile, would write in his own memoir about the Apollo conquest in the light of the only person he could think of who mattered.

"I was big," he said. "I had made it in New York."

But Gordy did arrive at an important conclusion about the Supremes after the first Motortown Revue finished up with a show in Pittsburgh and, mercifully, came home in time for Christmas. He, too, had seen the rise of a dynamic he had not planned for Ross, Wilson, and Ballard: They did not, and could not, fit the Motown mold. Whether they would rise or fall, it would be by playing against Motown type, as a Motown anomaly. They were not quite R&B, not quite pop, not quite *Motown*.

The "sophistication" angle was to be the new watchword for the group. If played right, it could add another dimension to his crossover dreams. If they couldn't possibly do the same kind of songs that Mary Wells, the Marvelettes, and the Vandellas did, their voices and the Motown rhythm section would move them to where the others could not go. To Broadway, that is—and, only incidentally, to Harlem.

Now, if only Gordy could find that vexatiously elusive song to move *this* vehicle down the road.

nine

SPLITSVILLE
IN
HITSVILLE

With Gordy wasting no time to get them back in the studio, the Supremes were barely able to decompress after the monstrously rigorous and profitable Motortown Revue tour of 1962 (all of the Apollo Theater box office records were broken during their eleven days there). Christmas was spent learning and rehearsing songs Gordy had cherry-picked from different writers and recording them under the aegis of different producers. This was, of course, a marker of Gordy's supreme problem: How to mold the Supremes' cosmopolitan brand while at the same time keeping them innocent and soulful enough for the girl-group and R&B markets.

Too soon a break from the Motown prescript—or too much of one—might have been counterproductive, given that the Supremes had actually become a favorite of the black deejays around Detroit, and Gordy needed them to keep playing the group's records. What's more, the Supremes factored into the entire Motown radio station strategy. When the radio stations sponsored sock hops and the bigger Motown acts were out on the road, the jocks and the promoters usually had no problem taking the Supremes in their stead. This was important for Gordy, who needed to keep all the local station managers happy, since the first, essential, stage in the national rise of any Motown record was lighting a fire for it locally. By assuring them that he still valued the local guys, and not looking beyond them, he kept them panting for Motown product.

Getting the Supremes, whose records were invariably Top Ten hits in Detroit, was a big deal. "I know I played all their records, and always got a good reaction, lots of requests," says Robin Seymour. "I always wondered during the first few years why those records weren't bigger national hits, and Berry did too. It really bothered him. He considered it a personal defeat. It just goes to show you the industry isn't a monolith. You gotta please a lot of people. And let's face it, a national hit can't be a record that sucks, they gotta be really good, and the truth was those early Supremes records weren't near as good as the Marvelettes' or Martha and the Vandellas' records."

"But again," he added, "in Detroit, Berry never had to beg me to play the Supremes."

Of course, that reality wasn't anywhere near good enough for Berry or the girls; but as long as they served as a useful tool in the local strategy, he was reluctant to change their M.O. After all, the Supremes needed as much promotional buzz as they could get. And when out-of-town radio guys needed to be convinced to take a second-string Motown act, the Supremes got the first call. As longtime Motown promotion director Jack Gibson explained, "Let's say a jock had sock hops on Friday and Saturday nights. He wants Mary Wells but he's told she's working the Apollo, but we got this girl-group the Supremes with this hot record. Just play it three, four times an hour and let everybody know they're coming."

For the gigs in other cities, Gibson would have the girls take a Greyhound, to Chicago, Cleveland, Pittsburgh, wherever. He'd put on his credit card the cost of bus fare and two hotel rooms—one for him, one for the three of them (except when Ross would talk him out of his room and let her sleep there, and he'd spend the night on a lobby chair)—and then he'd fly in, telling the promoters they needed only to pay the group's bus fare back home. Gibson would pocket the profits from the show and bring the money to Gordy when he got back.

For Gordy, this supplemental way of treating his artists like chattel— there were times when the Supremes would have to play nine shows *a day* on these impromptu treks—was doubly rewarding, as the appearances would garner record play and sales for their records. In fact, that the first half-dozen Supremes singles made the charts at all was likely due to this "underground railroad" of quid pro quo appearances.

For the time being, then, Gordy did not disrupt the basic flavor of the Supremes; they would still be mocha soul. The tune he chose as their next single was a blues ballad called "My Heart Can't Take It No More." Written and produced by two Motown heavy hitters, Clarence Paul and chief recording engineer Lawrence Horn, it had Ross singing the lead torch-song style, her slow and sensuous cadence and strained highs swathed by a deeply echoed backing track reminiscent of the Chantels' classic "Maybe."

For another Supremes single, Gordy lifted the unspoken injunction his "number-one son" had imposed against working with Ross. The stickiness of rejoining her and Smokey Robinson in close quarters was, he figured, made necessary by his need to find them a hit, though it was clear that failure would mean a permanent severance. And the song did seem to justify making Claudette Robinson's skin crawl for a few days. Hung with the longest title of any Motown song (and likely *any* song), "A Breath Taking, First Sight Soul Shaking, One Night Love Making, Next Day Heart Breaking Guy," was an extreme outgrowth of the cunning punning of Smokey's songwriting mien. It was also a naked call for attention.

And it was damn good, too. Smokey cut it in the now-comfortable samba beat of his Mary Wells records, and an increasingly confident Ross had an easy handle on the complexities of Smokey's lyrical flippancies, while Wilson and Ballard were each given fragments of the song's interminable title to sing solo—perhaps the best pure examples one can hear of Mary's sinewy alto and Flo's arching soprano on record.

Hopeful that with these sides he could at least flirt with the Top Forty, Gordy was again stymied. The first kick he took was when "My Heart Can't Take It No More," released on February 2, 1963, promptly tanked, getting stuck at No. 129. Not waiting for the verdict, he had rushed out the follow-up, with another Gordy trifling called "Rock and Roll Banjo Man" on the flip, only one week after "My Heart"; but with jocks giving little attention to the first release he feared the prolix title would further turn them off. Disrupting the roll-out of the record, he recalled the first pressings and reissued it simply as "A Breath Taking Guy," but the hiccup kept it from rising higher than No. 75 on the pop charts. Still, considering the snafu and the early death of "My Heart," Gordy was satisfied the group was on track and went ahead with a Supremes album he'd had in the works. The album, a compilation of their previous middling hits filled out with B-sides and unreleased studio detritus, was released in December.

The title of the album was telling: *Meet the Supremes*. After two years at Motown, Gordy was still pleading with the record-buying public to get to know "the girls."

In 1963, nobody in America with a radio or a Victrola had to be begged to meet Motown. The company profile was ascending as fast as the latest records by Mary Wells, the Miracles, the Marvelettes, and Marvin Gaye climbed the charts. Gross sales for the year were $4.5 million and the coffers were being fed by the double-dip of royalties from Motown song covers. In 1964, for instance, the Beatles' second album in America alone bore *three* covers: "Money," "Please Mr. Postman," and the Miracles' "You've Really Got a Hold on Me." This was serious business now. Gordy, far less patient with nonstarters in the "family," cut adrift deadwood, no matter if they were personal cronies such as Mable John, Sammy Ward, Shorty Long, even his brother Robert Kayli.

Then there were two other favorites who had failed to become assets as singers. One was the burly, pug-faced Lamont Dozier, who as Lamont Anthony hadn't caused a ripple. Early in 1963, Gordy teamed him with Brian Holland on a single under the name of "Holland-Dozier" called "What Goes Up Must Come Down." And while it stiffed, it was a fortuitous connection. Gordy had always wanted Dozier to do what he did best, writing songs—something he'd done as early as the late '50s with Mickey Stevenson when they were both teenagers. Now, Gordy had his way, the opening being that Freddie Gorman, Holland's old writing and producing partner, had followed Robert Bateman out the door, to produce records for Detroit's Golden World label (such as the Reflections' hit "Just Like Romeo and Juliet"). Keeping Holland-Dozier intact, but behind the scenes, Gordy was rewarded when they co-wrote with Janie Bradford two serviceable songs; one was "Contract on Love," which Holland and Dozier produced as Stevie Wonder's second single. The other, "Time Changes Things," was used as the B-side of "My Heart Can't Take It No More."

Gordy's consolidation also saved the other Holland brother, Eddie. He, of course, was one of Berry's closest "homeys," sticking with him through a mostly lean two years after returning to the fold following his United Artists detour. Early in '63, Gordy wrote and produced a song for Holland, "Jamie," a big-band-spiked, Jackie Wilson copycat record for which Gordy spared no expense, running his most elaborate session yet. This included a string section on loan from the Detroit Symphony Orchestra, the first appearance of violins and cellos on a Motown record.

The seemingly outdated song hit No. 30 on the pop charts and No. 6 on the R&B charts, but when ensuing releases came nowhere near that level, Gordy was faced with what to do with the "other" Holland.

He was no doubt relieved when Eddie lost his desire for singing. Part of that decision was said to have been owing to his severe stage fright. In a 1983 book about Motown history, *Where Did Our Love Go*, author Nelson George writes of Holland's "rough experience" at the Apollo Theater "before the notoriously demanding audience" as the last straw that convinced him he was on the wrong side of the microphone. The other side, he had come to realize, was where the payoff was.

"I was looking at my recording bill and I was like forty thousand dollars in debt," he was quoted as saying, "and my brother has got a royalty check because he wrote the songs. I just said, 'I need to start writing songs.'"

That was when Gordy implemented yet another immensely providential shifting of musical chairs: Eddie, with Brian pitching the idea to Berry, was assigned to intern with the Holland-Dozier team.

> EDDIE HOLLAND: I wasn't adverse to making money, but that thing about having stage fright, that's incorrect. That Apollo Theater story—that guy don't know what he's talking about. I enjoyed it at the Apollo very much, and other big theaters. And Motown kept putting out my records like into 1964. But it wasn't necessarily what I wanted to do for a living. It wasn't that I was scared. That's bullshit. I just didn't like performing live. I was uncomfortable with it.
>
> BRIAN HOLLAND: I wasn't either. We're alike that way. I didn't like performing at all.
>
> EDDIE: But we're different. Brian's a producer. That wasn't really my thing, charts, arrangements, chord changes. I knew words. I'm analytical—that's my accounting school background. I knew what I wanted to say in music. And I knew what Brian wanted to say but couldn't.
>
> BRIAN: Well, I *can* write lyrics, but I never could do it as well as Lamont and certainly not as well as Eddie. He has a way of coming up with the perfect lyric for any note progression, any mood. Give him a general theme and a melody and he'll come back with chapter and verse, with the right lingo, phrasing, vernacular, whatever you call it.
>
> Basically, that's what Lamont and I did. Eddie did the rest. Every girl-group song we did sounded like a young girl wrote it. 'Cause Eddie could get inside the mind of a young girl yearning for love, being protected by a guy, that whole mindset.

EDDIE: My brother is too humble. I could do it because Brian Holland has the best ears in the world. He is a very quiet, sensitive man who picks up feelings, vibes all around him. And he has ears dogs wished they had. Brian heard a word, maybe a title, and a note on a piano and he'd go off by himself and compose a symphony out of it, always fresh and unique in some way. And he would duplicate that complete melody in the studio exactly as he heard it in his head. He knew what he wanted and wouldn't deviate from it. Lamont would help on both ends. He'd get the first concept, play that first lick, and he'd do the charts with Brian and contribute to the final lyrics. I'd then coach the lead singer on how to do the vocal, exactly like *I* heard it in *my* head, and Lamont would work with the background singers.

We were doing this right from the start. We weren't following any plan, it just fell into place that way. Things happen for a reason, man. Berry didn't know it would happen that way, but he knew *us*. He knew Smokey, he knew Norman and Barrett. We were like his sons, so it was all very sort of hereditary. It was a natural thing.

Indeed, it was as if Holland-Dozier-Holland had sprung fully formed from Medusa's head. All through 1963, the troika rumbled in high gear. One of their earliest works, the Marvelettes' "Locking Up My Heart," released in February, hit No. 44 on the pop charts, 25 on the R&B. Then, without pause, came Martha and the Vandellas' "Come and Get These Memories," a song that they admit was a mish-mash. "We did everything different in that one," Dozier recalled. "We used 11ths and 13ths [chords], we used country, jazz, and gospel elements." When Gordy heard the tape, he demanded to know "Who wrote this?" Bracing for the worst, the three disciples let out a breath when he continued, "Wow, that's different. I like it." He liked it even more when the record went 29 pop, 6 R&B in the spring. The follow-up, "Heat Wave," with its infectious Charleston beat, established both group and producers as Motown elite-worthy, going No. 4 pop and hitting the top of the R&B chart; and the next, the nearly identical sounding "Quicksand," did almost as well, charting at 8 and 7. Between Vandellas smashes, HDH also hatched Marvin Gaye's astounding gospel rocker "Can I Get a Witness," which went to 22 and 3.

All these were pivotal benchmarks, proving that HDH had a way with a winking lyrical and melodic hook—more subtly amusing and musically versatile than Smokey's compositions—and no fear of rewriting pop boundaries. They could also ace that most elusive task, creating a convincing girl-group song.

Another early collaboration, though, wasn't as impressive. But Diane Ross had made it inevitable that the paths of the Supremes and HDH would cross.

In fact, Ross had had her eyes on Brian Holland for some time, as unconcerned that he was married as she had been with Smokey Robinson. The younger Holland may have been "cute," as Flo once remarked, but there had to be more to it for Diane to become involved with him. As much as she may have been attracted by the dumpling-cheeked, sensitive young producer—and he to the saucy, sexually aggressive young singer—her attention was focused not on Holland or his wife but, rather, on the Marvelettes.

Diane, of course, detested them for their slew of hits—all under Holland's direction—while the Supremes were stuck in the mud. And she could claim only picayune victories over them—by filching a dance step or two from them here and there or insulting Gladys Horton's looks or clothes. Indeed, it had not taken long before, inevitably, her loathing for Horton finally boiled over. The big boom happened on a 1963 Motown tour, when, during a show in Philadelphia, Gladys decided to turn the tables and dish on how Diane looked.

The Supremes were opening for the Marvelettes and had just concluded "Let Me Go the Right Way," to scattered applause, when Horton could be heard from the wings saying something to the effect that Ross's dress was so baggy, "it looks like a nightgown." As Mary Wilson recalled it, Diane came offstage "steaming." She marched up to Horton in the brief interim before the Marvelettes would go on and got in her face.

"Did you say our dresses look like nightgowns?" she asked angrily.

With perfect timing, Gladys twisted the knife. "No, Diane," she said, "I didn't say *their* dresses—I said *your* dress," and sauntered onto the stage.

Diane, whom Wilson nailed as having "a very high opinion of herself and a low tolerance to criticism," didn't let the matter drop. She scribbled "DIANE IS GOING TO KICK YOUR ASS AFTER THE SHOW" on a napkin and handed it to a stagehand with instructions to deliver it to the Marvelettes' dressing room.

The story that's been passed down through the years, more than likely with some embellishment, goes like this: After the show Horton was helping a blind boy (not Stevie Wonder) across the parking lot when Diane, stalking her from a distance, jumped into John O'Den's station wagon, which the two girl-groups were sharing. She fired up and gunned the engine and with a deafening squeal of spinning tires made a beeline right for Horton—braking just a few feet short of where Gladys and the unsuspecting boy were standing.

Horton squinted to see who was at the wheel, her famous voice bellowing into the night, daring Ross: "Come on—hit me, you crazy bitch!" If she was willing to take a few broken bones to get Diane Ross confined to a jail cell, Ross wouldn't bite. Instead, she flipped her middle finger in the air and drove away, her demonic laughter pealing.

Lost in the telling and retelling of this tale have been a few relevant details, such as what sort of *detente* the two bitter rivals could possibly have struck in the station wagon riding home after such a hair-raising episode. All Wilson says is that Ernestine Ross, who had come along as a chaperone, was "shocked" and "reprimanded Diane for her behavior," though Diane "didn't seem to be listening."

Horton, for her part, used to tell the car story herself. But in a 2004 biography of the Marvelettes, *Motown's Mystery Girl Group* by Marc Taylor, she is considerably more contrite, downplaying the parking lot contretemps as "kiddie stuff" and saying, "I have a lot of respect for Diana," cutting her slack as "just a girl who spoke her mind" and "a hustler who always knew what she wanted." Curiously, Horton's confrere Katherine Anderson says she doesn't remember this incident, though one would think it would be impossible to forget. But she acknowledges that Ross run-ins were common, and over the top.

"We had a lot of volatile situations with Diane because she thought she was the shit, better than everybody else. She was a bitch and when she wouldn't get her way she'd make a spectacle of herself and then run to Berry for support. It got very tiresome. We always wondered why Berry put up with it."

This time, at least, he didn't. When Diane called Gordy from the road, to preemptively tell him of the incident and somehow justify it as Horton's fault, he was horrified by the psychotic reaction and forced her to apologize to Gladys immediately. With a smirk, she did, the paleness of such a weak attempt to keep peace within the family obvious to all but perhaps Gordy. "When Berry wasn't around," wrote Mary Wilson, "he wanted Diane to learn not to get caught up in petty fights."

But as everyone at Motown knew, Diane did petty; it was one of her real talents. Which is why she had no qualms about trying to even the field with the Marvelettes by appropriating their producer, who, perhaps, could be pillow-talked into giving the Supremes some of those sure-fire songs that might otherwise have gone to Gladys Horton to sing lead on.

The relationship between Ross and Brian Holland warmed up in the last months of 1962. The drill was the same as with Smokey. The two of them, Wilson recalled, "would work late in the studio [and] before long everyone at Hitsville knew what was up." It was hard not to, since once again Diane indiscreetly boasted of her new "boyfriend." She'd even leave love notes on Janie Bradford's desk for Brian, not bothering to fold the paper so her panting prose was visible to all. Bradford, who found herself acting as the conduit in more than one secret tryst, has a good laugh as she says, "They paid me well at Motown, so I will not betray their secrets. But Diane never made it a secret."

For Ross, the romance may have been just another pit stop on the way up—nowhere in her memoirs does she profess the deep affection for Holland that she does for Smokey Robinson. Still, that Brian Holland was the fly to the spider puzzled many around the shop. Because while Holland was surely one of "Berry's boys," and thus seemingly inclined to use willing women whenever possible, Holland was a different kind of cat. Introverted and unassuming—"a real gentleman," says Wilson—he seemed not to be Ross's type of man. Her type was more the swaggering, hard-driving "bad boy" personified by Berry Gordy.

Still, Holland reeked of Motown power; for Diane, opportunity was written all over him. What's more, it appeared that he was attracted to her type; his wife, Sharon, was strong-willed and controlling, not unlike Ross. Then too, looks can be deceiving. Holland could seem meek and cerebral, almost nerdy, if one overlooked the great soul music he pumped out of his inner being. But word on the street was that as he became richer, more famous, and more desirable, he easily adapted to the promiscuous Motown culture, apparently carrying on a number of affairs; and that the Holland marriage was falling apart, either as a result of his philandering or because, as the talk went around the water cooler, Sharon "wasn't giving him what he wants."

All these years later, it is potentially perilous to broach the delicate subject with Holland, whose Buddha-like calm dissolves like a brioche if the attempt is made. Then, his narrowed eyes—and Eddie Holland's protective growl—end the probe before it begins. But the telltale fleeting, misty musings about the enduringly "pretty" Diana Ross emanate from the same place as does his music inspiration, deep inside him—right alongside the cleaved heart she may have left him with. Smokey may have stated for the record his long and genuine love for Ross, while obscuring how deep that love went, but one suspects Brian Holland actually *feels* it—so strongly transferred to "I Hear a Symphony" that he had to stop driving and sit there weeping. This emotional investment was a key element of the Supremes' oeuvre, and why it remains so convincingly heartfelt.

One would have needed to be psychic, however, to imagine such a profound long-term aftermath at the start of the affair. After Holland was persuaded to work with the Supremes and specifically asked Gordy to do so, HDH came up with a song for them called "Run, Run, Run." Taking the organ-based gospel intonation of "My Heart Can't Take It No More" further, when the song was cut on May 7, 1963, Holland added flourishes like the feverish piano triplets and windy sax straight out of Phil Spector's "Wall of Sound." Ross, a bit too preciously, emoted Eddie Holland's sermon of a lyric—"Come gather 'round me and hear the news," she began—while Mary and Flo chanted "run, run, run" behind her on the style of a C. L. Franklin choir.

Despite the HDH pedigree, though, Gordy sat on the song for nine months, worrying that the flop of another well-crafted R&B song might be one flop too many for the group to absorb. Before releasing anything by the Supremes, he wanted to send them back out on the road to sell themselves to a broader audience. The first means toward that end was the second Motortown Revue, to commence in the fall. By then, he needed them to have a more upbeat, poppy song to push. And when the new girl-group maestros composed a song in that vein, "When the Lovelight Starts Shining Through His Eyes," instead of giving it to the Marvelettes or the Vandellas, Brian Holland told Gordy it might be a good bet for the Supremes, just as Diane Ross had planned it.

HDH themselves thought the song wasn't up to their usual snuff. "It was okay, far from our best work," says Eddie Holland, but the demo with Eddie singing lead and Dozier pounding the piano bristled with energy. "We'd had success with the up-tempo stuff, the 'Heat Wave'–'Quicksand' groove," Brian goes on, "so we were in that mood and we just went all out with it on that song." Construing their lengthening track record as carte blanche on all song matters, they went all out on the title, too. Says Brian: "People said, 'You know, Brian, Berry had a problem with a long song title a few months ago.' I said, 'Tough.'

We didn't care what Berry or anyone thought." A laugh. "I think maybe we'd gotten a little arrogant."

Gordy stayed with the title, deferring to HDH, and the big-gun producers went into the studio with the girls on October 1—though judging from the way Brian and Lamont blew out the session, the Supremes were practically an afterthought. As it progressed, they ladled the tracks with great gobs of instrumentation, drums thundering, hands clapping the beat, and an adjunct background chorale with a new Motown group called the Four Tops grunting a loud "*yeaaah!*" at the break.

To more musically educated ears, the vital core of "Lovelight" was the inspired drumming of Benny Benjamin, who didn't always make sessions because he was frequently hungover, but when he did he filled out a drum part as brilliantly and eccentrically as James Jamerson did with the bass lines. Although he was Alabama born, Benjamin tried to jive everyone into believing that he was from the Caribbean, so fond was he of Caribbean jazz beats. Handed straight drum parts by Motown producers, he accented them with island beats that worked ideally with the Mary Wells songs. On "Lovelight" he hit a New Orleans–style "second-line" beat, an island riff popularized previously on the Ikettes' "Iko Iko." In fact, music historian and arranger Allan "Dr. Licks" Slutsky, who produced the magnificent 2003 retro-documentary about the Funk Brothers, *Standing in the Shadows of Motown,* says, "I hear Zigaboo Modeliste in that song," referring to the drummer of the celebrated New Orleans rhythm section, the Meters. "And all the rhythm section instruments—guitars, piano, Jamerson on upright bass, tambourine— shadow Benny's groove, as does Mike Terry's baritone sax, which also shadows the beat but in his own way."

Slutsky echoes what has become a bone of rabid contention for HDH—that the production of their nonpareil songs owed much, if not everything, to the Motown rhythm section rather than to their own genius. "It's doubtful that HDH knew about the second-line style," he speculates. "Probably what happened is they heard Benny messing around with the beat before the session and built everything around that." As the years wore on, sentiments like that would become fightin' words to the three music gurus, especially as the Funk Brothers took on mythic status *ex post facto.* (Never credited by name or even as the Motown house band on any Motown album liner notes until the '70s, they were known by few other than hardcore jazz and R&B denizens in Paradise Valley, and then primarily for their club work.) The influence of the Funk boys on all Motown producers, and vice versa, seems to have inflamed the egos of people who otherwise worked in perfect harmony, with each side seeking the last word. And (as shall be seen) the debate takes on added detail and clarity in light of HDH's future work with the Supremes.

When the track was done, HDH coated it with thick echoes, leaving little room for the vocals to breathe. Submerged in the din, the Supremes approached irrelevance, although Ross valiantly kept pace with the breakneck tempo, needing to upshift her voice to soprano level to do it. To HDH, the record is a reflection of their arrogant phase, and the lesson learned was not to drown out the Supremes, or any of Motown's wondrous singers. "We learned from every one of our songs," Eddie notes, "especially a song like that."

Even so, the HDH magic was still apparent. The chugging melody and big-band kick won quick approval from Gordy's Friday-morning panel of song arbiters; though again, when Gordy asked his famous one-criterion question regarding a side's release—"If you had a dollar, would you rather buy a hot dog or this record?"—the aye or nay votes by Mickey Stevenson, Janie Bradford, Barney Ales, Clarence Paul, HDH, even Smokey, mattered not a whit if Berry liked it and they didn't. Going unanimous on such open ballots at times like those was usually a wise decision.

"Lovelight" was released on Halloween, when the Supremes were on tour with the Revue and were promoted to the third act on the card behind Martha and the Vandellas and the fading Contours. But they couldn't possibly reproduce the densely layered cacophony of the record on stage and so they stuck with the raw emotion of "My Heart Can't Take It No More." At the Apollo gigs, they cooked up a dramatic affectation. Looking prim but sexy in taffeta knee-length dresses and wigs coolly angled to the side, they began with their backs to the audience, then turned as one on the opening line, Ross extending her left arm followed by Wilson and Ballard doing the same. Their voices were strong and cohesive, and if Diane was still making her eyes pop she also was more at ease than ever. The crowd gave them an appreciative, if still no more than polite, round of applause.

The tepid reception notwithstanding, during the show's finale, when all the Motown acts emerged to join in on the Miracles' "Shop Around," Diane quickly strayed from Mary and Flo on the far left end of the line of performers and elbowed her way next to Smokey, where no one could fail to see her singing and bumping hips with the star of the show—as if both were the headliners—while other acts looked at each other and rolled their eyes.

The upward flight of "Lovelight" justified that sort of preening. The single, backed with the soft, bluesy "Standing at the Crossroads of Love" (the title of which, but not the song, HDH would later recycle as "Standing in the Shadows of Love" for the Four Tops), quickly cracked the Top Hundred in mid-November. But its climb was abated, along with every other showbiz product, on Friday, November 22. On that day, everyone inside Motown huddled around radios, shocked at the tragic news that President John F. Kennedy had been murdered in Dallas.

Gordy was so distraught he sent everyone home for the day, canceling several sessions. Incredibly, even as the president was fighting for his life, and people around Hitsville shuffled about in an almost catatonic state, Marvin Gaye's thoughts were elsewhere. Peeved that his latest record, "Can I Get a Witness," wasn't making much noise on the charts, he had scheduled a meeting with Gordy for that day to hash it out. Ignoring the breaking news from Dallas, he barged into Gordy's office, where he chewed out Barney Ales's sales department. After Gordy had assured him they were pushing hard for him, Berry jocularly told him to "be a good boy, okay?" Gaye, irrationally taking it as a racial insult, screamed, "See! See, BG! That's a whole bunch of bullshit. You think I'm a boy just like the white man!" Exasperated, and in no mood to put up with Marvin's bullshit, not today anyway, Gordy snapped. With a roar, he swept his arm angrily across his desktop, sending papers, picture frames, and whatever else flying across the room. Then, getting in Marvin's face, he seethed, "Don't you realize the president was killed today?" before elbowing Gaye out of the way and going home to grieve for JFK. (By some accounts—but not Gordy's—he pinned Gaye against the desk, his hand around his neck, not letting him breathe before being pulled off of him by other Motown executives.) In March 1964, he would name his illegitimate son by Margaret Norton "Kennedy William Gordy."

Out on the road, the Motown tour dates were canceled for that weekend. The performers sat around in their hotel in a daze, crying while they watched the funeral services. For the Supremes, the timing of "Lovelight" also fell victim to the shots in Dealey Plaza, the ongoing shroud of mourning across the country blunting record sales for them and everyone else looking forward to a strong holiday market.

Admirably, "Lovelight," which likely would have flirted with the Top Ten, still managed to do well enough; it hit the Top Forty around

Christmas time, peaking at No. 23 (and 2 R&B) early in '64. Wanting to piggyback on it, Gordy now released "Run, Run, Run," only to suffer a setback when the song made it to only No. 93 on the pop charts and No. 22 on the R&B charts.

At that point, Gordy must have thought: "*Now* what?" The Supremes, a Motown commodity for three years, had not one significant hit. No other act there survived that long as a loss leader. Worse, the Ross–Brian Holland liaison seemed for a brief, ugly moment like it might backfire and wreck the Supremes' growing simpatico with HDH.

That moment occurred when Sharon Holland made up her mind to put an end to her husband's fling with Diane.

With none of Claudette Robinson's near-saintly all-forgiving nature, Sharon decided to have it out with Diane during a Motown event at the Twenty Grand in February 1964. That night, after eyeing Diane with a scowl, she began to thread her way through the crowd until she was standing nose to nose with her. Diane, talking with someone else, didn't know Sharon was right next to her. Turning her head, she was jolted by those two staring eyes. Making an effort to be nice, Diane was able to get out "Hi Sha—" when she was cut off by an eruption of profanity followed by a warning.

"If you don't stay away from my man," Sharon screamed, "you're a dead woman!"

Even with the noise in the club, she could be heard, and conversations and laughter were stilled as people paused to watch the fight— including an embarrassed Holland, who stood blank-faced, drink in hand, looking like he wished he could disappear. Diane, for her part, gave not an inch, standing tall as she could on her heels to meet the taller Sharon—"not a small woman," Mary Wilson recalled—at eye level.

"If he was your man," she hissed, "he wouldn't be with me."

Sharon answered with more expletives, spraying spit on Diane's face. This was usually the point when Ross would back off and slink away. But now her fists were clenched, as were Sharon's. With the fur about to fly, and no one in the room particularly eager to break them up, Mary and Flo—who themselves might not have minded seeing Diane get her hide tanned—did a quick huddle and decided to move in to shield her.

As Wilson tells it, she and Flo "circled around Diane, with Flo stepping right in the middle. Sharon kept saying she was going to kick Diane's butt, and for a few minutes we had to hold her back—she was raring to go."

Given the size difference, Mary and Flo were afraid Sharon would floor Diane and then "take a swing at one of us," but they were able to drag Ross kicking from the club and get her a lift home. For days, the incident was the talk of Motown, with the requisite conjecture about whether Sharon had made the same threats on her cheating husband's posterior, a likely circumstance considering that he and Ross thereafter agreed to be "just friends" and co-workers. That, however, may have had something to do with Brian shifting his philandering to another diva under his guidance—the tall, elegant, and equally ambitious Martha Reeves.

In fact, in the bramble bush of Motown intra-"family" carrying on, that affair had taken breath before the one with Diane was extinguished—leading Ross to relocate her loathing from Gladys Horton to Reeves, a subplot that would only intensify over the next year. It's a wonder, indeed, that Holland wasn't too winded to do his work. On the other hand, perhaps his tangled personal business supplied the motivation to turn in some of his finest compositions. The Vandellas' first hit, for instance, "Come and Get These Memories," was a bouncy but barbed farewell to a once-loving relationship (the guessing game being whether the old lover in the song was Diane or Sharon, whom he would divorce soon after).

It would be Diane, of course, who refused to leave his soul—not then, not four decades later. The affair may have been severed but the relationship wasn't, in contrast to the general studio *interruptus* with Smokey. Having learned that she could not burn another Motown bridge like that and prosper, going platonic with Brian was the proper, cosmopolitan thing to do, and she clearly had an easier time doing it than did Holland, the enticements of Reeves aside. But, for both, it would be the single most providential thing they ever did.

ten

A
"LOUSY
SONG"

Before that providence could come to pass, the Supremes would have to keep from falling off the earth. They certainly had a dim effect on the pulse of music as the seismic year of 1964 pressed on. This was so even though by mid-year the girl-group genre was in full flower, on a broad level helping to erect an effective firewall around the American record industry as the Beatles and wanna-be Beatles were invading the U.S. charts. Indeed, the extent of the Brit "takeover" and its immediate "new order" of music has been egregiously overstated through the years. Because while the Beatles did have six No. 1 hits in 1964, and Peter & Gordon, the Animals, and Manfred Mann one apiece, the year's fourteen other No. 1's were by American acts, including such swingin' "new" acts as Dean Martin, Lorne Greene (*Bonanza*'s Ben Cartwright), Roy Orbison, Bobby Vinton, and Louis Armstrong, who turned in the year's biggest seller with the Broadway show tune "Hello, Dolly!" Five No. 1's would be held by American girl-groups—the Dixie Cups ("Chapel of Love"), the Shangri-Las ("Leader of the Pack"), and three alone by a very long-overdue Motown trio known as the Supremes. And these were merely hits that went to the top; below the summit was a constant infusion of plasma by girl-groups that picked up where the Shirelles, Orlons, and Ikettes had left off when they ebbed, such as the Ronettes, Crystals, Chiffons, Cookies, Toys, and Jelly Beans.

The sun wouldn't shine on the girl-groups (with one notable exception) much longer; but as of mid-'64, they were no less than the buffer of American rock, padding record companies' bottom lines and easing their transition to the eon of the self-contained band and greater auton-omy for artists as the Brill Building model of centralized power drew its last breaths.

Motown, as a Brill pinchbeck, would need to alter its assumptions accordingly; one primary step would be the renewing of artists' con-tracts in 1965 with higher royalty rates. And yet, before the full mean-ing of 1964 had played out, at Motown and worldwide, the girl-group that would have the biggest impact of any American recording act on the industry had a tenuous place at the table.

For the Supremes it must have been like being seated at the kiddie table, permitted to speak only when spoken to. By one indication, early in '64 promotional flyers touting new Motown records were sent to the local deejays. The Supremes were not forgotten, but they were dwarfed by their more bankable shipmates. One such flyer bore a banner at the top reading "SURE-FIRE HITS!" Underneath were designs of two hearts, one large, one small; superimposed on the larger was "'Locking Up My Heart'—The Marvelettes, Tamla #54077." On the tinier one, requiring a magnifying glass to see clearly, was "'My Heart Can't Take It No More'—The Supremes, Motown #1040." Photos of each group were inside similarly lopsided hearts on the right border. Within this schematic was the "heart" of the Supremes' problem—they were a fac-tory second act, nothing "sure-fire" about them.

Some of Gordy's flacks wondered just why he was giving even that much play to them instead of to acts who'd delivered a good deal more, like Martha and the Vandellas. "We asked that, too," says Rosalind Ashford. "We had three big hits already and we not only had to put up with Diane's pissiness but also were getting less promotion than them, a group with no hits. It was hard to take, believe me." Apparently, con-siderations like budgetary allotments had to do with more than a young female singer finding her way to a mattress that mattered, since Martha Reeves would seem to have earned some Ross-like frequent-flier mileage by sharing Brian Holland's. The only reasonable answer to the riddle was that Gordy simply saw something organically tangible in Di-ane's voice that made her—and, oh yeah, the other two—worth wait-ing for.

While the Supremes were duly grateful, all the snide talk about what had to be going on *sub rosa* between Diane and Berry to attain this patronage began getting to them. It got to Ross, too, though of course she had sparked so many salacious rumors in the past. Recent whispers were that the Supremes would be dissolved so Ross could go solo, and while that normally might have excited her, she also worried about what effect such premature talk of that sort would have on Mary's and Flo's psyches. Mary, for all her anodyne compliancy about group matters, was terrified that the group might fail. And Flo, who was so insecure to begin with, had not gotten over Ross moving her out as lead singer. As much as Ross thirsted for a shot at solo fame, for now she had no desire to upset the girls and genuinely wanted them to taste the nectar of success together.

Attempting to re-cement her delicate bond with Mary, Diane agreed to go with Mary to Chicago where the latter's cousin was to be married. They hopped a Greyhound, on their own dime, and had such a good time they stayed on, living with Mary's relatives. Time flew, and they were still there two weeks later, happily isolated from the brain-scrambling Peyton Place on West Grand Boulevard.

"We were running away from Motown. We really needed to get away," Wilson said of the brief sabbatical, during which they had quickie flings with two members of the Chicago soul group the Dells, whom they met at a club. When they came back to Detroit, Diane was off again, hitching a ride with the Temptations, who were as spectacularly unsuccessful in their three Motown years as were the Supremes. They had gotten a gig in Atlanta, and they took off for their native Deep South, with Diane in tow.

"We were very close friends with Diane from way back," Otis Williams says. "She was like our kid sister. She said she wanted to go visit her relatives in Mississippi. We said sure, come with us; we'll drop you off, then pick you up on the way back." He continued:

> We were very protective of Diane. For all her reputation as a difficult person, to us she was always real vulnerable, breakable. Because we saw that side of her, which she didn't let others see. We would never let her walk anywhere alone on that trip. We'd be like her security guards.
>
> It was kind of refreshing, too, to see her in that context. She was just a confused 20-year-old girl, a sweet girl, not someone trying to be, y'know, Miss Diva. She spoke about how scared she was that the Supremes wouldn't make it. She thought she might have to quit the business and go to college like her daddy wanted.
>
> Hey, we knew how she felt. The possibility of failure was beating us all down. So we'd cheerlead for her and she'd do the

same for us. We'd say, "You're gonna make it big!" And she'd go, "No, you're gonna!" But Diane was really questioning herself. People rarely saw her that way.

During this abyss, Ross seemed to have convinced herself that everyone at Motown, with the sole exception of Gordy, was conspiring against her. A particular foil, she openly stated, was Billie Jean Brown, a young woman Gordy had hired while she was still attending Cass High School to write liner notes before he promoted her to no less than the gatekeeper of all recorded songs. "She was Creative Control," Eddie Holland says. "Meaning she'd listen to whatever tapes the producers had made and if she said, 'That needs remixing' or 'It sounds too slow,' you'd have to redo it. You can imagine how much she was either loved or hated, but Berry trusted her because she had really great ears. She didn't know anything about how to make a record but she knew if it sounded like a hit."

It was a thankless task, a monumentally unfair one to hang on a novice, and Ross's complaints that Billie Jean had it in for her were not atypical—especially since all Motown acts cut more records than were needed and very few were ever released. (By Wilson's estimation, for every Supremes release there were at least five others that sat in the can, where they sit to this day—even though the acts themselves were docked for the expenses of recording every one.)

Diane even moaned about it to Gladys Horton, looking anywhere she could for sympathy. Horton, stunned that her old rival was crying on her shoulder, of all people's, recalled her saying that "Billie Jean hates me." As Horton told author J. Randy Taraborrelli, "Next thing I knew I was comforting her, and crying with her. 'Don't worry,' I told her, 'you'll have your hit too, just you wait.'" In her assessment, "Diane was really complicated. She'd be runnin' your ass down with a car one day and then have you cryin' your eyes out feelin' sorry for her the next."

Horton was so sorry for her that when Diane, still wet-eyed, asked if Gladys would let the Supremes get star billing over the Marvelettes at one show, she acquiesced. "To me, it was nothing but a show," she recalled. Not so blasé was Esther Edwards, who Horton says got "angry at me because I begged her to let them star the show and the Supremes didn't have a hot record."

But that's how it went down, another small victory for Diane.

If Ross could use tears to connive, she had hardly lost her bravado, all her worries aside. This was always evident when the Supremes were

on tour with hotter acts, making her want to cut down the other performers by aggrandizing herself. Increasingly, her new obsession was
torturing Martha Reeves, who'd replaced Gladys Horton on her own
"hit list." Not by coincidence, of course, the Vandellas had taken off
under the tutelage of HDH. But adding fuel to Ross's ire was the fact
that there wasn't a soul at Motown who didn't think Reeves was a far
superior singer with a brighter future.

This was the prologue when, just before an engagement at the Howard Theater in Washington, D.C., at which the Supremes were booked
as the opening act for the Vandellas—another source of anger for
Ross—Diane did some nosing around and found out where the Vandellas had bought their dresses for the show. Placing a call to the dress
shop, she ordered three identical frocks in the Supremes' sizes, then
went and picked them up, paying with the money Gordy had wired her
as a clothing stipend after she cried to him that they needed new stage
wear. Wilson and Ballard, who knew nothing of the circumstances and
always deferred to Diane's educated sense of style and fashion, excitedly
slipped into them minutes before the lights went up.

This thievery went beyond Ross's dance-step-stealing. And when
Reeves saw them out there opening the show in the same dresses the
Vandellas were already wearing while standing in the wings, the steam
coming out of her ears could have melted her wig. After the Vandellas'
set, which as Diane no doubt hoped was less polished because their
concentration was disrupted by the dress issue, the Vandellas raced to
the Supremes' dressing room. There, Reeves banged on the door, then
kicked it open and glowered at Ross, sputtering "You did us dirt."

Mary and Flo were too startled to move in and defend Diane, and
besides they were terrified of Reeves, who with her oversized beehive
wig, long bony frame, and angry jut-jawed face was no one to mess
with. As they cowered, once more a fight loomed between Diane and
another woman in the Motown clan. But rather than get her back up as
she had with Sharon Holland, Ross almost by rote picked up a phone
and began calmly dialing Berry Gordy's personal line.

Probably thinking "What *now*?" when he picked up, Gordy listened to Diane's latest spin on an outrageous caper. When she stuck the
phone next to Martha's ear, he wearily intoned, "Now Martha, Diane
didn't mean you no harm. Just leave her alone," and defused further
fireworks by telling them with a sigh that he'd buy them all new dresses.

Reeves could only walk away shaking her head at Ross's childish-
ness. Nor did it end with this incident. During other Vandellas gigs at
the local clubs, they would be excited when Gordy would come

through the door to see the shows—until they'd see a giddy Diane on
his arm, preening like Nefertiti. She'd then make faces during their set,
indicating her displeasure at Martha's singing, and whisper her critiques
to Gordy, who'd take notes. For Reeves, the humiliation was almost too
much to stand. Diane, on the other hand, was loving every minute of it.

Gordy's habitual and, to some, delusional support for Ross brought
them in mid-1964 to the chain of events that finally broke them out of
their rut. The catalyst was an invitation in early May from Roz Ross,
Dick Clark's assistant, for a new Motown diva, Brenda Holloway, to
join the '64 edition of Clark's Caravan of Stars. Clark's was the mother
of all rock tours; running from Memorial to Labor Day each year; with
its two dozen acts and forty to fifty stops all over the country, it made
the Motortown Revue seem like an intimate gathering, and such was
Clark's cachet that any brush with his orbit was of inestimable value to
an act, especially one needing a boost. Indeed, most acts chosen for the
Caravan had a potentially big hit climbing the chart—as was Holloway's "Every Little Bit Hurts," which was actually recorded in L.A. as
part of a seminal West Coast Motown operation—and thus having a
place on Clark's bus was a double-bonus. An act could perform live
across the American landscape while its record was played on *American
Bandstand*. In fact, Clark flew back to Philadelphia one day each week
during the tour to tape a week's worth of *Bandstand*, armed with anec-
dotal evidence of the acts that were reaping the best reception.

One of the biggest benefits for black acts was access to white middle-
class record buyers. While Clark himself was clearly colorblind—his
tours were well integrated and even as far back as the '50s he'd been
heroic in booking black acts, including Motown ones, on *Bandstand*—
Motown had not been a presence on the Caravan. Perhaps this was a
matter of timing or, more cynically, had to do with Clark's close ties to
the Philadelphia label Cameo-Parkway, whose own roster of R&B acts
such as the Orlons, Dee Dee Sharp, the Tymes, and, of course, Chubby
Checker seemed to get automatic calls to sojourn with the Caravan.
Then there was the fact that while the Caravan, too, played many
Southern venues, its audiences were by and large white; it was this reality, Clark admitted in his memoir *Rock, Roll and Remember*, that guided
the tours' format, which, he wrote, "always closed with a white romantic teen idol, like Bobby Vee, Fabian, Gene Pitney, or Paul Anka."

Little known as she was, the sultry, drop-dead-gorgeous Brenda Holloway more than qualified as an exception, and indeed her inclusion was a major coup for Gordy. But he wanted more. He wanted another act on that bus—the Supremes.

As it happened, the timing was right for them, too. A month before the Clark Caravan entered the equation, the group had been tabbed to cut an HDH song with a standard relationship-breakup theme, its genesis being not Brian's breakup with either Diane or Sharon but Lamont Dozier's parting with a girl who, he said, "wanted more from me than a casual fling, a commitment I wasn't ready to make." Noodling on the piano, throwing out phrases that fit the mood, he matched to a punchy riff five words that would change his life.

"It hit me thinking about how something so strong as love could be so fragile and then go poof, just like that. It's like, where did our love go?"

Bingo! Another HDH song was born. A very different song, as it turned out. Far more melancholy and fatalistic than the kiss-my-ass declaration of independence of "Come and Get These Memories" and, as such, much more measured. Dozier and Brian Holland composed the charts as an unadorned melody, with the simplest eight-bar chord progression, and no frills. To the untrained ear, it would have sounded tedious, even listless. And Eddie Holland's lyric, on paper, only hinted at the blistered heart of the protagonist who sang, "Baby, baby, baby don't leave me," while contradictorily pining for a love that "stings like a bee" and for the lover who betrayed her by "leaving me behind."

It was an unmistakably adult plaint that rendered most Motown love found/love lost songs kid stuff; thus, because the song had to make the whole concept of love into an open wound, it would need to be carried, uncompromisingly, by the lead vocal. But who could do it?

Entrenched Motown lore has it that HDH intended the song for the Marvelettes, and that they hated it, whereupon it was shuttled to the Supremes as a table scrap. This narrative is recycled by Mary Wilson and Katherine Anderson, who remembers it this way: "HDH asked Gladys and Wanda to sing that song, but they didn't want to do it. We were not that kind of group to sing it. We were a very high-energy group."

Which is precisely why the narrative is fanciful—not least because it presumes, dubiously, that Motown acts, particularly the girl-groups, had any say about what to record. In truth, it is nigh impossible that anyone could ever have believed the languid sensuality and subtle ambivalence of the lyric could be accommodated by the Marvelettes' schoolgirl kitsch or overheated dance routines.

> BRIAN HOLLAND: No, we wanted that for the Supremes. Because we had already established a hit with them, a semi-hit, let's say, and we wanted to take them to the next level.
> EDDIE HOLLAND: Yeah, we wanted to come up with something different, something that hadn't been done with them. And it was a really different kind of song. Well, so what? Different is good. Shit, we knew that song was a No. 1 hit from the get-go.

Still, the choice of who would sing it wasn't necessarily Diane Ross. At least not for Eddie:

> I knew that Mary had a soft voice, and we needed a sweet, sensuous vocal for it. I mean, to me, I didn't care who the lead singer had been. All I cared about was getting the lead right. They all could sing, right? Well, Flo couldn't sing hardly that good, not for our purposes, 'cause we looked for a lot of depth and Flo didn't have that. I said, "Mary can sing this song." Because I'd never heard Diana sing that way. She'd always sung in that high, little-girl sound. I said, "We need the right feel for this. If we get the right feel, this is gonna be a monster hit."
> But I didn't know what I was up against. Brian and Lamont, they looked at me and said, "Are you crazy? Diane's the singer. Diane can sing soft and sexy, let's just drop her key, she'll sound older, sensuous." And I thought, well, they just don't wanna go up against Berry, because Berry had decided that Diane was the lead singer and that was that. It was frustrating to me, but I was outvoted. And when we got in the studio and dropped her key, I knew I was wrong. They were right. She had the sound. I hadn't seen what Berry had all along. Diana Ross is gifted with a beautiful and unique tone in her voice. It's genuine and commercial. She's completely unique as a singer. You can't find any other singer who sounds like her. That's why she can make any song her song. That's why Berry was so patient with them. He knew what he had in Diane.

Having been told by Eddie that she'd front the song, which would have been her first real lead, Mary was crushed. But she'd have been more so had she, and Diane and Flo, not agreed that this odd song would go nowhere. Rather than hearing any adult skew, they found it adolescent and silly—"a teenybopper song," as Wilson put it, with "a limited melody and no drive." There were rumors even then that the Marvelettes had turned it down before it came to the Supremes, which infuriated Ross.

Her cynical reaction: "So they want *us* to do this lousy song?"

At the session, on April 8, cutting the rhythm track went smoothly, uncomplicated as it was. As arranged by Brian, it came out with what Alan Slutsky perceived as a "swing feel," flavored by a two-bar piano line by Johnny Griffiths, Benny Benjamin's shuffle drum beat, and the mandatory (on all Motown songs, it seemed) Mike Terry sax solo. The real task was the make-or-break vocal tracks. Eddie had a hard slog with Ross, who was used to singing as her spirit moved her, according to the rhythm, not with every word and inflection tightly pre-ordered.

EDDIE HOLLAND: The thing is, an HDH song is unusual for any singer; it wasn't just Diane. There had to be a certain type of tone and sync to it. There were a lot of different beats, sharps, flats. The coloration was always more important than the note. The singers would come in and they were accustomed to singing to the beat, but in our songs they'd have to trail the beat, singing off of the beat in a sharp or flat key.

When I was teaching Diane "Where Did Our Love Go," the first time I sang it for her I was using some, shall we say, vocal gymnastics, overdoing it so she could feel the sound. And she said, "I want to sing it just like that." I told her, "No, no, no, no. It has to be sweet and sexy, and it won't be unless you do exactly what I say." And she did. She learned. It took a lot of time and work, but she did it. Remember, she was singing in a key she never had before. She had to take baby steps. She'd revert and start singing in the high register. I'd say, "Lower, Diane, bring it down." She'd say, "But it sounds more exciting higher." My retort would be, "I don't care if you're excited. You gotta make *me* excited."

I always harped on that, to keep songs in a lower key. I can't tell you how many arguments I had with Brian over this. When

I heard the first mixes of the tracks, I'd always say, "That vocal
is too goddamn high. Slow down the tape!" There'd always be
a tussle.

So finally we got Diana into the vocal booth, and she still
hated the fact that she had to do this song. She was not in a
good mood [laughs], and when Diana wasn't in a good mood it
meant one thing—she was gonna call Berry [hearty laughter].
She said, "Where's the phone?" and everyone, you know, rolled
their eyes. I said, "Diana, listen, you can go ahead and call
Berry. But if he comes down here, me and my brother and Lamont ain't comin' back in here for you girls, ever."

That stopped her in her tracks, but she just more or less
wanted to get it over with, and it came out really dry, not a lot
of emotion. The engineer turned around and looked at me,
like, "You wanna go on with this?" And I just said, "Leave it
alone, man, just let her go." Because it was the damndest thing.
What she was doing was perfect. She may have been thinking
the hell with this, but her voice had this natural quality that's
very hard to coax—very soft and beautiful, yet not pushing it
on you.

At the end she said, "Is this what you want?" She didn't
even know herself how good she was. I told her, "Thank you,
that's *exactly* what I want." I knew what we had.

Dozier, too, had his hands full with Mary and Flo's background
vocals, later calling that tutorial "a trying experience." The original
backing track was intricate, but the pair couldn't get down the call-
and-response pattern and so it was stripped back to only two parts—a
revolving chain of "Baby, baby" and the title phrase. To the girls, it
seemed like the most ridiculous song they'd ever heard. Wilson would
describe the lyrics as "childish and repetitive." And it might have remained so if Diane hadn't stepped before the microphone and made
something incredible happen. She not only nailed it, she epoxied every
single element of HDH's vision for the song into a two-minute-plus
trance. Her soft, sighing, almost diaphanous purring turned repetition
into emotion. The opening line made the sale: *"Baby, baby, don't leave
me, oooooh, please don't leave me."*

It was the *oooooh* that really did it. As HDH would discover, just
such an ephemeral, sexy-sad sonance, seemingly emanating from the
loins, could make the hair stand up on their arms—and thus stand as

the defining point of the song. And when she bled the line about having a "burning, burning, yearning feeling inside me," God only knows what went through Brian's mind.

Brian and Lamont had completed the session with no added intro; Diane came right in on bar one. Realizing afterward that they needed a buffer to prep the vocal, they wouldn't wait until the musicians were back for another date. Instead, improvising, they scrounged around for some makeshift sound that could fill space. Finding some wooden planks in a corner—part of the endless construction on the studio—they bundled two together, suspended them from the ceiling with piano wire to within a foot of the wooden floor. Then, Eddie and teenage studio hand Mike Valvano stomped on them with the heels of their shoes in a rough 1-2-3-4, 1-2-3-4 cadence. Fattened up with echo and overdubbed hand-clapping, the effect of a small army marching across a tin roof was just odd enough to accentuate the hard-to-soft contrast, and provided balance at the end, when it was reprised.

The rudimentary nature of the stomping aside, sheen-smooth grooves of the finished record spilled the very air of polished sophistication that Gordy had dreamed of for the Supremes. Upon hearing the final mix, he cautiously ventured that he had a potential Top Ten hit in his hands. HDH knew they'd done well when they played the tape for Barney Ales's salespeople. "They'd go, 'Man, that Diane Ross!' and then, like, smack their lips," says Eddie Holland. "It was like everybody wanted her because of how she sounded on that song." From that sampling (unscientific though it was), it was apparent that if the record was given proper play, not only the Motown teenage target audience would be broadened to more worldly ears but adult men, too, might be rather intrigued.

Ales himself had no doubt, and was even prepared to go out on a limb, using the Supremes in an attempt to blunt the potentially crippling loss of arguably Motown's biggest star. That crisis had arisen when Mary Wells, dissatisfied over Gordy's penury—and her ego swollen in the early spring of '64 by "My Guy," the massive No. 1 hit penned and produced by Smokey Robinson—walked out on her contract, claiming that since she'd been underage when she signed, she could do as she wished now that she was 21. With three years left on the contract, she signed with Twentieth Century Fox.

For Gordy, stung by this latest defection, it was small consolation that after he sued for breach of contract Motown was awarded part of Wells's royalties (of which there were few) for the next three years.

Needing to ease the distributors' jitters about Motown's stability, Ales told the big trade paper *Billboard* in July that while Gordy was "surprised and hurt" by Wells's walkout, it was actually Motown's "intensive" promotional campaigns that had made Wells a star (he left the issue of royalty compensation untouched) and a campaign just like that now awaited another deserving act. The article read:

> Ales, stating that he is aware that many offers are proffered to an artist who has had a top record, added that he would like to alert the industry to a group of young ladies called the Supremes, "who will have the next No. 1 record in the U.S."

Ales couldn't have gone out on a shakier limb than that; now, anything short of "Where Did Our Love Go" going high and mighty would be an enormous embarrassment, undercutting Motown's credibility and ability to seamlessly adapt to change. And if the Supremes wouldn't cut it, where then to turn? It wasn't as if they had a deep bench. One could feel Gordy's pain in the early summer of '64. As things stood, "My Guy" was the first Motown chart-topper since Stevie Wonder's fluke, live-concert version of "Fingertips (Part 2)" the previous summer. The Miracles' three releases that year stalled at Nos. 35, 27, and 35. Stevie Wonder's first two after "Fingertips (Part 2)" peaked at 33 and 29. The Marvelettes were in a slump. The Vandellas were waiting for a follow-up to "Quicksand." And Marvin Gaye was still waiting to crack the Top Ten.

Gordy was doing well enough financially, but the novelty and excitations of 1962 and '63 were receding into the past. The Wells exodus brought to a head Gordy's angst that he would now be seen as vulnerable—at about this time, Smokey Robinson was offered a million-dollar advance to jump to Scepter Records in New York by label president Florence Greenberg; and while his filial loyalty to Berry made the offer a no-go, it showed that the sharks were circling.

Gordy, a gambling man, now had no choice but to bet the store on a group that had never sniffed the Top Twenty and whose last appreciable contribution was singing backup on Marvin Gaye's "You're a Wonderful One," a spring hit. And so he and Ales would go to the mat with "Where Did Our Love Go." They'd hit up the distributors, flood the radio stations with copies of the record, lean on the station managers. But that wasn't enough. They needed to jumpstart Motown with the white market. And for that, they needed Dick Clark.

Contrary to Mary Wilson's Pollyanna-like assertion that "[w]e were flattered to know that Dick Clark . . . wanted the Supremes" for the Caravan, Esther Edwards had to pester Roz Ross for days to get it done. In nearly all editions of the Motown literature, Clark has been shaded as a hard-ass who finally gave in once Gordy agreed to pick up the group's expenses, whereupon Clark took them on at $600 a week, half of tour headliner Gene Pitney's fee.

The truth is exactly the opposite. Clark was actually extraordinarily generous to the Supremes, inasmuch as most performers on his tours, as he wrote in *Rock, Roll and Remember,* "didn't make more than $500 a week." What is more, Clark rarely if ever paid for any of the acts' hotel lodgings; instead, all but the biggest stars had to pay or arrange for their own accommodations. The Supremes, then, were doubly blessed: by two of the industry's biggest heavyweights. The upshot was that while most of the performers, as Clark noted, "were lucky if they had $20 a week to play with," the Supremes had $150 a week to do so—and the amount was that low only because Ernestine Ross came along as the girls' chaperone, meaning the money would be split four ways and not three. One can forgive Clark for being a mite unctuous in insisting that "[e]ven then you knew Diana Ross was something special." Yet there can be no doubt that, other than Gordy, no human being of that high-flown stature ever played a more pivotal role in the group's success than did Clark.

On June 8, the agreement and the accommodations made, the Supremes were driven by John O'Den to join the Caravan of Stars in progress in Cleveland. Light-headed in wonderment about the weeks ahead, they probably didn't fully realize that the weight of Berry Gordy's entire world now rested on the fragile shoulders of three girls from the projects.

eleven

ONE

B y the time the Supremes joined the Dick Clark Caravan of Stars, "Where Did Our Love Go" had begun to generate a small buzz. Hurried into release in early June, backed with a song called "He Means the World to Me," it spread from radio stations in Detroit to make the rounds nationwide. The next crucial step in the hit-making process was getting the song noticed in *Billboard*. According to the rules of that game, a record company was expected to spend liberally on full-page ads in the paper. Though the effect of such ads on record sales was highly debatable, given that mainly industry people ever read the trades, labels took to competing with each other to show whose ads could be bigger and snazzier. Not coincidentally, as well, the panjandrums at *Billboard* might have felt more disposed to return the favor when giving play to those companies' new records, in its "Hot Pop Spotlights" column, in which the magazine listed predictions for which new records would go Top Twenty or Top Sixty.

Gordy, of course, knew how to play the game. For a guy who never read a book until he was in his 40s, he could be seen most every day with his nose buried in *Billboard,* which had been his personal bible since back in his songwriting days. Dipping deep into the Motown till from the start, he had gained pivotal attention for the Miracles, Mary Wells, and the Marvelettes; now, in the spring of '64, came a new round of Motown ads, just in time for the big Supremes push.

A few weeks later, in the July 4 issue, *Billboard* finally took notice of the Supremes. In Spotlights, "Where Did Our Love Go" was judged a

Top Twenty candidate, with this bit of *Billboard*-ese explaining the selection:

> Music to hand-clap and foot-stomp to. Plenty of jump in this one. Beat is unbeatable and lead is in a true rockin' blues groove.

In the industry, a sentence like that—despite being written in semi-English—was worth a few thousand florid words, not to mention many thousands of advertising dollars. While most of the magazine's record and album reviews were nearly identical in language, it wasn't the prose but the mere fact they were *there* that got the records' distributors moving. Only a week later, in the July 11 issue, "Where Did Our Love Go" had already broken into the Hot 100, at No. 77; on July 18, it was No. 38; on July 25, No. 18; on August 1, No. 5; on August 8 and 15, No. 2. Then, in the August 22 issue, it rested at No. 1 on both the pop and R&B charts. It would stay there for two weeks, and be in the Top Five for another three.

Being far removed from the power centers of the industry, Ross, Wilson, and Ballard were, at first, unaware of the maelstrom.

"We knew it was out," Mary recalled, "but we weren't sufficiently interested in the business side of music to be reading *Billboard* or *Cashbox*, and without a radio on the bus we had no idea who had a hit."

Nor did Clark for a while. At the start of the tour the Supremes had pretty much the same status as on the Motortown Revues: They were among the "others" on the promotional fliers and programs, usually opening shows with "Where Did Our Love Go," or older material better known to audiences such as "Buttered Popcorn," to the same kind of lukewarm applause. This, even though they'd had a recent hit, or "semi-hit," in "Lovelight"; other acts such as teen idol-wannabe Bobby Sherman and the Brit group the Zombies couldn't boast even that. But it wasn't current hits that determined the pecking order on a Clark tour; it was name recognition. And, here the Supremes were eclipsed by everyone on the tour, including up-marquee acts like Gene Pitney, the Shirelles, the Drifters, the Crystals, the Dixie Cups, Major Lance, Bobby Freeman, Lou Christie, the Jelly Beans, and Brenda Holloway, as well as dimming bulbs like Johnny Tillotson, Mike Clifford, and Clark cronies Freddie Cannon and Dee Dee Sharp.

Still, perhaps not all the Supremes were insentient naïfs. One tour-mate, the Crystals' Barbara Alston, was so struck by Diane's ego-tripping that, later, when history unfolded to Ross's advantage, Alston assumed Ross knew it would go down just that way:

> I remember when they came on. We didn't know who they were but we'd heard their record and loved it, and we were excited they'd be on the tour. We liked them immediately—Mary and Flo, I mean. Because Diana just made herself unavailable to everybody. They were nobodies, and Diana was, well, strange looking, skinny with those pop-eyes. But Miss Diva thought she was somebody. She would recite over and over, like a mantra, "I'm gonna be like Lena Horne and Eartha Kitt, I'm gonna be in TV and movies." We'd all look at her like, "That girl is crazy."
>
> But I know now that she wasn't crazy. She just knew the plan that Berry Gordy was building around her. That had all been planned out. You don't brag on yourself like that unless you know someone's got your back. Why else was she sitting up there in front with Dick Clark? She never mingled with us peons in the back. It was like she was Dick's best friend. There had to be a lot of things going on behind the scenes that only she and Berry Gordy knew.

To be fair, another Crystal, Dee Dee Kennibrew, disputes Alston. "Diana was *not* difficult, not to me," she says firmly. "She thought a lot of herself, which she should have. She carried herself in a certain way and a lot of people think that means you think you're better than everybody. But that's from people who let jealousy get in the way. She could have walked around like Queen Elizabeth with a tiara on her head for all I cared, because it wouldn't have affected me. I was focused only on doing my own thing.

"And I *know* Diana didn't only sit with Dick. I have pictures of her sitting next to Lou Christie, falling asleep on his shoulder. Most of the time, Dick sat next to Ed McAdam, his tour manager. So you see how the memory can play tricks based on what happened to people much later, and what you want to believe."

Alston also believed that Flo herself could read what was just then being written on the proverbial wall:

> I became very close with Florence on the tour. She sat with me, we roomed together. I loved Flo, and I don't think she felt many people did. Not at Motown, not within her own group.

One thing that really upset her was that she felt she was being pushed back, that the Supremes were her group, she started it, and now Berry Gordy was making it Diana's.

She was definitely aware of what would happen. She knew things were going on between Diana and Berry, and that they were going to break up the group once it hit really big so that Diana could be a huger star. Florence knew she wouldn't be there for long.

She told me, "Barbara, please don't tell anyone about this. I'm not supposed to know any of this is happening." She felt they'd get rid of her in a second if she made trouble, so she kept it inside, all bottled up.

Mary was different. Mary may have known what was happening in the shadows—but she may not have *wanted* to know. She wanted to believe that Berry was looking out for all of them, so she just went along like a good little girl and didn't rock the boat.

But, listen, how hard was it to see what was gonna happen down the road? I mean, Diana didn't even try to hide it. She would say, right in front of Flo and Mary, "You know, girls, we're going to be called Diana Ross and the Supremes." That was the first part of the plan, right?

Whatever the subterranean machinations were, if the Supremes figured they'd stepped up in class with this tour, one glance in the direction of either of the two buses carrying the troupe no doubt disabused them of the notion. If anything, conditions were *worse* than on the Motortown Revue. The vehicles looked and smelled like garbage trucks, with litter everywhere, half-eaten food and Styrofoam cups lying in pools of unidentifiable ooze, and the strong odor of urine making it evident that more than one aboard had used the bus as a portable toilet; every now and then, Clark recalled, the driver would call out, "Whoever is pissing in the back of the bus, please stop," and Clark would add, "If you gotta go, please piss out the window." It's a wonder that Ernestine Ross didn't pull Diane off the bus and take her back home in a Greyhound the first day they arrived.

Moreover, whereas Gordy had a double standard about tawdry activity on his tours, Clark's only standard was pretty much anything goes. Booze flowed like water, with Clark himself footing the bill for forays to liquor stores. "We'd drink ourselves into a stupor by the middle of the night, riding along through some godforsaken Midwestern cornfield," he admitted. Even the driver, he said, would get sloshed, and if he couldn't focus on the white stripes of the road, one of the performers would take the wheel. Nor did Clark, or the putative chaperones, seem to care who was doing what to whom in the back seat. Just surviving the tour seemed to be the objective.

The Caravan's venues were a world removed from the Apollo or Howard Theaters; usually they were small school auditoriums, roller rinks, cheesy ballrooms, racetracks, or county fair grounds. In the South, the black entertainers on board faced redneck resistance at eateries and public bathrooms, and Clark saw to it that they were not hung out to dry by the majority of whites; by his decree, no one ate unless everyone was served, and often his *éclat* alone was enough to bend the Jim Crow laws. Sometimes, though, Clark could be seen getting in the face of a redneck who wouldn't bend, threatening to put him out of business. On one occasion, a claque of racists at a gas station came at the bus brandishing ax handles and clubs. In the nick of time, two highway patrol cars showed up and escorted the riders away.

"The Zombies couldn't believe what they were seeing," Alston recalls of the Brit group. "They were, like, 'This is America?'"

For the Supremes, of course, the sights and sounds of racism were hardly new, and they were able to keep their focus on their now-more-important act. In an echo of Stevie Wonder and his harmonica, they would practice their harmonies late into the night while everyone tried to get a few minutes of shuteye. Clark, too tactful to identify them as the possible culprits, told of his irritation in his memoir, saying, "Some dummies stayed up all night to sing their act over and over," times that he might not have thought Ross was so "special."

A tour not being a tour without a blowup between Diane and another woman singer, she traded angry words with Brenda Holloway and, nearly, punches with her newest foil, the youngest and most combative of the Crystals, Dolores "Lala" Brooks. Only 16 at the time, Brooks developed the same instant dislike for Ross as did Alston:

> Oh, she was such a pain in the ass. There was a sweet side to her that I could see, but because of Berry Gordy, he made her think she was superior to everybody—better than Mary and Florence, too, which was a terrible thing to do to them.
>
> You could see there'd be problems there once they got very popular. Mary and Florence would stay humble, but Diana was

a big showoff right from the start. I remember she'd call Berry, and he'd inform her of where their record was on the charts. And she'd sashay onto the bus and say to Mary and Florence, but loud enough for everybody to hear, "Oh, guess what? It's gonna be number so-and-so." Or, "Guess what? We're gonna be on *Ed Sullivan*." It was great for them, she had a right to be excited, we all were excited for them. But it was like she wasn't really happy until she knew she had rubbed our noses in it.

Brooks couldn't contain herself when after a show Diane made a crack about the Crystals' shoes, which, since that group had been on tour longer, were in less than pristine condition. Lala called her a smart-ass and soon fists were again clenched.

"She may have thought I was just a kid and she could cut me down, but I'm from Brooklyn. I wasn't about to back down. But then Florence got between us, and on the bus both Florence and Diana's mother came over to me, apologizing for Diana. I told them, 'She really pisses me off,' and they said, 'We know. She pisses us off, too. For everybody's sake, just cope with it.'"

The detente got only as far as the first chance Diane had to humiliate Brooks again. That happened after Bobby Freeman, apparently paying no mind to the term "jailbait," began cozying up to Lala. "It was nothing, he was just being friendly. But Diana saw it and she suddenly was sweet-talking Bobby, just to get my goat. So we got into it again and that's when Dick Clark separated us and put us on different buses, which is what Diana wanted."

Concludes Brooks:

That was Diana Ross to a T. I always thought she wasn't the greatest singer, but you have to give her credit for being manipulative. She didn't care who she stepped on or over. She was building herself into a product, a "look," marketing herself with the skinny look when it wasn't yet fashionable, the big eyes, the fashionable gowns, and great producers covering her faults as a singer.

For myself, their songs weren't that much. As a black woman, I didn't *feel* them. The Crystals' records had a lot more soul; the music carried us, not the image of the lead singer. And if I wanted to hear music, I'd sooner run out and buy a record by ['60s R&B singer] Baby Washington. But not many people have heard of Baby Washington, or Lala Brooks. Everybody on the planet has heard of Diana Ross. That took a whole lot of manipulation, to get there.

Cee

When the week of August 22 began, *Billboard*'s Hot 100 had a new leader. Having replaced the previous week's No. 1, Dean Martin's "Everybody Loves Somebody," the Supremes' "Where Did Our Love Go" was now king of the hot-wax mountain after a wild, month-long ride up the incline—and perhaps as a conditioned reflex among black record-buyers because of the soul dues the Supremes had paid, it achieved the distinctive honor of holding down the No. 1 slots concurrently on the pop and R&B charts, the ultimate crossover hit.

With the hottest act in the land on his bus, Clark had already moved the girls up both in salary—to $800—and on stage. By the climactic week, the formerly "no-hit Supremes" whom he had to be begged to take on the tour were top-billed in the programs and had gone from worst to first, now closing the show as the headline act. As soon as Diane would coo "Baby, baby," audiences began to whoop and holler, dancing through a sped-up, sometimes unrecognizable facsimile of the song to the clunky accompaniment of Clark's weary house band. Far cry from HDH's layered symphony or not, the crowds both black and white were in the palms of the Supremes' hands. In just a few weeks, the days of polite applause were gone forever.

The song would hang in the penthouse for two weeks and on the pop chart for twelve weeks—one week longer than the late summer's other big mover, "A Hard Day's Night." By the time it had fallen off the summit, displaced by the Animals' "House of the Rising Sun," the Supremes were also gone, from the tour, summoned home while in Oklahoma City and ferried back by plane, their way paid by Motown—perhaps the clearest signal of all that the days of the Supremes paying their own way on Greyhound treks to and from Detroit were over.

Gordy, having gotten what he wanted from the Clark excursion, needed to get the Supremes on other roads before they could have any time to cool off. Tracking their ascension to No. 1, in early August he had pressed and released the second Supremes album, mandatorily titled *Where Did Our Love Go*, which included their last three singles and B-sides and two fresh HDH productions cut early in the summer, "Baby Love" and "Come See About Me."

(Some clarification: The dates when many Supremes—and other Motown—songs were recorded are mysteries. Although required by the American Federation of Musicians to file with the Detroit local contracts listing the musicians and their union scale ($61 per session as of 1964), Gordy and Mickey Stevenson rarely did this promptly, as Gordy paid his house band more as salaried employees, and more still out of pocket on an informal basis when he cared to. The "Where Did Our Love Go" session—at which HDH also apparently cut the rhythm track for what would be Martha and the Vandellas' "Dancing in the Street"—is postdated July 15, 1964; "Baby Love" and "Come See About Me" were actually cut at the same session, according to the Hollands and an *ex post facto* session sheet dated, absurdly, March 10, 1965. On some of these sheets, some musicians who hadn't played were listed, either out of faulty memory or intentionally by Gordy and Stevenson to secure a few extra bucks for favored cats, and some who had played were left out, such as vibist/tambourine man Jack Ashford, who played a tangy vibe line on "Where Did Our Love Go" but is missing from the behindhand session contract. Remarkably, some contracts went unfiled until even the 1980s, when royalties accrued from songs used in the soundtrack of the highly successful movie *The Big Chill*.

Session sheets allegedly derived from in-house ledgers and such for latter-day album compilations are also unreliable, having been based mainly on guesswork, as Gordy and the producers generally did not preserve such minutiae. Thus on the Supremes's box-set, producer Harry Weinger, faced with the impossible task of adumbrating exact recording dates, ran with some problematic documentation, one result of which was that the liner notes insist that "Baby Love" and "Come See About Me" were cut at different sessions: August 13 and July 13, respectively. The problem being that the Supremes were on the Dick Clark tour on those days.)

The two new entries on the *Where* album were there because Gordy and Ales had chosen them as the follow-ups to "Where Did Our Love Go," and their inclusion would bring them to the public before they were issued as singles. And they'd need that sort of boost, having the unenviable mission of perpetuating the Supremes' newfound dynamism without merely replicating it, and milking the formula, before it—and the group—ran dry.

"Basically what we were trying to do was to keep them in the same ballpark," Eddie Holland puts it. "It stands to reason that you keep the same elements that worked before. You'd be stupid to divert from what worked so well; that's just part of marketing. That's what people like. But anybody's crazy who says that 'Baby Love' is a copycat song."

HDH would surely hear that critique enough through the years, given that elements such as the beat, the "Baby, baby" refrains, and the percussive effects right down to the quarter-note board-stomping on the intro were skimmed from "Where Did Our Love Go." But they were hardly identical. HDH could be ingenious in their variations on a theme. The song began with a round of brilliant triplets by veteran piano man Earl Van Dyke, another jazz master Gordy and Stevenson had imported from the Paradise Valley clubs. His riffs swirled brightly through the spatial image of the song, beginning with an interplay of piano, hand-clapping, and a bass-cymbal figure throb and then coming to a dead stop accentuated by a hard bang of the drum, preceding the entry of the board-stomping and Ross's newest vocal melodrama of burning and yearning—"Baby love, oh baby love, I need you, oh how I need you," she began, in the next instant complaining that "all you do is treat me bad, break my heart and leave me sad."

While the chord structure aped "Where," HDH got considerably looser and funkier with the rhythm. Van Dyke's riffs quickened as the second chorus swelled with horns and guitars, and James Jamerson's delirious bass licks thumped and pumped in a private concerto with Jack Ashford's bell-clear vibes. Riding above the tide, Ross again spread the gossamer, totally believable as the heart-cleaved inamorata, and Wilson and Ballard blended tightly but dreamily, echoing their mainly two-word iteration into the deep, dewy background.

Still, as with "Where Did Our Love Go," the first mix Gordy heard was lacking. As Gordy recalled, "I liked it but told Eddie it didn't have enough life and the opening wasn't catchy enough." The first problem was resolved by simply speeding up the tape a notch. The second was trickier. Having been floored by Diane's way of weaving that knee-buckling "*oooooh*" in "Where Did Our Love Go," HDH called her in to record an even sexier rendering of that syllable as the first verbal sound in "Baby Love," one that she deftly drew out to a pre–Donna Summer, pseudo-orgasmic moan, three beats in duration—"*oooooh-oooooh-oooooh*." It surely moved Gordy. "Brilliance," he said of the remix.

"Baby Love" and, in turn, "Come See About Me" had something "Where Did Our Love Go" did not—a fast track to run on. By the time "Baby Love" was rushed out on September 17, backed with the HDH song "Ask Any Girl," "Where Did Our Love Go" was still being hummed far and wide. The album bearing that title, containing "Baby Love," had gone to No. 2 on the pop album chart and No. 1 on the R&B album list; by far Motown's best-selling album up to that time, it stayed on the charts for over a year and by some accounts sold nearly 1 million copies.

Thus cushioned, "Baby Love" needed no extra push to receive a *Billboard* benediction. In the September 26 issue, the front page carried a photo of the Supremes—an honor (again, paid for by the respective record companies) given each week to an act considered to be the most popular of the moment—captioned in the paper's usual breathless prose, "THE SUPREMES, Motown Records' sensational singing group, are veterans of many Billboard Hot 100 charts. They are currently riding high with 'Where Did Our Love Go?' Their new album (by the same name) and new single, 'Baby Love,' will be released this week."

Inside, on the Spotlights page was a "Baby Love" rave that read: "A smash follow-up to their 'Where Did Our Love Go' click. The swinging harmony style keeps it rolling all the way through."

By Halloween, "Baby Love" was sitting at the top of the Hot 100, where it stayed for four weeks.

The autumn of '64 and winter of '65 stretched into an endless Supremes blurb. They made, for the first time, the pages of the teen-magazine press, their picture slapped on the cover of the February issue of *Teen Screen* alongside those of the Beach Boys, Righteous Brothers, and Manfred Mann ("Doo Wah Diddy"), intermingled with headlines like "Why the Beatles Can't Get Married!" and "World's Largest Color Pinup of Manfred Mann (& His Men)!"

The story on the Supremes cast them as a rare, prudish exception in the emerging rock swarm. Headlined "The Supremes Ask: What's Happened to Show Business," it was an inane but valuable PR move, calling them "the hottest female singing group in the nation" and throwing them huzzahs for how they managed to "keep themselves so fresh, neat, and ladylike while performing." Pronouncing himself as "immediately impressed" with them, the author quoted their prime rule in matters of appearance, "No tight dresses for us," noting with approval that "[t]he girls went on to say they felt that a contemporary performer did not have to utilize sex as a means of putting across a musical number. A female performer can look just as alluring when she's dressed as a young lady."

"We believe that this is an important part of a performer's image," Ross said. "Fans expect their idol to be a symbol. This loss of glamour, and of that certain air of mystery, has resulted in a loss of respect for many recording artists. The public has become blasé after seeing too many of their favorites in sloppy attire."

A couple of photos ran with the story, of the girls "checking each other's makeup" and posing with the Crystals during the Clark tour—the latter with the soon-to-be ironic caption, "'Big talent, but no big heads' would seem to be the motto for the Supremes."

Needing to keep the hit streak going, Gordy was riding the tail of "Baby Love" before it even reached the top of the pop and R&B charts. Four days before it got there, he put out "Come See About Me," for which HDH applied a harder, more direct tone heard from the outset with a fierce drum intro and carried by a still needy but defiant lead vocal. Diane, addressing the boy she had given up her friends for, only to see him leave, demanded that he'd better "hurry, hurry" back to her—though she couldn't help but reassure him that "no matter what you do or say, I'm gonna love you anyway." Mary and Flo, allowed to breathe a little more, got close to shouting their parts, further extending the amped-up emotion of the tune.

HDH had come to apply their "elements"—the hand-clapping, the resonant vibes, the clanging guitars—with such cohesion that the repetitive hooks of "Come See About Me" pounded out a lush, trance-inducing rhythm made for Ross's flan-light, chimerical vocals. For her, Eddie Holland was now writing more syntactically challenged lyrics; here, he had her sing of her tears not washing away the fear "that you're never ever gonna return to ease the fire that within me burns."

Eddie believed then, as he does now, that "Come See About Me" was miles better than "Baby Love," and he wanted it out as a single first. "There were arguments about that with Berry," he says. But the only reason it got out as quickly as it did is that a cover of the song by one Nella Dobbs was on the chart and climbing. When the real item came out, with "(You're Gone but) Always in My Heart" on the flip, it left Nella Dobbs in the dust on the way to landing in the No. 1 spot on the pop and R&B charts just before Christmas. It then fell to No. 2 behind the Beatles' "I Feel Fine" for three weeks—and moved *back* to No. 1 the week of January 16, 1965.

Gordy, not waiting for any moss to grow under their high heels, had the Supremes constantly in the public eye. An exhausting round of TV and stage appearances was planned, allowing almost no idle time. But Gordy would not send them on these long roads without making a few serious changes to ensure that they would come across as princesses, no longer urchins standing onstage in their makeshift dresses sewn by hand on Ernestine Ross's Singer sewing machine.

While the Supremes were more refined than the other wilder, gyrating girl-groups—sometimes to the discontent of audiences at some hard-core venues like the Apollo—their gawky movements and overall rube-like stage presence were a problem for Gordy. Now that they'd be playing some very high-visibility locales, which Gordy was working to extend to ritzy supper clubs and glitzy Las Vegas hotels, a makeover was called for. Just such an upper crusting of all Motown acts had in fact become a pet project of Gwen and Anna Gordy. Both of those very sophisticated ladies were habitués at posh, high-society affairs—for Gwen this was a way of life, having attended a finishing school as a young woman—and they were far more comfortable at a fashion show with a string quartet than at an ear-splitting, hip-grinding concert.

At first, their younger, unrefined brother regarded sending his rip-snorting performers to finishing school as a preposterous idea, antithetical to the barely controlled passion required of R&B. But then Berry, as he could afford the finer things in life, turned into a dilettante, lavishing his home with exorbitantly priced paintings by artists he'd never heard of—as well as (to the cringing astonishment of all who saw it) a floor-to-ceiling oil that he commissioned with himself posed in the image of Napoleon Bonaparte, one hand tucked into the lapel of a gilded waistcoat with big brass buttons. Indeed, he now fancied himself an arbiter of all that was tony and well-bred. It was Gordy who had blown his stack seeing a gum-chewing Marvelette on stage, and who bristled about anyone in his employ acting in a less than "high-class" manner (exclusive of his own gambling and philandering)—while the lower class that actually made him his money were charged for every expense, no matter how picayune.

Now that the Supremes had graduated to a rank in a higher order, Gordy needed them to act as such. He committed to the charm school concept—at first, just for his "girls." But that was inviting trouble.

How would it look if the Supremes were the only girl-group being given special treatment in grooming and style? Would it mean the rest would assume they were being consigned to the trash heap, good for filling seats in turbid R&B clubs but kept from the white stage? For now, anyway, even if Gordy was contemplating turning Motown into a platform mainly for the Supremes—and, eventually, Diane Ross—he knew that the consequences of such unveiled favoritism might rip the fabled Motown unity to shreds, before he was ready to risk it.

Thus, during the late summer and early fall of '64, Gordy hired a Chantilly-delicate, black former professional model, Maxine Powell, who as a young woman had attended the Detroit charm school where Gwen Gordy had also matriculated, and put her in charge of the new, corporate-sounding Artists Development division. Clearing space in a Motown-owned house across West Grand Boulevard, Powell began optional classes in etiquette and grooming that at first attracted few takers—until the Supremes were seen flitting in and out almost every day that they weren't on the road, for six solid months. Soon, the Vandellas, the Marvelettes, Brenda Holloway, and new arrivals like Kim Weston were receiving tutelage in the fine points of acting like a lady.

For the Supremes, who already regarded themselves as polished and fashionable, the classes, with their attendance mandated by Gordy, were laughable—a silly "game," as Wilson recalled. If, for example, "we were eating chicken and one of us picked up a piece with her fingers, the other two would cackle and say, 'Remember what Mrs. Powell said.'" Without a pause, the perpetrator would laugh and simply go on eating with her fingers. How could advice like that *not* be risible when Powell would tell them, say, how to handle fine china or how to get in a car like a lady (that is, without rear-end protrusion)—and few except the Gordys and their cronies owned either fine china or a car?

Powell did have a tangible effect on the Supremes' body language. Post-'64, they would smile a bit less, hold their nostrils in a pinched manner to look more haughty, and keep their bodies taut, tall, and erect. Diane, who needed the most work, "was taught not to 'soul,'" Powell once remarked, using a term of the era roughly equivalent to "styling," to describe Ross's tenacious habit of contorting her face and popping her eyeballs. "I told her that in first-class places like the Copa, no one's gonna pay good money to watch someone make faces."

The choice of the Copa—the oft-used short-form version of "Copacabana," the famed New York nightclub—as the Supremes' polar star was no accident. Gordy meant to drum the name into the girls' conscious and subconscious minds, as the ultimate meed waiting at the end of the rainbow. They were indoctrinated, while walking in front of Powell's mirrors with books on their heads, to "*Think Copa*," and that wouldn't change even if they were singing before winos at the Twenty Grand or the Roostertail.

To Mary and Flo, all this high-minded doggerel was a waste of time. Years later, Wilson had come to see the experience through an even harsher looking glass. Artists' development, she said, was "the Motown Myth," a fable that had grown out of the promotional piffle whereby "Berry took a bunch of ghetto kids with no class, no style, and no manners, put them through hours of grueling training . . . and then—voila—stars rolled out of Hitsville like cars off an assembly line. . . . Not only is this view incorrect, it's insulting."

"The truth is that Berry never signed anyone to Motown who needed to be 'remade.' . . . It's always bothered me that some people have assumed that by accepting what some consider 'white' values, we sold out. It's just not true."

Ross, too, resented the implication of Gordy as their shaman; with some pique, she wrote in *Secrets of a Sparrow* that beyond Gordy choosing their songs and contributing to "our direction," she gave him no credit for "the sophisticated elegance that we embodied. Or for the self-esteem, morals, and standards that we had. That's who we already were. Berry Gordy did not have to 'create' young ladies from ghetto teens, like some inner-city Eliza Doolittles. We were already ladies who had been brought up right." As proof of this, she offered the fact that Gordy took to "forcing" the other Motown women to "live up" to the Supremes' standards.

"We definitely started it," she said. "Our attitudes and our looks were organic to us, and Berry was smart enough to see that and to work with what was already there."

Back then, Gordy's staging of "My Fair Ladies" was amusing, but only to a point—the one at which Wilson and Ballard saw that the whole program was primarily intended for Diane Ross. This crude reality became apparent when Gordy quietly sent Diane, solo, to an even more tony pinkie-in-the-air academy, the John Roberts Powers School for Social Graces. There, deeper modifications were made. As recounted by Nelson George in *Where Did Our Love Go*, she was ordered to lose the low-rent vestiges of her "Brewster self," the first one being the "sickeningly sweet" Jungle Gardenia perfume she'd been wearing, by the bucketload—"It was said at Powers that if Diana walked in a building five minutes before you, you'd know it; her perfume would still be hanging in the air." Next to go were her "Minnie Mouse false eyelashes," her "three-inch blood-red false nails," and the irritating "giddy laughter" that "bubbled out of her whenever she talked of the places she'd been or the famous people she was meeting."

The Ross Rule was to make her not just glamorous but *warm* in a fine-spun way, as enticing and approachable (at least in theory) as she sounded on record—while at the same time as haughtily *unapproachable* in the real world as other crown princesses of pop like Barbra Streisand or Diahann Carroll. But all this did for the other two Supremes was to make Ross seem even colder and more calculating than before. Once more, Diane felt the sting of their discontent—much more so from Flo, since Mary's ire usually subsided quickly, capsized by the notion that, powerless as she was, she could be disappeared in a hurry, replaced without a beat.

Flo was less mollified by such unspoken extortion, according to the cousin in whom she regularly confided.

RAY GIBSON: Let me tell you something about my cousin. She never gave a damn about fame. That's not why she started singing. I can tell you that Florence never once told me, "Raymond, I'm gonna be rich and famous!" But she told me all the time, "Raymond, I'm gonna sing tonight!" And then they took that away from her. They wouldn't let her sing anything but "Baby, baby" in the background. The minute they did that, despite all the hits they were having, she really had no great attachment for the group.

Again, it had nothing to do with Diane being the star. Because when they started there was no star; it was just the three of them, together. And they were still making the same money, that never changed; they split the money, so it wasn't like Florence was unhappy with the money, especially when it started to really roll in. It was just that the whole feel was different. It was Berry's group now, not theirs. It was his vehicle to turn Diane into a star. That's all it was. Florence could never get her head around that.

If you look at Florence in the old films, that was not a happy woman. I knew she wasn't. We would still talk all the time. She would come off the road, which she hated because she hated to fly; it scared her to death. She loved being back home. And because she'd have all this pent-up frustration about not being allowed to sing, she'd come over and let it all out to me. She'd say she had no allies, that Berry would tell her, "You're all gonna be millionaires!"—that was supposed to fix everything. And Mary was . . . Florence would say, "Mary would never say no to Diane." So no matter what Florence thought, it didn't matter. Her attitude was, Why is it happening like this?

She tried to play the good soldier, she gave it a shot. Because she knew what was riding on it. She was making money, she was still singing. She didn't want to be the cause of this big hit-making machine breaking up. But no one at Motown ever took any time to talk to her, ease her mind. I'll tell you this, and I absolutely believe it. If Berry had just—one time even— sat down with her and said, "Florence, I just want to tell you how much I appreciate you and what you've done for the company," or, "If Diane goes solo, let's talk about what we can do." Or, "Someday you'll have a solo career, too"—anything like that, even if he didn't mean it, and you would have seen a very different Florence in those videos. But he never did. To Berry, Florence really didn't exist as a person, she was baggage. Excess baggage.

It was so sad to me. I loved her so much, and she was part of the biggest act in the world. I was ecstatic for her. I'd tell everyone, "My cousin is Florence Ballard of the Supremes!" And sometimes she'd be ecstatic, too, like she'd call me from the road and gush, "Raymond, guess what—we're gonna sing for the Queen tonight!" She'd sound like a little girl. But then reality would sink in, and she'd be depressed again. It was always like Florence was trying to climb out of a hole. Sometimes she would, but then she'd wind up falling back in again.

Diane, as she had before, felt transitory guilt about what her ascension was doing to Flo. However, she would usually construe it as an overreaction on Flo's part, or even a pathological defect. As Nelson George wrote, "With tears in her eyes, [Diane] told her instructors how paranoid Flo could be." Yet Ross apparently made little effort to distinguish between paranoia and Flo's pride being ripped apart. All Diane could see was a Flo who was teeming with "resentment about the time and money Motown was spending on Diane, and it upset [Ross]."

What upset her the most, however, was that Flo wasn't getting in line with the program.

Gordy reacted to the embryonic tensions between the girls as he always did—by covering them in yards of fabric. He gave Powell a generous budget to buy the Supremes a walk-in closet of new dresses for their upcoming appearances, everything from what have been lovingly described as "orange sherbet-colored cocktail dresses," "orange and beige balloon-shaped cocktail dresses," and "curve-hugging mermaid-shaped gowns" to "pert-looking frocks with box pleats and genteelly-scooped necklines." The gowns could weight down a mule at up to thirty-five pounds, and each would be individually sequined, beaded, flanged, and otherwise embellished by, as Diane joked, "little old ladies who went blind" staring into that psychedelic storm of colors.

It's doubtful Powell ever had in mind a sense of "autonomous" style for the black performers of Motown. In dressing the Supremes—always Job One—the grand objective was to prep them for audiences who were themselves awash in pearls, wing-tips, and Martinis. Her only cues were to approximate the hip fashion plates of the day, doyennes such as Jackie Kennedy or Gloria Vanderbilt, thus explaining why in that newspaper photo of them mincing through the Brewster project they were so tastefully appointed in their pill-box hats and elbow-length white gloves. At the time, as well, thin was not yet in; it would be Ross who would help make it so, down the line a bit. Curves were in. Playing to type, Powell inflated the Supremes with padded bras and hip pads—neither of which Flo had any need for, but donned anyway, frequently complaining that she was being made to look fat. That led her to diet, another thing she hated, further souring her growing irascibility.

Diane and Mary, meanwhile, were delighted to suddenly be given "womanly" figures for public appearances. Happily, Wilson recalled, "Diane added hip pads, and I padded my backside." When the new look padded Mary's ego a bit too much, she was deflated, literally; one day, when Lamont Dozier watched her wiggling around Hitsville, he found a knitting needle, snuck up behind her, and strategically inserted it. Not feeling a thing, she went on wiggling, unaware that the needle was appended to her embossed derriere.

The reality of the times was that there *was* no paradigm of fashion available to African-American women. (Black men, too, were mired in a one-white-size-fits-all cultural maw; just as black women believed they had to wear straight-haired wigs, men such as David Ruffin—for all the barbed-wire blackness of his songs—put off going "natural" and kept straightening their kinky hair with gobs of Pomade, a carryover of the black stagemanship of the '50s.) Many black entertainers, not knowing they were on the cusp of heavy social changes, borrowed liberally from proven and accepted cultural canons.

At the same time, few black girl-groups saw it fitting of the genre to imitate the most posh of the sophisticated white ladies. Mary Wilson can easily remember that "in those days rock 'n' roll singers were not really glamorous. We were totally into glamour and we did it all ourselves."

As guilty of hyperbole as Wilson is about the last part, there's no way of overstating just how radical the Supremes' approach was in 1964. Four decades thereafter, the Rock and Roll Hall of Fame and Museum in Cleveland went as far as to hold a retrospective exhibit of a dozen or so of the Supremes' spangliest outfits. Museum curator Howard Kaplan explained to the *New York Times* in 2002 why this mattered to rock's legacy. "Before the Supremes," he said, "the [girl-group] look was smart and simple, like the Shirelles; sassy and sexy like the Ronettes; or tomboyish and provocative like the Shangri-Las. But no one had ever done cocktail classy or set out to utilize certain visual signifiers that made them palatable to a white audience."

Moreover, this perceived audacity was ignited despite the fact that, mere months before the Civil Rights Act was written into law, more than a few record companies refused to put black performers' faces on album covers and 45-rpm record jackets. Little wonder the cosmetics industry didn't give much, if any, thought to women of color, even those who became wealthy. Even when the Supremes did, they had to go on buying their wigs at the beauty parlors on John R Street, the only places they were available—even as Maxine Powell was shelling out Gordy's money for Schiaparelli gowns at Hudson's department store (where of course Ross had waited tables only a few years before) or commissioning originals from designer Bob Mackie and his apprentice Michael Travis.

It was a bold play, and it would work. For the first time in the rock era, African-American girls and women would form a bond with an African-American group that was challenging the primacy of the biggest white groups. Here, one music critic would write, were the aptly named Supremes, "looking affluent, living the dream, looking impeccable and flawless to a fault." No one in this new generation had ever seen *white* stars portray the dream any better. That a trio of black women got there first left an impact that wouldn't stop, long after the music had ended.

They still had their shortcomings. No one could accuse them of being a distaff Temptations on stage, something that was all too obvious at the first show they did in the fall, a ten-day engagement at the Brooklyn Fox Theater from September 12 to 21, hosted by famous, fedora-wearing New York deejay Murray the K. Also on the bill were heavies like the British diva Dusty Springfield, Jay and the Americans, the Shangri-Las, the Ronettes—and, as it happened, the Temptations. Now produced by Smokey Robinson, they had finally rung up a Top Twenty (and No. 1 R&B) hit, "The Way You Do the Things You Do." Realizing the mesmerizing soul grit of David Ruffin, Smokey put him on lead for the follow-up, "My Girl," which Smokey wrote during the Tempts' Christmas gig at the Apollo Theater; by February, it would sit at No. 1 pop and R&B and endure as arguably one of the Top Five songs of the rock era.

At the Fox their repertoire of, by turns, flat-out wild and cleverly intricate steps only underscored the lack of same by the Supremes, who, to begin with, had no chance with the crowd in the backyard of the Ronettes, considering that their stage act was essentially a slightly toned-down pole dance.

Not that Gordy would ever have wanted the Supremes to try something like that; it would be out of their element and conflict with his vision. Still, their gawky hop-step cuteness just would not do. To remedy the situation, Gordy, early in 1965, would bring aboard a couple of veteran showmen to work with the Supremes when they arrived back home. That would be a while. After the Fox shows, they were off on their long road, a *very* long road, which would next deposit them 10,000 miles across the Atlantic Ocean—this time in the Beatles' backyard, London.

That road, Diane had resolved, would not be treaded unless one other small yet critical alteration was made, not to the group's image as a whole but to *hers* as a glamour-puss. Obediently, Gordy in early September instructed his promotion and publicity people that, from here on, the super-nova of the Supremes was to be identified in all Motown literature by the name she always swore was on her birth certificate and so much better reflected who and what she was.

Officially, in the periscope of popular culture, she was now *Diana* Ross.

twelve

THE
TWO
MOTOWNS

The timing of the Supremes' rising made the trip to England necessary and inevitable. Gordy had first seen the marketing value of a "Reverse Invasion" when the Beatles fawned on Mary Wells, calling her their "sweetheart" and favorite female American singer, and "invited" her to come to their country and tour with them. In mid-'64, in the wake of "My Guy's" worldwide success—including reaching No. 5 on the Brit chart—she did just that, opening for them at several shows and garnering rave notices in the rabid English music press. Further turning the spigot, Wells cut an album, *Love Songs to the Beatles*, that partly consisted of songs the Fab Four had written for her.

When Wells left Motown, she derailed plans that had been made for a second British tour scheduled for early October. But then "Where Did Our Love Go," released in the U.K. in September, caught fire. In fact, the record emerged as a cause célèbre in a "revolution" being fought over what records could be played on the government-run stations on the BBC. For years, in the guise of protectionism, these stations shafted "foreign" records, an injunction that seemed especially rigid— and cruel to discerning music lovers—when it came to records by black American artists, who of course had stirred the early work of the top Brit acts. In response, "pirate" stations began popping up offshore, broadcasting the "good stuff," with an early favorite being the Supremes' smash. When listeners began tuning out the BBC shows, the policy began to melt; now played equally by the pirates and the big stations, "Where Did Our Love Go" shot up the chart.

Switching the Supremes for Wells without missing a beat, Gordy also arranged a quickie album to drop some British chamomile into the Supremes' musical palate. He had them cover a number of Invasion hits by groups like the Animals, Gerry and the Pacemakers, Dave Clark Five, Peter and Gordon, and the Beatles. The twist was that they also did two Motown hits that had been covered by the Brits, "Do You Love Me" and "You've Really Got a Hold on Me"—a roundabout irony if ever there was one (and probably an inside joke on Brian Epstein, who, when his Beatles took three Motown songs for one of their early albums, had forced Gordy to accept a lower royalty than usual; now, he would piggyback off British songs to pump royalties on his own company's songs). Gordy produced the tracks himself and farmed them out to his L.A. producers Hal Davis and Marc Gordon to finish. But the album, *A Bit of Liverpool,* was a jolly old mess reeking of self-conscious preening, right down to the cover shot of the girls perched on the stoop of a trolley car clad in skin-tight Beatle-style "suits" while leaning on bumbershoots, and it was DOA.

With the album's failure (though it did manage to get to No. 23 in the States and, ineffably, to No. 5 on the soul charts), Gordy learned that an inferior Supremes product wouldn't go over well—not that this stopped him from repeating the mistake. For the girls themselves, it was an augury that by deviating from the HDH "formula" they'd see a word attached to them that would indeed "sting like a bee." That word, naturally, was "sellout," which Mary Wilson recalls seeing for the first time in reviews for *A Bit of Liverpool.* But not for the last.

The two-week British tour began on October 7 and proceeded along Gordy's scripted storybook tale. The dark-skinned American princesses—"*Negresses,*" as some in the British papers called them, not knowing or caring how offensive this was to the Supremes—arrived at Heathrow Airport, greeted by a small horde of fans assembled by the Tamla-Motown Appreciation Society, whose president had been called to Motown weeks before and given his marching orders. Everywhere the girls went, photographers were at the ready, and a rash of interviews had been set up.

The theme of the interviews was pre-ordered; as Wilson summed it up later with a pinch of cynicism, "We were exotic darlings, sexy and cute, and all the more interesting because we were black and hailed from what the [Brit] press liked to portray as a rat-infested ghetto."

Gordy, not bothered by that stereotypical spin—after all, he had created it, and watched it being played out in his own country—spared no expense in extending it in the light of how far these "ghetto girls" had come. The Supremes' rooms in London's swankiest hotels were lined with bouquets of flowers and buckets of champagne and caviar. Their gigs, held at mod clubs on Fleet and Carnaby Streets, were well attended—if ticket sales lagged at a particular performance, TMAS moved in with Gordy's money and made it a sellout—and reviewed more as social "happenings" than as concerts. They appeared on the TV show "Tops of the Pops" on October 15, warbling "Baby Love." A day before, there was also a side-trip to the Carre Amsterdam Club, where they ran through "Baby Love," "When the Lovelight Starts Shining Through His Eyes," and "Let Me Go the Right Way." (A live recording of that performance would surface over four decades later on the Dutch import album *The Supremes' Greatest Hits.*)

The climax, according to the script, was a meeting with the Beatles at the Ad Lib Club. However, only Paul and Ringo showed up for the event, pleasantly smiling for the cameras and exchanging a few words with the girls before splitting. For the pricey fortnight Gordy had lavishly footed, he got more than he imagined. By the time the girls boarded the plane to return home, "Where Did Our Love Go" had hit No. 2 on the British pop chart; and in late November "Baby Love" would hit No. 1—one of the very few American records to land in that spot in recent years, the most recent being Roy Orbison's "It's Over" in July 1964.

Now that Motown had conquered two countries, and Supremes records were flying off the shelves all around Europe, Gordy wanted even more. Plans were made to restart the Motortown Revue and fly it across the pond in March 1965. By then, the Supremes weren't merely Motown's hottest act; they would virtually *own* Motown, and Ross would own Berry Gordy, in all respects. And Gordy's allegiance to them—to *her*—would be indisputable, with their path superseding anyone else's.

The march toward that end could be seen when they got back to Detroit and were thrown right into the raging rapids of Gordy's crossover reveries. Over the span of the coming months, the Supremes would be practically the only Motown act regularly visible to the vast mainstream of the American public, this because they were about the only one with whom the network TV producers seemed comfortable enough to invite onto their shows. Again, this was a situation Gordy had no problem accepting.

Their first national TV appearance was at *The Steve Allen Show* on September 24, 1964, when they sang a breezy rendition of "Where Did Our Love Go." Next came an engagement that *did* include a couple of their Motown cohorts, preserving for now the soon-to-disintegrate Motown "family" ties in the historical freeze-frame of mid-'60s pop culture. This was at *The TAMI Show*, the short-form name for a concert put together by a sodality known as the Teenage Awards Music, Inc. The concert, showcasing a mélange of contemporary and past rock and soul acts, would be held at the Santa Monica Auditorium on October 26, and when it grew into a major convocation with a surreal cast that included the Beach Boys, Rolling Stones, Jan and Dean, James Brown, Chuck Berry, Gerry and the Pacemakers, Billy J. Kramer and the Dakotas, Lesley Gore, the Barbarians—and the Supremes, the Miracles, and Marvin Gaye—the producers added a second day to the show and got backing to shoot both of them for theatrical release *a la* Gordy's movies of the Revue's Apollo shows, not on film but rather on the newly invented medium of videotape, which was then "kinescoped" to film.

The crude, transfixing black-and-white images of *The TAMI Show* would transmit every ounce of energy from the shrieking teenage audience, but one of the most striking aspects of the film today is that the two *nouveau chic* acts, the Stones and the Supremes, look somewhat lost, buried in ennui compared with the reaction given most everyone else, particularly the two soul warhorses Brown and Berry. The Stones, pre-"Satisfaction," swagger and pout, the latter emotion perhaps caused by their having to follow Brown onstage, a decision they nearly came to blows over with the producers. The Supremes, who like the Stones were undeniably riveting, sang their three big hits somewhat mechanically, leaving a trace but not much excitement; reviews had little to say about them. Still, that they more than belonged in that company was confirmed empirically when "Come See About Me" became their third No. 1 hit—one more than the aggregate No. 1 hits by the rest of the cast at the time. (The other two were Jan and Dean's "Surf City" and Gore's "It's My Party.")

And so the invitations kept pouring into Hitsville. The most coveted of these, just as Diana had boasted, was *The Ed Sullivan Show*; the girls were booked to appear there on the day after Christmas. But if that was the penultimate mainstream milestone in Gordy's Supremes blueprint (behind only the Copa), the teenage market could not be ignored, not with the tons of record sales it generated. And so he took bookings on the new youth-oriented prime-time network shows, ABC's *Shindig* on November 18 and NBC's *Hullabaloo* on January 26.

In January, too, the Supremes flew back to California to film their prospective movie debut, at least technically, singing as themselves in what was intended as the fourth in the lightweight strain of Frankie Avalon–Annette Funicello "beach" movies with titles such as *Beach Blanket Bingo*, *How to Stuff a Wild Bikini*, and *Bikini Beach*, which while suggestive of sex-crazed teenagers cavorting on sandy beaches were classic teases and copouts, with no one going anywhere near all the way. These dim-witted affairs, produced on the cheap by B-film meister James H. Nicholson, raked in huge coin and in retrospect contributed some great rock videos in the Technicolor performances of James Brown and the Fabulous Flames, Lesley Gore, and, later, Stevie Wonder; the Beach Boys also did two knockoffs of the Frankie and Annette genre, *The Girls on the Beach* and *The Monkey's Uncle*, scoring a hit with the title track of the first. The Supremes were to appear in *Bikini Beach*, but it wound up on the shelf, never released. They would, however, be back; a year later they recorded the title track for *Dr. Goldfoot and the Bikini Machine*, and got their close-up—not in bikinis but in white cocktail dresses (and the wig on Diana's head perilously close to falling off)—in *Beach Ball*, along with the Righteous Brothers, Four Seasons, Walker Brothers, and Nashville Teens. When the movies would call again, it would be a much bigger deal.

Gordy, taking no chances that Motown would fall flat in these ventures, had put them through weeks of drills with his new hires, choreographer Cholly Atkins and—reaching back to the memories of his many nights at the Flame Show Bar—none other than Maurice King, the bandleader who'd mentored many a dud of a personality into a live wire on stage with a few well-chosen quips, some transitional storytelling between songs, and grand entrances and exits.

Atkins's days as a hoofer stretched back to the '30s when he danced with the Rhythm Pals and, then, as a team with Honi Coles weaving some tap magic performing with the Ellington and Basie big bands. Based now in New York, he had been tutoring acts such as the pre-Motown Gladys Knight and the Pips. Motown had met up with him when its acts played the Apollo and needed some big-time moves. After the Miracles bombed in their Apollo debut, he fancied up their footwork the next time they came in. Having also worked with Harvey Fuqua's Moonglows in the '50s, Atkins was receptive when Gordy sent Harvey to make him an offer for a salaried position at Motown.

Cholly had a rather high opinion of himself and a low opinion of most others, including Gordy—whom he considered a boor and a grifter living off the sweat of his young apprentices. He criticized the young performers themselves for their lack of training and discipline, and even for the accident of where they were born. "Kids from ghetto-like environments," he called them, and not sympathetically. Nearly everyone at Motown, in turn, detested him and derided Atkins as a "snob." But, given wide latitude to create dance routines at his whims, he did so with amazing variety, tailoring each group—each *song*—to a specific series of moves that advanced the mood. His was a classical, '30s pomp, meant to look effortless and light-footed, though the work involved was back-breaking.

If that style seemed very *un*-Motown, and anachronistic for the beat of the mid-'60s, it perfectly matched Maxine Powell's predilections—and thus, in the end, Gordy's. It was encouraged, and it worked. Lord, did it work. The difference was instantly apparent. Where before performers and house bands were at a loss trying to find the right tempo for a live audience—which almost always was different from the tempo at which the songs had been recorded—Atkins sent them out on the road, having rehearsed them to near-death on pacing and matching moves. Atkins and arranger Johnnie Allen wrote strict musical arrangements for the Motown acts to take on the road with them, so that the local house bands could keep the performances roughly consistent.

The most obvious beneficiaries were the Temptations, whose relentlessly practiced "white glove" dance moves were right up Atkins's alley. With his input, the routines now became buttery, visually and kinetically playing off their songs' narratives with clever pantomime. Their first hit, "The Way You Do the Things You Do," became a feast of literal embellishment: The line "The way you smell so sweet, you know you could've been some perfume" came with a dabbing of their fingers behind their ears, and in "My Girl" Ruffin would sing "What can make me feel this way" and suddenly grab a fistful of air before giving the answer.

For the Supremes, delicate femininity was preserved; if an arm rose into the air, it would be brought down with a flutter of the wrist—no better example being in "Come See About Me," on the line "Sometimes up, sometimes down." Flourishes matched to visually active lyrics would branch from their steady measures of hip-swaying and finger-popping. Most of the time, TV directors would place Diana in the middle. More and more, though, Motown passed the word that directors should feel free to place her off to the side—the right, only, because she photographed better turned slightly rightward; by this, the subliminal point would be made that she was separate and unequal.

One of the first fruits of the Powell-Atkins axis was the *Shindig* appearance in November. The "youth-oriented" TV shows only tangentially dabbled in soul music; their sensibilities were clean, wholesome, county-fair vanilla, with acts introduced between pimple-cream commercials usually by moonlighting disc jockeys in serge suits and skinny ties. The other acts on that *Shindig* episode included the Righteous Brothers, Donna Loren, a remarkably baby-faced Leon Russell, and *The Donna Reed Show*'s Paul Petersen, who had a hit song out at the time, a misdemeanor called "She Can't Find Her Keys," and who killed any good vibes in the audience by singing a morbid tear-jerker, "My Dad," just before the Supremes went on.

They came into the eye of the black-and-white camera looking like they'd just left high tea; wrapped in elegant tunic tops and ankle-length silk skirts, they stood feline-like, Ross between and raised slightly above Wilson and Ballard, arms bent identically at the elbow. As Diana trilled the "Baby Love" lead, Mary and Flo echoed her while they all executed perfectly timed foot shuffles that ended with their toes pointed outward, biding time until the next move. On the chorus "Don't throw our love away," they did a jump and pivot, to the back, then to the front. In a later segment, doing "Come See About Me," they wore knee-length fringe shimmies and mid-cut tank tops, infusing similar mini-moves without flaw.

Even now, before Maurice King developed their stage act for the supper clubs, they were *there*. Their smiles were fixed and genuine, their voices strong, their bearing commanding and causal. Most of all, they were *women*, not girls, surely young but with a sniff of mature detachment.

In truth, there were *two* Motowns now: the recorded tracks of Motown for mass youthful and biracial consumption, and for a much more select gene pool, the "sophisticated," grown-up, crossover Motown. With near-theurgic acts like the Supremes and Temptations, little adjustment was necessary to suit either target, beyond the injection of the odd Broadway show tune or evergreen pop standard. But possibly because Gordy believed he might lose the former when the latter became the more familiar identity, as a sop and reminder to record buyers he began appending to Motown record labels and album jackets the presumptuous codifying phrase "The Sound of Young America." By this, Gordy surely meant young black and white America—though that linkage would soon, and often, be questioned. Indeed, even as the inscriptions were being printed, his own focus was mainly the Supremes and how much they could make the "second" Motown *the* Motown.

While hit records were still the company's plasma, without which there'd be no Motown at all, chartings and the general bottom line seemed to pale before the vision of the Supremes mounting the stage at the Copacabana and in Vegas, and of Ross as Motown's "first lady," and the trail where *that* could lead. In fact, Maxine Powell and Cholly Atkins were repeating the word "Copa" to the Supremes as if it were a post-hypnotic suggestion. And, already, Atkins was putting them through their paces on routines appropriate for that venue, including never-ending drills with top hats and canes and singing the old Al Jolson chestnut "Rock-a-Bye-Your-Baby with a Dixie Melody"—hardly the sort of tune any self-respecting black performer would touch, unless of course being black didn't matter quite as much as it used to.

Powell, to be sure, set her sights even further down the road from Motown's original mission statement. Of the Supremes, she told someone, "We're training them for Buckingham Palace and the White House."

Ed Sullivan, whose long-running show was on the level of Buckingham Palace and the White House in showbiz terms, had never seen the Supremes perform, but contrary to appearance, the much-parodied, Gargoyle-faced newspaperman was a devotee of rhythm and blues and a frequent visitor to the Apollo Theater. He was also rightly proud of his star-making power, given the frenzy that surrounded the breakout appearances of Elvis and the Beatles on his stage. Oddly, though, he had not yet invited onto that stage a Motown act. The Supremes' hits and mainstream appeal made it an easy call.

During Christmas week, the girls flew to New York and checked into the posh Warwick Hotel. Following two days of rehearsals at Sullivan's Broadway studio, they came in on the Sunday of the show and sat in the makeup room, whereupon no one on the staff seemed to know how to apply makeup to these young black women, despite having no such confusion in tending to older black stars like Lena Horne and Diahann Carroll in the past. The makeup artists began slathering layers of mascara, eyeliner, and the darkest pancake powder they had, leaving the

Supremes looking like, as Wilson recalled, "black-faced singers in a minstrel show."

"Honey, I'm not going out looking like this!" Flo declared, and soon the three of them repaired to their dressing room where they washed the gunk off their faces and, as usual, applied their own makeup.

Little has been written of the Supremes' unveiling on the *Sullivan* show—when they were no more anticipated than the other main guests that night, Frank Gorshin, Leslie Uggams, the Serendipity Singers, and Rip Taylor—yet for them and Gordy it was no less critical a moment. This was the first time most of America laid eyes on these three talented black women barely in their 20s, and the first impression formed of them rested solely on their performance. Silly as it seemed to them, Gordy had been dead-on, grooming them according to his *Pygmalion* scenario just for moments like these as opposed to, say, singing in *Bikini Party*. Now, singing great soul music wouldn't be enough; it had to be sung with *panache*, fast becoming the new Motown paradigm.

In the end, though, Ross was right that neither Gordy nor any of his rented style- or stage-crafters made it work when the red light or the spotlight went on. That was the Supremes' doing. Embellished, yes, but at its heart an unscripted, unpiqued alchemy. It happened deep down somewhere when they joined voices on a great song; and for some reason, always had, as disparate and obviously unmatched as they were on a personal level.

Whatever it was, they grabbed millions of Americans on that December 26. Upon Sullivan's introduction, they were mid-stage, swinging and swaying in blue sleeveless dresses (that looked faded gray in black and white) against a geometric paneled backdrop, oozing "Come See About Me" and doing their twirls and pivots. Their smiles were so spacious that one could see Diana was missing a back upper molar in an otherwise perfect set of teeth, a curious, unwitting trace of humanizing usually purged from their act. The first impressions were of Ross as an ambitious chanteuse, shy, sweet, and ball-busting all in one; Wilson was eye candy, the inviting ingénue; Ballard was stately and striking, but a bit gawky, as if unwilling to commit all the way to the *shtick* and then doing it with a unseen wink.

By Wilson's reckoning, they were "perfect," and the "young people" in the audience, as Sullivan liked to say, clapped in time to the song and applauded loudly. When Sullivan waved for them to join him stage left, they expected he would swoon over them and perhaps engage in some light banter the way he had with the Beatles nearly eleven months before. Instead, he perfunctorily thanked them, though not by name, and shooed them off. Mary and Flo, walking on air, went right on beaming as they left the stage. Diana, however, looked peeved. Backstage, she kept muttering that Sullivan had "insulted" her, leading Don Foster, a Motown hand who'd been named their road manager, to tell her to hush up, that if Sullivan found out he'd never have them back.

Ross calmed down but would not let this perceived slight go; years later, she would recall—likely far more dramatically than it actually went down—that afterward "I just cried because I thought we had done something wrong" and that for a time in interviews she "really put down Sullivan because I was hurt." Yet someone who was backstage that night remembered not tears but a far more stringent Ross hissing that "We'll be back!" It was a promise, but it sounded more like a threat.

The Supremes' blitz continued apace into the new year, with appearances lined up as much as twelve months in advance. And, not by coincidence, Motown was getting fat as a whole, its "sound"—which by now, in no small part owing to the Supremes' run of hits, had weeded out the granular R&B of the early days—having made deep inroads into the mainstream. HDH had created yet another hit train with the Four Tops, a veteran quartet that had begun in the mid-'50s, led by the raw emotional tenor of Levi Stubbs (younger brother of the Falcons' lead man, Joe Stubbs). They'd had their first smash, "Baby I Need Your Loving" in the fall of 1964 and would crank out, machine-like, fifteen more Top Forty hits through the decade.

During this period, as well, Martha and the Vandellas enjoyed their biggest hit, "Dancing in the Street," cowritten by Marvin Gaye and Mickey Stevenson and produced by HDH, which went to No. 2 and was so molten that many—incorrectly—construed its call to take to the streets as an incitement to march, not dance. The dormant Marvelettes resurfaced to score a hit with "Too Many Fish in the Sea," co-written by Eddie Holland and Norman Whitfield and produced by Whitfield. Marvin Gaye delivered his first Top Ten hit, the HDH "How Sweet It Is to Be Loved by You." The Temptations had three more Top Twenty hits. The no longer "Little" Stevie Wonder was moving toward breaking out as a major act.

For now, despite the delirium surrounding the Supremes, the roster's collegial ambiance was still intact. Everyone, it seemed, was moving on up together, as Gordy always vowed they would. When Gordy extended the expiring Supremes contract in 1965 at a royalty rate 100 percent greater than before, he did the same with every expiring contract. Of course, Gordy knew exactly what he was doing. A look at the minutiae of the contract agate, which few if any artists ever did, would have shown that the "increase" was from half a cent per record sold to a whole penny—although this calculation was only theoretical because it was still subject to all those unspecified "expenses." Even with three straight No. 1 hits, Ross, Wilson, and Ballard had not yet seen a royalty check, and it wouldn't be until 1967 that Gordy would boost their weekly salary from $50 per week—apiece—to $225 apiece.

All the while that they were making many times that amount for the company, the Supremes had no clue about what they were officially making themselves from year to year, such information still deemed none of their business. Gordy continued to operate under the assumption that the acts were too star-struck to care—a justifiable assumption since, as Wilson recalled their thoughts at the time, "it really was like we were living a fairy tale. While most of our friends had gotten married, gone to college, or were working at boring jobs, we were in show business and having the time of our lives. It seemed like we were living under a spell." Under that spell, they didn't have to worry about things like buying clothes or paying taxes; ITMI did all that mundane stuff for them, unaudited.

Wilson would recall how she used to look out that big bay window at Motown and see Cadillacs parked up and down West Grand Boulevard, all belonging to Gordy and his executives. It would certainly have been enlightening to know how much of the Supremes' royalties had bought all that chrome—that is, if she'd ever thought about it.

Among the Motown shipmates, then, the Supremes may have been the wave runners, but they were still in the same dinghy with them, trailing behind Gordy's yacht. Not that Diana Ross wasn't even more insufferable than Diane Ross had been. Mary and Flo, in fact, pointedly kept calling her Diane, partly out of habit but also as a conscious slap at her flowering ego, sharing a silent giggle at her ruffled reaction. Nor did the rest of the company shrink into the Supremes' shadow. The day before they flew to New York for the *Sullivan* show, they appeared in a weeklong series of Motown holiday shows at the Fox Theater. In classic Gordy fashion, there was no special order of billing; seeking, as ever, to foment competition as motivation for inspired performances, he made sure the order was determined, in typical Revue style, by each night's audience reaction. All of Gordy's "children" were used to the practice, and were primed to pour out their guts on stage. In these gladiator contests, Ross showed that fame hadn't mellowed her cut-throat instincts.

The Supremes began the week third from the closing, behind Marvin Gaye and the perennial show-closer, Smokey and the Miracles. When they missed a couple of shows while in New York, they came back home to find they'd lost even that spot. Looking for an edge, Diana came on using a riff she'd purloined from none other than old flame Smokey Robinson. The irony is that the riff—in which Smokey fell to his knees and called out "A little bit softer now" until the band was playing at a hush, then escalated cries of "A little bit louder now" until it was at full pitch—was itself lifted from the Isley Brothers' "Shout."

"She's doing my whole bit!" he complained to Berry. "You gotta stop her."

Once, Gordy might have done just that. Now, not even Smokey Robinson stood before her in his line of sight.

"Smokey," he told him, "you're the star. You'll just have to come up with something else. There's no way I'm gonna stop her."

Smokey, from firsthand experience, knew the score. Laughing, he said, "I didn't think you would. As fine as she is, I wouldn't stop her, either."

Gordy would admit that his fixation with Ross, too, couldn't be stopped, and had developed into something uncontrollable. "I guess I loved her before I even knew it," he wrote in his autobiography. Unable to express it directly, he instead did it the only way he knew how, by putting it into a song, "Try It Baby," which he cut with Marvin Gaye in '65. In it, the guy broods about losing a girl who's "moving on up" and "leaving me behind," and tells her, "Take away your good looks and all your fancy clothes [and] you'll see that nobody loves you but me." Coming from a man who wielded power and wealth like an aphrodisiac, and could have had Ross with the crook of a finger, such self-tortured insecurity was clearly tied to his fear of love and rejection—a fear that never did recede, since the same neediness can be implied from the title of his autobiography, *To Be Loved*, in which he admitted, "I never told Diana she was the inspiration for that song. I found myself falling for her more and more, but I stayed cool, incredibly cool."

Of course, he was the only one around Motown who didn't know he was, another reason why not everyone—or more accurately, practically no one but Gordy and his executives—in the company was thrilled by the Supremes' astonishing breakout. The least thrilled likely being Martha and the Vandellas, who were still smarting from Ross having co-opted their outfits in Washington, D.C. As the next-biggest girl-group, the Vandellas could definitely feel the ground shifting as Gordy turned his priorities toward the Supremes. In fact, they believed, somewhat myopically, that the company "push" was almost totally responsible for creating that winning streak.

ANNETTE BEARD: That's what it's all about, promotion. It's not that we resented them for getting it. It's that we wanted it, too. Look at "Dancing in the Street." That got nothing like the promotion they were putting on the Supremes' records and it went to No. 2. If they'd pushed it, it would've gone to No. 1, easy, no doubt. Because that's the difference between being No. 2 and No. 1, the promotion. That's the hardest jump to make on the chart. So we thought we'd earned that push after that, because they said they would give it to us. And we waited and waited.

Our feeling was this: Motown was supposed to be this big, happy family. And we had three different girl-group acts: the Supremes, the Vandellas, and the Marvelettes, and all of us had huge hits. And we were hurt because we felt everybody should have gotten the same attention. But the focus was on the Supremes because Berry had this thing for Diana. He was getting them ready to be out there doing the better shows in the better places. We were told, "As soon as the Supremes open all the doors, you'll get your chance." It was like, "Wait in line and your turn will come." And in show business, if you wait too long, if you go cold, you're gone. So we thought, "Well, why do we have to wait? Why can't we all open the doors?" We were as good as the Supremes—better, if you ask me. To be honest, their songs never really knocked me out. When I heard them, I wasn't excited. I'm not saying they were bad. There are no bad Holland-Dozier-Holland songs, and they did a great job with 'em. But some, you know, had to grow on me. Because here we were doing "Dancing in the Street" and "Nowhere to Run." Tell me, can you compare "Where Did Our Love Go" and "Baby Love" to those? I mean, the Supremes' songs were good but, come on.

Beard is right that the Supremes didn't, and could not hope to, amass the brute sonic power of the Vandellas' two signature pieces. But neither did those songs, for whatever reasons, reach the top of the charts. Nor have the Vandellas lingered in popular music memory anywhere near as long or fertilely as the Supremes. That wasn't merely a function of which distributors were being pushed to sell more records; indeed, as great as Martha Reeves was, she didn't, and couldn't hope to, wear as well as Diana Ross.

Wilson, trying to put her finger on the Supremes' appeal vis à vis their closest Motown rival, told author Gerri Hirshey, "We weren't as— well, masculine is the wrong word. Maybe tough. The Vandellas were a bit more soulful than us, let's put it that way. More R&B than us, they'd move more, with different kinds of gyrations." She didn't need to make the point: The Supremes didn't gyrate. And no one, but no one, could ever call them *masculine*.

Dysfunctional as it was, while Motown was still a family affair, Gordy rolled the dice on his most ambitious idea: sending the Motortown Revue to conquer a second continent. The success of the Mary Wells and Supremes tours of England, coupled with the launch in early '65 of the Tamla-Motown international label, made a company tour seem a worthwhile endeavor. Gordy also added branch tours to France, Germany, and The Netherlands. The troupe would essentially be the same as before, with one major exception—the Supremes would be the unquestioned headliner.

They, more than anyone, had made such an undertaking possible, and thus there'd be no intramural competition over billing and stage order. Ross, Wilson, and Ballard would get the top spot on the marquees and billboards, in larger fonts, and would close the shows, sending Smokey and his Miracles into a supporting role.

And, this time, Berry would be there from the start, and clear on through to the end. There was no way he could pass up the chance to see his flock merging with the grandeur of the European Continent. He excitedly arranged to take along his children and Mom and Pops Gordy. What most excited him, however, was that these romantic locales might provide him with a shot of courage, at least enough to be able to say, "Try it, baby" to a certain lead singer who both consumed and terrified him.

thirteen

"ECSTASY
TO THE
TENTH POWER"

Motown's invasion of Europe was scheduled for March 1965, leaving ample time for the Supremes to continue their nearly nonstop pilgrimage across the pop culture landscape. However, the first order of business was the now-preponderant matter of following up three straight No. 1 records (a feat only Elvis had accomplished, twice, in the '50s en route to five No. 1's in a row, which the Supremes and the Beatles were concurrently working their way toward). For HDH, this was a tricky maneuver; if they stayed "in the ballpark," would the act run the risk of going stale? At the same time, going wide—more R&B, too much of a ballad, too sharp an edge—was just as risky. Realizing they could not change the park, only its dimensions, they went farther down the road of recycling the winning beat, while extending the newer elements they'd added in "Come See About Me."

Picking up on Ross's punchier but still imploring attitude on "Come See About Me," the three maestros wove a sequel of continued, angrier frustration out of another ember of Lamont Dozier's troubled love life. This time, he'd been caught cheating, and during what he described as a "tremendous argument," out of his mouth spilled the words "Baby, please stop, in the name of love, before you break my heart." The line was so sappy that both he and the girl erupted into laughter, but he had a final bit of sap in him when she spurned him. "Think it over" was his final plea. "Think it over."

Brilliant songwriters have an automatic retention for love-is-hell dialogue like that, and Dozier took it at once to the piano, initiating the talismanic teamwork with Brian and Eddie Holland. A session was eventually set for early February to cut the next Supremes tune—which by then had the title "Stop! In the Name of Love." Eddie's lyric, with its mandatory "Baby, baby" iterations, was kneaded into a dark, mocking stalk—"Baby, baby, I'm aware of where you go, each time you leave my door. I watch you walk down the street, knowing the other love you meet." The title hook was a clear threat.

The arrangement by HDH and the Motown arranger Paul Riser drove the *noir*-ish undertone, the usual bells and whistles of a Supremes song now sounding harder, meaner. Again, it would take a believably mercurial Ross to pull it off—to be this rough and still vulnerable enough to sing, "Each time we are together, I'm so afraid of losing you forever." And she was right on the money—though, in a twist, hers isn't the first voice heard on the song. The intro was an arching Hammond-organ glissando by Earl Van Dyke and a sudden concussion of sound with Wilson and Ballard throatily singing the title phrase backed by a thick vibraphone, chugging bass, and snare drum hammering on each beat. Fabulous eighth-note saxophone runs came out of the mist preceding the background choruses. The *chink* of an electric guitar meshed with the drum on the back beat, a '50s riff used on the Falcons' "You're So Fine."

Then came Diana, interchanging vinegar and custard. When the tracks were mixed—over a speaker sized to that of a car or transistor radio, which is how it would be heard by most—all the Motown Brahmins thought it faultless (save for an errant drumstick falling during the organ intro, inaudible on anything but a hi-fi system). In fact, after a year of trying, it seemed as if it all had become almost *too* easy.

Certainly, by 1965, all the conditions and personnel at 2648 West Grand Boulevard were geared toward optimally creating and channeling onto Ampax tape the now-consistent "Motown Sound." Gordy even took to calling his shop "Detroit's other world-famous assembly line" in promotional copy, though another metaphor—"black bubblegum"—was also catching on, much to his unliking. In '64, of the sixty releases put out on his four prime labels—Motown (including the Supremes and the Four Tops), Tamla (Marvin Gaye, Stevie Wonder, the Miracles, the Marvelettes, Brenda Holloway), Gordy (the Temptations, the Vandellas), and Soul (Junior Walker and the All Stars)—a full forty-two of them made the charts; and, amazingly, Gordy was putting out only about a tenth of the product he had in the can. Good enough, considering that of the twenty-five No. 1 hits on the *Billboard* pop chart in '65, five came from Motown—three by the Supremes and one each by the Temptations and the Four Tops.

The belt of the assembly line, of course, was Studio A, the room dank and constantly in disrepair. Several fires had broken out over the years when various tubes, wires, and speakers overheated and blew, usually on hot summer days in the un-air-conditioned studio and control booth, which operated twenty-two hours a day, seven days a week. (Sessions ran so continuously that the musicians now rarely knew what act each given track was intended for, since vocals were dubbed at later dates.)

But while Gordy kept the snake-pit atmospherics as they were, to retain the old R&B raunchiness, he also dropped a fortune on upgrading the equipment. He hired a small battalion of sound engineers to oversee state-of-the-art recorders, mixing boards, equalizers, and speakers. The chief engineer, Mike McLean, built a four-track stereo recorder in 1964, a tricky contraption he wouldn't allow anyone— Gordy included—to touch without passing an extensive tutorial on how to use it to, for example, "ping-pong," the process by which dozens of tracks were merged into one fat track for the finished mix, by bouncing them back and forth between two reel-to-reel machines. Those recorders could now hold 2,500 feet of tape.

A new echo chamber was installed, too, using a new German technology, as well as discrete vocal booths. On the studio floor, musicians were isolated by baffles and miked individually; instead of blending into a massive sonic fog, each instrument was heard over separate amps in the booth. In the mixes, the sound grew tighter, sharper, better balanced. On the early records, for example, the tambourine was too loud, because it was recorded on the same microphone as the drum, and reducing one meant reducing both. Now, each had its own mike, and was placed on different tracks.

The result of this progress could be gleaned on the Supremes' skein of hits. For "Stop! In the Name of Love," HDH were able to bulk up the rhythm, Phil Spector "Wall of Sound"–style, without muddling the mix, by adding instruments. One, a second bass, was played conventionally on the lower end of the scale, contrasting and buffeting James Jamerson's impromptu riffing on the higher end. An extra rhythm guitar doubled the back beat. In time, they'd use two drummers. As Alan

"Dr. Licks" Slutsky explains, the added instruments played "in the rhythmic holes left by the first," resulting in "a propulsive power groove"—the quality he says "drove teenagers to the dance floor all over the world."

By 1965, Gordy was seeing to it that the epochal Motown house band would be on call at all hours. The top cat, Jamerson—who was rumored to be earning something like a $100,000 a year from round-the-clock sessions and Gordy's largesse—was the constant from the beginning, his influence heard on virtually every Motown record through the early '70s. The other constants in the mid-'60s were Chank Willis, Robert White, and Joe Messina on guitar; Bongo Brown; Johnny Griffiths and Van Dyke on keyboards; Jack Ashford on tambourine/vibes; Jack Brokensha on vibes/marimba; Mike Terry and Hank Cosby on sax; Paul Riser and George Bohanon on trumpet; and Benny Benjamin and Pistol Allen on drums—the last coming on as a safety valve when Benjamin was too stoned or liquored up to play on or even make a date. Soon, when Benjamin couldn't make any dates, Van Dyke brought in the drummer from his outside jazz band, Uriel Jones.

"Actually, most everybody was high on something," recalls Jack Ashford, one of the few survivors of that tight knot of players in 2007. "There were no Boy Scouts in there, man. And Benny wouldn't know where he was, but he'd nail that beat like clockwork. His body just gave out on him." Benjamin died of a stroke at age 43 in 1969.

It was the endearingly garrulous, sometimes incoherent Benjamin—nicknamed "Papa Zita" after he babbled something like that while jostled out of a drunken stupor—who dropped the "Funk Brothers" moniker on the group as a whole, bellowing after a take, "You guys are the funk brothers!" "And that," says Ashford, "was the last time we ever heard that name until, like, twenty years later, when we were 'discovered.'"

In fact, the Motown house band, unlike Spector's "Wrecking Crew," was basically no-names to all but the most arcane industry types. The closest thing they had to a collective identity was the Soul Brothers, the name under which they recorded a 1965 instrumental album called *The Sound of Motown*; at other times, when some of them would go out on the road with Motown tours—an arrangement kept to a minimum by Gordy, who couldn't spare them from their studio work—they'd be billed as the Earl Van Dyke Trio or Sextet. That they normally labored in the shadows in real time was, Ashford insists, no accident: "In my mind, we didn't get honored like [Stax-Volt house band] Booker T. and the MGs because we were being held back. They did not want us to get the recognition, because they didn't want us to get offers to leave. But they wouldn't pay us, either. I don't know about Jamerson; those rumors might have been bullshit. I know I was making ten bucks a song at the start, and I never made much more than that the whole time I was there."

Ashford jovially admits he had something to do with a good deal of Motown B.S., serving as the prime font of Funk Brothers lore upon their renaissance. One of the most-told tales that began to circulate was that the Brothers used to take refuge between sessions in the funeral parlor next door on West Grand Boulevard, getting loaded on booze the undertaker kept for them on a table next to bottles of formalde-hyde. Another was that James Jamerson played the bass while flat on his back on Marvin Gaye's "What's Going On," too drunk to even sit up straight. Ashford laughs: "Those were mine. Not bad, huh?" One should not take his kvetching about the money too seriously; union scale not only grew to $61 a session by 1964, it paled next to the salary they were on and the alms Gordy gave them.

What was true was that the musicians felt like second-class citizens at Motown. "We were just sidemen, we weren't the writers and produc-ers," Ashford goes on. "They couldn't do a damn thing without us, yet no one knew who we were. And here Holland-Dozier-Holland were better known than the president of the United States! They just figured, hey, these guys are happy just to get work, don't build 'em up. Then they'd come after us if we did sessions on the side around town. I re-member we did [the Capitols'] 'Cool Jerk' at Golden World Studios, which Berry later bought out 'cause he couldn't stand having competi-tion. It was supposed to be a secret but who else could have played like that? Mickey Stevenson would follow us. If he caught us in another stu-dio, he'd dock us fifty bucks!

"The funny thing is, we didn't think Berry was discouraging us. We were always cool with Berry. We'd play cards and roll dice with him. But Mickey Stevenson, he was the henchman. Mickey Stevenson was an asshole. I told him he was, too."

Of course, Ashford's contention that the Motown creative hierar-chy would have been lost without those brilliant, savvy musicians is just the sort of thing that has been eating at Brian and Eddie Holland ever since the Funk Brothers' renaissance. And Ashford is only too willing to make the case for his old cronies:

How it worked was like this. The producers would come in with their song and they and Paul Riser or somebody would make up a sheet, a very simple sheet of chord changes. No intros, no turnarounds, bridges, anything. Those things would be done on the spot, and usually all emanated from the rhythm section.

The producers would really just lay the sheets down and then get out of the way while we played it. Sometimes a producer would come in and say, "Hey, guys, make me a hit," because they didn't know what to do. Not Brian, he could read music; he called out chords. Brian's a gifted guy. I don't want to take anything away from him. If the wrong chord was played, he was on top of us. But the truth is, every session the process was the same. It would start with Earl on piano. Earl would work it all out from the chords, he and James and Benny, and Brian didn't get involved with those conversations.

Earl would count it out, set the tempo, give us the key, and we'd play and get a feel for what the song would be. When I was on tambourine, I didn't have a part laid out. It was all up to me, what I felt. I'd be in the drum booth with Benny and I'd watch his foot moving on the beat. Benny was the greatest pocket player in the history of music. He'd hit that groove, man, and I'd follow him. And I'd hear Jamerson do his thing and play off his flourishes.

Let me tell you something. James was worth a lot more than a hundred grand. Those bass parts made those songs. *Nobody* could do what he did on the bass. You *can't*, because it ain't the way you're supposed to do it. He would play and his foot would be stomping to some other beat altogether. It was an instinct. Sometimes he'd take the sheets and throw 'em on the floor and start playing. He was just that good. But he didn't even know it. He just did what he knew was right. We all did that, just not as good.

Tellingly, the Holland brothers have little patience for such discussions. Although Brian and Eddie appear briefly in *Standing in the Shadows of Motown* waxing poetic about the Funk Brothers—"They were holding their children hostage," Ashord jives—when this author suggests, with caution, that they "relied" on the musicians, their reactions are such that they'd surely have wound up on the cutting-room floor.

BRIAN: Oh, bullcrap! They didn't come up with those songs. It's more than just chords. Those things have *melody*. They didn't create melodies. They were created by the songwriters and producers. That's a fact.

So, no, they didn't just do what they felt. Not for HDH, they didn't. Those bass lines, all of 'em we'd done on the piano first. We told them what to do. And if they didn't do it right, I'd stop that shit and say, "No, no, no. Play it this way." If I didn't want it, they didn't play it.

EDDIE: You been listening to the Funk Brothers too much. First of all, my brother is brilliant. The biggest arguments we had—which he always won—was because of what he heard only in his head, not what I heard or what the musicians heard. I'd say, "Brian, this part here is too dead, make it more lively." And he'd say, "You're crazy. Can't you *hear* it? I'd say, "No, I can't hear a damn thing." 'Cause I couldn't hear what he did. He'd lay out all these melodies, he and Lamont. Not the Funk Brothers. They didn't hear the melody he wanted, not until it was in the air.

It wasn't just chord sheets. If they were so good, why didn't they ever produce a record? What songs did they ever write? I will say this, to give them all due credit: They had the ability to *interpret*, and do what Brian wanted them to do. But it was tightly controlled.

BRIAN: For them, it was. When they played for HDH, they were.

Ashford, unmoved by the rebuttal, turns part of it back on the Hollands, particularly the producer:

He's on crack! Tell Brian I said he's on crack. You would have to have heard Jamerson to know. I heard him play on inside keys, outside keys, no keys. It was all in *James's* head. I'm surprised Brian said what he did. I can't believe it. And if *he* was that great, why the hell didn't they [HDH] stay hot after they left Motown? Why couldn't they do the same thing consistently with another bass player? Listen, for Brian to have in his head everything that Jamerson played, he would have to have been a master. If he even *thinks* he did, he's on crack.

"Stop! In the Name of Love," as with its three precursors, led a charmed life. Just after the new year, a month prior to its release,

Billboard's January 9 issue put the girl's back in the VIP cover spot, with the beneficial caption:

> THE SUPREMES, Motown Records' sensational group, are the first female artists to have three No. 1 records in a four-month period. Their smash LP "Where Did Love Go [*sic*]" is currently in the top five on Billboard's LP chart and contains all three of their No. 1 records.

Released on February 8 backed with "I'm in Love Again," the single was on the chart within four weeks, and in late March it, too, made it all the way to the top (pop and R&B), displacing the Beatles' "Eight Days a Week." There it stayed for two weeks, garnering the Supremes' second and last Grammy nomination, for Best Contemporary Rock and Roll Group Vocal Performance ("Baby Love" had been nominated for Best Rhythm and Blues Recording the year before) and leaving perhaps the most enduring aftertaste of any Supremes song—witness, for what it's worth, the nod that *Rolling Stone* gave it in 1988 as the tenth most important single in the rock and roll eon.

As their act took root, so did the schizoid nature of their great leap forward. On the one hand, the Supremes who drove those teenagers to the dance floor gratified that large slice of the market on dance-party TV shows both nationwide (the list now growing to include another *Shindig* on February 24, a Murray the K summer special on CBS called "It's What's Happening, Baby," and Dick Clark's new after-school show "Where the Action Is") and locally (in replicates of their periodic appearances on Robin Seymour's "Teen Town" in Detroit). On the other hand, the Supremes whom Gordy wanted to "go wide" alighted on the talk-variety circuit, singing and doing brief sit-downs with Steve Allen, Mike Douglas, Joey Bishop, and Johnny Carson.

And, most portentously, there was the motherlode of the mainstream, Berry Gordy's longtime dream of playing the Copacabana. After weeks of negotiating with the club's owner Jules Podell, Gordy finalized a three-week run beginning July 29. The lag time would allow him to gear up a massive marketing campaign culminating in the gig. More would happen in that interval, however, than he may have imagined, or hoped for. In fact, by the time they got to the Copa, both on an artistic and a personal plane there would be little mystery left as to who and what the Supremes—and certainly Diana Ross—were all about.

Much of that occurred as a result of the Motortown Revue tour of England. In mid-March the troupe—in this case, the Supremes, Martha and the Vandellas, Stevie Wonder, the Temptations, and Smokey and the Miracles, along with a group of Funk Brothers billed as the Earl Van Dyke Sextet—took off in a private plane bound for London joined by a horde of assorted Gordys and Motown functionaries, lawyers, accountants, promotions people, bodyguards, roadies, and chaperones. On the ground at Heathrow Airport, the Tamla-Motown Appreciation Society had assembled another welcoming mob to wave banners and scream nice things at the performers as they de-planed. When it was time to head for their quarters, the swanky Cumberland Hotel, it became immediately evident who the headliners of this tour were—and how the others' noses were going to be rubbed in it.

In truth, there'd been little doubt about this for some time. As the Revue winged across the Atlantic, the March 20 *Billboard* carried a two-page ad touting the tour, with "The Tamla-Motown Show Is on the Way" splashed along the top in white letters against a solid black background and bubble insets of each act. Inverting the order of the old Motown ads, the Supremes' bubble, sitting top left, was the biggest. In England, *The New Musical Express* worked up a cover story headlined "THE BEATLES' FAVORITE ARTISTS ARE COMING TO BRITAIN"—their "favorite" conveniently not Mary Wells anymore but the Supremes.

In London, Gordy's favoritism was clearly on display, as was the fact that the "Others" on the roster were now everybody else. No longer as concerned with competition among acts as with capitulation to his biggest act, he had the girls ride in his stretch limo and nosh with him on caviar and champagne, accompanied by their personal hair stylists, makeup artists, and valets. Meanwhile, even Esther Edwards and the Gordy brood had to ride in one of two buses, the rest of the troupe in the other bus.

At the Cumberland, the Supremes were checked into a penthouse suite down the hall from Gordy's, accessible by a private elevator that bypassed the rest of the company on lower floors. Most of the interviews set up with the British press were with Ross, with a peep here and there from Wilson and Ballard. It was as if all of Motown had turned out in England as courtiers in the court of Queen Diana.

This was abasing to most, but for Martha Reeves it was humiliating. Reeves, after all, had been the stimulus for the Revue's first gig on the tour, a March 18 appearance on a BBC-TV show, "The Sound of

Motown." This, an hour-long special produced by the weekly program *Ready, Steady, Go* and hosted by Dusty Springfield, had come about because Springfield was enamored with Motown and especially with the Vandellas' butch but slinky lead singer. When the show was pitched to the BBC, Springfield wanted the Vandellas to be the featured act, an idea that was nixed by the network and by Gordy.

There may have been more to Springfield's preference than merely her musical tastes. Early on the tour, she was in Martha's room and fell asleep. Reeves later recalled that "I just let her sleep and I covered her with a comforter as any friend would." The next morning, Mickey Stevenson came to the door to inform Reeves of a schedule change and when she opened the door, he saw Dusty, "with one of her legs sticking out from under the comforter—fishnet stockings and all." Stevenson apparently couldn't wait to spread the news and in no time "all the men kidded and teased me as though something odd had happened."

The story became a spicy staple of Motown lore, reprised when Springfield came out of the closet years later, leading Reeves to finally address that "odd" night in London by saying, absent of a direct denial, "I was amazed at just how others regarded our friendship, but I couldn't care less what anyone thought."

Reeves and the Vandellas were permitted to do a duet with Springfield on the show, but in rehearsals the producers and director fawned on the Supremes. For the finale, when all the acts were onstage as Smokey and the Miracles would perform a wild, extended version of "Mickey's Monkey" in stage center, the Vandellas, Temptations, and Stevie Wonder were to line up stage left; the Supremes were placed prominently, alone, just to the right, where they could be seen interacting with Smokey—this time, unlike at the Apollo, there'd be no need for Diana to elbow her way to get next to him. They'd also be given three numbers to sing on the show, including the first public unveiling of "Stop! In the Name of Love."

Even so, Diana, as in the past, grew frantic watching the other acts in rehearsal going through their electric paces. Realizing the Supremes couldn't get away with their quiescent "little kicks" in this setting, according to a tale in *Call Her Miss Ross*, she charged into the men's room while the Temptations were in there making a pit stop and, between the urinals and stalls, bellowed, "We need some choreography quick for 'Stop! In the Name of Love!'" whereupon the guys zipped up and taught her what would become the Supremes' signature gesticulation: right hand straight out, palm forward, left hand on hip as they jointly and dramatically emoted "Stop," then slowly lowering the right arm, with fingers snapping in a cool, circular motion—a freeze-frame of precious, adorable haught, which, when prefaced by the story of a blinkered Ross barging into a men's room to make it happen, seems a perfect allegory. If only it wasn't perfect balderdash.

"Nah, it wasn't in no men's room," says Otis Williams, "although Diana was bold enough to do that. It was at the Cumberland. We were all rehearsing in the ballroom and Paul [Williams] saw the Supremes doing the song and had an idea. Paul was a great idea man when it came to moves. It was really Paul, not Cholly [Atkins], who choreographed the Temptations. And he knew he had a killer move for the girls, and that the word 'stop' was the crux of the whole thing; everything had to come to a stop with a nice visual effect."

"Paul told them, 'Hey, do this here'—and made like a traffic cop. He worked it out with them in, like, five minutes and they had their move. They loved it, too. 'Cause they always wanted to do more physical stuff than Berry or Cholly let them do."

This, Williams believes, was an indicator of a deeper resentment of how overly processed they had become. He went on:

> They'd gotten to the point where they were getting to hate the Broadway-Vegas kind of thing. Even Diana. I mean, she's often blamed for the group going in that direction, but that ain't so; it was all Berry. Diana wanted to be a blues singer, like Billie Holiday. She was actually very rebellious of doing all that "top hat" stuff. All of them were—hell, we were, too, 'cause they made us do the same thing when the Supremes were such a success with it.
>
> Flo hated it the most. Flo just wanted to go out and sing and not have to smile like a Barbie doll. That wasn't Flo. And, I'll tell you, I think she held back a little on those numbers. You can see it in the old videos. She'd be a little off, a little stiff. She was a good dancer so she could pull it off not giving her all, and she'd give you that little look, that gleam in her eye, that all this was bull. That was Flo, man. She was the most real, funniest person I knew. She was really good-natured and down to earth, not like what they wanted the Supremes to be. People loved that in her. But I think as time went on, Berry didn't like it.

The tour proper began on March 20 at the Astoria Theatre in Finsbury Park. From there, it ran nearly nonstop until the April 13 finale in Paris at the Olympia Music Hall, with only two days idle in between. Along the way, the Revue would come through country towns and working-class ports, including Hammersmith, Bristol, Bournemouth, Leicester, Sheffield, Luton, Cardiff, Wolverhampton, Liverpool, Manchester, Portsmouth, and Leeds. On April Fool's Day, it hopped across the border to Glasgow's Odeon Theatre.

The whole time, no one had to guess where Gordy's allegiance was. As Mary Wilson recalled, "Berry never let us out of his sight, and I began to think of him as the fourth Supreme." Separating frequently from the troupe, the "four Supremes" headed off for private receptions at castles and palaces, having tea and crumpets with the likes of Lord and Lady Londonderry, in whose grand estate they all stayed for a week between shows (though for some reason Gordy didn't take them when he was called to meet the Beatles at the Pinewood movie studio where they were filming *Help!*).

It was, said Wilson, astutely, "like living in a fairy tale, not only for us but for Berry, too. We [all] realized that we were going to make it—and bigger than we ever imagined."

Nor did it seem to matter to Gordy that there were three other big Motown acts somewhere in England, as well, who might have wanted to tell him, "Hey, Berry, remember us?" Or that the tour turned into what Wilson calls a financial "flop." The first two weeks, it became evident that the Brits weren't overly interested. Some shows were sold out, some embarrassingly undersold. Plainly, Gordy had read too much into the record sales racked up by Mary Wells and the Supremes across the pond. That, and all the testimonials in the world from the Beatles weren't enough to sell seats in a land where Motown was still a hazy entity, its artists not regularly heard on the airwaves until recently.

Things picked up in the third week when the BBC-TV show was broadcast, but even so the most warmly received act on the bill each night was the middling British singer Georgie Fame and his band the Blue Flames, whom Gordy had contracted to warm up the audiences. In the end, Motown lost several hundred thousand dollars on Gordy's ambitious idea, though it did help establish the Tamla-Motown brand in Europe.

Gordy, though, seemed for once not to be thinking primarily of the bottom line (never mentioning that aspect of the tour in his memoirs), too focused was he on getting Diana's bottom line into one of those an-

The Primettes, circa 1959. In the beginning, there were four. But Betty McGlown, at far left, decided to get a real job. *From the author's collection*

Milt Jenkins, the hustler who created the Primettes, flashing a million-dollar smile, poses in one of his quieter suits in his "office" at the Flame Show Bar, where a fist hole in the wall was just part of the decor. *Courtesy of Maxine Ballard*

Hitsville, U.S.A. was the hub for young Detroit soul singers, and where the Primettes hung out trying to get noticed by Motown president Berry Gordy. *From the author's collection*

The new fourth, Barbara Martin, entered the picture when the Primettes were signed by Motown and renamed the Supremes. When Martin quit, they continued as a trio. *From the author's collection*

For three years, they were the "No-Hit Supremes," but not for want of trying, as Gordy pushed them hard—to the discontent of more popular acts—in Motown ads like this one. *From the author's collection*

One of the "no-hit" flops: "I Want a Guy," cowritten and produced by Berry Gordy. The 45 was originally released on Tamla Records. *From the author's collection*

The record that made them the "Number-One Hit Supremes" in 1964: "Where Did Our Love Go"—a song they loathed but which changed the face of Motown and pop music. *Courtesy of John J. Grecco, Red Bird Entertainment Inc.*

A fateful pairing of threesomes: The Supremes and the songwriting/producing team of Brian Holland, Lamont Dozier, and Eddie Holland take five in front of Motown, with Brian and Diana, at least seemingly, lost in their own thoughts—perhaps about the affair they were having? *Courtesy of HDH Music*

In the mid-'60s came guitarist Robert White, left, and piano master Earl Van Dyke, center. *From the author's collection*

The unsung heroes were the Funk Brothers, the long-uncredited Motown house band that turned simple chords into chart gold. An early edition of the "brothers" included, clockwise, drummer Benny Benjamin, incomparable bassist James Jamerson, pianist Joe Hunter, and sax men Hank Cosby and Mike Terry. *From the author's collection*

Signs of success: Making the cover of the teen fan magazines, like *Teen Screen* and *KYA Beat. Courtesy of John J. Grecco, Red Bird Entertainment Inc.*

A proud Berry Gordy holds aloft the Supremes' second album, which seems almost literally to be propping up Hitsville, U.S.A. Figuratively, the group's ongoing sales did just that. *From the author's collection*

While the Fab Four were invading America, the "Fab Three" were conquering England, making appearances on TV shows like the BBC's popular *Top of the Pops. From the author's collection*

The "big, happy Motown family" included the Temptations, Stevie Wonder, Smokey and the Miracles, and Martha and the Vandellas. Diana usually found her way to the center of attention, right next to Smokey, as the others steamed. *Courtesy of Tom Ingrassia Productions*

Going where other black acts in the sixties couldn't, there was always room for the Supremes on the tube—above, sharing the stage on a 1965 *Hullaballo* episode with Sonny and Cher, the Lovin' Spoonful, and host Sammy Davis Jr., who seemed to like Diana the best (left).

Both images courtesy of Tom Ingrassia Productions

Soul goes mainstream: The Supremes, looking classy, cool, and confident, segue from Motown to Tin Pin Alley tunes on the *Dean Martin Show* in 1965. *Courtesy of Tom Ingrassia Productions*

With the Supremes as his army, the megalomaniacal Gordy could feel like he looked in this painting of himself in a Napoleonic guise that he hung on his mansion wall—as ruler of the entertainment world. *From the author's collection*

Continuing to bridge musical generations, the Supremes back up legendary composer Richard Rodgers for a 1966 TV special, and also cut an album of Rodgers & Hart tunes. But the old master still thought their music was tedious. *Courtesy of Tom Ingrassia Productions*

There was never a doubt who Gordy's "Josephine" was. At occasions like this gathering at a Detroit nightclub, Diana would be at his table while Mary and Flo would be on their own. *From the author's collection*

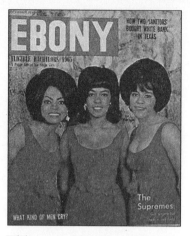

Opening more important doors, the Supremes became the first black act in the rock era to play the storied Copacabana nightclub in 1965. The live album of the engagement hit No. 11 on the pop chart. *From the author's collection*

While commercial crossover was the name of the game, maintaining "cred" in the black record-buying market was a must, as shown by this cover on the country's biggest black magazine in 1965. *From the author's collection*

Oozing sophistication and charm during a 1966 show at San Francisco's Fairmont Hotel. *Courtesy of Tom Ingrassia Productions*

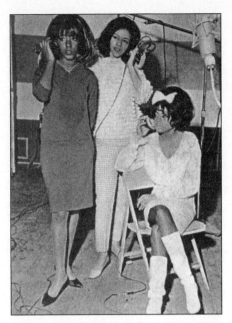

Even in an airless studio, being fashionable was essential. *Courtesy of Tom Ingrassia Productions*

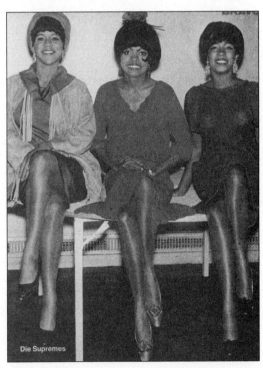

Bavarian cheesecake: Earning fame worldwide, Motown's ambassadorettes displayed their assets for this German magazine cover in 1966. *Courtesy of Tom Ingrassia Productions*

Vogueing in rhinestones, gobs of mascara, and chandelier earrings. Even in padded bras, Diana couldn't stack up, but because of her thin, she would become "in." *Courtesy of Tom Ingrassia Productions*

Shwing! In this outtake from the photo shoot for the 1967 *Supremes A Go-Go* album cover, the "happening" Supremes donned appropriately groovy pastel designer gear and gyrated like the cast of *Laugh-In*. *Courtesy of Tom Ingrassia Productions*

Looking drunk with power, a dapper Gordy basks in the limelight with his "girls" during their 1967 gig at L.A.'s Cocoanut Grove nightclub. As always, Diana beams for the camera, but, reversing their usual roles, Flo looks like "the sexy one," while Mary just looks drunk. *Courtesy of Tom Ingrassia Productions*

A seamless transition: In July 1967, Flo was out and Cindy Birdsong in. Supremes fans didn't notice a difference in their dazzling act, which continued on at venues such as here at Berns Nightclub in Stockholm, Sweden. Few knew that only Diana was now singing on their records. *Courtesy of Tom Ingrassia Productions*

While Flo sang on the *Reflections* album, one wouldn't have known it by the cover when it came out in early 1968 and Cindy Birdsong was the only "third Supreme" in a photo montage with Diana and Mary—the start of Motown's revision of history to erase Flo from the past. *From the author's collection*

Political theater: The Supremes throw their weight behind Hubert Humphrey for president in 1968, but they couldn't quite take him to number one. *Courtesy of Tom Ingrassia Productions*

Trying to keep in step with the socially conscious times, the girls traded high fashion for ghetto chic on the cover of their November 1967 *Love Child* album. While Diana passed off the jarring image of her in a sweatshirt and torn cutoff jeans as an "act," it was convincing enough to take the title track to number one. *From the author's collection*

Pop and circumstance: America's princesses live out a fairy tale (though Mary seems somewhat unimpressed) as they're greeted by Princess Margaret during a November 1968 tour of England. *Courtesy of Tom Ingrassia Productions*

Appearing somewhat haggard and a good deal less glamorous than usual, the road-weary Supremes arrive at Stockholm's Arlanda Airport in November 1968. And there was still a year of exhaustion and aggravation to come. *Courtesy of Tom Ingrassia Productions*

Even across the pond, the burning issue of 1969 was making headlines in the papers. *From the author's collection*

While plans moved forward for Diana's solo career, Motown squeezed every last drop out of the Supremes by pairing them on two TV specials, four albums, and four singles with another hot act, the Temptations. The juiciest was "I'm Gonna Make You Love Me," which hit number two on the pop and R&B charts in early 1969. *Courtesy of John J. Grecco, Red Bird Entertainment Inc.*

The last gasp for the Supremes—the result of a happy accident—allowed the Supremes to go out on a high note, when "Someday We'll Be Together" went to the top of the charts at the end of 1969 just as they gave their final performance. While their legion of fans have held out hope ever since, the title would not be prophetic. *From the author's collection*

tique four-poster beds he was sleeping in. The romance of escorting his leading lady over hill and dale and polo grounds intoxicated both of them. Concurrently, most in the company actually came to detest England—no one more than Flo, who for all the grandeur of the Supremes' own primrose lane, complained about the cold, dank weather, the bland food, the lukewarm pints of ale (she never was the champagne type), and the lack of rhythm by the British go-go dancers on the BBC show and in the nightclubs. Even for Mary, the fairy tale wore thin; later, she insisted she'd been "appalled" by, among other major inconveniences, the British toilet paper—"thick and brown, like wax paper"—and the seeming lack of a single ice cube to be found in the whole country. Her post-tour verdict was that England "wasn't anyone's idea of civilization [even though] people carried on about it like it was the end of the world."

There were at least two such people on the tour—Lady and Lord Gordy. One night, the Supremes and the Vandellas were invited to London's Top Hat nightclub to see Eartha Kitt in concert. After the show, they were taken backstage to meet the leonine Kitt, whom Ross had long called one of her idols. Reeves recalled Kitt sitting imperiously at her dressing table, "looking every inch a 'diva' in full command," when Diana, not waiting to be addressed by the veteran star, made the moment about her.

Stepping ahead of others, she blurted out, "Eartha, a lot of people tell me I look like you!"

Said Reeves: "You could have heard a pin drop. Eartha said not one word in reply. In the icy silence we were all suddenly nervous and uncomfortable." After a long pause, Kitt got up, told her mockingly, "I'm not half as beautiful as you are," and swept out of the room.

To Martha, hardly a Ross fan before, scenes like this were really Gordy's fault, for sequestering the Supremes, and especially Diana, from the rest of the pack—and any semblance of reality. For Reeves and most everyone else along for the ride in England, the entire experience was a downer, and traceable in retrospect as the beginning of the end of Motown as they—and Gordy, once—had known it. As a once-integral part of Gordy's "master plan," Reeves would rue that she'd "watched [his] dreams grow to full realization," only to watch him now write her out, concluding that "I never questioned his directions or his motives—until this trip to England."

In his reveries, for Gordy the trip would be a fantasy come to life, marking a change in his life that he regarded only as beatific, not to

mention the release of several years of pent-up sexual frustration about
his leading lady. Never mind that he had a live-in girlfriend back home,
Margaret Norton—a fine-print matter that concerned him, it seemed,
only when he confided to his lackeys his feelings for Diana and swore
them to silence, lest Margaret hear it through the grapevine.

By his own admission, Gordy became even more enthralled with
Ross in Europe. For much of the time, with eyes fixed, they took to
calling each other by the bizarre pet name of "Black"—as in "Hey,
Black, what are we doing today?" "Well, Black, let's go to Buckingham
Palace," dialogue that made the rest of the company want to toss their
cookies. In Manchester, he insisted that the Supremes perform the vacuous "You're Nobody 'Til Somebody Loves You," a recent hit by Dean
Martin and the kind of mid-road potboiler he wanted them to use in
their act on the way to the Copa. For weeks, the girls had rehearsed a
jazzy version of it arranged by Gil Askey, a trumpet player and big-band
leader who'd been named music director and conductor for their stage
act. But whenever they had sung it on stage, the audience sat inert, and
Diana blamed Berry for the embarrassment of the girls—and mostly
her, as the leader.

"I don't know what you're trying to do," she raged at him during
one intermission, "but I'm not gonna let you ruin my career!"

Gordy, always thrown by her hellfire tantrums—something only
she could get away with—meekly tried explaining that the song "could
open the door to everything we've wanted." When she continued balk-
ing, he gulped hard and gave her a "do it or else" ultimatum before the
Manchester show. While that normally brought her into line, this time
he wasn't so sure it would, worrying even as he spoke the words that he
may have lost the group right there. They were, after all, big enough
now to conceivably go out and fish for offers from other labels, contract
or not; indeed, if Mary Wells could walk out the Motown door under
the same circumstances and legal risks and get a big deal, what sort of
ungodly deal could the Supremes score?

In truth, Gordy had nothing to worry about on that score. Ross,
Wilson, and Ballard were in his thrall, too; they were, in their minds,
every bit his product, his delegates, his children (something that, of
course, only added to his angst about ever getting it on with Diana).
Then, too, Diana's ballsy demeanor in standing up to him made him
want her more than ever. What to do, indeed? His head spinning with
contradictory feelings and directives, he sat down for the show and—to
his infinite relief—the band struck up the intro to "You're Nobody,"
meaning that the girls had cued the song to be played. When Diana

then began to sing, he would say, "It almost brought tears to my eyes."
Little wonder, since it meant his "master plan"—making them, as he
said, "the biggest female singing group in the history of the word"—
was again ensured.

Even better was Ross's final word after the show.

"I still don't like it," she said of the song. "I did it for you."

She said it without emotion, as if it were her wifely duty, but to
Gordy it was the ultimate turn-on.

Thereafter, throughout the rest of the fortnight, he looked for the
courage and the right time to make a move on her. One natural opening was the night he threw a lavish party in honor of her 22nd birthday,
March 26, after a show in Kingston's ABC Theater, but he held off—
and kept doing so until time was running out. With only two days left
to the tour and the Revue in the world's romance capital, he couldn't
think of a better time and place.

The April 15 show at Paris's Olympia Music Hall, the tour's sign-
off, was given before a full house that included screen legend Marlene
Dietrich and soul singer extraordinaire Sarah Vaughan and was filmed
for French TV. During the afternoon, cameras followed the Supremes
as they pranced down the Champs Elysees while lip-synching a song,
snarling traffic and leading the gendarmes to roust the whole crew from
the street. For a few tense minutes, the cops held the Supremes, whom
they hadn't heard of, while they debated whether to arrest them for
causing a disturbance. Flo, who seemed to be enjoying the incident,
wondered aloud whether their image would be damaged by any bad
publicity. Esther Gordy Edwards, who was with them at the time,
thought just the opposite.

"As long as they spell your name right," she said, citing the first rule
of show business—one that her brother might not have agreed with in
this case.

Fortunately, after a few calls, the decision was made that no action
would be taken, and the tour's last show went into the books. It
couldn't have ended fast enough for most of the troupe, but Diana
wasn't quite ready to go home. No doubt sensing Gordy's amorous affections, she coyly suggested that they stay in Paris, just the two of
them, after the Revue flew back. "I was," he would say, "rocketed off
my feet. April in Paris. Alone? Phenomenal!"—knowing that this could
only lead to him literally being off his feet with her.

In such an "excited state" that he could barely remember his name,
he found himself alone with her in her hotel room that night, exchanging
champagne toasts with each other. That's when he went for it, initiating

a round of kissing that culminated in an overheated ripping of clothes and clutching of flesh, at which Gordy recalled thinking, "This is it!" However, standing there in the altogether was altogether too much for him to handle. With performance anxiety the only thing rising, he admitted, "Everything stopped working," mortified that the "big man" was anything but behind that closed door.

"I think it would be better if we just stayed friends," she intoned, almost pityingly, given the role reversal.

He nodded timidly and fled in shame to his room. But she was not about to follow her own advice; she had come to believe they really did love each other, at least as much as they loved the notion that they'd boost each other to the heights of success. Besides, she was absolutely intoxicated playing Lady Gordy, and *that* depended on being more than friends. Much more.

The next day, their last before going back, they said not a word about the embarrassment of the night before and "did Paris." In the afternoon, he rented a speedboat and they ran the waves up and down the Seine. At night, with her on his arm, they went club-hopping, listening to jazz bands. Back at the hotel, she serenaded him as they got high on expensive Cabernet Franc.

Evidently, that was the ticket. What didn't work the night before worked just fine now.

And so on April 15—appropriately, income tax day—the two biggest assets in American popular music became lovers. Gordy remembered the moment decades later with poetic license, obviously still feeling the tremors.

"We fit perfectly, like a carefully choreographed dance," he said, calling it "ecstasy to the tenth power!" He added: "And after that it only got better," not specifying if he meant Motown, the master plan, the music, the sex—or all of the above.

fourteen

"BABY, JUST POUR"

ordy's true confessions about the making of Diana Ross—in the biblical sense—revealed details no one seemed to know, or were willing to talk about, either back then or for years afterward. Even Ross, breaking form, didn't brag around the shop about it, biting her tongue at the time and keeping quiet to this day. Of course, everyone had known something happened between them when they were on their own in Paris—a liaison that would eventually produce an out-of-wedlock daughter—but it was too touchy a subject for them to want to indulge it, usually to protect Gordy, in deference to his power and his wish to keep it from the public. Indeed, even in Mary Wilson's "tell-all" memoirs, she told almost nothing of this monumental shack-up beyond the hazy euphemistic recollection that Diana and Berry "began dating" sometime around early '65, making their convulsive affair seem more like a prom date.

In truth, what Diana was doing was sleeping with the boss, and because the company was aware of this, it's a stretch to believe that Gordy was somehow able to keep it from Margaret for more than five minutes: How, for instance, could he possibly have explained his unexpected "layover" in Paris with Diana? Provided she didn't live with her hands over her ears, it's only logical to assume Margaret, unlike Claudette Robinson and Sharon Holland, accepted being cuckolded as a consequence of owning Gordy's part-time attention. As far as is known, she never staged any confrontations or psychotic scenes or let fly with any "it's either her or me" ultimatums.

For the rest of the Motown family, the Gordy-Ross union was as much a part of the environment as the "Hitsville, U.S.A." sign. There is one story in the Motown literature that Diana, dying to blab about it lest she implode, told Flo, "I got him!" Barely stirring, Flo asked, "Who?" Exasperated, Diana gushed, "Berry! I got him!" Flo's yawning response was, "So?" If this dialogue really happened, Flo's diffidence could have been a false front, hiding her own envy. Or, just as likely, it could have been that Flo had grown up and wasn't capable of squealing in excitement like a pig-tailed teenager at the idea of a grown woman spreading her legs for her employer, no matter how far it got her.

If it was the latter, Flo was not alone. For most of the entrenched crowd at Motown, all of them older and wiser, affairs were a fact of life; but this one so violated Gordy's little-followed rules of propriety that it reduced him in their eyes from benevolent despot to moral reprobate. The proof wasn't so much that he couldn't keep a professional distance from one of his stars but, rather, that he couldn't see what effect his Supremes obsession was causing. The thud that Martha Reeves had felt on the England tour had been felt even earlier by Marvin Gaye, who would recount for author David Ritz shortly before Gaye's 1984 death during a violent dispute with his father: "No one was prepared for the Supremes' [success]. It flipped Berry out, like he was playing the slot machines in Vegas and three cherries came up ten times in a row. He was gone [and] the rest of us felt his interest turn. Professionally he turned toward the Supremes and romantically he hooked up with Diana."

Accordingly, he went on, "[e]veryone saw it coming." And when it did, all of Motown became consumed with jealousy toward Ross, with Gaye—no less than Gordy's brother-in-law and delivering hit after hit himself—feeling as if he were on the outside looking in. Incredibly, he had been left home when the Revue flew to London, told that he'd sold too few records over there and that solo acts were lagging behind the group acts (Stevie Wonder apparently being an exception). That ruling, he said, "hurt me" and led him to forgo single work for the next two years, nearly exclusively racking up monster hits singing duets, first with Kim Weston, then Tammi Terrell.

Ross, he said, "had a power I lacked. I had Anna to talk to Berry, but Diana had Berry himself." In a sense, Gaye, like all the increasingly forsaken Motown artists, became as caught up with Ross as was Gordy, admitting, "I became obsessed with Diana's stardom. I resented the attention [Gordy] lavished on her."

But was Gordy so wrong? Even if he could have summoned the courage to keep his pants on when with her, did he even have an option in giving Ross the keys to the kingdom? Marvin Gaye wondered about that himself. "[H]ow could I blame him?" he concluded. "The Supremes were making him a fortune. Besides, with Diana's drive and class, he knew this was only the beginning."

And the consequences be damned. Raynoma Liles, with whom Gordy had made peace and financed a small record label for her to run, remembered coming back to Detroit and being startled by the devolution of the company she helped get off the ground into quite nearly a one-woman band. "So many talented people were discarded" during the interval when Gordy became fixated with Diana's "hungering, driving ambition to be famous," she recalled. That detour would be a money trough in the short term; in the long run, she said sadly, "it would cause irreparable damage to Motown."

In catering to Diana Ross, Liles believed, "Berry was shaping a monster."

The way the Supremes' TV rounds were rigged now, they were to provide context for major upcoming events. In late February, a few weeks before the England tour, the group made a return engagement on *Shindig*, but only with the proviso that it could promote *A Bit of Liverpool* by performing "Eight Days a Week" and "You Can't Do That" sandwiched around the mandatory "Stop! In the Name of Love"—not that the girls seemed any more excited to sing those songs, turning in rather listless renditions of the Beatles songs, though they would never look hotter than they did in the skin-tight pants suits they wore for "Eight Days a Week." It was possibly their sexiest TV appearance ever, even if it was musically forgettable.

Positioning them for their summer Copa run, and beyond, Gordy began prepping them by having them perform standard pop fare along with their hits; for their second *Hullabaloo* appearance on May 11, 1965, Gordy insisted that the producers allow the girls to sing the reviled "You're Nobody 'Til Somebody Loves You" along with their hits—if not, no Supremes, period. Rare indeed was a TV show they performed on that didn't contain this hybrid approach; in the fall, after the Copa gig, they would do a *Hullabaloo* redux, including a top-hat, soft-shoe rendition of "Toot Toot Tootsie." The following year they'd be seen on *The Dean Martin Show* crooning a medley of elevator-music standards ("If This Is Love," "Love Is Here to Stay," "Let There Be Love") with geriatrics Dino, Jayne Morgan, and Imogene Coca, and on *The Sammy Davis Jr. Show,* sharing the stage at one point with the aging Andrews Sisters—who had sold no fewer than 5 million records in their day—with each group performing some of each other's hits. Those who could remember the Supremes singing "Let Me Go the Right Way" might have winced watching them camp it up on "Roll Out the Barrel," "Apple Blossom Time," and "Bei Mir Bist Du Schön." Other bookings in '65 included the Steel Pier in Atlantic City, the Miami Orange Bowl Parade, and the opening of the Houston Astrodome.

For anyone at Motown who was more than a little uncomfortable about the racial bastardization of his preeminent act, Gordy had only one answer: Get used to it. Motown, he knew, would always have its black market. But not until the Supremes went "broad" did the company clear $40 million a year in sales, as it would in 1965. The days of R&B purity in the Motown Sound was over. Gordy never regretted it, not as filthy rich as he would become. But for others, it would be something like a tragedy.

In the spring of '65, too, the Supremes could finally put Brewster-Douglass into the past tense. Though they'd been on the road so much that hotel rooms and not the rusting tenement had been their homes for the past year, the move was clearly past due given their diamonds-and-pearls lifestyle. After Esther Edwards had scouted appropriately tony neighborhoods, Motown put down payments on a number of homes along the well-heeled, lightly integrated Buena Vista Drive (which in the local idiom is pronounced "Byoona Vista"). The mainline of the neighborhood ran roughly twenty blocks, with the homes mainly two-story brick Tudor estates lined with leafy trees and immense lawns and yards. Given a choice of which ones they wanted, the girls, in the manner of all four Beatles living on the same street in Liverpool, wound up within steps of each other; Diane was across the street from Flo, and Mary a block and a half away.

It was only beneficial to Motown to be able to cast this propinquity as continued proof of the Supremes' "sisterly" nature, which in fact had only fleetingly existed. Indeed, their inter-relationships while in their new $30,000 homes remained much the same as they had been back in the projects. Each of the Supremes lived with her family, taking them along in a kind of mass liberation. And most of the broods lived there in style for years, with Motown accountants paying off the mortgages—and the Cadillacs chosen by the girls dressing up their driveways. Not that any of these appurtenances were endowments from a big-hearted Gordy; every cent doled out for their lavish lifestyle was deducted from their still unspecified "expenses," including the thousands of dollars charged to sessions for and master tapes of unreleased records. (Although that suggests they owned those tapes, in truth they did not; only Gordy did.)

Amazingly, Diana's house was the *least* pretentious, quite likely because it was set up by Fred and Ernestine who, with her brother and sister, were given the ground floor to live in and decorate as they wished. Diana took the upstairs, which she basically turned into a massive storage bin for her gowns, dresses, shoes, and jewelry. One bedroom was used entirely as a closet, with mirror-lined walls so that she could see herself from all angles when deciding what to wear. When she was home, she usually hunkered down in the master bedroom and rarely came out.

Flo, across the street, would refer to her as "Greta Garbo" when people came to visit her. One frequent guest, Flo's cousin Ray Gibson, can recall with a giggle that while Diana wouldn't deign to come out of the house, as did Flo and Mary, when their fans would gather outside and wait for autographs, she would gayly talk about the dozens of gift packages that would be left on her doorstep.

"Flo would tell me, 'Honey, I see that door every day. And I've never seen even one package out there.' She'd also be in hysterics because when Diana would have to come out and the fans would be in the street, she'd run up to the ones in front of Flo's house and make a big show of her appreciation. She'd say, 'Oh, are you here to see *me*?' One time Flo said there *was* a big package by Diana's house—and it was left out there for a week, so everyone could see it."

That Flo had become offended by just about anything, small or large, what Diana was doing was becoming all too obvious. "Oh, definitely," says Gibson. "You could feel it. And you just knew it was going to get worse, a lot worse."

Flo, aptly, had laid out her house exactly opposite from the way Diana did. She put her huge clan upstairs and ruled the roost downstairs, where she created a cross between country calico and urban chic. There were airy white and baby-blue walls, four-inch-thick plush white carpets, Oriental vases, crystal chandeliers, and in the basement a "nightclub" with cocktail tables and jazz bric-a-brac.

The shock was that meek Mary Wilson turned her digs into a playpen that Hugh Hefner could have decorated. Not incidentally, she moved her family—her mother and two cousins—to a separate, smaller house on the block. Living on her own, she went a bit wild. The decor was contemporary swing-club, with inviting sectional sofas, gaudy yellow and orange walls and matching drapes, open bars, and in her bedroom a huge round bed fitted with a remote button that, when pushed, activated the encirclement of sheer curtains for additional privacy. Even Caligula himself, Berry Gordy, blushed when he heard that Mary wanted to mirror the ceiling over the bed.

Aghast at what such a revelation would do to the girls', and Motown's, image if it ever got out, he told her firmly, "Mary, I don't think that's a very good idea. It's not going to sound right."

She obeyed, but overhead mirrors or not, hers was the place to be for the Motown "in crowd." After billing the company for building a dance studio in the basement where Mary and Flo would rehearse their moves—Diana usually passed it up—she rented the basement to Cholly Atkins and his wife, Mae, who also had a home on the street. Consequently, other acts would come over to rehearse, as well, and if Wilson was at home she'd throw a party; soon, the house would be teeming with more guests and crashers. Frequently the Four Tops were among the revelers, upon which Mary started a fling with Duke Fakir, a married member of the group.

As she wistfully recounted in her autobiography, "Duke was a man's man, and many times when we were home he'd call and say, 'Sweetpea, I'm bringing some of the guys over for dinner.' . . . Duke was known for making a knockout punch, and we'd have what we called 'sloopy parties.' I can't count the mornings I woke up to find a guest lying face down on the black bear rug in the den."

Flo would normally join in on the festivities—Diana almost never—as well as throwing her own bashes, at which she'd make a grand entrance, a la Loretta Young at the beginning of her TV show, in a billowy gown, at times carrying a silver tray of goodies she herself had cooked up. Still, Mary's was the party center, and she herself wasn't lonely for long in that circular, curtained bed. She was the "love 'em and leave 'em Supreme," taking up with a string of paramours as if making up in quantity what Diana had in quality; for a time, and periodically over 1965 and '66, Duke Fakir moved in with her during his regular separations from his wife. That meant all three Supremes were involved on and off with nonsingle men in the Motown "family," Diana of course with the "big man" and Flo with Otis Williams.

OTIS WILLIAMS: My marriage was on the rocks anyway, but it was not just a fling or whatever with Flo. She may have been the only woman I really, truly loved. We always made time to see each other on the rare occasions we were both home at the same time. Flo didn't have many people she could talk to about her problems. She couldn't do it with her family. In fact, she would come over to my place just to get away, be in a quiet surrounding.

Flo was a passionate woman, I won't kid you. She had a lot of, let's say, *energy*, because she kept so much pent up inside. She took me on some wild rides. I'd love her openness about it. She had these great expressions for doing it, like she'd say we were gonna "shoot the habit to the rabbit." I'd never heard that one before, and I'd been around, man. She'd give me that big sexy smile and call me, "Big Daddy," and that was all I needed.

But it was more than sex. I knew Flo was depressed and I feel that when she came over she wanted to just get away from all her problems. So we wouldn't talk about any of the shit she was going through. That time was just for us, to share some beautiful moments. We just didn't have enough time with our schedules. And there wasn't enough time for Flo to get away from those problems.

The PR campaign that would carry the Supremes into the three-week Copacabana engagement was under way by now. One goal was to take them further into the mainstream media than any Motown act had gone, and Gordy came up aces when reporters from the devoutly establishment *Time* magazine sent reporters to Hitsville to interview him and the girls—a huge breakthrough given that only within the last year or so had Motown drawn just modest attention in the press, even in the Detroit press. Granted, part of that neglect was due to the nearly annual labor vs. management warfare that led to strikes at the city's two biggest newspapers, the *News* and the *Free Press*, which were shut down by strikes nine straight years, the most recent from July to November

1964. But even the black press had little to do with Motown, save for some passing mention of a hit song here and there in the pocket-sized *Jet*. The black *Michigan Chronicle*, its offices on nearby St. Antoine Street, virtually ignored one of the most significant exemplars of black capitalism right down the street on West Grand Boulevard.

Motown PR man Al Abrams remembered that even when the Supremes were to do the *Sullivan* show and he believed it would be a snap to get them on the cover of the *News*'s Sunday "TV Week" insert, the editor told him, "We can't put black people on the cover of a TV magazine." That kind of neglect could be measured nationwide, with very few papers' TV listings bothering to include the Supremes as one of the acts on that *Sullivan* episode (most, however, found room for the Czechoslovakian Folk Dance troupe). By mid-'65, it still was not a sure thing. Abrams was finally able to get that "TV Week" cover for the Supremes, an important step since regional editions of the section were published by the *New York Journal-American, the Houston Chronicle,* and the *Washington Evening Star.*

"I believe when that happened, the Supremes became the first African-Americans to be on the cover of a TV magazine," Abrams said. At about that time, the same *News* editor was doing a big story on Motown and wanted to meet Berry Gordy. When Abrams introduced them, the guy gushed, "I've wanted to meet you. I've heard so much about you." Gordy replied, "You have?" "Yeah," he said, "my maid listens to your music all the time."

And then, suddenly, there were the Supremes on the cover of the May 21, 1965, issue of *Time*, in pictures and words and quoted along with Gordy in the accompanying article. The article hardly reversed the tide of racism in the mid-'60s—and in fact the faux-hip prose indulged in some typical passively racist prose itself—but it did put black faces into the center lane of American pop culture. On that milestone cover the Supremes broke into a collage of the (white) rock elite, side by side with the Beach Boys, Herman's Hermits, Petula Clark, and the Righteous Brothers. The article, titled "The Sound of the Sixties," read in part: "[T]he best brown sound is, of course, that sung by Negroes. . . . Next to the Mersey Sound, the 'Motown Sound' currently dominates the rock 'n' roll market. It is a swing, city blues sound, propelled by a driving beat." The Supremes, it went on, were "the prize fillies in Gordy's stable," and Ross "[is] envied for the torchy, come-hither purr in her voice."

Of course, much of this come-lately revelation was already dated by Gordy's fine-tuning of the Supremes. But now, the seal was broken on all fronts of the mainstream media. For Gordy, it couldn't have gotten any better. In fact, with his mind freed of the obsession of getting Diana into bed, he returned to his original obsession, the business one. Almost as soon as he got out of bed the morning after in Paris, he was different, his sights elsewhere; while the affair would continue back home, he became progressively more distant toward her. Falling back into the paternal Berry, he was frequently domineering, insensitive, even nasty, as if consciously reestablishing his credentials as the master of all who breathed in Motown, including the woman he'd lost his breath and nearly his mind wooing so arduously.

Superseding Cholly Atkins, Maurice King, and Gil Askey, Gordy took to handing down the last word on the Supremes' choreography and stagecraft. Often he could be found at rehearsals or at local gigs the girls did at the clubs, furiously scribbling notes on a thick legal pad as they performed. He'd then go backstage and, with not a word of laudation, start in on his critiques—mostly of Diana—which could be brutal. As Ross would recall, his litany seemed intentionally harsh but rarely constructive, along the lines of "Tighten up the act," "You're singing wrong," "You're not moving together," or "You're not smiling." Soon, Diana could take no more.

"Leave me alone! I know what the fuck I'm doing!" she screamed, *really* torchy, after one such chew-out session.

Although she was the only one at Motown who could come at him like that and get away with it, usually such bravado would recede into contrition. Not now. Regularly, the two of them would be seen bickering and sniping at each other, temporarily resolving the flare-ups in bed but solving nothing in the long term.

"It was just like they were an old married couple," laughed Otis Williams, who saw the same scene carry out at Motown picnics, parties, recording sessions, photo shoots, anywhere Berry and Diana found themselves. "It's a good thing the girls were on the road so much, 'cause if not, those two woulda *killed* each other."

The "marriage" would endure for over two decades, with varying degrees of dysfunction, at times with and without the "under the sheet" music, and the relationship mutated into something more like an addiction to mutually assured torture than anything resembling love. Which might account for why the passages about Gordy in her otherwise saccharine *Secrets of a Sparrow* read like an exercise in self-therapy, as if Ross was trying to ease Gordy withdrawal by striking a balance between mandatory declarations of love and fealty and shooting daggers into his hide.

There was the Berry who "related to me" and who "could see him-self in me," a man who inspired her to such inane cosmic jive as "the greatest connection between Berry and me was our powerful life en-ergy." And there was the Berry who "behaved like a tyrant . . . heavily judgmental . . . discouraging," who was "very hard on us." She also had no problem granting herself absolution for her pariah status—by pin-ning the blame for it on Gordy. "He played favorites," she wrote, "and [that] set up an unhealthy internal climate." She remembered hearing him harpooning other Motown artists by using her as the poison tip, going into tirades like "Why can't you be more like Diana? She makes her plans, she works really hard, she rehearses all day long, she records all night. Why can't you be like her?"

The assumption, naturally, was that he was merely repeating what *she* had told him, and she could never convince Motown denizens other-wise. But she maintained her innocence. "Comparing is a terrible thing to do in a family situation," she concluded. "It produces crippling sib-ling rivalry [and] it became a very difficult situation for me." Those who couldn't measure up to her—meaning, everybody—subsequently "turned not only on Berry but on his chosen one."

Missing from Ross's self-pitying tale of woe, of course, is that there's no room for her pre-success presumptions in which she, in effect, put the company on notice that no one *would* be like her. Gordy only held her to it—without objection from her, at the time. But in the nuclear-driven Gordy, she had the cover she needed for plausible deniability. "I am quite clear," she stressed, "that I am not responsible for anybody else's success or failure."

Not that the lesser Motown mortals had much sympathy; they'd never heard a word suggesting that Diana cared a whit about anyone else's fate. But Ross from here on in began to, as she recalled, "live un-der constant stress," manifestations of which would soon become evi-dent. Without pause, however, the beat went on.

The next song from HDH was "Back in My Arms Again," early tracks for which were cut in late December 1964 and completed with the girls' vocals in late February. Cutting it in the same quarter- and eight-note beats as "Stop! In the Name of Love," but with a freer, bluesier gait, HDH—let's say *with* the Funk Brothers—made Studio A rever-berate, buffing up a melody that was driven by a simultaneous line of

Earl Van Dyke's nifty honky-tonk piano riffs and Ashford's vibes, which in turn played off Mike Terry's honking sax, blaring trombones, and thunderous drum and bass lines.

Eddie Holland's lyrics had Ross going beyond her usual pining, yearning, and burning; now she could strut triumphant and smug, ignoring pleas to "break away from the boy I love" and risk suffering the "heartache he'll bring one day." Having "lost him once" by listening "to my friends' advice," she adamantly swore that "it's not gonna happen twice." Most cleverly, the lyric identified the meddling friends, with "How can Mary tell me what to do when she lost her love so true? And Flo, she don't know, 'cause the boy she loves is a Romeo."

"See, that's how girls talk, they put the blame on their friends for screwing up their love lives," Eddie says. "I always tried to write to that kind of voice and attitude with those songs."

Whether intended or not, it was a perfect match for Ross's attitude. On a more subtle level, it was even a mild homily of her "de-friending" of Wilson and Ballard, not that anyone perceived it that way, least of all Mary and Flo, who saw it mainly as a welcome, and overdue, recognition that they, too, were Supremes—one that allowed them a taste of the acclaim Diana lived with 24/7. Released in mid-April with "Whisper You Love Me Boy" on the reverse, "Back in My Arms Again" was only nine days later the lead song on *Billboard*'s Spotlights page, its breakout so breakneck that the showbiz bible didn't have time to get the title right—calling it "Back in Your Arms Again"—in pegging it a "[h]ot follow-up to 'Stop! In the Name of Love,'" with "a strong lyric and powerful vocal performance pitted against a hard rock background in full support. A winner all the way!"

Billboard seemed genuinely ready to swoon at just about any Supremes product by now. Just weeks before, it had boosted onto its "Breakout New Albums" page *The Supremes Sing Country, Western and Pop,* the oddball mélange produced by Clarence Paul that had sat on the shelf for a year before a belated release to cash in on the group's popularity (to no avail; it stiffed, on merit, rising no higher than No. 79)—one of three Supremes albums issued between March and July. The others were the intriguing *We Remember Sam Cooke*, covering hit songs by the recently murdered soul singer (e.g., "You Send Me," "Chain Gang," "Twistin' the Night Away," "Bring It on Home to Me," "Shake")—which stalled at No. 75 on the pop album chart but made it to an impressive No. 5 on the R&B chart—and the obligatory *More Hits*, another compilation of hits and filler that would ring in at No. 6

pop, 2 R&B. And two *more* LPs were cut and cataloged—a live album and the other of Broadway show tunes called *There's a Place for Us*—but both were held back and never issued.

The very listenable and marketable "Back in My Arms Again" shot up the pop chart, almost *too* fast; it was in the Top Forty by early May and in the top spot on June 12, to be bumped after a week only by the equally meteoric trip of the Four Tops' "I Can't Help Myself." With the Copa a month away, and riding a trail of five consecutive No. 1 hits—something achieved only by Elvis until then, in 1956–57 and 1959–61, and which the Beatles were working on en route to six in a row by early '66—the girls were called back into the studio to record another current ditty to coincide with the big gig. Reaching into the HDH barrel, Gordy came out with "Nothing But Heartaches," another winner but with blemishes, one of which was familiarity. Indeed, the HDH-Supremes "ballpark" was in need of expansion. Though perfectly catchy power-pop, it left a somewhat tiring effect after one listen, as if it had been heard—because it *was,* in "Back in My Arms Again." Then, too, after the happy ending of "Back," the brooding despair of "Heartaches" and its fatal-attraction lyrics—"He brings nothing but heartaches / Ooh, nothing but heartaches / But I can't break away / Oh no, keep a loving him more each day"—and the vision of Diana Ross "crying myself to sleep" were downers.

For once, a Supremes record wasn't a must-have; released in July backed with "He Holds His Own" and hurriedly included on *More Hits*, it didn't move onto the charts until after the Copa gig and peaked at a disappointing No. 11 in late August. While Gordy tried to ameliorate some of the damage by claiming the record sold over a million copies, as best as could be determined by the RIAA it managed to sell only around 600,000.

The downer of "Nothing But Heartaches" was the least of the Supremes' problems in the run-up to the Copa, the subtitle of which, right up to their entrance on the stage there, could have been "Nothing But Headaches." The expectations were high from the start, only to intensify as July 29 approached. Gordy, turning *Billboard* into a PR arm, was able to get them on the front page of the July 17 issue, when the caption noted not only that "the hottest recording group in the world" had a new single but that "New Yorkers will have an opportunity to see this exciting act when it opens at the famous Copacabana night club July 29 for three weeks." A week later, ads run by the club popped up in the New York dailies; bannered "THE COPA RAINS SUPREMES" with their picture, they gave lower billing to stand-up comic Bobby Remsen and "the world famous Copa Girls," and at the bottom touted "full course dinners from $5.25 . . . 2 shows nightly 9 & 12, 3 shows Fri. & Sat. 8, 11:30 & 2."

Things were moving so fast and furiously that Diana, prodded and exhorted by the relentless Gordy, looked like she might not make it to New York. Pushed to the limit every day in rehearsals, all three girls were run ragged—only days before the show Flo came down with a case of the flu—but Gordy worked Diana the hardest, putting her under tremendous pressure by telling her that she was the whole act and that success or failure rested solely on her. Overtired and too nervous to eat, she lost weight on her already undernourished frame; at five-foot-five she normally carried 103 pounds, but now she was down to 90, her face hollowed, her legs spindly.

Of course, the "emaciated" look was in vogue, thanks to the British model Twiggy and her concentration-camp-survivor appearance. If that was the new paragon of fashion and glamour, Diana was relieved, as she no longer would need to enhance her waifish figure with those padded bras and such. Neither was Gordy averse to the idea, in his drive to imbue her with elegant sophistication. What concerned him was possibly having to postpone the Copa, which at this point would mean financial disaster for Motown after so much money had been shelled out to publicize it. Such was his terror that *he* couldn't eat either; nor did he want to even *think* about leaving the Copa in the lurch and perhaps never being allowed back in. And so he consulted dietitians to prepare special meals for Diana. Thankfully, she got strong enough and recovered, as did Flo, who flew to New York two days before the gig. Still, nearly everyone at Motown kept their fingers crossed that Diana would make it through the next three weeks in one piece.

For a 400-seat nightclub, the Copacabana had a Vatican-like imprimatur in the showbiz community, and Motown was at its mercy negotiating with Jules Podell, the cigar-sucking, Runyonesque tough-guy character who owned the quarter-century-old watering hole on East 60th Street. Even though the summer was the time new acts were booked in lieu of the big names who took their shows to the Catskill Mountain hotels, Podell nonetheless would give little ground on the Supremes. Never before had a "rock" act played that most important of

VIP venues, nor for that matter had any act seemingly younger than 40, its marquee a dependable gleaning of '50s cool and first-name recognition—Frank, Sammy, Tony, Ella, Peggy, Nat—with mass appeal to the mainly middle-aged tourists who jammed into the place night after night to drink like fish in a Brazilian motif complete with jungle palms, coconuts, and murals of banana boats.

Rumors that Podell was either part of or a cover for the Mob were something he shared with Gordy. And if the Copa was starting to lose a bit of its luster, along with that of the New York club scene, Podell was still baronial in 1965. To be sure, he had Motown over a barrel in giving his stage over to the Supremes, more so knowing that Gordy would agree to just about anything. It turned out to be a contract that would bring the girls in for three annual engagements, the first for a three-week run for a flat payment of $3,000. At sixteen shows a week, including that killer thrice-a-night weekend schedule, this came to all of $180 a show—or $60 each. In truth, Gordy would have taken three subway tokens, but at least the handout would be bumped up to $10,000 a week for the second year and $15,000 for the third—that is, if Podell chose to have them back, a decision that was all his. At the same time Gordy could justifiably claim that Motown was being ripped off, since he had to foot all production costs, not to mention throwing parties for the New York industry crowd and his distributors, and putting up the large Motown contingent in suites at the Plaza Hotel.

Basically, all Podell had to do was turn the lights on and off each night. As Gordy would recall with lingering distaste, "Knowing what a major launching pad his club was, Jules made us pay for everything. . . . No discounts on food or drinks; you paid full price, no matter who you were—manager, musicians, or star." He called the Supremes agreement "a slave contract," as ironic a complaint as there possibly could have been from Gordy.

For many reasons, the opening was as much an ordeal for Gordy as for the girls. Just days before, he was called back to Detroit when Loucye Gordy suffered a cerebral hemorrhage and a day later died on the operating table. With the most contrasting of emotions imaginable, the Gordy family attended a funeral on the morning of July 29, then flew to New York for the opening—one of the saddest moments in Berry's life followed almost immediately by one of his most exultant. Somehow, he was able to put on his game face and cheer on the Supremes, fully expecting them to ease his grief by tearing the roof off the joint.

Ross, Wilson, and Ballard hardly needed to be put under any more pressure; it was more than enough that the future of Motown, as Gordy saw it now, was riding on them. And if anyone ever doubted that Diana Ross was a trouper beyond compare, the most convincing rebuttal of all would be that Copa run of shows. Programmed as she was by Gordy, Atkins, King, Askey, and Powell, and kept sharp right up until the opening—while they were in New York, he booked them into a small club in northern New Jersey for several nights rather than have them sit around the Plaza—it was a wonder she could come out and be any-thing close to natural when she'd get her cue at the Copa. But, consid-ering that she'd waited twenty-one years for this moment, there was also no way she would not be ready for her grand entrance.

At the same time, if anyone failed to understand the continent apart the Supremes were from their—and Gordy's—musical roots, a small ad in the New York papers the day of the opening brought it home. Hours later, while the Supremes were making history at the Copa, the world they'd left behind carried on: At the Apollo Theater that night, the Shirelles, Wilson Pickett, Shep and the Limelighters, and Garnet Mimms would be on those grimier boards, as would the Marvelettes an evening later—representing the Motown the Supremes and Berry Gordy had turned their backs on.

Down at the Copa, black and soul were quaint notions. With Gordy and the Motown cognoscenti at the head VIP table sat tastemakers of their new world, scribes like Ed Sullivan and Earl Wilson, Sammy Davis Jr., Joey Bishop, actor Jack Cassidy—though Gordy did not for-get the honchos of his distributing companies and the still-important solons of the radio such as Murray the K and Frankie Crocker of New York's all-black station WBLS. He also invited his boyhood idol, Joe Louis. Over the course of the evening, he would shell out $10,000 for drinks—charged to the Supremes as "promotional expenses."

Everything was in place and ready as Bobby Remsen finished warm-ing up the crowd—everything, that is, except the Supremes, who were frantic backstage because their chosen dresses for the opening, blue with green and yellow feathered flowers at the advice of Maxine Powell, had still not arrived. Rummaging through "leftover" dresses in a tizzy, and Diana starting to unravel to the point that Mary thought she had a "weird look in her eyes," Mae Atkins, who'd been responsible for pick-ing up the dresses from the designer, ran in at the last minute holding the boxes under her arm. Powell practically pushed her aside, grab-bing the boxes and tearing them open so the girls could hastily shimmy into their clothes. Then, with Gil Askey giving the downbeat to the orchestra, the Supremes smoothly sauntered onto the floor singing the Cole Porter chestnut "From This Moment On," a message-sending song if ever there was one for the group at that particular fork in the road.

Indeed, the next order of business was a perfunctory, distilled medley of "Baby Love," "Come See About Me," and "Stop! In the Name of Love"—the only hits of theirs that would be heard that night. Following that came "The Girl from Ipanema" and the show tune "Make Someone Happy," which Askey had arranged to be a showcase for Diana, with some of the stage patter written for her by Maurice King. Introducing her mates while standing to their right, she began: "I know if there were teenagers in the house they'd know our names. [Audience laughter.] But if you don't know us, on the end is Florence Ballard. She's the quiet one." [Sardonic grin from Ballard.]

"In the middle is Mary Wilson. She's the sexy one." [Wide grin and a wiggle from Wilson.]

"My name is Diana Ross." [Extended pause as audience grows expectant.] "I'm the intelligent one." [Laughter and applause as Wilson and Ballard look at each other and roll their eyes.]

That, however, was a mere warm-up for her. During a seemingly endless break between verses of "Somewhere," the *West Side Story* tearjerker, she delivered an excruciating soliloquy about there being "a place for each of us, a place of peace and quiet . . . where love is like a passion that burns like a fire," going on in that vein for a full two minutes as Mary and Flo hummed the melody in a whisper behind her spotlight-illuminated visage. It was all very cheesy and scripted right down to the last comma. In fact, the only moment of spontaneity was when Flo—contradicting Gordy's prescribed rules on conduct for the show—took it upon herself to ad-lib during the closing number, the ever-present "You're Nobody 'Til Somebody Loves You." When Diana hit the line "But gold won't bring you happiness," Flo broke in with "Now wait a minute, honey. I don't know about all that."

It was classic Flo sass, executed with perfect timing, the kind of one-liner she'd done a thousand times before, and it prompted the bucolic Sammy Davis Jr. to chime in from his seat, "All right, girl! You tell it like it is!" as the audience hooted and clapped. Diana, momentarily thrown by Flo's deviation from the script, also broke up and, ad-libbing too, remarked affably, "She's always been like that." As delightfully genuine as the interlude was in a sea of staged hokum, Gordy, so wound up that he'd forgotten how to enjoy a good line that wasn't prefabricated, sat stonily, mortified that Ballard had upstaged his diva.

The balance of the show was filled out with detritus: the hat-and-cane-twirling softshoe of "Rockabye Your Baby" that Flo detested so much, the Barbra Streisand tune "People" (featuring Flo on lead), "Queen of the House" (a reworking of Roger Miller's "King of the Road"), and a couple of songs from the Sam Cooke tribute album. After three encores, the Supremes took their final curtain call to a sustained standing ovation. For the Motown entourage in the electrified room, there was nothing but exhilaration. Gordy, for the first time in months, could finally exhale. Backstage, having traded their soggy dresses for terry-cloth robes, Mary and Flo were ecstatic, crying and exchanging hugs with the Hitsville VIPs. Diana, jubilant, kept excitedly asking people how she did. When Gordy came in, he cut through the mob and kissed Diana on the cheek. That was when she knew she'd done well, very well.

The next day, the reviews certified it. Earl Wilson's *New York Post* column—randomly identifying Ballard first, Wilson second, and Ross third, to Gordy's consternation—reported that the "rhythm and blues singers from Detroit" had won an ovation from a star-studded crowd. In the *Daily News* Ed Sullivan said the Supremes were "the greatest of the new singing trios," a typical half-aware Sullivan rave—in actuality, there were few rock trios around—but one the Motown PR people would eagerly attach to their press releases. Leonard Harris's *New York World-Telegram and Sun* notice read: "The girls are good musicians [*sic*], good performers and good looking" and called Ross "a devastating vocalist with a hypnotic presence."

When *Billboard*'s August 7 issue hit the stands, there were *two* reviews on the same page, one by no less than the publisher Hal B. Cook titled "SUPREME SUPREMES," stating that "[t]he lovely Supremes shook up the entire block with their fantastic performance. . . . This group has had fabulous success on records. We had heard of their great 'in person' ability. Now we have seen it. If you get the chance, catch the Supremes in person." In the other, titled "COPA PROVING GROUND: AS AN ACT FOR ALL AGES SUPREMES BLOOM OUT," Aaron Sternfield foamed that they'd "put on a performance the likes of which the famed bistro has seldom experienced." Noting that "the Motown beat was polished, refined and arranged to a fare-thee-well"—an observation that might have made the company's nonelitist fans want to cringe—he went on to say that the Supremes "have all the equipment—poise, polish and a comic sense—and that equipment was working flawlessly." Most gratifying for Gordy, though, was Sternfield's emphasis on Ross, saying she had "emerged as a solo talent to be reckoned with. . . . Her distinctive phrasing and amazing vocal range stamps her as one of the best in the business."

And there was this: "While the Supremes will probably keep their teen-age following for some time, there appears little question that the act will last a lot longer as staple adult fare, not too dependent on the chart position of their latest single."

Except for the irrelevance of hits—a premise that violated every instinct he had—Gordy couldn't have said it any better himself. Nor could he have played the mutual scratch-my-back game with *Billboard* more successfully.

The Supremes continued to shake up the block for three weeks, with every show a sellout and bolstered by growing word of mouth. It seemed everyone who was anyone in New York knew they were there and were the talk of the town. During the run they were asked to be on the popular CBS Sunday-night quiz show *What's My Line* as the collective mystery guest, and were guessed quickly, though panelist Arlene Francis asked, "Are you Twiggy?" Diana, proof of the new axiom that "thin is in," coyly replied, "I'm shorter."

However, not even in the blissful atmospherics of this triumph did Gordy behave with any tact in singularly promoting Diana Ross—and slighting Florence Ballard. The two were surely on a collision course for some time, with Flo of the mind that even in her diminished role she was integral to the chemistry and personality of the group, as shown on opening night. And she was right, far more so than Gordy knew, or wanted to. It may well even have been that the Supremes' unfathomable winning streak had kept him from seriously considering a radical move, such as a solo Diana Ross project—something all of Motown believed was an inevitability and never dismissed by Gordy.

The streak was also a palliative for Ballard. She had done all she could to get on with Diana; she'd stepped aside as the leader for her, and sought to keep the old, albeit never strong, "sister" vibe going by trying to include Diana in the parties on Buena Vista. Now, she worked extra hard mastering routines that clashed with her style and music sensibilities, rehearsing herself right into a sick bed, just as Diana had. The difference was, when the latter had taken ill, Gordy did everything but act as her wet nurse. For Flo, perhaps looking for a reason to question her commitment to the Supremes, he couldn't spare even a phone call.

Neither did it seem a coincidence when Diana began openly questioning whether Flo was even very sick at all. When Flo had to delay going to New York, Diana cattily spent the couple of days that Flo wasn't there with her and Mary telling people that if it were *her*, she would "collapse on stage" at the Copa rather than be felled by a "head cold"—though there was never any doubt that Flo would not have missed the opening. That was the sort of nasty accusation that Flo never would have made about Diana, and was so personally cruel that Flo had to assume that Diana took a cue from Berry.

"The one thing about Florence was, she was very, very sharp; she had antennae, she could read people's intentions," her cousin Ray Gibson believes. "When she was sick before the Copa thing—that was the first of many times she'd get sick—she could sense things that were happening. It was like they wanted to use it to insult her, to make her seem like an outcast so they could use it against her later. Hell, they knew she wouldn't miss the Copa. They would have had to kill her for her not to be there. She was incredibly excited about it. She'd tell me, 'Imagine that, Raymond—I'm gonna be singing at the Copa!'

"So all that bullshit made her stronger. She wasn't going to let them stop her from having her moment, any of the great moments the Supremes had. I think the objective with Florence was that Berry wanted to make it look like she didn't care about the Supremes, and that was the furthest thing from the truth. That was her group, her dream. And here it was like they were trying to take it away from her, and she just never knew why. If they had to do that, tear her down, never say a good word about Florence, because they wanted to make Diana stand out more, that's the height of cruelty. Thinking about it all these years later, it still turns my stomach."

Otis Williams believes that "Flo never could reconcile having all that success, being one-third of something so special, yet not being able to sit back and enjoy. She couldn't figure out why it had to be so hard. She understood about Diana being the lead singer because she had a voice that sold records. But she couldn't understand why she was so unappreciated by the Motown establishment."

It was surely a weird dynamic. Onstage, fans seemed to have more affection for her than they did for Diana and Mary; regularly, shouts of "We love you, Flo!" or "Sing it, Flo!" would resound in the hall. But then she'd get back to Motown and be ignored as the "establishment" fell all over Diana, and even Mary, whose low-pitched voice was almost always recessed and was really now no more than that of a good-looking mannequin—whereas Flo's human qualities were both vocal, in the high, ringing notes she could let fly, and visual with her slightly against-the-grain ingenuousness. This certainly explained why club owners out on the road also loved her, far more than Gordy did while seeing her refracted by his obsessions with Ross. Indeed, those shouts of "We love you, Flo" may have had something to do with Gordy's waspish attitude toward Ballard, given that Ross rarely, and Wilson never, were the recipient of such hosannas from Supremes fans. Gordy's plans meant he had to get that kind of reaction for Ross, even if he would have to manufacture it.

It wasn't just paradoxical that he could have regarded any form of adulation for the Supremes as a threat to his blueprint; it was beyond absurd. But the fate of Florence Ballard seemed to show that it was standard operating procedure around Motown, as Ballard became known as a "problem."

The more adrift Flo became, the more she found the means to gauze the hurt—with a glass in her hand. For most in the Supremes' entourage, Ballard's increased consumption of alcohol meant nothing other than that she was a good-time girl who liked to get the juice flowing for everyone. At the Plaza, she set up a wet bar in her room, making Suite 811 the place to be. Here, every day, room service was instructed to roll in her standing order, which was described by one reveler as "a bottle of everything, one Scotch, one vodka, one gin, one rum, one rye, and several dozen canapés"—along with a dozen each of champagne glasses, water glasses, highball glasses, and shot glasses, and three ice buckets.

Everyone just took it as a road-show version of the basement bar she had at home, with the same intent—to provide spirits for people streaming into the room at all hours. As always, she meticulously set up the bar, pouring all the booze from their bottles into the decanters and serving the drinks herself, every inch a lady who could keep waves of guests entertained for hours. Flo would imbibe freely, but while she could drink them all under the table she seemed to be able to hold her booze, too, and almost never appeared to be drunk.

But being around all that alcohol was a comfort, too, and during the Copa run Flo Ballard needed comfort as her grand dream turned sour. Even in the opening-night afterglow, before the orchestra had stopped playing, Gordy was messing with her about her amusing ad lib during the final number.

"About that one-liner you dropped in," he began, uneasily. "Real funny stuff."

But he didn't say it as if he really thought it was funny; to Flo, it sounded sarcastic, meant to cushion what he wanted to say, and her suspicion was well founded when he added, "Diane loved it," something Flo couldn't have cared less about.

"Oh, she did, did she?" she said.

He then told her it was a good idea to keep the one-liners in the act, but that "maybe we'll give Mary a line, too." Pause. "And, next time, I want you to say—"

Before he could utter another word, Flo was in high dudgeon. "Hold it, Berry," she said, raising a hand "Stop! In the Name of Love" style. "I'll do it my way. That's *my* thing, nobody else's."

Gordy, not wanting to create a scene, and typically at a loss when a strong woman refused to shrink before him, mumbled, "Fine, suit yourself," and went off to mingle elsewhere in the room.

Flo, against what her instincts told her, hoped that would be the end of it. Taking it as a victory, at the second Copa show she moved her one-liner up, to when Diana did the introduction of her as the "quiet one." Waiting for it, she chirped, "Honey, that's what *you* think!"— only suggesting to the audience what Motown already knew, that when Flo Ballard had something to say, quiet she wasn't. The reaction in the house was the same as during the previous show, but this time Diana didn't break up and riff off it. Eyeing Gordy, she saw him wince, at which point she moved on, afraid that kibitzing with Flo might elevate "the Flo line" to a fixture of the act—which she knew Berry did not want, never mind that it always went over so well, because it encroached on Diana's turf as the group's "hostess."

Gordy needed some way short of a face-to-face confrontation to show Flo who was boss. Days later, it became evident. During a dress rehearsal at the Copa, Harvey Fuqua came in, silenced the musicians, and announced that there would be a change in the show—"People" was out of the repertoire. Flo was incredulous, as were those around the group who knew what that tune meant to her—that as her only lead vocal on stage, "People" was the last thin reed of her leadership role that she could hold on to. And also that dedicated Supremes fans had come to expect the song at shows, and would often call out for it from the galleries. There was even a live track of the tune on the shelved *There's a*

Place for Us album. With all this as context, Fuqua's explanation that Gordy made the move because there were "too many show tunes" in the act seems vacuous, since obviously any other show tune could have been killed. The only criterion for killing "People," it seemed clear, was that it was "Flo's song."

For Flo, there was only one explanation: It was payback from Gordy. And she wasn't going to take it "like a lady." According to Tony Tucker, who at the time was a teenager recently befriended by Ballard and employed as a flunky, a ballistic Ballard stormed off the floor and in full costume headed for the front door, letting it be known who she believed was behind the back-stabbing. "She'll never get away with it!" she screamed—the "she," everyone knew, being Diana, who with Mary stood in place, their mouths hanging open as Flo blasted through the door.

Pushing her way through lunch-hour crowds on Fifth Avenue while running to the Plaza a block away, she began "ranting and raving" things like "Flo's not taking this shit!" and sputtering at Ross. Recalled Tucker: "People are slamming on their brakes, she's not waiting on lights, she's just yelling about 'that bitch.'" In the Plaza lobby, realizing she'd left her purse with her room key at the Copa, the "quiet one" loudly banged her fist on the front desk and shouted, "I want the key to my suite now! I'm a Supreme!"

Up in her room, Flo lay out on a white sofa, crying and covering her eyes with an arm over her face. Hearing Tucker come in, she pointed to the decanters sitting on a table and gave him a directive.

"Baby, just pour."

fifteen

A SYMPHONY IN BLACK AND MOSTLY WHITE

For Flo, the degradation would only get worse. Having stuck the knife in her, Gordy twisted it during the final Copa week by ordering the reinstatement of "People" to their set—but, in an even unkinder cut, it would be with Diana on lead. In the practical sense, this was not really a radical transition; as the song had evolved on stage, Flo and Diana came to sing one verse each, Flo the first, Diana the last. But in symbolic terms, Diana's annexation of the other verse, as well, must have felt like a child being ripped out of Flo's arms. Now, she would have to endure singing backup on her pride and joy—"That's *my* song," she would say by way of protest, to much nodding within the Motown entourage, but without effect.

The wonder is that Ballard was able to remain functional—and sane—for as long as she did. Not once through '65 and into '66 can anyone remember her faculties being less than keen on stage or in the studio, her footwork out of step, her vocals anything but firm, all those smiles that would hurt her face less than warm and endearing. Mary may have been the official "sexy one," but even if Flo didn't have a knockout quotient, her brand of sexiness—escaping grittily from deep within and not out of a makeup jar with a studied, plastic superficiality—seemed to appeal to an equal reservoir of male Supremes fans.

If anything, Flo Ballard was the "underground" leader of the group, without the Cinderella qualities of Diana Ross but with a kind of "Everywoman" depth that made it an almost involuntary reaction to cry out, in Sammy Davis Jr. style, "You tell 'em, girl!" This was, and should have been, all well and good—except that in the prism through

227

which Gordy and his staff of yes-men looked at the Supremes, it resembled treason, and Flo was something like an apostate.

It's likely even Flo didn't fully comprehend why she had such populist appeal as she was trying to conform to the vacuous strictures of "class" and "elegance," but she perhaps naively believed it was a lever of power she could use against Gordy if he had any ideas about booting her out of the group—which many others at Motown saw as an inevitability after she stood up to him at the Copa. Seeing what she could get away with would become a matter of great pride to her.

The problem was that, popular or not, she wasn't in the same galaxy as Ross, who, as Marvin Gaye noted, had not just Berry's ear but Berry himself. Thus, it wasn't only Berry she was up against. And as early as mid-'65, it wasn't necessary to merely assume Gordy would someday take Ross solo; locked in bliss and business with Diana, he almost seemed determined to prepare everyone's awareness of that inevitability. For one thing, there were the gifts he was now lavishing on her, many of which were so ostentatious that they meant he would go to any lengths to keep her happy. (The most storied was a long white fur coat on which, some swore, he insisted they make love.) By now, too, he didn't even care who overheard him when he talked up his plans for Ross. At the Copa opening, for example, he couldn't contain himself when Diana hit a particularly pleasing note, leaning over to tell Mickey Stevenson, loudly, "She ain't gonna be in this group too long. She don't need those girls."

Which was exactly the theme he wanted to come out of all future articles about the Supremes in the big magazines. When interviews were set up for the group, Gordy let it be known that Diana would be the one who would answer the questions. During one interview with a European magazine, Diana, as if she'd been prompted to do so, reminded the reporter that she was to be called "Diana," an odd request since her name change had been in place for a year. Mary would recall that as a ham-handed way of "putting more distance between her and us" by rubbing the new identity in their faces. An identity she trusted would flourish way beyond the Supremes.

By sheer coincidence, Berry Gordy felt precisely the same way. "As Diana Ross goes," he was fond of saying, "so goes Motown."

For the sub-Supremes, all that remained in the wake of Diana Ross's smashing notices at the Copa were idle wishing and hoping.

"Flo and I were still hopeful that we might be singing more leads, or more solo spots in the live shows," Wilson would write in her memoirs, adding ruefully, "Little did we know that our fates were sealed."

Actually, Flo did know it, during the Copa run. Seeing what was going down, with Diana being given de facto solo star status, she tried appealing to the Supremes' other sub-class member to stand with her.

"Mary, she has all the talking lines," Flo told her. "We're just standing there."

Wilson, though, who rarely if ever had any on-stage lines anyway, was not about to do anything that would undermine the Copa high. Not that she, too, wasn't sympathetic, or didn't agree that Ross was accountable for purloining "People" from Flo—"How much more of the spotlight did Diane need?" she wrote years later. "Everyone knew that Flo was very sensitive and that [performing the song] meant a lot to her. Berry's taking it away from her like [this] was just vicious."

Moreover, Mary herself had felt Gordy's sting. Every once in a while over the previous months she'd ask him if she could sing a lead, even if just at the back end of a set. Finally, annoyed by her peskiness, he brushed her aside like a mosquito.

"Oh, Mary," he said with not a care for her feelings, "you know you can't sing."

Wilson recalled being "devastated," so much so that she would need years of therapy "to overcome my gradual loss of confidence" when she could not forget the nasty diss thereafter.

Yet at the time she could never muster the nerve to join Flo in common peonage, falling before the reality that, as she later put it, "I couldn't beat the system." Nor did she have the stomach for risking her own job and financial security by giving it a try.

That left Flo out on a lonely limb, something she came to resent Mary for almost as much as she did Diana. "Mary Wilson," she is quoted by Tony Tucker as saying during those convulsive three weeks in New York, "has lowered herself to being cute for a living, but I got talent. I'm the one with a voice around here, honey, and I want to sing. I don't just want to hum."

She was much harder, however, on Ross, scorching her at every turn—"That bitch doesn't even know how to sing that song!" she would tell whoever was around at the time, referring to "People." If there were too many show tunes in the act, she asked with perfect logic, "Take out one of Miss Thing's songs," using a poison pen name for Ross that she would often employ.

Nerve was something Flo had plenty of. One time she was hanging around the Copa lobby after a show when Diana and Berry came through, hand in hand. Apparently just the sight of them acting so carefree and smug filled Flo with rage. Spotting her glaring at them, the

King and Queen of Motown moved toward the door before a scene was created. Flo reveled in their fear.

"That's right," she mocked them, "get walking. You better get walking!"

Naturally, none of this inner discord showed itself on stage or in their records. Ballard was far too professional for that. Even her one-liners weren't practiced with malice; rather, she believed the audience reaction made them an effective part of the show, Gordy's contrary opinion carrying no truck with her. No one ever knew what she would say, and when, but it always seemed to play well, delightfully unrehearsed as it was. Once, when Diana did some prefabricated patter about "thin being in," the curvaceous Flo, who thought it absurd that her size-6 figure was somehow a fashion faux pas, riffed that "thin may be in, honey, but fat is where it's at"—a barb aimed at Ross's emerging role as a *nouveau* goddess of emaciation chic, and the fact that Mary was now cutting calories trying to become acceptably gaunt, though she would never quite get there. (The anomaly is that Ross was actually a bigger woman than most observers realized: At five-foot-five-and-a-half she weighed around 105 pounds—no Twiggy by any means, though her swizzle-stick arms and legs made her look smaller.)

In fact, everything about the act remained smooth, unruffled, and classy. And after the Copa no important music venue seemed out of the Supremes' reach. After the Copa and a second guest shot on *Ed Sullivan*, they were jetting across the Atlantic again to appear at the Grand Gala du Disque festival in Amsterdam, a kind of global talent competition with acts performing for their home countries. First prize went to the girls from Detroit. The next day, Jack Thompson wrote in the *New York Journal-American*: "The Supremes were the winners in the international sweepstakes. . . . They held the huge audience in the palms of their hands for three-quarters of an hour."

That was followed by stops in Brussels and another sojourn in England, with appearances on the TV shows *Top of the Pops* and *Ready, Steady, Go*. Then, back across the pond they went, to New York for a show at Arthur's discothèque and a milestone one-nighter on October 15 at Philharmonic Hall at Lincoln Center for the Performing Arts. The Hall, home to Leonard Bernstein's New York Philharmonic Orchestra, was not your typical pop venue, its acoustics built for classical opuses by

Mahler, Stokowski, and Copland, and it had been interrupted by the "lower classes" only sparingly, in 1964, for the Beatles and Bob Dylan.

Thus the gig was another check mark on Gordy's wish list of "legitimate" mainstream music hubs, and for the Hall's management it was a boon, the house selling out quickly even at the top ticket price of a pricey $6.50. For the night the gross ticket sales would exceed $15,000— a record at the time for the Hall, and a nice night's work for Gordy, whose cut after "expenses" left little for the girls. For them, in fact, the affair left a taste as sour as some of the notes had sounded in a hall with acoustics meant for bassoons, French horns, and kettle drums. A very nasty *Variety* review of the proceedings punned that the Supremes were "an echo of their selves," given the "lack of a recording studio echo" and "the toe-tapping beat of their platters" in this "pretentious" setting. The audience, similarly underwhelmed, gave them what the paper called "a moderate kind of pandemonium [that] didn't quite match the zealotry of the Beatles fans, but then it was more than Leonard Bernstein gets from his audiences."

As it happened, the girls had recently crossed paths with the Fab Four, who were in New York to play their Shea Stadium concert during the same month the Supremes were appearing at the Copa. As when the girls were in England the year before, promotional people arranged a meeting, now in the Beatles' opulent suite at the Warwick Hotel.

When the Supremes arrived there in a limo, it was a pop culture clash. As the car door opened, a tidal wave of teenage girls surged toward them, a frightening moment that receded when the mob saw the Liverpool lads weren't inside. Upstairs, the Beatles, all four of them this time, sat around in dirty jeans and T-shirts looking rather out of it in a room that, Wilson recalled, "reeked of marijuana." The girls, decked out in elegant day dresses, hats, and jewelry, and each wrapped in fur— Diana in mink, Mary in red fox, Flo in chinchilla—couldn't engage them even in small talk. While John sat in a corner staring into space, Paul, George, and Ringo mumbled a few questions about the technicalities of the Motown sound that the women didn't know how to answer. After a few long, surreal moments, said Mary, "we wanted out" and bid a hasty adieu, leaving the world's two biggest rock music acts not thinking much about each other.

Many years later, Wilson would visit Harrison in his home in England. Remembering the brief meeting, and the stereotype bred during the Supremes and Motown Revue tours of England that American "Negresses" were ghetto-bound musical geniuses, he told her, "We

expected soulful, hip girls. We couldn't believe that three black girls
from Detroit could be so square."

Their squareness angle worked just fine for Gordy, who wanted to
limit their racial identity—outside of Motown's black buyers—to the
rags-to-riches tales cranked out by the promotions people. To be sure,
the Supremes *were* square as the new rock and roll class went. At the
same time, though, being black had its advantages in the more politically informed rock music culture, and so he needn't have lifted a finger
to keep his black bona fides in order. Stevie Wonder, for instance, exploded from near obscurity in 1965 as a social symbol, the empty-
pocketed "poor man's son." This, even as other Motown acts followed
the Supremes' path into white-oriented bastions like the Copa—to the
great displeasure of Marvin Gaye, who only under protest had cut albums of Nat King Cole standards and another of show tunes called
Hello Broadway, and of Smokey Robinson.

To the record-buying public in general, Motown acts were relevant
by habit and by simply being black. While the Supremes' main demographic now was young white women growing out of their teen years—
and definitely not turned on by the electric guitars in a Byrds' cover of a
Bob Dylan song or by the apocalyptic prophecies of Barry McGuire's
"Eve of Destruction"—they were still held in esteem in the black community, accounting for continued high rankings on the R&B charts.
This, helpfully, not only allowed Gordy a ready comeback to his critics'
"purity" arguments; it also let white record buyers pretend they were
cool and clued in to "race music" by buying Supremes records.

As Mary Wilson pointed out, Gordy "saw us as the golden key to
any door he wanted to open. We were now BLAPs—black American
princesses," but in a way that Lena Horne, Eartha Kitt, and Diahann
Carroll hadn't had the luxury of: tapped into a white market.

The downside for Gordy was that, having pushed them into the
deepest mainstream waters, his own race consciousness had diminished.
Before the Supremes changed his stratagems, he considered Motown an
algorithm of the cause. In 1963, for example, he signed the great black
poet Langston Hughes and recorded him reading works such as "Of
Freedom's Plow" in an album called *Poets of the Revolution*. The same
year, Motown released *Great March to Freedom*, an album of speeches
from Martin Luther King's March on Washington, as well as a single of

the "I Have a Dream" speech backed with a choral rendition of "We Shall Overcome." But Gordy dithered over putting out the Hughes work, and killed it as the company's priorities changed.

In 1965, while Gordy was preoccupied with the Supremes, a good portion of black America was concerned with more pressing matters. In March, the "Bloody Sunday" outrage in Selma, Alabama, when state troopers opened fire on marchers on the Edward Pettis Bridge, was followed a day later by the murder of civil rights workers Viola Liuzzo and James Reeb. The bloodbath led President Lyndon Johnson to go before Congress demanding passage of the long-stalled Voting Rights Act, which finally was enacted on August 6 but changed little overnight. Just two days after, the arrest of a black man for driving drunk in L.A. erupted into a ten-day rampage in the Watts ghetto in which 34 people died and over 1,000 were injured.

The fires of the Watts "disturbance" were doused on August 21— eight days before the Supremes went on at the Copa, 3,000 miles and at least as many light-years from Watts and the seething within the black community that placed a half-dozen other big cities on the edge of going up in smoke next—including, of course, Detroit, the martyred Viola Liuzzo's hometown. By then, Gordy's ties to the movement were more an obligation than a moral imperative, to be satisfied with not much more than contributions to the NAACP. Accordingly, some students of the black social evolution, understandably, would not take kindly to his having gone missing in action when the ghettos became tinderboxes, not that there was much he could have done about it in any case. However, Gordy—as ever—would catch a break even on this count, when something strange happened beyond his control, or even his ability to comprehend.

As Suzanne E. Smith wrote in her 1996 book *Dancing in the Street: Motown and the Cultural Politics of Detroit*, even though Gordy's "basic business principles" caused "ambivalence about his role [in] the 'Negro revolt,'" the music coming out of his shop, no matter how off-white it got, fit a need for the proliferation of all black cultural forms—in effect, being accorded protection from the community.

"[A]s [Gordy] continued to pursue white crossover audiences," Smith noted, "the civil rights movement continued to look to 'market' black culture as a tool of the struggle. . . . [And] as its 'popular' music began to resonate with the racial and political upheavals of its time, declarations of black consciousness . . . were often read into the lyrics of a Motown song."

Just such an unwitting declaration had been read into the Vandellas' "Dancing in the Street" in 1964. Now, racially deep meaning would be projected into Motown's grooves and embraced in the almost exclusively nonpolitical love-gained-and-lost themes of the Four Tops, Temptations, Marvin Gaye—and, yes, the Supremes. Of the latter Smith writes, "[They] always negotiated, rather than transcended, their racial identity." Yet, even as they "conquered different musical genres and appealed to new audiences, they always contended with larger cultural assumptions about race and music."

Gordy may have been too busy blending the Supremes' brand into the corporate landscape to grasp this concept of passive racial identity, such was his success in getting them those Coca-Cola commercials. And he must have been far gone indeed if he didn't find the time for a private wince, or a hysterical laugh, at another of the girls' commercial promotions—when their faces were screened onto wrappers of Wonder Bread. Wonder white bread.

Still, he knew enough to leap at the chance to pimp the role that Motown soul played in pop music for an ABC documentary on February 15, 1966, *Anatomy of Pop*. This, a high-minded dissection of pop's debt to blues, jazz, and soul, had cameos by Duke Ellington, Tony Bennett, drummer Gene Krupa, bluesman Jellyroll Morton, blues singer Billie Pierce, and famed songwriter Richard Rodgers (kvetching about rock's "repetitiveness"). But a major theme was "the Detroit Sound," featuring some of the only film clips ever seen of the Supremes (and the Temptations) in the studio; in chic leisure wear, the girls mouth a song amidst the Funk Brothers, with Eddie Holland lurking in the background and Brian Holland in the shadows of the booth as the narrator says, "The formula: a strong gospel and blues feeling with a rocking beat." Gordy, put on camera to analyze his "sound," leaves it at "Soul is something that comes from within."

The girls' success was certainly a useful tool to Gordy in maintaining his street "cred." Late in '65, he was more than willing to "loan out" the Supremes when the Advertising Council in conjunction with the government's Equal Opportunity Employment Commission solicited Phil Spector to produce a promotional single to be heard on radio stations. The result was a song called "Things Are Changing" (actually an aborted track Spector had cut with the Beach Boys' Brian Wilson called "Don't Hurt My Little Sister") that was recorded in three versions, by the Blossoms, Jay and the Americans, and the Supremes, who flew to L.A. to lay down the vocals. (However, while it's great fun hearing them sing Ronettes-style in front of the "Wall of Sound," Spector was never in the studio with them; the single—which appears as a curio on the Supremes' 1996 *Anthology* album—was produced by Spector associate Jerry Riopell.) To push the campaign, the Ad Council executives posed with the Supremes for a *Billboard* cover shot.

But not everybody was buying the notion that Motown truly had a racial and social agenda. The criticism Gordy took for "selling out" would not abate and, indeed, became more barbed as "purer" forms of soul caught a groove in places like Memphis and Muscle Shoals. But, for now, Gordy could have it both ways, black and white, and as Mary Wilson could personally attest, open any door he wanted. It was a drunkard's dream, seemingly without end.

◯ℓℓ

The Supremes had come farther than Milt Jenkins ever could have foreseen or imagined back in 1961. In fact, a measure of this distance was the diametrically opposite direction of Jenkins's life in the years since. After both the Primes and Primettes had left him for dead, Milt lived as modestly as he had once lived large and loud. The bling went from his fingers to the pawn shops on John R Street; his snazzy threads were replaced by the overalls he wore to his job working for Detroit's Parks Department cutting grass at the public parks around town. The shiny Cadillac that was parked at the curb outside the Flame Show Bar was traded in for a Buick Skylark now parked in the driveway of the small home on Richton Street where he lived with Maxine Ballard Jenkins and their two children.

Milt still hung around the periphery of the music scene, promoting talent shows at the Twenty Grand bowling alley and managing Maxine's attempt at a singing career, writing for her a song she recorded called "Black of Face." But he was resigned to the reality that his big dreams were gone. Motown had changed the lay of the land for the old hustlers, all of whom would have given their spleens to be a part of it—all except Milt Jenkins, whose pride refused to let him use the old Primettes card to curry favor with Berry Gordy and land some sort of job with him.

Conceivably, he could have sued Motown on the grounds that his contracts with Ross, Wilson, and Ballard—as well as with Eddie Kendricks and Paul Williams—had been legally binding, which likely wouldn't have gone far in the courts considering how he'd abandoned them when he took ill, though he might have squeezed a few bucks from Gordy in settlement. Often, Maxine urged him to do just that. Instead, he let it go—out of family loyalty. "Baby, I can't do that," Maxine remembers him telling her. "You're my wife and Flo is your sister," the implication being that Motown might hold it against Flo, by association.

Of the Supremes, only Flo, because of her sister, maintained any contact with him, and out of pity she offered to kick in some money to help him out when things got tough. Milton wouldn't hear of accepting charity. Taking his pride into account, Flo then suggested that she pay him to come over to her place and mow and tend to her lawn. As degrading as it still may have been to him, he could live with himself doing this and took the job, at a hundred bucks a week for cutting the grass on Monday and Thursday. Maxine would pick up a check for him every Friday at Motown. Not once did Milton himself go to 2648 West Grand Boulevard. A "matter of principle," he told Maxine. But it was probably more the case that the man who had created the Supremes couldn't bear walking into Berry Gordy's office asking for what amounted to a handout.

℃ℓℓ

To the credit of Gordy and HDH, they didn't stand still with the Supremes product. The so-so showing of "Nothing But Heartaches" was a danger sign of possible Supremes fatigue, and it led Gordy to issue one of the sillier memorandums ever to make the Motown rounds. Written in Gordy's semi-literate hand in the autumn of 1965 to the entire creative staff, but really intended for HDH's eyes, it read:

> We will release nothing less than Top Ten product on any artist; and because the Supremes' world-wide acceptance is greater than the other artists, on them we will only release number-one records.

Gordy never said whether he was referring to the tepid "Nothing But Heartaches" here, or whether he believed any previous Supremes records had somehow been made with any less care, commitment, and expectation of success. But it was clear how much he had riding on the girls now. After dropping hundreds of thousands of dollars during the three-week Copa adventure, he needed to put everyone in the shop on notice that there would be no coasting with the Supremes.

HDH apparently got the memo. Having normally conducted their business with little or no input from Gordy until the first tape masters were in the can, they immediately rethought the follow-up to "Heartaches," which originally was slated to be "Mother Dear," a ho-hummer from the *More Hits* album. But in late September, they had a better idea, after finding a new groove. A groove that came from outside the Motown pool.

Though HDH almost never looked beyond their own purview, they were beguiled with a song they heard on the radio, the Toys' "A Lover's Concerto." This, a lovely parting gift of the ebbing girl-group genre, retrofit a rock beat to no less than "Minuet in G Major" from Bach's "Notebook for Anna Magdalena Bach." Written by two Brill Building tunesmiths, it was all pop and circumstance, with lilting strings, Van Clyburn–like piano flourishes, and horn riffs right from the Motown playbook, swirling around a lyric that fused the macrocosm of nature—birds, trees, bees, flowers, rain softly falling on the meadow—with romance and love in a grand symphony.

"A Lover's Concerto," released on a small independent label, DynaVoice, owned by Four Seasons producer Bob Crewe, was not a notable hit when HDH went to work on their *grand bouffe*—"I Hear a Symphony," the title (cribbed, too, in part, from Phil Spector's stately Ronettes' song "I Can Hear Music") more than a mere suggestion of "Concerto"—likely not anticipating much competition from the latter. (Not that the Holland brothers will acknowledge ripping off "Concerto," which Eddie Holland calls a "great song" but nothing like "I Hear a Symphony.")

Indeed, when they cut the song in late September, it surely had its own cachet, having toned down the pomp and pandemic lyrical sweep of "Concerto" into a "tender melody" of a girl being pulled ever closer into the arms of her lover until "your lips are touching mine." Rather than crash in with full symphonic might, the intro crept in with a lullaby of vibes, delicate cymbal-tapping, and a heartbeat-like bass. Diana's vocal entree was a part-spoken, Gilbert and Sullivan–style intonation: "You've given a true love / And every day I thank you love / For a feeling that's so new / So inviting, so exciting."

Now came the fluff and the force. Brian Holland's arrangement—"Bach swing," as Alan Slutsky calls it—took a typical HDH eight-bar chord repetition and sax solo on the break and ladled it with dollops of sweet cream; for example, when the girls would sing the chorus hook—"Whenever you're near I hear a symphony"—the last word was drawn out, melding into an echoed font of violins—a first for a Supremes record. And at intervals there were dramatic piano runs by Earl Van Dyke. From start to end, the intensity steadily built, the strings ultimately supplanting the early vibe runs in soaring octaves on the fadeout.

Four sessions and days more of mixing, remixing, and overdubbing were needed to get it right. And though it took Brian two decades to realize just how deeply the song burrowed into the gulch of the heart—especially his heart, reluctant as it was to stop yearning and burning for Diana Ross—HDH had no doubt they'd cleared the bar that Gordy had set so high.

"Listen to that song. *Listen* to it!" Eddie Holland instructs a fellow who made the mistake of wondering if, under the veneer of Bach, the core of "Symphony" was the raw vital force of simplicity.

What Brian did with that thing, he threw everything in—different modulations, different keys, different sounds. That thing sounds amazing even now. So there is nothing simple about that song. There is *nothing* simple about them lyrics, man. [Begins singing:] *"Those tears that fill my eyes. I cry not for myself. But for those who never felt the joy we felt. . . ."*

When I hear that song today, I hear lyrics I didn't think I was capable of writing. It was like therapy forcing myself to go way inside me, my heart, my soul. That song opened the way for me to break out and really express myself. I think that's what Berry wanted for the Supremes because they weren't teenage girls no more, they were women with more complicated feelings. So it was good for everyone all around that Berry pushed us like that.

Mesmerized, too, Gordy rushed the song into release in early October, backed with "Who Could Ever Doubt My Love." Powered by the usual all-out sales and promotion campaign, "Symphony" quickly hit *Billboard*'s October 23 Spotlights page, with a blurb reading "No problem rushing up the chart with this well-written rhythm ballad with pulsating and top vocal work. Block buster!" After the girls sang the tune on *Hullabaloo* and at a huge celebrity benefit concert for the U.S.O. in New York's Madison Square Garden, it cracked the Top Forty on Halloween.

By then, though, "A Lover's Concerto" was already Top Forty, having entered the list in early October. This could have spelled trouble for

"Symphony," coming so soon on the trail of the other pomp-pop song. Happily, however, there was more than enough room for both. "Concerto" would turn in a three-week run at No. 2 in late November, kept from the top spot by the Rolling Stones' "Get Off My Cloud"—which, in a roundabout irony, was then knocked out by "I Hear a Symphony" on November 20, the first of two weeks it held the brass ring.

Cee

In the fold of '65 into '66, one could have gotten the feeling that the Supremes were lurking around every corner, at least when the Beatles weren't there. Gordy, no dummy, pressed *three* more Supremes albums in December alone, putting out two—the live *At the Copa*, with liner notes by Sammy Davis Jr. (No. 11 on the pop chart) and a *de rigueur* Christmas album (No. 6 on the holiday album chart) that yielded a two-sided holiday hit, "Children's Christmas Song" and "Twinkle Twinkle Little Me"—while shelving another called *Tribute to the Girls*. Not far behind, in February came *I Hear a Symphony*, which included their next single, "My World Is Empty Without You" as well as a mishmash of L.A.-recorded covers such as the Beatles' "Yesterday" (produced by Norman Whitfield), "Unchained Melody," "Wonderful Wonderful," "Stranger in Paradise," and—as a sop to Bob Crewe—"A Lover's Concerto."

Not for nothing did Gordy take out an expensive full-page ad in *Billboard*'s year-end issue that was basically a love letter to the Supremes. Bannered "AMERICA'S NO. 1 RECORDING ARTISTS," the ad copy proclaimed: "6 gold records in two years . . . records broken wherever they appear . . . outstanding reviews," and pitched their upcoming TV gigs and international concert tour. (Of course, the gold-record claim was pure Gordy blarney—in truth, they had none, officially, due to his boycott of the RIAA.)

Nor did it matter much that "My World Is Empty Without You" didn't clear the high bar, stalling at No. 6, perhaps a tad too turbid, brooding, and pre-"Symphony" formulaic to go the extra mile on the chart. That slight dip—though a charting most acts would kill for—was indicative of how immensely difficult it was for the group to keep topping itself. Yet that would be precisely the marching order for everyone involved with the Supremes, including the girls themselves. Two of them would be able to endure the hideous pressure. One would progressively need to numb it.

sixteen

AN ITCHING
IN THE
HEART

I f Gordy could have, he would have taken Diana Ross solo as early as 1966. By then he had already talked himself into believing that Mary Wilson and Florence Ballard were excess baggage, cosmetic accessories rather than necessities. Indeed, a reference point had already been established for him to make that argument. Though the fact of Ballard's absence was kept tightly under wraps, she did not sing on "My World Is Empty Without You." Whether there was a mix-up and she didn't get word of the session, or whether she was still pissed off at Gordy after the Copa humiliations, Flo didn't show up at the studio for her backing vocals. With the track and the lead vocal recorded, HDH couldn't wait for her and called in Marlene Barrow of the Andantes, the trio that backed nearly every Four Tops record, to join Wilson.

When no one could tell the difference on the record, Gordy had the perfect opening to suggest the possibility that the change be made permanent. What's more, he had Diana cut some tracks without Ballard *and* Wilson for an album he produced in tribute to Loucye Gordy, *In Loving Memory* (unreleased until 1968)—technically, Ross's first solo recordings. Another opening presented itself when Flo again became ill with the flu in February and couldn't appear at a Supremes show in Boston. Once more, Barrow filled in, much as Flo had done with the Marvelettes. Gordy was so excited that he ordered up publicity pictures of Barrow with Ross and Wilson—and more excited still when, Flo's popularity aside, the pretty, talented Barrow received a warm reception, after deferentially announcing from the stage that she was there in Flo's stead for the night.

Convinced, Gordy called a meeting to ask what his adjutants thought about moving Flo out and Marlene in. But the feedback couldn't have pleased him—basically, everyone in the meeting told him that in messing with a winning hand, the hand that fed Motown, he had lost his mind. That Gordy didn't already know this was preposterous to the other executives, who couldn't believe they had to tell *him* why the act was so successful. All Berry ever saw was Ross. Even the Barrow-Ballard matter was small next to his main obsession: Ross as a solo act, whereby the smaller change of the girl-group genre would be dwarfed by the glitter and gelt of a pathway the likes of Lena Horne, Ella Fitzgerald, Peggy Lee, and Judy Garland had treaded to and from music and motion pictures. In fact, pondering the replacement of Flo, Gordy was hardly naive; any tinkering that diluted the Supremes' original chemistry would make it easier to separate Ross. The Motown boys were well aware of the unspoken truths, and did not hold back telling him that while Ross had become a very high-profile diva who was surely capable of going it alone, the act was the *Supremes*, not the *Supreme*.

However, Flo at times seemed determined to make it easier for Gordy to take the first step of firing her. One of the Supremes' first important gigs of the new year was their return engagement at the Copa, booked for one week, March 17 to 23—their first prime-season engagement at the club. But as it approached, Flo's continuing health problems made for a queasy déjà vu; again, unable to go to New York with Diana and Mary, she missed days of rehearsals.

Along with her flu, questions persisted. Weeks before, when she missed the Boston show, Gordy demanded to speak with Flo's doctor. He told him she was indeed ill with the flu, and while he would allow her to go to New York for the Copa shows, she would not be able to endure the next scheduled Supremes event, a brief tour of Germany and Scandinavia. Gritting his teeth, Gordy postponed the tour. And when Flo held off coming to New York, he became furious at her, insisting to people that even Flo's doctor had told him her biggest infirmity was that she was "lazy."

Fitting right in with the theme of déjà vu, Harvey Fuqua—whose opinions were given to him by Gordy—emerged, not to announce but to propose a change in the act, broaching the idea to Diana and Mary that Marlene Barrow go on for Flo at the Copa. Diana—who, like Gordy, was livid at Flo—was willing to let Barrow "share my stage," as she put it. Mary, who in the past could be counted on to at least verbally defend Flo, simply shrugged and said she didn't care. Being caught in the middle all the time, between Diana and Flo, and now between loyalty to Flo and the well-being of the act, had begun to wear on her. As did having to constantly reassure people that Flo wasn't a problem.

"Don't pay attention to what Florence says when she's mad, especially after she's had a few cocktails," she told Tony Tucker. The contretemps with Flo, she insisted, "would blow over." Any day now, went the chirpy refrain, "Flo will be back to her cheerful self."

Very little was cheerful about Flo by early '66, however, and so Wilson stood aside when Gordy, through his Tonto of a companion Harvey Fuqua, decided to replace Ballard at the Copa—a move that everyone knew would be tantamount to junking her altogether. However, now is where the story becomes less clear. According to the J. Randy Taraborrelli book *Call Her Miss Ross,* Gordy's plans for the Copa shuffle "were thrown into turmoil by Jules Podell," who, when he "discovered Florence would not be on stage, became angry. He enjoyed Florence tremendously, remembered that she was a crowd pleaser during the last engagement, and made it clear that he wanted the three original Supremes. If Berry could not guarantee the presence of all three, the commitment would be canceled. Both Berry and Diana were quite amazed at this turn of events [but] Berry had no choice but to call on Flo."

Even more amazed was Shelly Berger, a young former actor and talent manager who was hired by Motown's L.A. office in 1966 and put to work using his TV and club connections in the furtherance of the Supremes.

"I don't know who came up with *that* story," Berger says, fairly jumping out of his seat. "I will guarantee you, categorically, that Jules Podell never fixed it. Berry Gordy didn't have to run anything by Jules Podell. He could have done whatever he wanted. Listen, I was very close to Jules Podell. I'd known Jules for years before that. With the Supremes, with the exception of Diana Ross—if you said, 'Oh, by the way, Diana Ross is not gonna be singing,' Jules would've said, 'What the hell are you doing?' But even so, that wasn't his business. And if it was one of the backup singers, he wouldn't have even cared."

"It was Berry who made that call. And of course you would want Florence. She was a Supreme. The only reason you wouldn't have Florence was if she couldn't make it, which would be the case more and more. But not at the Copa."

Florence did make it. She joined the Supremes at the Copa, and the engagement was as big a hit as the last time. To Gordy's credit, he retroceded on replacing Ballard rather than callously dismissing the evidence of her charisma with the public and the advice of nearly everyone except Harvey Fuqua. That the group had risen so far, so fast, so illogically for a girl-group and a black act certainly carried a deeply personal and satisfying sense of satisfaction for Berry. As myopic as he was in seeing the group as an extension of Ross's interests, he knew that his own guiding hand had been responsible for their apotheosis, with just a little bit of help from Ross, Wilson, and Ballard. Having taken all three for the ride, he was soul-mated with them—all of them—now, and for the foreseeable future.

Cee

The first attempt to fire Ballard averted for now, Gordy would wait it out. Not that he didn't want Ballard banished, and not that he'd forget about it, but nothing would happen until the time was right. The same applied to the master plan—separating Ross from the group and depositing her, alone, on the big stages she pined for. But that would take even longer, when he could feel it in his bones that the group was about to ebb, yet before Ross had lost any of her cachet. Whereas that would be a tricky bit of maneuvering, the first part of the equation was all too easy. By now, no one could get enough of the Supremes, and their itinerary ran the length of Gordy's arm. Just in the first three months of the year, they were off to shows at the Deauville Hotel in Miami Beach, the Fairmont Hotel in San Francisco, the Roostertail Club back home in Detroit, the San Juan Hotel in Puerto Rico, and a return engagement of the Motown Revue at the Olympia Music Hall in Paris that was recorded for a live album. Their TV appearances included the Dean Martin and Red Skelton shows, as well as Johnny Carson's *Tonight Show*. The once-quarantined Motown was able to sell a syndicated special, "The Supremes at the Copa," broadcast on March 18, 1966 (though *Time*'s review of the broadcast pricked "the best-known evangels of the Detroit Sound" for "frequently abandon[ing]" their "Sound" to "adopt some Broadway airs").

A whole new audience presented itself when, in a *Billboard* poll of college students, the Supremes came in second only to the Beatles (though just who these students were could have been questioned, since even the Rolling Stones didn't make it onto the list of thirty acts). The girls had made only one appearance on a campus, a December 1965 show at Bridgeport University that sold out in six hours. Seeing the potential, Gordy chartered a massive Motortown bus tour of some two dozen colleges—the "Hitsville U.S.A. to Collegeville U.S.A. Tour"—in the early spring of '66, ingeniously tapping into both the nostalgia quotient of the generation that had been weaned on Motown as early teenagers and the secondary sociopolitical messages—real or imagined—of all black music forms in the mid-'60s. Ironically, the Supremes were about the only Motown act *not* on the tour, so busy were they elsewhere.

There was, as well, superstar-worthy media exposure, with Supremes stories coming out only two months apart in *Time* and then *Look*, both articles trenchantly different from previous press treatment of the group in that the focus was on them, not the company and its grand aspirations. *Time*'s March 4 piece, "The Girls from Motown," hit all the salient talking points, from their "Negro ghetto" genesis to their "Copa cup runneth over"—and the comforting observation that "the trio's childhood friendship, surprisingly, shows no suspicion of strain." Despite the big league they were in, having made $250,000 each in 1965, which "may hit $400,000 this year," their "modest duplexes" were "luxuryless" and "just spartanly comfortable," reflecting the girls' "sensible, unawed view of their instant riches."

"You know," Ross was quoted, "my father didn't want me to get into this business. When I left, he said, 'If you don't make it, don't come crying around here asking for help.'" (Not mentioned was that these now fully grown women weren't permitted checkbooks, bankbooks, or any information about their tax returns or access to their money.)

The May 3 *Look* article, "The Supremes: From Rags to Real Riches," contained some of the same financial details, obviously spooned up by Motown. But portions of the whitewash peeled off in unguarded and, for Gordy, unexpected moments of candor. Diana, for example, still smarting over Ed Sullivan's lack of proper deference on stage to the Supremes, started right in with a diva-licious tirade:

> I can be anything I want. I'm ready to do all the extra things—acting roles, be the star of a big Broadway show. But where are the offers? We had six [actually five] number one hits in a row but we're still treated like some ordinary rock 'n' roll group, except in clubs.
>
> On TV shows like "Ed Sullivan" we're pushed on and off the stage like we were nothin', and there are the Supremes cryin' behind the wings. On "Hullabaloo" they gave me a cue card with a stupid speech to say. How dare they do that? I

could be the mistress of ceremonies, but they never ask me. I see all the phonies who never even had one number one hit runnin' around actin' like the stars. I've got something they don't have and the kids know it. I'm for real, and every time I sing a song, it's part of my body.

Mary fretted about impending burnout, with a helpful suggestion:

Every once in a while, I look at our work schedule, filled every day into next year, and I say, "Boy, your life is really going away, Mary." But it wouldn't make sense to work seven hard years like we have and then quit. . . . We're so different and yet so alike. . . . Diana is a rather lonely type. She'd go out and conquer everything, just to have something to do. We've got to take the load off Diana. It's endangering her voice; we must even things out.

Florence takes things in easy stride. She'll go along, but she wouldn't go out by herself and make something happen in her career. She's a very lovable person, but some people don't understand her. They think she's haughty and vain. When I first met her, she was the swingiest girl in Detroit. Now, she doesn't like to party.

What we have now is what other girls want to have, fame and money. But we don't have fellas. I guess there's time for that stuff later, when it slows down. But I'm so tired. I'm glad we're young; we are leading such a fast life, traveling and no rest, and all our mothers are worried about us.

Flo, echoing the change-of-life trope, spoke with pride of her founding of the group, and with lament of the simple things in life she had missed out on:

I was the one who got the whole thing started with our careers. I rounded up Mary, who rounded up Diana, and later on, I even picked the name, The Supremes. . . . When we started out on the road for Motown we were excited and self-conscious. We used to dress up and wear hats on planes; now, we wear slacks and anything comfortable. . . .

I used to be a swinger myself and knew every new dance. Now, when I listen to our records, they give me a feeling of wanting to move, the feeling you just want to get up and dance. . . .

I'm the motherly type. I think a woman needs six to eight children to make her happy. . . . We all wear engagement rings—we're married to Motown. When I see somebody I like, I take it off real quick. . . . When I used to live in the projects, I always thought it would be fantastic to have a phone. [I would] dream about getting out of the projects. It takes a while, but it comes sometimes. At least, it came for me and for Diana and Mary. We had nothing much before. Now, well, now we're the Supremes.

Gordy loved all the free publicity but hated the straight talk— which was repeated in a *Chicago Tribune* piece written during a trip to the Windy City for a show at the Aire Crown Theater. The paper's reporter, allowed to accompany the girls on the plane and in their limo, chronicled Diana's fits of temper and her facetious answers to questions she never believed would be put into print. Asked at one point about what she dreamed of at night, Ross mockingly riffed, "Frightening, terrifying things. . . . One night I dreamed of a cat leaping on me, digging his claws into my skin." She also unthinkingly divulged that her mother had tuberculosis—something Ernestine did not want even her own friends to know, as in those days TB was lumped in with other bestaining "social" diseases like leprosy. When Ernestine read the article, she was in tears.

When Gordy saw it, and the *Look* quotes, he was furious. Scolding all the Supremes, he lit into Diana in particular for her lack of discretion, telling her she was "crazy" for talking about Ed Sullivan like that—"Do you know how hard it is to get you on that show?" he raged. Not again would such *vérité* glimpses, or seditious chatter about "taking the load off Diana," be permitted. Media access was restricted, tightly, and the girls would be made available for mere minutes at a time, to channel prescribed pabulum to any given query.

They were, after all, the *Supremes*.

While the long road seemed smooth and paved with yellow brick, there were potholes ahead. For one thing, recent Supremes' songs, contrary to Gordy's "No. 1's only" dictum, hadn't moved great amounts of vinyl.

This even though elements in "My World Is Empty Without You" were breathtaking, such as the haunting ensemble string arrangement by conductor Paul Riser.

The latest HDH unveiling, "Love Is Like an Itching in My Heart," had, in its title and lyrics, a dash of Eddie Holland cheekiness that may have been too clever by half for another wail about the burning and yearning of heartache—something that for many Supremes fans had become trite. Indeed, one might have assumed that "Itching in My Heart" was a parodic send-up of the thematic obsessions of most every HDH song, with a classic blues hookline that if not done right might come off like a punchline—"Love is like an itching in my heart, and baby I can't scratch it." However, the assumption would be wrong.

EDDIE HOLLAND: There was nothing light-hearted about it. Humorous, yes, but only in a funny-sad way, not a funny ha-ha way. Both Brian and I were going through some heavy shit in our personal lives at the time, and the lyrics were coming from two broken hearts. Think about it. Love isn't only yearning and burning in the heart; it's an itching that you can't make go away, it taunts you. It tickles you to death. And that makes you angrier and angrier because you feel completely impotent. That's what the song is about, completely hopeless frustration.

Accordingly, Brian and Lamont Dozier produced the track with a hard edge, a gruffness not usually heard in their records. Alan Slutsky defines the tune as "one of the most simple, direct and in-your-face grooves" in the Supremes' catalog, its sneering staccato stabs of rhythm topped by Earl Van Dyke's hammered piano licks and bottomed by James Jamerson's thudding bass, which at times becomes fuzzy in over-amped distortion. In fact, over four decades later when Slutsky produced the deluxe edition of the *Standing in the Shadows of Motown* CD, featuring instrumental remixes of several hits from the original multitrack tapes, he included "Itching"—even though, after stripping the vocals, leaving only the naked tracks, he was mortified by what he heard.

The bass track sounded like shit. Actually, there were *two* different bass parts, Jamerson's and probably Tony Newton, a backup bass player of the day. Jamerson played the deep bottom, Newton the upper bottom. But they were out of tune with each other and didn't mesh well at all in terms of pitch and rhythms. I thought, "How could they let a track like this go to vinyl?" But when you placed the track into the total mix, it sounded perfect! That was the genius of HDH. They were cutting in eight-track, which was high-end at the time, but they didn't care about the technical proficiency of a track, only how the song sounded as a whole. They wanted *music.* That song would never have made it out of the studio today like that. They'd have to get all the levels right—and it would probably sound like crap with all that perfect technology.

The capper was Diana's urgent delivery on lead: From the opening lines about how the "love bug done bit me" and the resulting "burning sensation," Eddie Holland's overwrought imagery—"Love is a nagging irritation / Causing my heart complication / Love is a growing infection / And I don't know the correction / Got me rockin' and a reelin' / And I can't shake the feelin'"—is so convincing that it makes you want to reach for some peroxide.

The record, released on April 8 backed with "He's All I Got," received the usual warm reception from *Billboard* (in which Gordy took out a full-page ad touting the new record), highlighting it on the Spotlights page as "[m]ore exciting sound from the girls in this slow rhythm rocker with a solid back beat. Should top their 'My World Is Empty Without You' smash."

That, however, did not happen; "Itching" would go only as high as No. 9 in late May, four notches below the apogee of "My World"—which, rather than being a "smash," was regarded at Motown as a semifailure. Such was the lofty footing of the Supremes, and the irrationality of Gordy's "No. 1's only" fiat, that two Top Ten records could be a letdown. Years later, that "distorted reality," to cadge a phrase from a future Supremes hit, still leads HDH to defend those "underperforming" hits:

EDDIE HOLLAND: Listen, we didn't need no orders to write No. 1 songs. We wanted every song we ever wrote to be No. 1. Like I say, we didn't write songs; we wrote *hits.* But I'll say this: Making a hit is a collaborative process. And by that time the Supremes were hardly ever there. They were always out on the road, doing this club, that TV show, this hotel. The only time they saw Detroit was when they flew over it. We'd have to grab them for a few hours at a time every two, three months. And they'd be tired and really didn't want to come in.

It wasn't just the Supremes. It was happening with the Tops, too. I mean, those guys were never around. You had to catch lightning in a bottle with them, all of them. I'd have, like, an hour to rehearse with Levi and then go right in and have him lay down the vocal. Thank God he could get it right on the first take. Diana needed more work, but she got it, too. Me, I personally didn't think any of those records suffered. But, shit, you can always make a record better, if you had time. Since we never had that, we had to get it right the first time, every time.

Perhaps the most amazing achievement of HDH was that under these circumstances, and with the crushing pressure on them, they would get a second wind with Supremes songs that kept the group on top of the heap—and, ironically, further delay the inevitability of Gordy taking Ross solo. For Brian Holland, it was hardly a shock. "We always rose to the challenge," he notes—a contention met with no objection. But there would be a price to pay for it. For HDH, redoubling their efforts with the Supremes meant they would have to cut bait with the Four Tops in 1967—ending, with "Bernadette," their run of five Top Ten hits as they turned to recording cover songs without success.

A similar fate awaited other once-proud Motown acts like the Marvelettes, who had given the company its first No. 1 hit; after being "put on the back burner because of the Supremes," as Katherine Anderson puts it, they would hang around, racking up a couple of mid-level hits written and produced by Smokey Robinson before disbanding in obscurity in 1969.

Motown was in an odd state during these years. There were, as of 1966, around 200 acts signed to the company, a good number of them white, most unknown (rock bands like the Underdogs and the Messengers), some known but otherwise baffling (TV mediocrities Paul Petersen, Irene Ryan ["Granny" on *The Beverly Hillbillies*], and the warped kiddie-show host Soupy Sales, now working out of New York), and un-Motown-like black club singers like Diahann Carroll, Barbara McNair, and Leslie Uggams. Rounding out this cast of odds, ends, and factory seconds were comic actors Scatman Crothers and Jack Soo.

Yet only four acts meant anything, and they monopolized the top songwriting/producing teams: the Supremes with HDH, the Temptations with Norman Whitfield and Barrett Strong, Stevie Wonder with Henry Cosby and Sylvia Moy, and Marvin Gaye with Harvey Fuqua and Johnny Bristol. And even in this rarefied chamber, the Supremes drained almost all the oxygen in the room; there were times even the bigger acts weren't given more than half-hearted promotion—not even Motown Vice-President Smokey Robinson. He and his Miracles, after "Going to a Go-Go" late in '65, would release ten singles over the rest of the decade, only one of which, "I Second That Emotion," became a hit. Martha and the Vandellas, after "Nowhere to Run" in early '65, would release thirteen, with only two hits ("Jimmy Mack" and "Honey Chile").

Martha Reeves didn't need to do the math to know what was happening.

It all changed, she said, "when Berry finally got somebody who he could depend on and wouldn't turn on him and say, 'I don't want to go there' when he tried to push them." Reeves added, "He found [Diana Ross], and she would go where he wanted to put her, and sleep with her, too."

She went on: "First it was the learning group [the Marvelettes]; the second group was a commercial asset [the Vandellas]; and the third group was the prize that he showed off like you would a German Shepherd—purebred, of course." For Reeves, the fall from star to has-been was more than she could handle; in the late '60s, she had a series of nervous breakdowns and, reportedly, was put in a strait-jacket for a time.

Motown, essentially, had evolved into a two-headed creature—the Supremes and everyone else. But even as HDH were digging deeper into their creative well for a last few rounds of immortal genius, the darker view of life that they had begun to mine and brand into the Supremes' sonic dreamscape—an ingenious and even necessary commercial segue, to be sure—was in itself an ominous signpost, and one tied to their progressive enmity for Gordy.

At the same time, there were strains building between Gordy and Mickey Stevenson and Harvey Fuqua. Which is why, even if Gordy didn't sense it, there was a crisis on the way at Motown, with the Supremes—and by extension, the entire Motown realm—squarely in the cross-hairs.

Cee

The hiring of Shelly Berger would shift the center of Motown's axis. Berger, at 27, was a short, brash, and hyperbolic former actor who had talked his way into managing acts either not-yet-famous like insult comic Don Rickles or erstwhile-famous like the Kingsmen and Dick and Dee Dee. Good fortune smiled on him early in 1966 when he walked into a big L.A. talent agent's office one day just as the agent was on the phone with Ralph Seltzer, Motown's chief accountant and lawyer and overseer of its bare-boned L.A. operation.

Berger recalls, "He was saying, 'No, I'm not interested,' then, spotting me, continued, 'but you know who would be great for the job? Shelly Berger.' I said, 'Yeah, I would.' When he hung up, I said, 'Oh, by the way, what job am I perfect for?'"

It was, it turned out, with Motown, trying to line up work for the company's performers on TV shows and in movies—still not the easiest of tasks in the real world outside of the Supremes, which was no doubt why the big agent declined. Berger, up for any challenge, didn't. When Seltzer took the advice and called him with the offer, he quit Rickles and the has-been rockers and began talking up Motown acts all over Hollywood. He didn't meet Berry Gordy until he came to Detroit to drop in, uninvited, at the July 4th Motown picnic. Gordy was shocked to see the elfin white stranger arrive in the back seat of Gordy's ex-wife Thelma's car, having waylaid her on the way by claiming he "ran Motown's West Coast office." When Berger introduced himself, Gordy kept his distance, wondering why Seltzer had hired this loon.

SHELLY BERGER: At the beginning, Mr. Gordy and I thought each other were crazy. I thought his memo that the Supremes could only record No. 1 records was the most insane thing I'd ever heard of. When we sat down, he asked me, "Can you get our acts on TV?" I said, "Not only will I do that, but we're going to produce our own TV specials and movies." At which point he excused himself, called Ralph Seltzer, and told him to fire me. I was informed that his exact words were "Either he's on drugs or he's an idiot."

Because it was so far-fetched. But it was something I truly believed. I knew what Motown was capable of. It had giant potential. It just didn't have anyone who could work full-time on it. Mr. Gordy tried to do it himself, but he had a record company to run. Left to his devices alone, it never would have gotten done. For many reasons. Look, there's no need to sugar-coat it. There was resistance to black acts. We live in a racist country, back then much more so. We were up against Sammy Davis, Louis Armstrong, Ella Fitzgerald, all the "standard" black performers who got all the work there was for black acts. We were the rock and roll kids.

Mr. Gordy realized all that; and that he had nothing to lose with me. And I think we both learned to believe that each of us was at least partly sane.

Gordy became convinced Berger was onto something when, within weeks, he'd gotten Dick Clark to do an entire "Where the Action Is" show from the Roostertail Club featuring no one but Motown acts.

The Motown operation in L.A. was a cramped room in a small office building at 6290 Sunset Boulevard. "Actually," says Berger, "the West Coast office was basically Brenda Holloway," the only act of consequence to record out of L.A. The staff there consisted mainly of producers Hal Davis and Marc Gordon and songwriter Frank Wilson, their work confined to cutting Holloway records and Motown album filler. Now, it became a hub of outgoing and incoming calls, with Berger, a phone in each ear, carrying on several conversations at once with TV producers. Leaning on Ed Sullivan's head man Bob Precht, he was able to secure a deal for the Supremes to appear on the *Sullivan* show four times a year; in time, every other big-name Motown act would make it onto Sullivan's stage, too.

Berger's old friendship with Jules Podell also paid dividends; the original Copa contract with the Supremes was torn up, replaced by one that broke the "glass ceiling" of Podell's pay scale. "I gave Jules an additional year on the Supremes," Berger explains, "and an added year on the Temptations, and I broke the top, which was $10,000. I believe we got $17,500 for the Supremes' last engagement there. Nobody, not even Sinatra, had ever gotten near that, even near $15,000. It happened because I was one of the few people Jules Podell would talk to. He didn't do me any favors, he just listened to me. He didn't ever really listen to Mr. Gordy. He didn't really even know who Berry Gordy was. Jules spoke to me, Lee Solomon at William Morris, and Buddy Howell at GAC. So that was the bonus that Motown got when they hired me."

With barely a breath in between negotiations, Berger enlisted the independent TV production team of George Schlatter and Ed Friendly (who would bring *Laugh-In* to the small screen in 1968) to package a Supremes-Temptations special and present it to the networks, and began dickering with ABC's Saturday night stalwart *The Hollywood Palace* for the Supremes not just to perform on the show, as they had already, but to host the glitter-filled show several times a year.

By 1967, L.A. would be more than a nominal piece of lint in the Motown back drawer. Its weight, reflecting that of the West Coast itself as the show-business capital of the world, was pulling Gordy toward a new vital center. That would mean a recasting of the Motown brand, from a community-based enterprise to a multi-market, multi-media combine, from brown-bag lunches to power lunches at the Beverly Hills Hotel. It would be a long, long way from John R Street to Hollywood and Vine.

Just as with the ultimate design for Diana Ross, however, Gordy would need to go slow, since eventually these transitions would mean that the palm tree–shaded, avocado-flavored Motown would have no use for the rapidly rusting Motor Town itself—nor for most of the Motown acts. Still, Gordy would drop plenty of hints as to what was coming. As early as June of '66, *Billboard* crackled with a page-one story headlined "MOTOWN EXPANSION IN HIGH GEAR WITH B'WAY, TV, MOVIES"; not incidentally, the paper noted that the "first step in the grand plan is the hiring of Shelly Berger."

Gordy found other ways to keep Berger busy and away from the phones. Needing a proxy high-roller to fete industry executives and assorted showbiz VIPs at high-visibility Supremes concerts—not to mention a human shield to keep the Supremes separated from the press—he began sending Berger on the road with the girls. By the autumn of 1966, when the Supremes embarked on a tour of the Far East, Gordy had made him manager of the group, handing over the affairs of the second-biggest act in the world, just as Florence Ballard was fast becoming Motown's biggest headache.

seventeen

"PUT THE MONEY ON DIANA"

ey to all of Gordy's plans for the Supremes, and Diana Ross, was the unending production of hits—not just big hits but *No. 1* hits. HDH did their part by ushering the group back to the seat of power on the charts. When Berger came to Detroit on that July 4th, the girls were putting the finishing touches on two new songs, then titled "This Is Where I Came In" and "Pay Back," after spending months of tracking and overdubbing.

Clearly, no Supremes song would go out now with any hedges or shortcomings; those unmatching bass lines on "Itching in My Heart," as well as they were integrated into the overall mix, were now the kind of thing that was *verboten*. Hours, then supplemental sessions, were eaten up getting every note right. And because the two songs were nothing alike, each required a different sort of tinkering.

The former—renamed "You Can't Hurry Love"—backtracked to a more soulful, gospel feel and engendered a less decorous arrangement, one that Alan Slutsky pairs with no less than Ravel's "Bolero" as "a simple rhythm that had a dramatic influence in the music world." If Motown grooves were normally meant to mesh like the workings of an automobile engine, with small parts playing off each other, each instrument in "Hurry" was melted into a giant slab of rhythm, the syncopation provided only by the *chank* of a guitar and the clanging vibes on the backbeat; as always, the anchor was James Jamerson's fat, sassy bass licks—including arguably the second most famous bass intro in history (behind only Jamerson's three-beat preamble on "My Girl"), a 1-2-3, 1-2-3-4 figure (cribbed years later on Hall and Oates's "Maneater").

Ross eased out a gossamer-soft opening incantation: "I need love, love to ease my mind / I need to find, find some someone to call mine, but mama said, . . ." before checking off the litany of maternal caveats—that "You can't hurry love, no, you just have to wait," that "Love don't come easy, it's a game of give and take," and to "Just give it time no matter how long it takes." The swelling urgency of Diana's voice, and the frustration of her priceless elongation of the "no" into "noooooo" on the first piece of motherly advice made clear that "my poor heart" would break if she had to wait any longer for "that soft voice to talk to me at night" and "some tender arms to hold me tight." Mary and Flo, meanwhile, were of no help, peppering her with the taunting admonition that "You just have to wait." The theme was of course a classic girl-group cliché, but also something new and fresh.

The latter tune—renamed "You Keep Me Hanging On"—was a kind of primordial pop-funk. It had a looser, harder-driving arrangement, tempered by the sense of angst that leapt from Eddie Holland's lyric sheet. The intro, equally as striking as that on "Hurry," was a mercurial high guitar burst by Robert White that sounded like Morse code, met by a haunting organ and then an explosive Pistol Allen snare drum roll that unleashed a torrent of long, ringing chords, spiked by White's persistent dot-dash-dot "code" and Jamerson's sinewy bass clomping on the bottom.

The Supremes, too, let loose. Giving voice to Mr. Holland's monumental opus of love trapped inside possession, Diana wailed, "You don't really love me, you just keep me hanging on," cajoled the guy to "be a man about it" and "set me free" because "You don't care a thing about me, you're just using me," and was reduced to practically shouting, "Go on, get out, get out of my life, and let me sleep at night." Mary and Flo joined the fray, bellowing the choruses. It was a two-minute, forty-seven-second psychodrama, unlike anything ever heard before at Motown.

The conundrum for HDH was which of the two songs to put out first, a colossal decision given the pressure. They, and Gordy, went with the more upbeat, tighter "You Can't Hurry Love." Released on July 25, 1966, backed by "Put Yourself in My Place," it burned up the charts, reaching No. 1 the week of September 10 and staying there for two weeks. It also returned the Supremes to the top rung of the R&B chart for the first time since "Back in My Arms Again"—which was pure gravy, given that their R&B days were long over.

Indeed, Shelly Berger wouldn't, and couldn't, position them in an R&B fold. "Mr. Gordy and I never discussed it but it was implicit to me: The Supremes were a white act," he says. "They were immediately mainstream. That was due to Holland, Dozier, and Holland more than anything else. It wasn't only the Supremes. Look, there's a reason why Motown was the only major record company that didn't have an R&B division."

One can quibble that Motown's Soul and VIP labels, created as homes for harder-core R&B artists—Earl Van Dyke and the Soul Brothers, Jimmy Ruffin, Shorty Long, the Originals (Soul), the Velvelettes, the Elgins, the Monitors (VIP)—more than qualified for that distinction. However, Soul, too, bent with the flow of Motown's priorities, its product distilled for maximum hit-making potential such as that realized by Junior Walker and the All Stars and Gladys Knight and the Pips; and VIP simply floated along, taking on distinctly nonsoul acts such as white singers R. Dean Taylor and Chris Clark.

"Mr. Gordy had many labels, because it was easier to get all the acts air play," explains Berger. "If everyone was on the same label, a radio station wouldn't play more than a fixed number of Motown or Tamla songs. He also put out the album of Martin Luther King's speeches, but that was a personal thing to Berry. The whole company plan was that he did not want to be pigeon-holed just because he was black. Really the only record that went out at Motown was a pop record. That's why the Supremes were so perfectly emblematic of Motown."

Berger considered his mandate to obliterate the line between black and white—and did so quite literally in one respect.

"I was the one," he says, "who changed the standard Motown contract. I put a clause in that if there was a segregated audience for any show, the act or acts would be paid in full and we wouldn't play. It wasn't necessary once we got to the '70s, but it stayed in the contract up until the end of the '80s. Berry remembered those early tours through the South; it left a mark on him, the divided auditoriums, the singing for whites on one side, then blacks on the other side, all that shit. He said, 'Never again.'"

All this racial de-emphasis crested with the Supremes, about whom there was a kind of subliminal obeisance to certain virtual realities. Berger, for example, never fielded a single offer for the girls from anyone but a white promoter. The contrast was especially stark when in 1967 Berger became the Temptations' manager. "Then, if a black promoter was on the line, it had to be for the Temptations. And not one black promoter ever called and said, 'I want the Supremes, too.' Never. It was understood that the Supremes' audience was white."

As of 1967 they were still the hottest female act under the sun—the hottest, period, in the public eye now that the Beatles had given up touring to concentrate on studio work. "You Keep Me Hanging On," released on October 12, 1966, with "Remove This Doubt" on the flip, raced just as fast and far as "You Can't Hurry Love," careening to No. 1 on both the pop and R&B charts the week of November 19—again, for a healthy two-week run. Their latest album, *The Supremes A Go-Go,* became the first Supremes album to go No. 1 (and the first No. 1 R&B album since *Where Did Our Love Go*), its inclusion of "Love Is Like an Itching in My Heart" and "You Can't Hurry Love" making up for the filler of mainly Motown covers—"Baby I Need Your Loving," "I Can't Help Myself," "Get Ready, "Shake Me, Wake Me," "Come and Get These Memories," "This Old Heart of Mine"—and of Nancy Sinatra's "These Boots Are Made for Walkin'" and the McCoys' "Hang On Sloopy."

Not for public consumption were the fissures within the group caused by Diana's rising star and Flo's envious, booze-fueled antagonism toward her; that was effectively plastered over in the "glitz, glam, and gowns" fable of the Supremes. Yet under the literal and figurative "Snow White" patina, any tranquility in the group was only temporary, and fast becoming a rarity. By now, the three Supremes had drifted into their own camps, each of them, along with their personal lackeys and hangers-on, openly contemptuous of the others. Flo had come to so detest Diana that even in public settings it was hard for her to keep from letting fly with a cutting remark. Whenever Diana had an objection to a bit of Cholly Atkins's choreography, Flo, watching her get all ruffled, would yowl, mocking Ross's adopted name, "Uh-oh, Miss *Di-an-ah's* gonna run and tell it, just watch." Everyone knew what she meant: Diana would complain to Berry and get her way. The comment was, as ever, right on the mark, and a hoot, and inevitably would play out like that; at the next rehearsal, the choreography would be done as Diana wanted.

Ross, for her part, simply acted as any diva would, pretending Flo wasn't even there, or else glaring at her with disdain, muttering not quite under her breath about Flo's lack of class—meaning perhaps her lack of deference to the star of the act. Communication between the two ran between mechanical shop talk about dance moves and utter silence. More and more now, that awkward situation was handled by giving Diana a private dressing room, with Mary and Flo sharing another one. For Flo, that was just fine.

"It's not as if me and Mary want to look at her skinny little ass," she remarked one time to her go-fer Tony Tucker, who would hear Flo talk trash about "that Diana woman" all the time, such as that "[s]he's always been snooty and looking for a fight." Flo also relished relating the story of Ross aiming the front grill of a car at Gladys Horton in the parking lot of the Howard Theater, when, Flo insisted, "[s]he tried to run over a little blind boy!" A favorite Flo aphorism went like this: "That woman is like a fire engine. It don't care about who gets in the way. The only thing to do when you see it coming is move."

Flo had done just that when Gordy anointed Ross; now, every day, she had to move further out of the way for Diana. In doing so, she told herself, and anyone who would listen, that Ross wanted her and Mary out of the way rather than have to compete with them.

"She's just jealous, plain jealous," she said, according to Tucker. "She's a jealous woman. She's jealous of Mary for being pretty and she's jealous of me because people around here are my friends, which is more than anyone can say for her, honey."

With Flo becoming more unhappy and unstable, Diana, as with Gordy, had little sympathy for whatever may have been a cause of her disruptive behavior and her drinking. In fact, mired in mutual contempt, whenever the two were in each other's company off-stage, each seemed to lose her mind a little. During one of the Supremes' engagements at the Copa, Flo often would tell the driver to stop their limousine so she could get out and greet fans who regularly trailed after the car following shows. For all of Diana's showy attestations of "love" for Supremes fans while on stage, she generally avoided such impromptu human contact in uncontrolled situations, and would huddle in the back seat, hiding behind Mary, who would make an effort to cheerfully wave to the fans.

Knowing how uncomfortable Diana was, Flo would take her sweet time, sometimes even leading groups of fans down the street and treating them to slices and soda at pizza parlors. Worse, one time when a construction gang was hooting and whistling at the girls as they got into the limo, Flo held back and began doing a sexy catwalk down the middle of the street. Diana, dying of embarrassment, hissed to Mary about Flo's "disgusting" display. "She's making a spectacle of herself! How common!" To which she added, "I've never seen anything so shocking." Diana then ordered the driver to leave without Flo. When he hesitated, she shouted, "Do you hear me? Do you want to be fired?!"

It wasn't the only time Flo was left behind. Whenever she was even slightly tardy leaving a theater or club, Diana would issue the same order, leaving Flo on the street having to hail a cab back to the hotel. At least Flo wouldn't have to ride with Diana, an interlude that always seemed to bring on a spat between them.

Flo got her revenge after one of the Copa engagements had ended and the girls were being driven to JFK Airport for the trip back home. Suddenly, Flo yelled to the driver, a Motown road manager named Phil Wooldridge, "Pull over! Let me drive this car."

"No, Miss Ballard, you can't drive," he told her, apparently having been briefed to that effect by Motown, in case she might try something like this.

"I *know* how to drive," she sassed. "I'm from Detroit where these cars are *made*. Let me at that wheel!"

Bounding into the driver's seat as Wooldridge scrambled out of the way, she soon had the car fired up and the pedal to the metal, in the thick of heavy traffic on the Van Wyck Expressway. Weaving in and out of lanes, with her purse dangling from her arm, she spun the wheel back and forth, creating chaos on the road and a very dangerous situation as the car's tires screeched in tune with the screams of terror from those inside—especially from Diana, whose eyes were as big and wide as hubcaps and was shrieking, "You're going to kill us all!"

For twenty hair-raising minutes, the future of Motown—not to mention the life of each Supreme—was riding with that car. For Flo, it was a rush, maybe not least of all because the Supremes were back in her hands again, even if just for the duration of this ride. And just seeing Diana turn ashen with fear seemed to make it all the more exhilarating. At one point Diana, prayer-like, wailed, "Oh, Jesus," over and over. Even speeding down a highway, Flo had a ready one-liner. Turning her head around, she chastised Ross, "Never take the name of the Lord in vain."

Still not easing up on the accelerator, she overshot the airport exit. Flipping into reverse, she backed up against oncoming traffic. Finally, she stopped at the entrance to the terminal, the car's front wheels on the sidewalk. In the back, Diana and Mary were entangled and moaning. Diana's wig was half off her head, causing Flo to break out laughing. A skycap, who'd nearly been run over, dashed over to the car to see if anyone was hurt. Squinting through the windshield, he forgot everything else when he saw the familiar faces.

"You're the Supremes!" he gushed.

Flo didn't much care who was in the line of her ire, including Big Daddy himself. She had taken to derisively calling him "Napoleon," riffing on that ridiculous painting he had in his mansion, using it as a scalpel to chip at his corpulent ego, as in "Hey, Napoleon, how are the troops doing today?" If she really wanted to get under his skin, she'd call him "*Little* Napoleon," knowing how sensitive he was about his height. Not irrelevant, too, was that Gordy had made it clear that when business associates, and even his Motown flock, spoke to him, he was to be addressed as "Mr. Gordy," *not*, as had been the case from day one, Berry or BG; in the corporate Motown mindset, Berry was no more.

Mr. Gordy rarely went back at Flo, fully aware that she seemed to enjoy making a big scene out of nothing. Usually, his response to her cracks would be an Edgar Kennedy–style slow boil. But he now began to level criticisms about her performances, either that she was singing too loudly on stage, overwhelming Diana's softer leads—something he and everyone else believed was intentional on her part—or that she was gaining too much weight. The latter, of course, would become a central catalyst of her demise, legendarily so, and Gordy may well have played that card expecting the obstinate Ballard to gain *more* weight, out of spite, and thus put herself in greater jeopardy of remaining a Supreme. No one at Motown ever denied Gordy could be that cruel if he chose to be.

Predictably, Flo accepted none of the criticism. On the weight matter, she shot back one time, "I am *not* getting heavy! Diana is too *thin!*" Then, as a parting shot: "And you are just too damn short to know what you're talking about!" At times, as well, she would tweak Gordy by reminding him that she, too, was a world-famous Supreme, as opposed to his more limited fame. "Don't nobody know you!" she said, digging into his fantasy of omnipotence.

Ballard had not been fond of Gordy right from the start, but could easily play him off with charm and proper deference. For several years, in fact, the two would enjoy hanging together, with Gordy taking her to lunch or on shopping sprees. Now, however, so fixated was he on Ross that he'd all but filtered Wilson and Ballard out of his awareness. Worse, he seemed not to realize how much he was rubbing the other two Supremes' noses in it when he ceaselessly invited himself to accompany the group on most of their tours—rather than letting Diana out of his sight and possibly becoming amenable to other men's flirtations. In so doing, he made sure no one could breathe with him around, not just Diana.

Seeing him every day fawning over Ross was insufferable to just about everyone in the troupe, but far more so to the already obstinate Flo. On those excursions, not only did she not speak with Diana but she and Gordy couldn't contain their contempt for each other. As Tony Tucker wrote in *All That Glittered*, "He went all over the world with them [and] you couldn't help but notice the tension when he was around because he and Flo would be constantly but quietly bickering."

For Flo, making a fuss was the only way of dealing with the avalanche she felt coming down on her. However, it was Ross, not Gordy, who was the villain; if he was to blame for anything in her view, it was allowing Diana to castrate him—and it was driving her half-mad with paranoid delusions. She insisted that her backing vocals on "You Can't Hurry Love" had been toned down or even erased, and that she had laid down the lead vocal for the cover of "These Boots Are Made for Walkin'" on the *A Go-Go* album only to have it scrubbed so Diana could have every lead on the album. Rewriting her personal history, she would claim that Diana had "never cared about Berry until she knew I was interested in him," and that "[h]e and I used to get along just great until that bitch came along."

The most galling thing for her was that "that bitch" now had everyone at Motown in her thrall. That was no delusion. Mickey Stevenson said that if Gordy had ever proposed that the wealth of the Supremes be spread around to buoy the other Motown acts—"so that we could all go out of business together"—he would have told him, "You're crazy. Put the money on Diana because she's a winner and I want to be paid on Friday."

Gordy himself, as Tammi Terrell sang in "Ain't Nothing Like the Real Thing," seemed to be "not in reality" when he was with Ross. Even as he (needlessly) carried on the ruse that they weren't fooling around, he flaunted her everywhere they went. In Puerto Rico and Las Vegas, he'd have her on his arm at the gambling tables, high-rolling and even letting her take over his hand at poker games. She was, in every respect, his good-luck charm, his Josephine. Not even her name-change could do justice to the stratum she was now on. During an interview Ross was giving late in 1966, when the writer addressed her as "Diana," Gordy, who was with her, interrupted, saying, "Call her Miss Ross." The same instruction soon went out to all Motown department heads.

To Mary and Flo, it was rich—that only a few years removed from the projects, Diane Ernestine Ross was now too good for a first name, not far removed from "Mrs. Rockefeller." The same honorifics did not apply to them. But then, they had never been on the arm of "Mr. Gordy."

Even the strenuously temperate Wilson was rankled by his tunnel vision about Diana. Like many women, she had been captivated by the man's roguish charm and spontaneous displays of generosity, such as when he surprised Mary and Diana by flying their younger sisters to New York for one of their Copa engagements as a graduation present. But his verbal cruelty and insensitivity rarely were given a rest, and he was just so damned hypocritical. Ignoring his abundant moral failings, he ragged Mary constantly about her partying and laundry list of sexual partners.

True, Mary liked to play, one reason her love life never seemed to stabilize. Late in '66, Duke Fakir moved out to go back with his wife and was replaced in her bed by another of the Four Tops, Obie Benson. But neither of these relationships ever satisfied her hobby as a collector of the male gender, which was always obvious by the volume of overnight visitors to her room on the road.

If anything, this was just another mirror of Big Daddy's own habits, which Wilson observed almost like a student. For instance, though he went to great lengths to hide it from Diana, he was already cheating with Chris Clark, the white Motown singer who happened to be a gorgeous and sexy blond. Not willing to wait until he was back in Detroit to fool around with her, he would sometimes fly Clark to where he was on the road and have roadies smuggle her into his room—which, with a sense of danger and betrayal that must have been perversely exciting, was always right next to Diana's room, an adjoining door away from his Queen, who would be kept busy elsewhere as a diversion. As Wilson wrote in *Dreamgirl*, "The road managers and musicians were my friends so I got the scoop on these things."

Had she been a man, Gordy probably would have looked the other way—after all, he did that even when all of Motown knew, and recoiled in disgust, about David Ruffin's horrible physical tormenting of Tammi Terrell. But his parochial paternalism led him to assume the role of a church pastor when lecturing her on the subject.

"Mary," he told her one time, "I think you're making yourself too available."

"I like to be out," she said.

With not a crumb of irony, or shame, he went on: "You should be more like Diana—untouchable, unreachable."

She had to laugh out loud at the notion of Diana Ross as a role model of chastity-belt sensibilities—knowing that Diana kept her nose clean on the road only when he was there to stifle her. Before Gordy started to come along on tours, she had been plenty "touchable," carrying on "boy in every port" romances, including one with a white record promoter in D.C., Eddie Bisco, who would travel to see her on Supremes stops in northeastern cities (until Gordy found out and threatened to take Motown acts away from him if he didn't keep away from her). Regarding Gordy's right to pontificate, Mary could have answered him with two words—Chris Clark.

Gordy pulled the same pious rap on her in London after Mary and Flo hit the town without security and didn't get back to the hotel until the crack of dawn. The next day, he began to chew her out—but not Florence, who could intimidate him. Wrung out and hung over, Mary was in no mood.

"Flo and me, we like to have fun at night," she snapped at him. "Don't make us go to bed early just because you're jealous of Diane," whom, of course, he prohibited from such nocturnal meandering.

It was the kind of thing *nobody* said to him, except Flo. That the winsome Wilson had nailed him with an essential truth—one he wouldn't admit to—left him at a loss. All he could do was force out a laugh and say, "Mary, that's the dumbest thing I've ever heard in my life."

Realizing she'd struck a nerve, she drilled further in. "She's the one who needs to save her voice and get sleep, not us. She's the *leader*. All we do is [sing] doobie-doobie-doo. If you're jealous of her, that's your problem. Don't make us suffer."

"Mary," he said, trying to end the matter on a light note, "you'd say anything to get out at night."

Gordy, plainly, was unpained about the corrosive effects of Diana's Norma Desmond–like vanity and how he was always enabling it, not least by letting her walk all over him. All Motown suffered for it. Marvin Gaye would later recall that he'd been "sick of hearing about Diana all the time from Berry." If a non-Supreme, and Gordy's brother-in-law, felt that way, one can imagine the depth of revulsion experienced by Wilson and Ballard.

In fact, despite Gordy's cheating and sudden bursts of blithe indifference and cruelty—which didn't spare Ross, about whom he felt the need to denigrate publicly, and absurdly, in a 1966 interview as "lazy"—it was as if he lived in fear of her leaving him, rather than the other way around. Given Ross's ambivalence and periodic self-loathing about the "secret" relationship through the years, his fear was well

justified. Confessing she never knew who wore the pants in that unhealthy coupling, Wilson put it like this:

> Seeing [them] together, I never knew exactly who was directing
> whom. When changes occurred, we never knew which of them
> had instigated them. But Flo and I could see that whatever Di-
> ane wanted, Diane got. In Flo's mind this was unfair, and her
> resentment began to consume her. . . . [N]either Diane nor
> Berry gave a damn about what we wanted, and Flo made no
> bones about feeling betrayed and lied to.

It's telling that in this indictment "Flo and I" becomes merely "Flo"
when dealing with the personal repercussions of those changes—with
Wilson not willing to admit that she might have been "consumed" by
resentment or felt "betrayed and lied to." In the end, Mary always
thought better than to stand too closely with Flo in her defiance toward
Gordy, which put Ballard out on an even shakier limb. But as differently as Wilson and Ballard handled their slightings, they were equally
sick of Ross pulling rank on them, turning all those smiles on stage into
frozen masks. The tragedy of it was that there were times when the ice
and the hype melted and they were suddenly sisters again. During a
show in March 1966 at Bilstrub's Supper Club in Boston, Diana began
weaving while singing "I Hear a Symphony" and appeared faint, mum-
bling, "What's happening to me? I feel so small. I'm getting smaller,
smaller, smaller." A road manager rushed out and half-carried her off
stage as the audience gasped and Mary and Flo stood rooted, not knowing what to do or say. The show was halted while, backstage, Diana was
placed on a couch in her dressing room, an ice pack on her head, crying
out, "I can't go on . . . it's too much."

That's when, according to a lengthy telling of the incident in the
book *Call Her Miss Ross*, Flo became mother hen. Sitting down on
the couch and placing Diana's head on her lap, she rubbed her temples
and calmed her, saying, "You don't have to go on any more, honey.
We're all here for you." In this telling, as Mary stood crying hysterically
over them, Flo, taking charge, demanded a phone and rang up Gordy
back in Detroit.

"What's happening?" he asked.

"Diane's sick, that's what's happening!" she barked, then ordered
him to cancel the rest of the two-week engagement. When he refused,
she spat out "Son of a bitch" and told him, "This is all your fault!"

Gordy would fly to Boston the next day and, seeing Diana's condition, did cancel the gig. He flew Diana home and put her in Henry Ford Hospital to recover from her "breakdown." Flo was said to have visited her whereupon they had a teary heart-to-heart talk, with Diana suggesting that Flo sing some more leads and Flo asking her if she would be leaving the Supremes to go solo.

"I don't know, Flo," she allegedly said. "What do you think? Berry probably thinks I should."

"Who cares about what Berry thinks," Flo replied. "Who's gonna take care of you if you leave? Not Berry, no way! He don't care about you, Diane; all he cares about is money."

(A mandatory note of caution: There is some doubt about elements of this story. Author J. Randy Taraborrelli, in an endnote, attributes as sources "many observers" and the road manager Sye MacArthur—none of whom were directly quoted—as well as a 1972 interview with Ballard. However, he allows that "it may be possible that she was confused" about certain details—and that Ballard herself asked that he not print the story, saying, "I think I may have said some things that are too personal." Moreover, Flo's actions as described here are not corroborated in the Motown literature—including the writings of Ross, Wilson, and Gordy—or by any source consulted for this book. Unconfirmed, too, is that Ross had a "breakdown," as Flo apparently called it; she may have been suffering from exhaustion due to the Supremes' hectic schedule.)

Any such heartwarming moments, however, were fleeting; in an eyeblink the infighting and cattiness were back. Gordy would try to keep peace between them as best he could, usually by trying to induce some sympathy from Mary and Flo for the diva. Diana, he told them one day, was "miserable" because she felt "isolated from her friends," meaning them.

"We're the ones being isolated," Mary pointed out. "She gets out there on stage and acts like we're not even there."

"Yeah," Flo added. "She ain't nothin' but a show-off."

He couldn't disagree. "But she's *always* been a show-off," he said, while insisting that "[s]he loves both of you"—and beseeching them to "work it out." Though they had to wonder why it was that *Diana* was unable to tell them those things herself, they said they'd try. But more and more the sword of Diana hung over their heads, as the issue of whether she would go solo gained pitch and fever in the media. Each Supreme had to deal with it in different ways. Diana, who most assumed was behind the whole idea, actually was quite torn, so insecure was she that she might be a catastrophic failure on her own in such a highly visible and surely over-hyped endeavor. Further, like Gordy, she was less than sure the time was right just yet, or if it ever would be.

Wilson, always looking for reasons not to worry, took that ambivalence as assurance that she needn't. The back-biting, she recalled thinking, was a "phase" that would soon "come to an end." Flo, surprisingly, for all her anger, was even more convinced nothing would change. In her biggest delusion of all, she believed Diana would stay put for the same reason that Flo could get away with anything she laid on Gordy: that individual personalities and schemes bowed to the oneness of the act.

"Maybe that bitch is fixing to be the only diva in this group but she ain't ever leaving, and Flo ain't either," she vowed, according to Tony Tucker.

What Flo, and Mary, didn't know was that these things had already been decided. Only the timing of the move was in doubt. From henpecked Gordy's perspective, the act was nothing more than, as Shelly Berger says succinctly, "a lead singer and backup." With all the money riding on the lead, for one of the backup singers there'd be only small change; for the other, a lump of coal.

eighteen

"SHE'S OUTTA HERE"

When Gordy let his mind play out the scenario of Diana going solo, he pegged the Supremes' Las Vegas debut at the Flamingo Hotel, to run from September 29 to October 19, 1966, as the group's "farewell" event, bathed in all the appropriate mawkish rites of joy and sadness as a new fairy tale would be born and the old one refit. According to the plan, Ross's breakout would be accompanied by the announcement of the "new" Supremes, which in the manner of the "old" Supremes would be fronted not by Mary Wilson or Florence Ballard but by a fresh lead singer. While no final decision had been made, for that role Gordy was leaning toward Barbara Randolph, a muscular-voiced former member of the Platters who was now on the Motown Soul label. Her tall, slinky "Supremesque" carriage made her a logical choice. Meanwhile, Shelly Berger would go on managing the revamped Supremes, but his main thrust would be Ross.

"A lot of things were already on the fire," Berger says. "We were already starting to develop the *Lady Sings the Blues* movie for Diana. In fact, we had Diana come out to Hollywood and we took her around to the studios, meeting directors, producers, acting coaches. She met Doris Day, which Diana said was the biggest thrill of her life. We wanted everyone to know that Diana Ross was the next biggest thing, and to get on the bandwagon. The impetus for all that was her going solo."

However, Ross's insecurities and the Supremes' ever-expanding bottom line put all that on the back burner, with Gordy holding back on the move he desperately wanted to make. The Flamingo run was still a smashing success—though not without its hurdles. The most vexing, as usual, had to do with Flo. Although she posed no problem early in the run, after one particularly long night of drinking she was still asleep when the other two Supremes arrived at the hotel for the night's shows.

"I'll never forget [that night]," Ross would recall. "Mary and I were thrilled to be there, it was one of the places that we never imagined at the beginning of our career we'd get the chance to play. But here we were, as excited as we could be, and then Florence showed up, late and drunk. Our costumes were tuxedos. Florence had gained so much weight, her stomach was bulging out of her costume. We were embarrassed to go onstage with her."

Gordy, who could barely watch, buried his woes at the blackjack tables. But even with his lucky lady on his elbow, he lost something like $25,000 and his credit was cut off, forcing him to call Motown and have more cash wired out to Vegas; also, Diana blew several thousand more on her own.

The mixed bag of their Vegas debut was a proper augury of the Supremes' path ahead. As Gordy looked beyond to the terrain of 1967, the future suddenly seemed considerably less titillating. But there was a definite upside. Because Gordy had intentionally held back on booking the girls, anticipating what would have been a gradual break-in period for the "new" Supremes—and with his own time surely to be dominated by all matters Ross—the "same old" Supremes actually had little else to do *but* record songs in the studio. Following their Christmas gig at the Eden Roc Hotel in Miami and at the New Year's Eve King Orange Jamboree Parade, the only time they left the Detroit area the first three months of '67 was to do an *Ed Sullivan Show* on January 22.

That suited HDH just fine. Over that winter they cut a hardy flow of vinyl, including an album that seemed the height of egomania but which in reality was simply a sure-shot profit-maker for them and Gordy. Titled *The Supremes Sing Holland Dozier Holland*, it was for many casual fans the first time they'd heard of or seen the names of the tunesmiths behind the thrones; and for those who *had,* a bit redundant—hadn't the Supremes been singing Holland-Dozier-Holland for years? For Gordy, though, it offered a unique and irresistible lure— a secondary bonanza of royalties on old hits by having his biggest artists cover them. Mixing HDH evergreens like "Heat Wave," "It's the Same Old Song," "I Guess I'll Always Love You" and "I'll Turn to Stone" with "You Keep Me Hanging On" and the latest Supremes single—"Love Is Here and Now You're Gone"—Gordy had himself a low-overhead cash cow.

Predictably, the album, released on January 23, quickly went to No. 6 on the pop charts and No. 1 on the R&B charts, and even brought the Supremes back onto the British album chart for the first time since *Meet the Supremes*, at No. 15. Concurrently, "Love Is Here and Now You're Gone," released two weeks prior with the aptly titled "There's No Stopping Us Now" on the flip, ran all the way up to No. 1 the week of March 11, making for a telltale triumvirate of No. 1 hits in succession, with "Ruby Tuesday" coming right before it and "Penny Lane" right after. It also provided the strongest proof yet that the Supremes were on such a roll that even a song that deviated from the forensics of the hit-making machinery could still come up aces.

It wasn't that the HDH formula was different but, rather, a matter of where and with whom it was carried out—not Studio A and not the Funk Brothers. In fact, "Love Is Here" may be the best rebuttal HDH could make in the dust-up about who was most responsible for their sound. The song was recorded in L.A. after Gordy, thinking ahead to future session work for his big acts on the coast, had sent HDH out in the late summer of '66 so they could test the acoustics of the studios (mainly Hollywood Sound Recorders, a virtual copy of Studio A, converted from a garage in a two-story home by its owner, engineer Armin Steiner) and connect with West Coast musicians.

Those sessions were historic, in that they were apparently the only known instances when some of the later musicians from Phil Spector's "Wrecking Crew"—pianist/keyboardists Don Randi, Larry Knechtal, and Mike Rubini; guitarist Tommy Tedesco; bassists Carole Kaye and Bill Pitman; drummer Earl Palmer (who went back to the mid-'50s with Fats Domino's band); and arranger Gene Page—also played for the second most famous producers in the world (as opposed to cranking out Motown filler for Hal Davis and Marc Gordon, as had the legendary West Coast drummer Hal Blaine).

While "Love Is Here and Now You're Gone" sounds not a bit discordant from other Supremes songs, Motown scholars and purists can immediately discern it as an "outside" product. Allan Slutsky, for instance, says, "You can tell it's an L.A. session just by listening to the drum and bass, which sound great but lack the round fatness the Detroit players were known for. And the guitars and tambourine are pulled back far beyond what was the norm in Detroit." The tempo was glacial, even maundering, with an electric harpsichord intro featuring Wilson and Ballard in a high soprano wail melding into a mass of strings and horns—nearly Spectorian in its hollowed stateliness. And

Eddie Holland's grim tract of a woman wooed, won, and abandoned—including three spoken soliloquies, a novel and even daring gimcrack for the times—was every bit as hopeless as "My World Is Empty Without You."

What made it fly farther was the hazy prettiness of Gene Page's arrangement and Diana's uncanny knack for tapping the very nuanced range of emotion of that lyric; while she made the usual wounds burn through the radio, so did her sense of optimism that she and the cheating dog would work it out; that she wouldn't let it *not*. Just acing those three Lady MacBeth proto-"raps"—which with their over-the-top melodrama could easily have been laugh-out-loud funny—was a world-class coup, intoning as she had to with dead seriousness a bathetic line like "You closed the door to your heart / And you turned the key, locked your love away from me," and stamping the pity of it all with a knife-in-the-heart glottal gasp, something that would emerge as a signature Ross vocal affectation (and years later for Michael Jackson, who shamelessly cribbed it).

So delighted were HDH, and Gordy, by this accidental gem that the auteurs returned to L.A. trying to strike gold again on the next Supremes single, which actually made perfect sense because the girls would be recording the title song of a new movie—moving Motown's footprint further into the Hollywood community. The flick, a Columbia Pictures kidnap-ransom farce called *The Happening*, starring Anthony Quinn and Faye Dunaway, had the pedigree of producer Sam Spiegel, he of *Lawrence of Arabia* and *Bridge on the River Kwai* fame, and its plot blurred good and evil. As such, it was intended to attract audiences on the cusp of the late '60s counter-culture wave—a focus that, clearly, had nothing to do with the Supremes other than the fact that they were, well, "happening."

For HDH, the problem was that the title track, as composed with the film's musical director Frank DeVol, was supposed to be the aural image of a swirling carnival, its pipe-organ feel simulated by piccolos and a Herb Alpert–style Tijuana brass. Laying down early tracks in L.A., they couldn't catch the groove. Needing a stronger, funkier bottom and backbeat, they started over again in Studio A in March. That was when the missing element was found—James Jamerson's mercurial bass licks, meaning that Jack Ashford may have been right, after all, about Jamerson's bass being intrinsic to the Motown sound. It's an argument that will never be settled.

"The Happening" single was another against-the-grain winner, its sprightly cadences matched niftily with nonsensical jibber like "I saw the light too late / When that fickle finger of fate, yeah came and broke my pretty balloon / I woke up, suddenly I just walked up to the happening" and a repeating killer hook—"Ooooh, and then it happened"— by Wilson and Ballard mid-song. The record far outran the movie, which tanked at the box office when it opened in late March—when there was a gala opening at Detroit's Adams Theater, with the Supremes entering on a red carpet—whereas the concurrent release of the single, with a song called "All I Know About You" on the reverse, soared.

In fact, it was the first time that a title song had stolen a movie since *Love Is a Many-Splendored Thing* in 1955. *Time* even savaged the picture by citing from the song's lyric—"Is it real, is it fake? Is this game of life a mistake?"—answering snarkily, "Indeed it is, at least in this film." Not so the song. The week of May 13, a bare two months and a day after "Love Is Here" had held the spot, "The Happening" went to No. 1.

That made four No. 1 hits in a row, with radically diverse material each time. There seemed nothing they could do that would disturb their still upward spiral—until Gordy's "Broadway airs" took them too far afield. He had them record an album of show tunes, as they had two years before with the unreleased *There's a Place for Us,* but with the gimmick that all of the songs were Rodgers & Hart show-stoppers—the same Rodgers who had slapped down rock and roll as a repetitive bore.

The album would be released to coincide with the Supremes' appearance on an ABC TV special "Rodgers & Hart Today," to run on March 12, 1967, in which the famous duo's songs would be performed by contemporary acts, the others being Bobby Darin, Petula Clark, the Doodletown Pipers, and, keeping it real, Count Basie. It was such a vanity project for Gordy that he returned to the grind of the studio to co-produce the album in L.A. with Gil Askey. Some two dozen tracks were made with the girls, enough for him to consider turning it into a double LP. The sessions ran through October of '66, then most of December back in Detroit for the overdubs.

For Flo, it was especially torturous. Expecting no alms from Gordy, she was pleasantly surprised when told that she and Mary would have one song each with which to emerge from the background shadows: Mary would get a co-lead on "Falling in Love" and Flo would have a duet with Diana on "Manhattan." But while Mary's made it onto the finished LP, Flo's didn't; unhappy with the track, Gordy first stripped her vocal, then junked the cut altogether along with twelve others—two of them with titles Flo could have related to: "Bewitched, Bothered and Bewildered" and "You Took Advantage of Me." What remained included the likes of "Blue Moon," "Where or When," "This Can't Be Love" "My Heart Stood Still," and one more that Flo would surely regard as ideal for Diana, "The Lady Is a Tramp" (which in fact had become a fixture of the stage act).

But Gordy would not release a single from the album, wisely, no doubt realizing that while the tracks were well done and more than adequate as examples of the Supremes' versatility in the bombastic, string-swelled, big-band idiom, overall it was shlock—a judgment confirmed when the album rose no higher than No. 20, mainly on the strength of the Supremes' brand—though with not a shred of logic it hit No. 3 on the R&B charts. (It would also become a lingering curiosity through the years, with all but two of the unreleased tracks—which were used on *Diana Ross and the Supremes' 25th Anniversary* album in 1986—appearing on *The Rodgers & Hart Songbook* a year later; and all twenty-five tracks on *The Supremes Sing Rodgers & Hart: The Complete Recordings* in 2002.)

Having seen "People" snatched from her, Ballard, upon being double-crossed on the album, lost another little piece of sanity at a time when she seemed to have calmed down a bit, perhaps because the time off the road cut down on the time she had to spend with Diana, whom she could avoid at home since background vocals were usually cut separately from the lead.

"She was never as happy as when she'd come home from a tour," recalls Ray Gibson. "She would decompress; you could see her change before your eyes. She'd lose the anger and tension. She could just be with the family, go and record, and come home. The funny thing is that Diana was right across the street but they never crossed paths; she may as well have been thousands of miles away."

There was something, or someone, else that kept her happy to be home. Recently she had taken up with a tall, mustached fellow who was one of Gordy's drivers, Tommy Chapman, another pairing in the never-ending procession of canoodling within the Motown "family." (A further one was Flo's cousin Winnie Brown, a Supremes' hair stylist, who was fooling around with the married Paul Williams.) It seemed to many around the shop that this was a step down in class for Flo. But after a brief fling with Obie Benson ended when he turned his affections to Mary, Flo fell hard for the driver who had been pursuing her for months before. On the Supremes' Far East tour, she gave in and took him into her bed. Chapman had nerve, for sure. But he was also the only one she could find who encouraged her skirmishes with Ross, in effect taking sides against his own boss. When she'd go on about Diana, Chapman would nod like a metronome and say, "Yeah, she's a bitch," at regular intervals. He'd then tell her to "ignore the bitch," that Flo's day would come, that Berry would come begging her to stay in the group and maybe let *her* have a solo career.

It was either a grand match of soulmates or a grand illusion, a con played by a low-level bunco salesman seeing an easy mark in a sad, vulnerable woman slowly losing her mind. Wilson believed it was the first. Flo, she said, "seemed happier" with Chapman, who she thought was "very nice" and "seemed to empathize with Flo, and he loved her."

Just that Flo could love a man, any man, was a welcome event for everyone in the small ring of people who knew of Flo's rape and its lasting scars. Although Flo had no trouble having meaningless, recreational sex, she had a deep aversion to letting herself get close to anything like love. Now, that guard was being let down. "Knowing how difficult it was for Flo to be intimate with a man," said Mary, "I was happy that she had Tommy." Happy for Flo, and happy for the Supremes, since "[w]henever Tommy was around, she stopped obsessing about Berry and Diane."

Ray Gibson, though, had his doubts. "Thomas Lorenzo Chapman," he says, stretching the syllables with a pained laugh before turning his mind back in time.

I always thought Tommy was a nice guy, but he just didn't get it. It was really strange, because everybody was telling Florence, "Don't get involved with him," but she was in love with Tommy and you wanted it to work out for them. But then you'd see his temper and how he was already telling her what to do, and you'd go, "Uh-oh." Because he was presenting himself as her manager, which he later became. And if you knew Tommy, you'd know the last thing he was qualified to do was be anybody's manager. I don't think he could manage himself.

It didn't seem to be the healthiest relationship. But Florence had come to feel she was all alone. Diana and Mary weren't there for her. Berry Gordy wasn't. Her family was, but she needed someone in the outside world who took her side. And here came Tommy, all dashing and full of big talk and smooth ways, and before you knew it they were inseparable and talking about getting married! It was crazy.

That, it seems to me, was more indicative of something unhealthy; it was out of touch with reality, something that could only make things worse. It didn't *feel* like real love. To me it was like addiction. I think they were both addicted to each other, for their own separate reasons: Florence needed to be loved and Tommy to find a pot of gold.

Flo was so hooked on Chapman that when she would go on the road, and he didn't come along as a driver, she'd mope around moaning, "I miss Tommy so much." That, added to the stress of tight scheduling and rarely a moment before a plane, a PR appearance, or a show, led her to her real best friend—the bottle. Wilson in her memoirs cut Flo some slack, claiming that she "never drank before a show"—a conclusion disputed by others, Shelly Berger for one—and that even with the grind and often no more than two hours' sleep, "we were never less than perfectly gracious and beautiful"—a point disputed by no one.

In fact, Flo seemed proud that she could get sloshed in the folds of the itineraries, usually at post-show parties and wee-hours nightclub forays, and not act like a falling-down drunk. She could steel herself, act out the role of a carefree but classy Supreme, and get back to the hotel intact; then pour herself into a stupor, crash, and still be able to wake up the next morning and make it to the next function, laughing to herself that she could do the drill while hungover. She surely had an impressive constitution, and it threw a good many Motown people off the scent.

When Ross and Wilson, for example, gently pressed her about her drinking, and practiced little artifices trying to rein her in—pointedly declining any booze when they were with her, or milking one drink for hours—Flo would be hip to what they were doing. "Flo wasn't dumb," Wilson said. "She was touched by our efforts." Making sure to ease their fears, she would tell them, "Don't worry, I'll be all right." And she no doubt believed that.

She was indeed not dumb. If she believed she would be okay, she didn't con herself that it would be easy to get there. According to Gladys Horton, with whom she had remained close, Flo bared her inner torment to her just as she had years before about her rape. Saying she was "miserable," she 'fessed up that she was bringing it on herself because "I'm an alcoholic behind all of this," though the main reason for her drinking, she said, was her fear of flying. "I got to get stoned to get on those planes," as she put it.

Brutal as that mea culpa was, Horton was bowled over when Flo dropped another bomb. "She told me she was ready to quit," said Horton. "I was shocked. I thought she had it so good."

This was a clear signal that, for all her "And I tell you I'm not going" bravado—the virtual epitaph of the resurgent "Flo" character in the *Dreamgirls* play and movie scripts—Ballard was clear-headed enough most days to know how worn out she was by her battles with Ross and Gordy; and how much her sanity was being battered. Fighting it out didn't always seem like the best idea to her; going home and lying around the house with Tommy and a bottle for a year or so, now *that* seemed like a pretty fair trade-off. Still, it wasn't only her pride that kept her battling; it was a sense of duty only she could see, that the honor of the Supremes was being ravaged by crass commercial pimping, and by God she was gong to defend it.

RAY GIBSON: All the talk about Diana leaving hit her hard, but not because she was jealous of Diana. It was that she could see Diana and Berry making decisions based on what was best for *them*, not the Supremes. They didn't care that the Supremes would be broken up, and Florence didn't think that was fair. In her mind, it was like her responsibility to keep the group together. As it happened, they *did* stay together longer than anyone thought. Now that may be a stretch, that it was Florence's doing, but that's how she looked at it.

So incorruptible did she consider herself on this count that she believed in the reverse of the old saw about might making right; for her, right would make might. Once, when Mary tried to caution her about constantly giving lip to Ross and Gordy, Flo indignantly replied, "I'm fightin' both of them, and I'll win."

"You won't win, Flo," Mary sighed. "No one ever wins."

At the same time, she was so eager to fight the good fight that she seemed blind to the trap Gordy had set, leaving him no choice but to cut her out. Then again, a frank truth about Ballard was that another of her motivations for continuing to make war was less than altruistic. Quite plainly, she had come to love the money, and with it the furs, the El Dorados in the driveway, the shopping sprees, the shoes. As Gibson readily notes, "Florence knew if she left, she'd lose all that. She was honest about it. She'd say things like, 'As long as the money's the same for all of us, it's fine for Diane to sing all the leads.' Or, 'Berry said we're all gonna be millionaires, that's what I'm in it for.'"

"So she was caught in so many contradictory thoughts and impulses. And when it all came out of the blender, what was left was that she felt betrayed by everybody—especially Mary. Florence always said, 'At least one thing I know about Diana—Diana will be straight with you, I know where she's coming from. But Mary, she'll tell you one thing and then do another.' That hurt her a lot."

To the Motown brass, Ballard wasn't all that complicated. "Florence was a drunkard" was all Shelly Berger could see at this point. "I don't know at what point you become an alcoholic, or why. But I know I can't stop someone from drinking if that's what they want to do.

"Florence was drinking heavier all the time. She and Paul Williams had the same problem. In '67 I became the Temptations' manager and lived through it with him, too. For some people the more the pressure becomes the less they can handle it, it eats them alive. It was just amazing, the change in them. When Paul started out he never drank a drop. Then he got to the point where he was drinking a fifth of Courvoisier a day.

"It hurts you to see people you really love killing themselves like that. But, like with Florence, you just can't stop them. Sometimes, they just want to kill themselves. You have to remember, too, that it wasn't like it is today. There were no 'designer' Betty Ford Clinics. It made you very sad and frustrated, but we weren't these people's keepers."

Gordy, of course, passed down that laissez-faire approach to his acts' personal foibles, his credo being: Just don't do it on company time. And he dealt with the subject of Ballard's drinking with a few diffident sentences in *To Be Loved*, shouldering no blame for her descent—and, incredibly, claiming he hadn't known she was drinking so much because Ross and Wilson kept it from him, as if he didn't keep tabs on all of his performers. His response when they told him? "Everybody knew how I felt about drinking and drugs," he wrote airily. "They had heard me say many times: 'It's easier to stay out than to get out.'"

If empty bromides like that were all Gordy could offer Flo, even he admitted it was woefully inadequate: "It seemed the harsher the warning, the more flagrant Flo's behavior became."

Gordy did try some preventive measures to turn Flo's spigot off. When they went on the road, he would give orders to the management of the hotels where they stayed not to send liquor to her room. Flo, though, was too smart and cunning for that. She would simply have lackeys smuggle booze up. Once, in New York, she was going to send Tony Tucker to the liquor store for a fifth of Bacardi. Realizing he was too young to purchase alcohol, she instead had him ask his mother to do it, on the pretext she would be giving it to a friend as a gift. Naturally, the Bacardi never left her room.

Beyond these half-hearted attempts, no one at Motown appeared compelled to make an effort to understand *why* Ballard was in such a sad state. Four decades later, Eddie Holland regrets that:

> When I look at it, I think that if someone had done a little bit more, had a little bit more time for Florence, maybe things would have turned out different. Somebody had to be more attentive to her, to stop all that. But she really needed a psychologist, a psychiatrist. What I knew about Florence was that she loved to sing, that she never came in to sing drunk or anything like that. But it wasn't enough. She was really frightened, a frightened little girl. It was like she had a lot of demons she was running from.

If it occurred to anyone who knew her that Flo's excesses were a plea for help, it was a fleeting thought. Of course, that conclusion would become common much later. But even then, Ross, like many at Motown, took the cop-out route; in *Secrets of a Sparrow* she assented that Ballard was "not well" and had "serious emotional problems"—but insists "we didn't know that then," no matter that she had cried with Flo after her rape. The Flo as she saw her back then was an "angry woman who drank too much and wouldn't take responsibility for herself," who "blamed everyone else for the things that were not working out in her life"; but playing dumb about why that was, she cut herself the break that "I never knew why it happened. I never understood her. Florence's life was always shrouded in mystery to me."

Ross went on like this, with a rather breezy cruelty, for more than a few discomfiting passages when, attempting to be "frank," she eviscerates Ballard with no mercy, while begging off any "responsibility" for having, or needing, to understand her "problems"—or, worse, helping to cause them with her own insensitivity. Her words are more than frank; they're actually hurtful because they're meant to allow Ross to duck any blame. Consider this remarkably self-serving and intentionally myopic—or even flatly dishonest—memory stream:

[W]e were also frustrated because we were none the wiser about what had caused the emotional roller-coaster. She was secretive about her feelings, so she was the one everybody tried to appease. . . . With Florence, there always seemed to be a problem; nothing was ever right no matter how hard we tried to please her. . . . Mary and I both cared for her, and we wanted her to be happy. I wanted everyone to be happy. . . . When we were getting lots of press that started to mention only my name, it was difficult for her. The articles would refer to "the skinny little girl who . . . ," and that hurt her very much. She started acting out in a big way.

Of course, it would have been a revelation for Ballard had she known she was the one being appeased, not Diana. But in the cloister in which Ross lived, it was really pretty simple to make sense of Flo's descent: By merely inverting reality, she could pretend it had nothing, absolutely nothing, to do with Diana Ross. "We wanted to be able to enjoy it all," she wrote, "but Florence . . . ruined it for everyone. . . . [W]hatever energy we had was being drained by Florence's moods. . . . She was constantly letting us down."

It was the Motown mantra when it came to Ballard. As Brian Holland pronounces, "What happened to Florence was sad and touching to me, but all she did, she did to herself."

That is the easiest conclusion, and also an inarguable one. Even her staunchest defenders have only shades of disagreement with it.

RAY GIBSON: A lot of people played a part in it, but it all came down to Florence herself. My cousin had a big heart. But she could be very stubborn and not do what was right for her, and as a result she made some very bad choices. She thought she was strong enough to live with her mistakes, but she was wrong.

With the drinking, I was still young enough to grasp the entirety of it. She would never drink around me. But I knew she wasn't right. She didn't look or sound or act like Florence to me. She just had so much pain, felt so betrayed, that she just sort of gave up.

She was pulling away from reality.

Part of that reality was that if Gordy had little to say about her booz-
ing, he never seemed to have enough to say about her weight. Even his
rare compliments were like rabbit punches, damning with the faintest
of praise.

"You know, for a fat girl," he told her one day, "you don't sweat too
much."

Flo took as many of these foul-natured jibes as best she could,
silently responding by eating more, blimping up to a robust size 12
early in 1967.

"She *was* too big," Ray Gibson says. "They were right. She was up
to around 150 pounds and didn't look good. But the problem was, she
couldn't do anything right for them. I remember when she got sick
again and she must have lost about 30 pounds. And then they said she
was too *thin*. She couldn't win. So she ballooned up again."

The yo-yo dieting, indeed, contributed to her brittle state, physically and mentally. Trying to shed pounds in a hurry, Flo had begun to
take diet pills prescribed by her doctor, who also prescribed Valium
to reduce her anxiety. Tony Tucker said he would see her shoveling
clumps of pills into her mouth at once and washing them down with a
swig of rum or bourbon. Assuring him, she said the pills were vitamins.

But, as Gibson noted, whatever weight Flo lost never elicited a positive reaction from Gordy. Again, he may well have used the issue to set
up her eventual ouster, knowing all along he would provoke her into
fits of anger that he could hold against her. If so, he got more than he
bargained for when he spotted Flo one night at the Twenty Grand with
Tommy Chapman, a Martini in her hand, feeling no pain. She'd dropped a few pounds and people were telling her how great she looked.
Then, for some reason, Gordy thought it would be a good time to rag
her again.

After a perfunctory greeting, he told her, with a nastiness that could
only have been intentional, "Diana's right. You have to do something
about your weight, Florence. You are much too fat."

Wincing, Flo produced the most memorable Motown moment at
the Twenty Grand since Sharon Holland's almost-cat-fight with Diana.
Turning her face to his, she gave her retort.

"Fuck you! I don't give a damn about what you or that bitch thinks!"

As quickly as Gordy used to throw a left jab, her right arm jerked
and before he could react his face was covered in gin and vermouth.
Blinded temporarily, he blinked his stinging eyes, his beard now a dripping sponge. When he could see again, her stool was empty, vacated

when Flo scooped up her sable coat and made for the door with Chapman, the both of them laughing like hyenas.

That was, for many, the exact moment they knew Florence Ballard was a goner. It *had* to be. Gordy could not possibly tolerate a breach of his authority like that—at least by anyone other than Diana Ross. Yet, remarkably, he did not fire her, or Tommy, on the spot; nor did he weeks later, for a couple good reasons. One being that the Supremes were about to go back on the road with major gigs set for the spring: at the Deuville and Eden Roc Hotels in Miami Beach, the Hollywood Bowl, back at the Copa, at Symphony Hall in D.C., and the Cocoanut Grove in L.A; as well, there were impending appearances on *Ed Sullivan* May 7 and 21 (the latter broadcast from Expo 67 in Montreal), and *The Tonight Show* May 22.

It would be a mistake to shake up the Supremes now—or ever, it could be argued, as Shelly Berger did. "Mr. Gordy was sold on the idea that Florence had to go," he recalls, "and I have to tell you, I was against it. I was against any changes in the act because from my experience any time an established act had been changed, the act had fallen apart. And now, it was written in stone that both Florence would go and Diana would go solo. So I was totally panic-stricken."

The case about the fatal nature of change was arguable; group acts like Billy Ward and the Dominos and the Drifters had lost lead singers without commercial loss—sometimes becoming even more popular. At Motown as well, both the Marvelettes and the Vandellas had replaced members without harm. However, Gordy was looking far beyond Ballard and the small change of a remade Supremes. Nearly his entire purview was tied to the windfall that would accrue to Ross on her own. Still, Berger tried his best to get him to hold off on casting Flo adrift.

"I made out a list of reasons why it would be a mistake," he says. "And he looked at the list and said, 'Shelly, this is incredible. You're right on the money.' Then, in the next breath, he said, 'She's gotta go.'"

Before Diana and Mary were made aware of the decision, Gordy believed they needed a proper indoctrination. After endless recitations to each, such as "Flo is making you look bad" and "She's taking you down with her," he revealed that he was going to fire her, but they were pledged not to let on to anyone—most of all Flo—while a new third Supreme was being recruited. They both complied, with far different emotions. Diana, nowhere near as grateful to Flo as she may have been after her "breakdown," had actually given Gordy the talking points about Flo's effect on the group, having spouted them often during their pillow talk; thus she was so giddy about the change she could hardly contain herself. Mary, on the other hand, was sick with guilt that she had to keep the secret from her old friend, yet she, too, had come to conclude that Flo's work had become sloppy and was tarnishing the technical precision and pristine surface glitter of the Supremes.

That was the result of Flo's many missed rehearsals, through either illness or hangovers, necessitating that the girls wing it on stage and, at times, making them look somewhat ragged—in fact, Marlene Barrow and Barbara Randolph, kept on standby in case Flo had to miss a show, knew the latest Supremes routines better than Flo did. Unfortunately, one such messy performance came in full view of the whole world, or so it seemed, when they did the January 22 *Ed Sullivan Show.* Keeping time to the beat as they sang "You Can't Hurry Love," each of them gradually branched off and did pretty much their own moves. Seeing that, Gordy flew into a rage.

The *Sullivan* show, in fact, seemed to bring out the worst in the Supremes. While they always sang in full and perfect throat, and their gowns always glittered against the pastel sets—still effortlessly playing off the cool chic of high glamour and pimple-cream angst—something about the heightened pressure and demands of performing before a live nationwide audience tripped the wire of sanity. For Flo and Mary, in fact, the sore was still festering from the *Sullivan* show on February 22, 1966, when at the end of "My World Is Empty Without You" Diana, situated between Wilson and Ballard, raised her arms upward at a "V" angle so that her hands obscured their faces; Mary and Flo thought it was intentional, having noticed that Diana had thrown her head back so she could see the monitor hanging overhead, and thus see her handiwork. What's more, it would become something of a habit on their TV appearances.

Another, more ominous, snafu developed on the *Sullivan* show of September 25, 1966, when during a rehearsal one of Flo's earrings came loose and wound up on the floor and Diana, almost certainly by accident, stepped on it. As she and Diana gazed down at the crushed pearl and metal, Flo's eyes got wild. She charged like a puma up to Diana, tore off *her* earrings, and her wig, and began yanking her by her real hair across the stage like a Raggedy-Ann doll. Fearing for her life, Diana screamed "Help me!" over and over. It took two bodyguards to pry Flo off her. Thereafter, Diana was physically afraid of what Flo might do to her if she snapped.

When the Supremes would return to the *Sullivan* stage on May 7, 1967, they would be even more of a powder keg, with the potential for Flo setting a match to it exponentially greater.

Cle

The train wreck that was Florence Ballard could not be hidden any-more. Alternating between open contempt for Ross and Gordy and the altruistic mission, in her view, as savior of the group's pride and iden-tity, each day—each *hour* at times—could bring a different Flo.

Shelly Berger saw up front what effect this had on the act when he accompanied them to Miami Beach in mid-March for their engage-ments at the Deauville and Eden Roc hotels. Those shows went on without a hitch, but with Ballard progressively drinking harder, disaster awaited them as they trekked from Miami to play several college dates across the South. It was, Berger says, like a trip through Hades:

> We started in Atlanta, then went to the University of Tennessee in Murfeesboro and on through Memphis and down to New Orleans at Loyola College. In Murfeesboro, the Holiday Inn kitchen closed at 10 PM, but there was a pizza place across the street. Diana said, "Come on, let's get a pizza and take it back to the hotel." So we went over there and as I was ordering, she was standing at a juke box and a bunch of Bubbas were spout-ing off. Diana came over to me and said, "Did you hear some-body say 'nigger'?"
>
> I hadn't, but a minute later a guy kind of snuck over and told me matter-of-factly, "There's six guys at that table over there who're coming to beat you up. Just don't fight with them, because they'll kill you."
>
> At that point, Diana Ross became Joe Louis. "Oh *yeah?*" she said, and damn if she wasn't going to go fight six rednecks with tire irons! I had to get her the hell out of there. I grabbed her by the arm and flew out the door like Jesse Owens just as they were coming to get us.
>
> And that was the *fun* part of the trip. Because Florence was drunk all the time. In Memphis, we had to go on a half-hour late just getting Florence in some kind of condition to stand up on stage. Then, in New Orleans, it was just a nightmare. Flo-rence couldn't even make the show. Diana and Mary went on as

a duo. We were relieved the audience was forgiving because if they demanded refunds we would have had to give them and lose a lot of money.

Everyone was just in a foul mood on the flight home. We all knew this couldn't go on much longer with Florence. And then, as I was sitting with Diana, a stewardess handed a note to Diana. It was from Florence and it read: "I just can't do this anymore. I have to leave the group." Not too many people know that story.

Wilson recalled that fateful journey a bit differently. Leaving Memphis, she said, Flo hadn't come down from her room for the ride to the airport for the flight to New Orleans. The road manager, Don Foster, was sent to fetch her and found her sitting upright and fully dressed in her bed, clearly inebriated and refusing to move. He managed to get her up, threw some water on her face, and half-carried her to the limo. On the flight, Flo began raving semi-coherently that Gordy wanted her out of the group but for that to happen, "they're gonna have to put me out," though Wilson recalls nothing about a note from Flo asking out. On the ground in New Orleans, she said she called Gordy in Detroit, who ordered that Flo be put on a plane home at once, leaving Diana and Mary to go on alone.

"Diane was furious [but] I was sad and disappointed," she related. "Flo was digging herself into a hole she would never get out of."

Ross looked back at that night as if she were still stigmatized by it. "Mary and I were frantic; we ended up having to go on without her. We abandoned the regular choreography, and, after grabbing the hand mikes, we walked around the stage and sang, just the two of us." Any concern she and Mary might have had for Flo, personally, as she was falling into an abyss, was left unsaid.

Whether or not Flo did write that note, Gordy had heard from enough people, who swore she had used similar language, to use that as a rationale to dismiss her—which he was ready to do, having decided on her replacement. This was Cindy Birdsong, an obscure background soprano with Patti LaBelle and the Blue Belles, a black girl-group quartet from Philadelphia that had a No. 15 pop hit in '62, "I Sold My Heart to the Junkman" (though a different group had actually sung on the record) and two middling hits in '63. But it wasn't Birdsong's voice that won her the Supremes job; it was an eerily close facial resemblance to Ballard. Four years older than Florence, five years older than Diana and Mary, she also had a seasoned air of poise and maturity at a time when the Supremes were getting a bit long in the tooth for the teenage burning-yearning pulp.

Yet Gordy still was squeamish about putting Flo's neck under the blade. With important engagements on tap, he envisioned nasty publicity if the change was made into a scandal—if her alcoholism became public knowledge, what would become of the Supremes' undefiled image? And if Flo could not be convinced that she wanted out, and appeased—for real, not just in Ross's inventions—would she raise a stink in the press and lacerate a seamless transition?

These were the kind of land mines Berger had warned Gordy about. But just as Flo made it easy for Gordy to want to fire her, she was making it easier all the time for him to actually do it. This was made clear when the Supremes were summoned to Gordy's gigantic French-colonial manse in the *crème de la crème* of Detroit neighborhoods, the 5100 block on West Outer Drive, where all but the most upwardly mobile blacks were kept from owning property by banks' egregious redlining practices. The girls weren't invited there to partake of the Olympic-sized swimming pool or the bowling alley or movie theater in the house, but for a climactic showdown of the Ballard problem. Flo, expecting be humiliated, brought along her mother so she wouldn't be alone against the wrath of Gordy, though Lurlee had no idea about the severity of her daughter's troubles.

Flo, however, did not fully realize how tenuous her hold on her job was—not until she entered the house and the first person she saw was Cindy Birdsong sitting silently in the den outside Gordy's tureen of a living room. The two women knew each other in passing, from past contact on the touring circuit, and Flo was startled to see Cindy who, because Gordy was so furtive, had been told only that she was going to be added to the Supremes; if she was to replace any of them, she thought, it would be Diana when she went solo.

"Flo!" she gasped. "What's going on?"

"Damned if I know, honey," Flo said, but her confusion gave way to a pained look on her face, no doubt reflecting her understanding for the first time how much trouble she was in.

Even so, as she and her mother went into the living room and sat together on a settee, she wanted to believe the same thing Cindy did.

After a few minutes, Gordy descended from a spiral staircase, with Diana on his arm, a sight that always made Flo's jaw and gut tighten. Mary came late, as she often did for meetings, but Gordy didn't delay. Dropping with Diana onto a bench next to his grand piano, he made an announcement. There would be a "change" in the group, he began. "From now on, the group will be known as Diana Ross and the Supremes," going on brightly that this was "great news." Now, he said, there would be "two stars"—one being Diana, the other the group as a whole. With great excitement, he explained how this would translate into greater appearance fees. Everyone would share in a new Supremes windfall.

Flo, who'd heard rumors of just such an alteration for months, was somewhat relieved that this was Gordy's big news, though she couldn't help but glare at Diana, who, putting her acting lessons to use, acted surprised at the announcement, fooling no one. But if that was it, Flo could live with it. Now, though, Gordy cleared his throat. He had more to say.

"Now, about Blondie. . . ."

Mary, maybe hoping she would miss the whole meeting, arrived to hear him rattling off the litany of Flo's offenses: her drinking, her weight, how she was undermining the Supremes, how the group depended on an image of class and squeaky-clean femininity—"three Cinderellas" for a generation of young women around the world. He brought up the unpardonable sin of Flo missing that show in New Orleans; things like that, he said, "get around" and lead promoters to shy away. Millions of dollars were at stake. Flo had "gone too far," he said, and forfeited her right to be a Supreme.

As Wilson recalled it, Gordy treaded carefully, "sticking to the facts. There were no insults or accusations; he knew better than to provoke Flo [because] she had a violent temper. He just wanted to get it over with."

But get *what* over with? Because he was so circumspect—or so afraid of Flo—he never actually fired her. Instead, his wimp quotient peaking, he suggested that "it would be best if Florence left the group." He then threw in her own iterations about wanting to quit, hoping—as was Diana, who now seemed bored and looked mostly at her nails—that Flo would get the message and do it right now.

Hard as it is to believe, Flo would later assert that she was "totally shocked" at Gordy's action, and that she—the sassy Supreme who had an answer for everything—could find no words to say in her own defense. She began to perspire heavily and felt sick to her stomach, and when those in the room looked at her all they saw was Ballard being, as Wilson put it, "cold and distant." Finally, Lurlee spoke up for her. "Flo wants to be in this group," she said. Knowing nothing of Flo's old friend's duplicity, she turned to Mary, who was nervously avoiding eye contact with Flo. "Mary," she asked sadly, "don't you want Flo in the group?"

Mary, close to tears, pulled herself together and recited by rote part of Gordy's indoctrination. "Mrs. Ballard, Florence does not want to be in this group" came her reply in a shaky voice. That was the unkindest cut of all for Flo—later, according to Tony Tucker, she would recall the "*et tu Mary*" response and rage, "Who told that black bitch *that*?"

With tears in her eyes, Lurlee slumped on the settee and sighed, "Well, if that's how you want it." Flo, still inert, remained silent—a minor miracle and a blessing for Gordy, who had prepared himself for the ultimate Ballard blowup. Surely it was an odd vibe in that room. Flo had always sworn that Gordy would have to "drag me" out of the group, that she'd never go quietly. Yet here she was, dazed and confused, as if narcotized. Perhaps it was a deep-seated fear of crossing Gordy, or that she was just feeling too ill to think straight; or that on some still-functioning level of acuity it was a new way to show defiance. Then again, on the opposite flank, she might have calculated that not protesting would be taken as contrition, and the whole thing would blow over.

Whatever the forces at work inside her head, her mystifying silence allowed Wilson an artificial justification for stepping on Ballard when she was down. Never mind that she had led Flo to believe she would stand by her if it ever came to this. With supreme disingenuousness, she would years later actually blame Flo for not standing up for herself. "Flo was waiting for me to rescue her," she wrote in *Dreamgirl*, "[but] refused to defend herself," which she construed to mean that "[s]he wanted out more than anything, and she knew that I knew it." What's more, she noticed that Flo "seemed satisfied with the outcome." What she did not say was that she apparently never asked Flo if these impressions were true.

But again, just what was the "outcome"? With all the emotional bloodletting going on, Gordy played Flo's submission as a catharsis. Trying to sound sincere, he asked Flo if she was all right, then bent over and hugged her before walking the two Ballard women out to Flo's car, with an arm draped around each. As they left the living room, they crossed before a very puzzled and uncomfortable Cindy Birdsong. Having heard only now the truth of why Gordy had recruited her, she felt terribly guilty, and worried that Flo would think she had a part in her being humiliated like this. Birdsong would admit in retrospect, "I wondered what I had gotten myself into."

Once Flo was out the door, Diana—who at that moment Mary described as "giddy"—came running over to Cindy, grabbed her hands, and began gleefully jumping up and down like a schoolgirl just named prom queen—a show of *schadenfreude* Birdsong could not make sense of, given Lurlee Ballard's tears and the dank sadness in the room.

Ross, as would Gordy, took the easy way out of reliving the emotional tension of that day—by simply making it disappear from her memoirs, in which she tossed off Flo's ouster in one factually inaccurate sentence: "At the beginning of 1967, by mutual consent, Florence left the group." At other times through the years she would tow the Motown party line that Flo had "left" out of a desire to get married and settle down and raise a family.

But Flo was not out, not yet. She didn't quit that day, nor would she ever. When Gordy returned to the living room, he called in Birdsong and spoke of "getting Cindy ready"—Mary, he said, would tutor her on the routines, Diana on the makeup and stage wear—and it was generally assumed that Flo at some time or other in the near future would fall on her sword, that is, after removing it from her back where Mary had planted it. But when this didn't happen by a month later, the notion had congealed around Motown that Flo was on some sort of "probation" or "trial."

Never during that time did Flo speak of going away; indeed, it was as if she had outwitted "Napoleon" by keeping quiet at the mansion. Telling Tony Tucker of the scene at the house, she was as brazen as ever, saying, "I'm *not* gonna quit! If they want me out, they'll have to throw me out!"—and that if Gordy did, "I'm going to create a big mess and nobody in the world is going to like it." Neither did she reel in her verbal lashings of Diana and Berry. It actually seemed as if they might come to blows. When Gordy, one time, stuck an open palm near her face in anger, she screamed, "If you raise your hand to me, you're gonna pull back a bloody stump!" Another time she raged at him, "I'll cut you too short to shit!" He, in turn, stopped calling her by her name, or Blondie. Instead, he would ask, "Where's that Ballard bitch?"

How could Gordy have made it more awkward? Or more trying for the group? In truth, Flo, when she wasn't stewed, was too smart to think she was in the clear, or on any sort of trial. She knew Gordy had to ease Birdsong in. "He just wants to cover his dirty work over with roses for the public," she told intimates. In the meantime, Flo was the walking dead. But she'd be nobody's corpse. Since Gordy still needed her for now, she had a free pass. She'd be damned if she'd use it to be a good little girl now.

Even more untidily, Gordy actually tried to make the Birdsong-for-Ballard move, but it failed to take, because of his own mistakes. It went down when the Supremes flew to L.A. for the April 19 Hollywood Bowl show, a charity affair for the United Negro College Fund that included other acts like Johnny Rivers, the Fifth Dimension, and Buffalo Springfield, and Gordy told Flo to stay home to "rest." Not that many in the Bowl knew it; because the stage there was situated far from the rows of seats in the audience, and because Birdsong was a ringer for her, those who knew who Ballard was assumed it was her. Even most of the newspaper critics were duped. One who did know, writing in the *Los Angeles Times*, touted Birdsong as a "strong sub" with whom Ross and Wilson "blend[ed] effectively." *That* must have caused a few double-takes when the spectators who'd been there read it the next day.

Gordy, naturally, wanted the transition to proceed this way, with no muss, no fuss, and barely a notice. While the name change to Diana Ross and the Supremes was obviously planned to grease the way for Diana to go solo, a secondary consideration was to overshadow any negative fallout from —or even any mention of—Ballard's being cashiered. The name change was scheduled for a late June rollout in Vegas when the girls would return to the Flamingo Hotel, and on vinyl with their next single, to be released a month later. Ideally, Birdsong would be comfortably phased in by then, having, according to the plan, already performed with the group on the May 7 *Ed Sullivan Show* and at the Copa May 11–24.

However, Gordy earned himself more heartburn by signing Birdsong as he did, with no caution paid to her contract with the Blue Belles. As was common then, she didn't know much about her legal obligations, and Gordy may not have cared about these himself when he signed her to Motown. But when word got out in the trade papers, and her active role as a Supreme was confirmed at the Hollywood Bowl, the Blue Belles' lawyer rang up Motown's lawyers, waiving Birdsong's original contract and an injunction, which took effect during negotiations to buy out that contract—thereby effectively putting her in limbo for weeks.

Gordy couldn't throw Marlene Barrow or Barbara Randolph into the high-level engagements only to have to make a *second* change when

Birdsong was free; how'd *that* be for a quiet transition? With no choice, he had to turn again to the foil he'd just *replaced*. And hope like hell he would get through it.

Because Flo knew the score, that she had not been taken back out of regret or because Gordy had second thoughts about letting her go, she was under no illusion that she could prove him wrong. *She* was the stand-in now, and doing Gordy a favor by carrying out that role. Thus, while it might have seemed logical that this new "reprieve" called for a change in behavior so as to go out on a high note, she didn't appreciate the constant haranguing from Gordy that one more slip-up and "You're out. You retire peacefully, that's it."

It would get worse. The group came to New York for *The Ed Sullivan Show*, always a beaker for the Supremes' dysfunction, on May 7. Just before they went out and performed "The Happening," Diana, on her own, pulled out a brand-new wig, a Twiggy-style, short-cropped number with a "peek-a-boo" curl partially covering one eye. As she'd told Mary and Flo nothing of this alteration, they were left with their "old-school" bouffant wigs. By this, Diana was further separating herself from them, making herself the main attraction. Out of spite, when they came back on later to sing a medley of "Roaring Twenties" songs, Flo wore *no* wig, appearing with her own short hair, which actually was perfect for the "flapper" motif. But it left Ross and Wilson hung out to dry and violated Motown's girl-group protocol of always being seen publicly under a wig. When reminded of this by Gordy, Flo said—accurately—that the wigs were "plastic" and out-of-date for 1967.

"I ain't gonna wear no fake white-girl hair," she huffed, a rather trenchant observation of how racially *jejune* those wigs were—something that, sadly, had not occurred to Berry Gordy, who bridled when he found out that Flo continued appearing *au natural* at other gigs.

Unfortunately, that noble sentiment was obviated by other manifestations of her new fashion sense, which arose not out of any couture standards but from her corroding physical appearance. For example, she had begun ladling on gobs of mascara and eyeliner to divert the gaze from her bloodshot eyes, and layers of pancake makeup to buff her sallow complexion, lightening her skin to the point where she nearly appeared Caucasian. Somehow, though, they got through the two weeks at the Copa in style, with a *Variety* review rhapsodizing that the act was "polished to a high gloss." That was followed by a five-day Midwest college tour and the Symphony Hall show.

But the Band-Aid covering the tensions could have come off at any moment. It nearly did when they appeared on *The Tonight Show* on May 22. Diana, sitting closest to Johnny Carson, was to do most of the talking, though an ebullient Flo would cut her off when she'd begin to speak, injecting her Pearl Bailey–like witticisms. Johnny brought up that there'd been a "stand-in" for Flo at the Hollywood Bowl and the ensuing rumors that the Supremes were going to break up. Flo jumped right in. "Listen, honey," she drawled, "if all the rumors were true we'd have six children and would've been married six times" to much laughter.

Diana, feeling she had to address the subject in a more serious way, added that the group had "two young ladies," meaning Barbara Randolph and Marlene Barrow, "as stand-ins." "The show must go on," she said. "Except for me. They can't stand in for me." Mary blinked her eyes at that, having not until then heard that there even *was* a stand-in for her. "That was news to me!" she recalled.

(Ross, as well, was less than truthful about no stand-in ever being used for her. Jack Ashford can recall a gig in '65 when several of the Funk Brothers went out on a brief road swing backing the Supremes. "We did it as the Earl Van Dyke Trio," he says. "I don't remember where we went but it was a real classy atmosphere, a Bill Gates–type crowd, the smell of money. And Diana didn't want to do the gig, she refused. So you know who they used in her place? Telma Hopkins [later of Tony Orlando and Dawn], and she sang her buns off. The crowd didn't care that Diana Ross wasn't there.")

Gordy was still praying to the heavens nothing would go wrong when the Supremes pulled into L.A. for the eleven-day Cocoanut Grove gig. He needn't have worried, as the engagement went like a charm and drew the usual round of rave reviews, the *Los Angeles Times*' notice saying the show was "bombastic." The reviewer should only have known how much so. The *real* fireworks didn't go off until the next engagement, back in Las Vegas for two weeks at the Flamingo Hotel.

This turn of the road would mark the end of the line for Florence Ballard and, for the Supremes, a very tangible sense that they really mattered to the rock pantheon. For one thing, on Opening Night, June 28, 1967, the marquee read "*Diana Ross and the Supremes*," taking the first step in the separation process for Ross. For another, Gordy flew in for the opening, now with the ink dry on the settlement giving Motown exclusive rights to Cindy Birdsong, who had been fitted for the same gowns the Supremes would be wearing during the run. Cindy, who had unnerved Flo for the past several weeks by sitting visibly in the audience of each previous stop, would be in the wings, in full stage dress, for every show, and there'd be a rack for her gowns alongside those for Ross, Wilson, and Ballard, and her own dressing room. Incredibly, Gordy thought he was actually keeping Cindy's presence a secret, putting her up across the street at Caesars Palace so she and Flo wouldn't cross paths.

Flo couldn't refrain from stirring up trouble. Prior to opening night, she was skewering Gordy about his "dirty work" in giving Diana what she wanted and putting her name above the group. Knowing that Flo was not going to survive the engagement, he turned from confrontation to comity, sentimentally recalling the old days and telling her to "look at where we are" and "We made it as a *family*." Cringing at his Sammy Davis–style "peace, love and togetherness" rap, and expecting the axe to drop at any minute, she responded in a way that was anything but sentimental. "Mr. Berry Gordy," she seethed, "you'll be sorry you started this war with me."

Gordy didn't know what to make of the oblique threat; nor, at this point, did he care. All he knew was that he was going to put her out of the group, though he held off at least for the opening show, not just out of sentimentality but also for a practical reason: By allowing her one more taste of glory, he hoped she might go more quietly when he dropped the axe. However, he regretted that decision. Seeing that dastardly marquee must have broken Flo's will, because she seemed not to have made any attempt to go on that night with a clear head.

When the spotlight went on, there were two Supremes and an imposter from Central Casting. Plainly inebriated, Ballard had the clown makeup on, her wig was off-center, her eyes bleary. The outfits chosen for the first of the night's two shows were—maybe not by coincidence—completely inapt for her: mod, silver lamé pantsuits with a shocking bare midriff. Next to Diana and Mary's board-flat stomachs, Flo's full belly was more than conspicuous.

Worse, much worse, Flo decided to use her flab as a comic prop. At the point in the show where Diana did her "thin is in" line, Flo's "ad lib" that "fat is where it's at" came with an impromptu bit of choreography—pushing her distended middle out even *further* and undulating like a freak-show belly dancer. While the audience hooted in delight—it *was*, after all, *Vegas*, not the Met—Diana and Mary tried hard to keep their smiles frozen despite their mortification. At his table, Gordy was beside himself. Already grimacing over Flo's voice, which he said was scratchy and flat, he was unable to sit still. Bolting from his seat, he stalked backstage. Pacing furiously, at one point he yelled to nobody in particular, "Get her off the stage now!" Watching the show, everyone pretty much ignored him.

Indeed, the audience, merrily chugging drinks and enjoying every sight and sound of a high-octane, glittering performance from one of the world's elite acts, found nothing amiss. The *Variety* review of the opening show would laud them as "superb," and the run would be extended for a third week to accommodate the demand for tickets. However, like Gordy, Gil Askey, and Diana and Mary, Flo knew better. It was inconceivable that she could have believed she even belonged on stage with the Supremes—with *anyone*—now. When she stumbled offstage, she blew by the stagehands and the Motown leeches, scowling. She headed for her dressing room, slamming the door behind her. There, she sat alone, knocking back straight shots of vodka.

An hour later, zombie-like, she forlornly changed from the pantsuit to the more "Supreme-like" sequined chiffon gown for the second show, and went out to the wings where Gordy was standing alongside Ross and Wilson. A second later, Cindy came hurrying out of a dressing room, wearing the same gown they were. Flo began to walk toward them when a glowering Gordy stepped in her way.

"Flo," he said sternly, "don't you go up on that stage. You're finished. You're fired."

"Berry, you better get the fuck outta my face," she slurred, trying to push past him.

Diana, acting neither neutral nor surprised any longer, poked her nose in, telling Flo: "You're too fat! Why don't you stop drinking so much? Look at yourself. You're as big as a house!"

"Why don't *you* shut the fuck up? Why are you so goddamn mean all the time?"

Gordy steered it back to Flo. "You look terrible on stage," he went on. "Look at Diana and Mary. You're not holding up your end."

Tired of being picked on, she turned diffident. "Oh, I don't care. Just leave me the fuck alone."

"I'm serious, Florence. You're fired. If you go on that stage, I'm going to have you thrown off."

"Bullshit. I got a show to do."

He motioned to some bodyguards, who surrounded her and began guiding her away.

Her head was spinning so much that she didn't know which direction she was being led. Taken through the kitchen, with hotel workers happily waving at her in a surreal scene, she then was led into a service elevator and finally deposited in her room. Dumped on her bed, she was able to peel off the soggy gown and wig and slip on a blouse and Capri pants. She then crashed cold. It wasn't until around noon the next day that she was awakened by the telephone. Pulling it to her ear, she heard the stern voice of Gwen Gordy.

"Joe Schaffner's waiting downstairs," she said. "Pack your bags. He'll drive you to the airport. When you get back to Detroit, someone'll be waiting for you who'll take you to Henry Ford Hospital. Berry wants you to rest."

Later, Flo would recall that the only thing she could think of at that moment was that she *needed* a rest, a *long* rest. That was, of course, one of the cover stories Motown would promulgate by way of explaining for public consumption why Flo had "left the group." But it wasn't entirely wrong, either. Indeed, as Flo tried to sort out what was happening, it again didn't seem like a firing but rather something like another reprieve. In any case, not having to perform at the Flamingo came as a great relief.

It was again Don Foster's chore to take her from her room. Just as in New Orleans, he dragged her from her bed and washed her face. He collected some of her personal items like toiletries, makeup, and light clothing and stuffed them into a carry-on bag. Throwing a mink coat over her shoulders, he eased onto her face the oversized sunglasses she always wore outside to cover her red eyes and led her down to the lobby, passing her off to Schaffer, who eased her into the limousine. Flo, in a deep hangover, said nothing the entire time. Later in interviews she would remember that on the way downstairs a Motown staffer, whom she did not identify, egged her on not to "take any shit" from Gordy, and that she should "go out on that stage tonight."

"This is Vegas," she said he told her. "He ain't gonna go out on the stage and drag you off. Go and tell those people out there what they're doing to you. They came to see you, not Cindy Birdsong. Don't let him break you, Flo."

It could have been sheer persiflage, a good story told for effect and sympathy, but she insisted that for a fraction of time she considered doing just that, to shove it down Gordy's throat and go out in a blaze of glory—something he seriously feared could happen right up until the lights went up that night. But the thought quickly passed, when she came to the realization that, as she told Tony Tucker, "I had no fight left in me. They won."

Now that the war was over, the only thing she wanted to do was go home.

Ce

To some, at least, the change was jarring. Shelly Berger had gotten to Vegas too late for the first show on opening night:

> Nobody told me what had happened when I got to the Flamingo. Everyone was acting matter-of-factly, like everything was routine. So I sat down at my table with Berry, the lights come up, the orchestra starts playing and there was Cindy, not Florence.
>
> I thought, "Couldn't somebody have told me this? I'm only the manager of this group." Of course, the show was absolutely fantastic and very few people in the house had any idea a change had been made. That's how good Cindy was, and how proficient Diana and Mary had become. Life just went on, un-interrupted, like nothing had ever happened. And I never saw Florence again.

nineteen

A
DISTORTED
REALITY

The Supremes' ability to continue uninterrupted would have to endure a setback even more serious than the erasure of Florence Ballard. In fact, though Gordy had done his best to ignore warning signs, his empire was beginning to splinter. While he globe-trotted with the girls and spared little time for anything or anyone else, the daily grind at 2648 West Grand Boulevard was winding down, most ominously threatening to dry up the lifeblood of the Supremes' fortune—a seemingly endless supply of hit material.

A grim portent of that, though few knew it, was the first Supremes single to go out in the post-Ballard interregnum—"Reflections." While it had Flo's voice in its grooves, having been recorded before her termination, the song was so anguished and convulsive a confession about lost hope and dreams that it can be heard today as the theme song of Motown's deteriorating soul—and, for the Supremes, of a group that in mid-1967 had reason to look back more in sorrow and pity than in accomplishment.

And yet at the cutting edge, "Reflections" was conceived in a narrow frame, almost as a private matter between HDH and Gordy, as it was composed early in 1967 just as a rupture was severing the relationship. Such a rift had been inevitable given that the Motown *über*-structure was unchanged from 1961—Gordy at the top, mostly everyone else at the bottom. While Eddie Holland had renounced a singing career because he wanted to be cut in on the kind of bread his brother Brian was making, when the HDH triumvirate exploded into space the trio were chagrined to find that they were being kept at a distance from the real money.

Even now, as arguably the world's best writing-producing team, they were still not permitted to own the copyrights to their own songs. They were still paid on a salaried basis, and not a half-bad one, now up to around three grand a week apiece, landing the Holland brothers in luxurious digs in the exclusive Palmer Woods section of town. But when *The Supremes Sing Holland Dozier Holland* brought in several hundred thousand dollars in sales, they'd have been able to see the writers' royalties only by looking in Gordy's bank vault, since Jobete Music owned all the rights, sales, publishing, and writing.

Gordy, who reveled in the role of benevolent dictator, swore to himself he was being generous to a fault with his writers, with spontaneous raises, bonuses, and gifts. In *To Be Loved,* he posited that all this would have been more than enough, if not for Eddie's avarice. Early on, he recalled, Eddie had come to him saying he would be representing HDH.

"For what?" Gordy asked.

"Business. I'll negotiate for all three of us."

Gordy asked what he could conceivably want to negotiate. "Oh, I don't know," he said Eddie told him. "Brian and Lamont aren't moneyminded. I have to keep them motivated." When Gordy then went to Brian to confirm this, he was told, "I hope you understand and have no hard feelings. But that's my brother and you know how it is."

Gordy noted "Eddie's constant requests for added incentives through the years," adding, "They were great as a team and I knew I had to pay an additional cost to keep them happy. It was part of doing business." This included, he said, "serious readjustments" to the trio's compensation package. While the Hollands won't revisit such details, the sour look on their faces and their acrid laughter speak for them. What Gordy forgot to mention, they know well, was that his payouts, as with any other advance, had to be earned back or else deducted from future earnings—and, furthermore, that he docked them for unspecified "expenses" on sessions at which they cut tracks that never were given to any act to record and sat on the shelf.

There was also the thorny issue of stock options in Motown Recording Corporation, which grew—with no small thanks to HDH—to an enormous value. Gordy shared those only with Gwen and Anna and to a lesser degree with his children. Not even that most loyal adjutant Smokey Robinson was given more than token equity in the company he had gotten off the ground and served as vice-president for until Gordy sold it in the '80s.

Operating in the ether of his Supremes idyll, Gordy either didn't know about or pretended not to be aware of a growing unease among those in his steerage class. By early '67, HDH were only one of the rising headaches. Another restless native was Mickey Stevenson, his go-to guy in A&R who ironically had kept the acts contented in the feudal system. But Stevenson himself was quite unhappy over the fact that Gordy wasn't giving him writers' credits he believed he deserved for ideas that saved more than a few records that had hit a snag in the studio, and that his salary hadn't kept pace with the company's growth. The last rip was when Gordy refused to do more with Kim Weston, whom Stevenson married in 1967.

Weston, whose gritty R&B style had fallen out of favor at Motown, hadn't had a single released since early '65, despite her mild hit with HDH's "Take Me in Your Arms," and a larger one when paired with Marvin Gaye on "It Takes Two" in early '67. Behind Gordy's back, Stevenson brokered a deal for Weston in L.A. with MGM, which also offered him a production deal with equity. He went to Gordy looking for the same and when he was offered only a raise, he walked with Weston midway through 1967, though not to any great future success at MGM.

Next it was Harvey Fuqua. Once Gordy's biggest yes-man, he had saved the day by moving in Tammi Terrell for Weston as Gaye's duet partner and producing the pair's hits "Ain't No Mountain High Enough" and "Your Precious Love." But friction had been mounting between Gordy and Fuqua as well, perhaps spilling from the latter's rocky marriage to Gwen Gordy. A year later, when he left Gwen (who kept the Motown inbreeding farm going by taking up with G. C. Cameron of a newer company group, the Spinners), he needed to get away from all the Gordys and wound up taking an executive position at RCA Records in New York. In addition, Clarence Paul was losing *his* patience with Gordy's penury; within two years, he, too, would walk.

By the end of '66, even Maxine Powell, with little to do, had left the company.

With his creative braintrust crumbling around him, Gordy filled the A&R gap left by Stevenson's exit by elevating Eddie Holland to head of the department, and Brian Holland to head of Creative Control when Billie Jean Brown took leave after getting married. These were moves that Gordy would admit he regretted, and almost right from the get-go other producers began to grouse to each other that HDH would give priority to their own records and not theirs. The once-tight creative structure at Motown was turning into a malleable mess. And for HDH, the promotions did nothing to address their dissonance about being stiffed, and nothing to pacify the unease that had crept into their work—most dramatically and fatalistically in "Reflections."

> EDDIE HOLLAND: Let's just say there were a lot of different emotions running through our heads starting in early '67, the time when we did that song. Listen, we loved Berry Gordy, we'll always love Berry. The man is a genius. He's the reason we achieved what we did. That's what made it so much more emotional and crazy. You try to separate business from everything else, but things carry over, they get emotional and out of hand. It's like you end up hating your own father, who you love dearly, and you hate yourself for hating him. You feel unloved by him.
>
> How do you deal with heavy shit like that, when it's tearing you up inside? Maybe you try to deal with it by writing a song.

Enter "Reflections," a tormented-to-the-max, three-penny operetta of mourning, ostensibly about lost love, that contrary to other Supremes vinyl lovelorn confessionals did no reaching out burning and yearning for reconciliation; its damning and dooming finality about "the way life used to be" and "the love you took from me" cut right to the bone from the opening stanza—"Through the mirror of my mind, time after time / I see reflections of you and me"—and only became more lacerating, with visceral elegies of being "all alone now, trapped in a world that's a distorted reality" where "the happiness you took from me has left me alone with only memories." Some of these verses may, along with those in "Bernadette," incorporate some of the most Bard-like rock poetry ever penned—"Through the hollow of my tears," "I see a dream that's lost from the hurt that you have caused," "After all the nights I sat alone and wept, just a handful of promises are all that's left of loving you." But the killer was this:

In you I put all my faith and trust
And right before my eyes, my world has turned to dust.

Normally a man not given to understatement, Eddie Holland says of his work on "Reflections" that "I was getting heavy then," more so than anyone knew. As Dozier recalled, "When we started at Motown . . . miracles were realized, love was good, but then it went bad. Disenchantment spoiled the dream and memories were all that was left." If Gordy ever really *heard* the song, he might have realized that the "distorted reality" Diana was singing about with icy contempt was his own; and the world turned to dust, what he'd left behind for many of the flock. If he ever did hear that in the song, he never let on.

Because of the exposed nerve of the song, Brian and Dozier stripped the arrangement to its essentials. This was now *adult* music; gone were the *chink-a-chink* electric guitar backbeat and the honking sax, leaving a throbbing Jack Ashford tambourine, a dark Wurlitzer electric piano line by Earl Van Dyke, and a subtler drumbeat by Pistol Allen. Jamerson's nimbly brooding bass filled the bottom; swelling, stabbing strings the top. There were dead stops, long notes echoing into silence. And a whacked-out intro not to be believed to this day.

Seeking a sci-fi effect to almost literally reproduce disturbing brain waves, something like the theremin Brian Wilson used on "Good Vibrations" the year before but less kitschy, they used an electronic oscillator, a juiced-up version of the common instrument that merely measures sine waves. The amped version gave them a sound—at low power Sputnik-like beeps, at higher power futuristic swirling like something out of *Plan 9 from Outer Space.* That very jump, in a six-second sequence, became the intro. But not before Brian, thinking it might be a tad too cheesy, nearly nixed it.

"I wanted to kill him," Eddie says. "'Cause it just blew me away. It was perfect! *Through the mirror of my mind . . .* that was the sound! I told him, 'Don't you dare take that out!'"

There were also more practical reasons to leave it in, what with the rising commercial niche of songs suggesting a drugged-out feel. "It made that song sound psychedelic. It was like a person on a high, being in a whole other space in their own body."

"Remember, this was about the time of *Sergeant Pepper's Lonely Hearts Club Band*, when all the rules were broken. We wanted to tap into that and we could do what we wanted to do, no matter how crazy, if it made sense to us."

The Beatles' influence in "Reflections" is obvious in other, technical ways—Alan Slutsky speaks of the "Beatle-esque chamber music texture in the low-register strings" and the "shifting meters of the melody." But it surely was the mild psychedelia—to be taken much further by Norman Whitfield's brilliant late '60s and early '70s Temptations productions like "Cloud Nine" and "Psychedelic Shack"—that bought it and the Supremes a little sanctuary in the "Summer of Love."

This alone was no small feat: that the Supremes of the Copa and the casinos could sound cool to the flower-power crowd as well as to the cigar-chewing carnivores of the clubs. One can add to that list soul devotees and both sides of the Vietnam War divide; in '67, a *Time* dispatch from the combat front noted that Supremes songs were heard echoing in the jungle on soldiers' transistor radios, having had no difficulty getting through the Armed Forces Radio censors. Two decades later, "Reflections" was used as the theme song of the retro-Vietnam TV series *China Beach*.

The Supremes, in the wake of "Reflections," had become all things to all people—the perfect commercial equation, at least. Not that they could have had a place at the Monterey Pop Festival that summer between Janis Joplin and Jimi Hendrix, or even the Mamas and the Papas and the Association, or that they could ever have been seen taking hits of Monterey Purple. (The only Motown artists who could have fit in with that scene were Marvin Gaye on style and, on substance, Stevie Wonder, who had dragged Motown into the loam of its own community, using a ghetto street milieu on the cover of his '66 *Down to Earth* LP, which included period-relevant songs like "A Place in the Sun" and a cover of Dylan's "Mr. Tambourine Man.")

Yet the widespread reach of "Reflections" was an important hurdle to clear at a time when Motown was, in some circles, approaching excursus. It had begun not to be good enough to some rock critics, and the general record-buying market, that the label "belonged" simply by its black birthright. Indeed, within the soul market, many had written off Motown in favor of the "real deal" of the Atlantic Records' Stax and Volt labels that mined soul gold from the studios of Memphis and Muscle Shoals. Atlantic seemed to have no interest in going "wide," not if it meant sending the likes of Sam and Dave, Wilson Pickett, Otis Redding, Solomon Burke, and Aretha Franklin to Vegas casinos and the Copacabana. With much cheek, Stax-Volt pointedly dubbed itself "Soulsville," in living-color contrast to the more generic Hitsville, where too many soul acts had gone to die. It had a right to gloat on this point; without a single No. 1 record in the decade, save for Aretha's cover of Redding's "Respect," the Atlantic stable was spanking Motown on the "purity" issue.

This was the price Gordy had to pay for its taking crossover appeal to unimaginable, even unseemly heights in the first place. That aim, once admired in the community, had come to be reviled. Washington University professor Gerald Early, author of *One Nation Under a Groove: Motown & American Culture*, recalling the Motown records of the middle to late '60s, remarked that "[t]here was a feeling that whites were sort of co-opting this music and there was no longer a sense of pride that whites were playing the music. There was this sense that Gordy was making a mistake by trying to make his music have this integration-assimilation appeal. I remember one kid I knew, he said, 'This music shouldn't [have been] called The Sound of Young America. It should [have been] The Sound of *Black* America,'" which was of course what Gordy had studiously avoided.

And, indeed, "Reflections" hardly silenced the growing chorus chanting "sellout," which only became more voluble when real-world events made a mockery of the Motown model of "assimilation"—the most immediate and traumatic being one that literally hit close to home. On July 23, 1967, while Gordy, the Supremes, and most of the Motown hierarchy were still hunkering in the desert oasis of Las Vegas, living large and white, Detroit began to go up in smoke. This was sur-prising in only one respect: that it took so long to blow.

Of all the inner cities in America, Detroit's had probably eroded the fastest and hardest. By 1967, the old urban romance of Paradise Valley was perfect urban rot. As if boxed in by the ugly steel-gray erector-set maze of new highways, the Valley was a hypoxic ghetto in every sense: From a population one-third white when the Supremes were born, it was now almost completely black, poor, and neglected, its last thread of pride stripped when the highway construction necessitated that most of Hast-ings Street be obliterated. On John R, Beacon, 12th, St. Antoine, War-ren, nearly every street, apartment buildings were subdivided so that six families could occupy space once barely sufficient for two families.

Most of the great old clubs where Louis Armstrong, John Lee Hooker, T-Bone Walker, and Bobo Jenkins—and the Supremes— wailed were either rubble or abandoned, starved out by too-high rents and increasingly dangerous neighborhoods. The sirens heard every night in Brewster-Douglass were the music of the streets now. The Flame Show Bar, where Berry Gordy and Maurice King incubated, went down in '63. The Twenty Grand and the Roostertail and the Graystone Ballroom—the latter still owned by Motown and used to record string arrangements, but in an increasing state of disrepair— were hanging on for dear life, their days numbered as their neighborhoods crumbled around them.

With blight and crime came the usual suspects, at least for "the Man." Since the early '60s, the DPD's "Tac Squad" of four-man patrol cars had been raiding bars and busting streetwalkers. With shouts of "Hey, nigger," the police pulled innocent people over and asked them to show identification; if they had none, they'd be run in and held for as long as deemed necessary. In '64, a prostitute who had leaped from a police car was shot in the back and killed. Beatings, even deaths, in custody were not uncommon, more so as jobs in the auto plants dried up, clubs closed, and more people were on the street. In response, militancy rose; in early July '67, the Black Panthers' "Justice Minister" H. Rap Brown famously vowed that unless America, and Detroit in particular, didn't come around, "we're gonna burn you down."

On the 23rd, it happened. The spark was a raid on an after-hours club on 12th and Clairmount during which eighty-two blacks were arrested. Outside the club, a seething crowd began vandalizing stores, looting, and setting fires. Within forty-eight hours, when the National Guard and the 82nd Airborne were called in to quell a conflagration, the fires burned through the days and nights, including on West Grand Boulevard.

Inside Studio A on the first day, the musicians smelled the musky smoke outside and said the hell with the session; running for what they thought were their lives, guitars and horns dangling from their arms, they made for their cars, some with their pistols drawn.

"When we heard what the whole thing was about," recalls a still-shaken Jack Ashford, "we were afraid Joe Messina would be shot in the street for being white. Hell, we didn't know if we'd *all* be shot. Joe didn't know what to do, where to go. I had this sport jacket, why I don't know 'cause it was, like, a hundred degrees and gettin' much hotter out there. So I threw the jacket over his head and said, 'Joe, just come with me.' I had him under my arm, leading him through the smoke to my car. And, man, you could hear them gunshots gettin' close. I took him home and wouldn't let him leave 'til everything was calm."

That took five days, when the grim toll reached 43 dead, nearly 1,200 injured, and over 7,000 arrested. Out in Vegas, Gordy—who, after he sent Flo packing, had nothing more serious on his mind than which VIP party to attend, including grand galas hosted by the Mr. and Mrs. Johnny Carson and Mr. and Mrs. Milton Berle—heard of the riot on the news and tried to get back home, but the airport in Detroit was closed for the duration. When he finally could, he was deeply relieved that no one in the Motown family had been hurt and that, amazingly, none in the row of company buildings were damaged. (Some would subsequently wonder quixotically if perhaps the rioters spared Motown out of some kind of residual debt to Gordy—though why scores of black businesses *weren't* spared isn't answered by this chimera.) But he was, as Marvin Gaye once said, "freaked" by the close call and soon moved the central operation of the company a half mile away to the Donovan Building, a fortress-like ten-storey office tower on Woodward Avenue, then began selling off most of the townhouses that had been used for peripheral business. Studio A, with its new twenty-four-track recording machine and other expensive upgrades, would still be the recording site. But even that vital center of Motown gravity, and of American popular music, was becoming a casualty as circumstances and lives changed all around it.

By the fall of '67, Gordy, as did the Supremes, existed in a weird bilateral holding pattern in which immense success seemed to indicate impending change. For all the flak he took for being so spectacularly successful in what he did, "Reflections" had opened yet another door for Motown, through which would follow other "serious" work such as Whitfield's with the Temptations and Marvin Gaye. Meaning that if Gordy still had a "purity" problem, at least he didn't have a relevancy problem. Or, certainly, a financial one. By the end of '67, Gordy would tithe his Taj Mahal on Outer Drive to his sister Gwen and move on up to an even bigger, more ostentatious household, an Italian Renaissance mansion on five acres along ritzy Boston Boulevard with underground tunnels between the main and guest houses and the indoor and outdoor swimming pools—"Gordy Manor," he would grandiosely dub it. At the same time, he had commissioned top Beverly Hills realtors to find an appropriate "second home" for him in L.A., as well as one for Diana in the same neighborhood.

His meal ticket, the endlessly relevant Supremes, meanwhile, were still so popular that Gordy, paradoxically, was prevented from being able to bring about Ross's solo breakout. As long as the hits and the bread were plentiful, he could afford to wait. He trusted that HDH would keep that ship sailing. He would turn out to be wrong.

Ce

The frisson of "Reflections" aside, it fell short by a tick of meeting Gordy's "No. 1's only" rule of order, breaking the Supremes' second streak of chart-toppers at five. Released on July 24 backed with "Going Down for the Third Time," it sprinted upward during the week of August 26 before making it to No. 2 on the pop charts and No. 4 on the R&B charts, blocked from the summit by the four-week occupancy of Bobbie Gentry's "Ode to Billie Joe."

Even so, "Reflections," almost certainly selling nearly a million copies, extended the continuity factor of the group, buffering any potential fallout from the Ballard mess. Trying to manage how that story would be played in public, Gordy ordered that nothing be said of the reason it happened, explaining years later that "[i]n the sixties, alcoholism was not dealt with the way it is today. It was something to be kept secret." Instead, he sicced Motown vice-president and head of publicity Mike Roshkind on the media.

Roshkind, a 40-ish, well-connected flack who had once been a PR advisor to John F. Kennedy during his presidential campaign, was an accomplished "fixer," doing Gordy's bidding with a blend of courtly charm and thinly veiled threats of future noncooperation. Roshkind fed reporters and editors spin that Ballard had left on her own, with no bad blood, and that everyone was on the same page, which wasn't being turned but continued. It might be best, he suggested, if they'd just leave it alone. Most newspapers, magazines, and radio stations did just that, the story being confined to a mention here and there, with the prescribed spin. In the September 4 issue of *Soul*, a small-circulation black tabloid, for example, the headline was "FLORENCE ASKS OUT." (Less sanguine was a take in the pocket-sized black tabloid *Jet* that wrote titillatingly of "a hair-pulling, knock-down-drag-out fight" between unnamed Supremes in Vegas "over the change in billing," a fight that did not happen.)

In truth, the page *had* been turned, months ago; from now on, Mary Wilson would be downgraded from co-Supreme to stage prop, which was what Cindy Birdsong was hired to be. Neither would object openly since the Supremes were still working under the terms of the original communal contract, which evenly divided all monies three ways. While that seemed patently unfair to Diana and Mary, given that Cindy had not sung a note on a Supremes record, and never would, Mary nevertheless considered herself fortunate that Diana wasn't getting what she really wanted, and bugged Gordy endlessly to effect—namely, the lion's share as the "star." Gordy, though, refused, having concluded that the group had been through enough strain and needed to act and think as a team again—not that his continuing gifts on the side to Diana, the latest being a white Rolls-Royce, made that any easier.

In any case, because the "third Supreme" position had been smoothed into anodyne superficiality—with the second Supreme not far behind—Flo was often still assumed to be there (aided to no end by Birdsong's uncanny resemblance) or else happily off finding domestic tranquility. In the end, did it even matter? That was the operative question in the fall of 1967, when the Supremes and/or Motown were accorded a spectacular succoring in the media that all of God's and Gordy's money couldn't have bought. First, in September came breathless articles published in *Time, Cosmopolitan,* and *Fortune,* and in December in the *New York Times Magazine.* This was the ultimate quadrifecta, covering the four bases Gordy cared most about: upscale Americans, upscale women, upscale businessmen, and upscale urbanites.

All had been written before Flo's dismissal, and fortunately three focused mainly on Gordy, the *Time* piece titled "HEAVYWEIGHT FEATHERWEIGHT" and *Fortune* "THE MOTOWN SOUND OF MONEY," with the latter describing him as "a Negro [who] owns his own company in an industry still almost entirely white owned." The *Times'* 20,000-word paean, "THE BIG, HAPPY, BEATING HEART OF THE DETROIT SOUND," read like one of those paid-for *Billboard* inserts, complete with images of eight Motown album covers—and pictures of several acts, including the Supremes, one of which showed Ballard applying makeup.

Gordy could live with that, especially with passages such as "It is sometimes said of the Supremes that they have a 'white sound.' Diana rejects the description. 'The white sound means the commercial sound,' she explains a little hotly, as if to say, 'This is our sound, baby, not theirs,'" and, "'A Supremes record will sell almost 500,000 almost automatically,' Gordy says. 'Kids buy their records without even listening to them. We are putting something into their homes sight unseen, so we want it to be good.'"

But Rona Jaffe's *Cosmo* piece had been calculated as center-ring treatment for the girls. Titled "THE SUPREMES: THEY MAKE YOU

BELIEVE AGAIN," it cast them in a hip-to-be-square light, as "the most unusual pop vocal group in the country. They don't take pot or LSD, talk hip language, or attend love-ins and protest rallies." And in the text arose the ghost of Florence—"a tall, *zaftig*, earthy honest, completely un–show business, more woman than girl, constrained, private . . . the 'Quiet One' [who onstage] is suddenly radiant, more radiant than a mere audience could ever make a girl [but] painfully shy."

"We've been together nine years," she is quoted. "I can't believe it's gone by so fast. If I had stayed home and been a nurse or something, I'd probably be saying what a long time it's been."

The irony of those words was likely lost on most, and for Gordy the minor embarrassment paled before the marquee value of the publicity, including Jaffe's final panting paragraph: "The Supremes sing and the Ice Age cracks wide open. It is the cracking of the ice that has covered all our hearts in the cool, cool sixties. It is a sound that makes you believe again in love." So what if it actually made Ballard believe in anything but? In the larger lens, the Supremes were much bigger now than the sum of their parts. In fact, because Ballard's departure was never framed as a firing, it wasn't completely clear that she wasn't just on sabbatical. When the *Detroit Free Press* touched on the matter in its September 1 edition—more than a month after she was canned—the headline ambiguously read: "SUPREMES FLO BALLARD: IT'S SAID SHE'S LEAVING."

Thus, the Ballard blurbs in the *Times* and *Cosmo* came in rather handy, keeping her ghost lurking in the periphery, for those who might care. Because Cindy wasn't yet being introduced regularly on stage (the "sexy one–quiet one" routine was put in moth balls), maybe that third Supreme was Flo. Or, as Diana had told Johnny Carson, maybe she was just a stand-in.

While the charade played out, the real Flo seemed to be adapting to life on the outside with a mixture of relief, resignation, and cynicism—but surprisingly little anger.

> RAY GIBSON: Florence still felt betrayed, but she was definitely happier. It was like she could breathe for the first time in years. She got out of the hospital and had all this energy. She wouldn't have to be flying, she wouldn't have to be tormented by Diana

and Berry. And, frankly, she was expecting to kick back and live off all that money she was supposed to have. She'd given seven years of her life to her work and through all that time Berry would say, "We're all gonna be millionaires." So now she said, "Okay, where is it?"

Gordy had thought of that, too. With the fine print of Ballard's firing needing to be worked out, he didn't even wait to let the flames of the riots die down before arranging a meeting with Flo for July 26. To avoid the sticky situation of Flo coming to Hitsville, he chose the Northland Inn in Southfield, Michigan, for the meeting. As it happened, Motown was still closed on that day and Gordy not yet home from Las Vegas, but the meeting went on as planned, with his place taken by Mike Roshkind. Anticipating that she would be settling up with the company, and that she would leave with her freedom and her money, Flo came in without a lawyer, though that may have been at Motown's insistence, with the assurance that this was a "family" matter and that lawyers would only prey on her naiveté and steal her money— their assumption being, evidently, that only the Motown lawyers had a right to do that.

Indeed, the first sign that this was to be something other than a family gathering was the sight of Roshkind. Flo didn't know who Roshkind was, or of his reputation as Gordy's attack dog, but she found out right away why he was there when the squat, scowling flack immediately started browbeating her about the clause in her contract that denied her any usage of the Supremes' name if she recorded for another label. This meant there could be no billing with the words "former Supreme," no albums with titles using the word "Supreme," no liner notes that even mentioned the group, or even her association with Motown.

This, of course, wasn't merely petty posturing but just plain nonsense. There were ways of getting around that proscription with creative wordplay; besides, wouldn't anyone who would buy a Flo Ballard record know exactly who she was? But it was the way Roshkind came off, his "or else" tone of voice, that shook her. At the time, she was just out of the hospital and still on medication for her nerves, which made her feel weak and did little to alleviate her paranoid tendencies.

"I'm scared of this white man," she told Tommy later.

The meeting got nastier when money was discussed, or rather, not discussed. Roshkind, with no interest in what Flo had to say, told her she would never see another dime in royalties from the Supremes' future work—but could stay with Motown, provided that she sign a contract extension and have the company handle her career. If she left, Motown was prepared to "settle up" at $2,500 a year for six years against future royalties of her old Supremes records. While Flo may not have known how much all those hits brought in each year, $2,500 sounded more like a weekly cut, just from radio plays alone. As for what was being held by Gordy in escrow, much of her fortune from ten No. 1 hits, Roshkind said nothing.

As intimidated as she was, Flo could see through the muddle of Gordy having fired her from the Supremes only to turn around and want to extend her service. What he really had in mind, she reckoned, was to keep her out of the way and quiet, "or else." Roshkind actually had the nerve, or gall, to tell her that if she didn't re-up with Motown, "Berry won't have anything to do with you."

"Do with *me*?" she replied with a rising laugh. "I don't care if I ever see that man again!"

Still, she was bullied enough to agree, and walked out of the room shaking and in tears, with nothing in her hand but a carbon copy of the royalty agreement that would net her a paltry fifteen grand. "Is that all I'm worth?" she moaned to Tommy when she got home. He, too, had left the company, claiming that Gordy assured him he could have his chauffeur job back any time he wanted—which, if so, might have been a "divide and conquer" mind game being played by Gordy.

Now, as he and Flo made plans to marry in early '68, she had time to think about Motown's very nearly sadistic personal humiliation of her—the kind never faced by Mary Wells or other Motown expatriates who had the temerity to jilt the company. Realizing that she'd been cheated at the Northland Inn, and that she had no family at Motown, she did what she should have done before being dressed down by Mike Roshkind. On August 24, Ballard retained at a 20 percent commission the Detroit firm of Baun, Okrent, and Vulpe, making the lead attorney, Leonard Baun, her business manager, even though he was not practiced in entertainment law and had never written or seen a show-business contract.

Already hamstrung by Flo having signed the royalty agreement, Baun had little leverage but was excited by the chance to shake loose some of Motown's millions, even if he would have to go up against the assembled might of Gordy's legal representation. He had confidence, and Flo liked that. He told her he knew Ralph Seltzer from when they'd both worked at law firms in the same building downtown. Meetings were quickly set up between Baun and Motown lawyers George Schiffer and Sydney and Harold Novick. To Flo, Baun was just the kind of heavy hitter to go toe-to-toe with them.

Reasonably hopeful that her money was just around the corner, she expected that her grievances with Motown would be taken seriously. Actually, she had more grievances than she knew. For instance, there had been movie offers for her, alone, that had come in to Gordy and were quashed out of hand because only Diana could be in a movie. Just as there'd been scuttlebutt in the New York gossip columns that Broadway producer David Merrick had his eye on Flo for an all-black production of *Hello Dolly*. With a big-time lawyer on the case now, Flo was convinced that projects of that kind would be hers for the taking, in addition to a solo singing career. Her old sass returned, with lines to friends like "My tomorrow looks promised" and "Lord knows, my bread is buttered."

By the end of summer, her bitterness had eased toward Diana and Mary, but not toward Big Daddy, whom she routinely referred to as "that evil Berry Gordy." When the Supremes played the Michigan State Fair, drawing a record 20,000 people to a free concert, Flo and Tommy were in left-front-row seats, with an animated Flo loudly singing along to her old songs and glad-handing fans who recognized her. In the *Detroit News* that day, Diana was quoted as saying of Ballard, "We're still good friends," with Mary attributing Flo's departure to the result of "the hard work and traveling all the time." To all appearances, the schism had healed.

Two weeks later, on September 15, Baun's sessions with Motown netted results. Gordy released to Baun $75,689 from the ITMI escrow account for Ballard at the Bank of Commonwealth. With the money Baun opened a trust fund account under the name of Talent Management, with Flo listed as president, Tommy Chapman as vice-president, and Baun as treasurer. This was a wise move, as it kept Flo from being able to take the money all at once and possibly squander it. Baun explained to her that periodic withdrawals would mean compounded interest and less tax to pay, and that solid investments could be made.

Flo thought she was benefiting from sound fiscal advice, from someone who got things done and cared about her interests, as opposed to "evil Gordy." And Baun kept coming through. On December 5, Motown released some token stock that had been kept in Flo's name. Baun had put her on an allowance of $2,000 a week—four times what she was paid as a Supreme—and, as Gordy had, authorized payments for occasional luxury items like clothes and a new El Dorado. He also obtained credit cards for the officers of TM—the first credit card Flo ever had. She even had a stock portfolio, after Baun invested $10,000 in 34.3 shares of the Dreyfus mutual fund.

There was still a good deal of unfinished business with Motown—namely, the official termination of her contract and an equitable settlement (i.e., all funds due her from the escrow account). Things were proceeding smoothly enough for Flo to turn her attention to singing again. Chapman began putting out feelers to record companies about getting behind the career of the first Supreme to go solo. It was a clever sales pitch, framed so that Flo would beat Diana Ross to the solo-artist market, and in December ABC Records in New York, using former Motown promotions man Lou Zito as a conduit, sent word to Chapman: "Let's talk."

Only then did the negotiations with Motown hit a snag—and hardly by coincidence, Baun suspected. Clearly, the last thing Gordy wanted at this point was Florence Ballard receiving accolades and reaping hits so soon after her departure from the Supremes, which would put her in competition with the Supremes she had left behind and in a position to step on Ross's endlessly impending breakout. However, denying her any stated connection to the Supremes hadn't scared her away; and if releasing her funds piecemeal was an inducement for her to literally keep her mouth shut—given that a final termination agreement was necessary for her to sign with any other label—when ABC made a hard offer Motown couldn't pussyfoot around anymore. The offer was modest by Supremes standards but decent for a relatively obscure singer: For recording two intended singles and an album of material, Ballard would receive a $15,000 advance on royalties.

Throughout the negotiations, even as it was releasing monies to Flo, Motown had never acknowledged that Flo was, in fact, no longer a part of the company. Her contract, they insisted, was still binding—and what's more, whether Flo knew it or not, by signing the future royalty agreement at the Northland Inn she had legally accepted the extension, because those weren't separate agreements at all but linked together. Baun never took that argument seriously, regarding her signature that day as invalid, as having been coerced without benefit of an attorney present on her behalf. But the claim allowed Motown to sit on its hands for months, effectively stalling the ABC deal. Gordy's mouthpieces stopped speaking with Baun altogether, leaving his calls unanswered and refusing all requests to check Motown books and documents. At one point, they insisted that the Supremes' original contracts could not be found—and, in any case, there may not even have *been* any.

As best as Baun and his co-counsel Ralph Jewell could piece together, the Supremes had grossed, all told, $1.6 million for the first eight months of 1967 alone. Theoretically, that would mean Flo would be entitled to at least $500,000 that year, before those notorious expenses. By a conservative estimate, it was reasonable to place her overall career share at something like $1.5 million, even if Motown's accountants could be believed that the Supremes had not received any royalties until 1965.

A complicating factor—and yet another reason for Flo to be paranoid—was that she was under investigation by the IRS. Because Motown accountants had prepared her income tax returns, Baun had no records for her and had to estimate, and pay back taxes on, earnings she may not have been paid. As if all this wasn't enough, Motown claimed, *ex post facto*, that because Flo had actually agreed to the contract extension by signing the royalty agreement at the Northland Inn, freeing up some of Flo's escrow money proved only that Gordy had sole discretion on such matters. To Baun, the claim was pure *chutzpah*.

There'd be more to come. When Baun contended that Flo had a monetary interest in the Supremes' name, having chosen it herself, Motown denied she had ever done any such thing. It also maintained that royalties for Supremes records would fall drastically in the future, a canard that Baun would credulously stipulate during negotiations. Early in 1968, however, Baun decided to go over the lawyers' heads and appeal directly to Gordy, who refused to take his calls. When Ralph Seltzer learned of the calls, he was incensed and he, too, refused Baun's calls, telling him he could go tell his case to a judge.

That is exactly what Baun wanted to do, pressing Flo to agree to let him file a civil lawsuit against Motown and subpoena all relevant documents and records. But with the ABC deal in peril—the company lawyers having nullified their offer while Flo fought it out with Motown, fearing Gordy would sue *them* for tampering—she believed that would create further delay and cost her huge legal fees in a case she couldn't win. Indeed, Sydney Novick seemed to be daring her to take Motown to court. Of the fifteen grand she'd agreed to, he sniffed to Baun, "Take it or forget it and start your lawsuit."

Instead, Flo had Baun continue to push for a settlement. Turning up the heat, he began giving Motown a preview of what it could expect if the case did go to court, blistering Gordy for keeping Flo in "chivalry servitude" and making her a "vassal." This incendiary terminology made Gordy chafe as he tried to reckon how it would play against Motown's mostly white top brass. And what might Flo herself say on the stand in open court? The PR hits he stood to take made him shudder. Accordingly, Motown came back to the bargaining table in mid-February 1968, wanting now just to be done with the whole affair. Following an intense several days, on February 22 Baun signed off on the terms of a nine-page termination agreement—terms that fell far short of $1.6 million.

It was agreed that three checks signed by Harold Novick would be made out to Baun for deposit in Flo's account, broken down this way: $134,809.40 from "Motown Record Corporation" for the balance of Flo's escrow account—though no books had been opened for Baun to inspect, nor opened to an outside auditor; $5,000 from "Diana Ross and the Supremes" for the value of gowns Flo had been fitted for but was never given; and $20,195.06 from "Supremes Vocal Group" for unpaid royalties, which would supplant the $15,000 she'd previously agreed to.

Combined with the $75,689 December disbursement, this outcome meant that Motown, which had made untold millions from the group she founded, had dismissed Ballard for $235,693.46—a bargain indeed, at mere pennies on the dollar. Still, Baun believed it was the best he could do without taking Motown to court and with Flo in an understandable hurry to begin her solo career. A protracted legal battle with court-ordered audits and postponements could have taken years—as HDH would find out—and cost Flo not only immense legal fees but her limited window of opportunity to be a "relevant" act.

When she and Baun went to the new Motown office in the Donovan Building on February 26 to sign the final papers, Mike Roshkind straggled in without his game face on. Trying to be sincere, he urged Flo "as a friend" not to take the money in a lump sum and instead let Motown pay it out over time. "Otherwise," he said, "the government is going to kill you." This of course was excellent advice—just as it had been when Baun first advised Flo at the time he set up her trust account, which is why Baun took offense at the remark as a slap at his integrity. Reminding Roshkind that he was sheltering Flo's money, he then tapped into Flo's resentment and suspicions of Motown, saying, with a sneer directed at his adversary, "Don't worry about it" and that "a clean break" from the company was "the best way to go."

Roshkind laughed. "Yeah—the best way for *you*."

But he could have saved his breath. After the way Motown had humiliated her and made her fight for every dime, Flo was not about to let Motown have any say over her money. Roshkind, making a final effort at parting as "friends," threw his arms around her, but Flo didn't reciprocate, standing rigidly, arms at her side. He then wished her well, grandly assuring her she could call him or Berry any time. "I mean it," he said.

"Okay. Then I wanna call Berry right now," she parried, leaving Roshkind to nervously shuffle papers until he was sure she wasn't serious, at which point Flo went on, "And if he's so concerned about me, why ain't he in here right now sayin' goodbye?"

The flummoxed flack had no reply, and as she and Baun turned for the door, the silence in the room stood as Motown's goodbye and good riddance to the founding Supreme. But Gordy was not through messing with Florence Ballard.

twenty

FOREVER
CAME
TODAY

Three days after her divorce from Motown, Flo and Tommy Chapman flew to Hawaii to elope. Though her family and friends were disappointed they wouldn't get to see that rare day of happiness in her life, no one begrudged her wish to get away from it all without delay and be with the man she loved for a few days in paradise. But only for a very little while, as it turned out. They spent a good part of the honeymoon arguing, something that was common for them but which escalated after they were married.

RAY GIBSON: The truth was, Tommy was always a little snippy with Florence, but when they married it was like he took it as a license to control everything she did. I mean, he was telling her to shut up and all that—how do you talk to your new wife like that in public? But he had to be the boss, to be the man, to be like Berry Gordy.

Like I say, Tommy could be a nice guy but he just didn't get it. He loved Florence, but that was only one part of the bargain; a nobody like Tommy Chapman sees a woman with more money and talent than he would ever have, that he'd be nothing without her, and maybe deep down he resented her for it.

His behavior just sort of confirmed what a lot of us thought, that Tommy was playing an angle with Florence. The most heartbreaking part of it was that Florence, God bless her, couldn't admit he was doing that. I'd see her with her eyes all red from crying about something Tommy said or did, and she'd always make sure to say how much she loved him and he loved her. And there *was* that, which was good enough to her because she didn't want another part of her life to be a failure.

But here she was supposed to be happy. She had a new career, she was married, she was gonna have kids. And yet I sensed that her life was more desperate than ever.

The ABC deal was reinstated in late February after the company received a copy of Flo's termination agreement. Holding off on the signing, Tommy flew to New York for some last-ditch pitching of Flo to other labels, but not a one expressed any interest, their reasoning quite likely having much to do with the inside industry knowledge of her drinking and "troublemaking" at Motown. Consequently, Flo knew that the ABC opportunity would likely be her last shot at the brass ring.

ABC's interest came only because the music division of the giant broadcasting corporation was looking to make a large leap. In ten years, as Am-Par, then ABC-Paramount, it had released fairly standard pop fare, its biggest hits being Paul Anka's '50s "teen idol" fare. And yet, with some irony, ABC-Paramount released black-and-proud anthems by the Impressions ("I'm So Proud," "Keep on Pushing," "Amen," "People Get Ready") that Motown wouldn't have dared broach; and its iconic jazz sub-label, Impulse, was home to John Coltrane, Art Blakey, and McCoy Tyner. In '67, it commenced a bid for expansion by acquiring the West Coast Dunhill label, bringing the highly commercial Mamas and the Papas and Three Dog Night to the table.

Ballard was thought pertinent to this growth. When she and Tommy flew in early March to New York to sign the two-year contract, one year with an option on a second, company executives told her that what they wanted was a "Supremes-like sound." Considering that the very word was restricted from use, this objective was easier imagined than done. And far, *far* too heavy a burden to put on a still-far-from-whole Blondie Ballard.

An even bigger burden was now on the actual Supremes. By early '68, post-Flo, the group was losing altitude. Although Ballard's departure had little to do with this turn of events, surely some would have spun it that way if she'd made a mark as a solo artist. It would be the easy thing to do, running along an agreeable story line of vindication and pay-back, and Gordy couldn't say he didn't ask for it.

What caused Motown to ponder this nightmare scenario was that the follow-up to the stunning "Reflections" was arguably HDH's most flyweight Supremes effort, "In and Out of Love." Not that it didn't have some typical ingratiating HDH quirks—mainly in the strum-ming acoustic guitar riff on the intro that satisfied the Hollands' pet yen to drop a country-western feel into a Motown record before the strings and horns took over the sonic field. Nor was the bouncy beat anything less than a smart pivot back to the toe-tapping reverie of "The Happening."

The rhythm track was cut in L.A. in April with the working title "Summer Good, Summer Bad," then completed in Studio A in early June—with Flo having put in her last hours there. Not just was the old HDH "feel" diluted, but Diana's cyclical repeating of the lyrical core, "keep falling in and out of love," didn't quite make clear whether she was happier falling in or out of love, or why it was supposed to matter.

Released on October 25, 1967, with "I Guess I'll Always Love You" on the flip, it ran out of gas at No. 9 in early December, not a disaster but also not enough for Gordy. Yet when he looked to HDH for an-other rebound, they were nowhere to be found. As he wrote in *To Be Loved*, "I was told HDH had stopped recording and were in some sort of strike." Lamont Dozier himself has used the term "strike" in describ-ing HDH's actions. (Another time, asked what he did that summer, he responded, "I mowed the lawn.") The Hollands prefer "slowdown." Whatever the semantics, it was a double blow for Gordy, given that HDH controlled the creative ship of state at Motown, at A&R and Creative Control.

In fact, Gordy's judgment about which records to green-light seemed to be slipping as he drifted further from the day-to-day grind to galavant with the Supremes. Incredibly, overruling the Friday group meeting verdict, he had nixed the release of Marvin Gaye's first single in nearly a year, "I Heard It Through the Grapevine," co-written (with Barrett Strong) and produced by Norman Whitfield and perhaps the single best piece of work ever to come out of Motown; instead, possibly as a favor to HDH, he went with their Gaye record, "Your Unchanging Love," which became only a minor hit at No. 33 in mid-'67. Whit-field's re-cut, up-tempo version with Gladys Knight and the Pips went to No. 2 later in the year, becoming the top-selling Motown single up to then—until eclipsed by the too-long-belated release of the magnificently brooding Gaye version late that year, which stayed at No. 1 for seven weeks.

While Gordy waited for HDH to show, he had to stretch the soup to put together the Supremes' next album, *Reflections*, including with the title track and "In and Out of Love" a hash of second-tier HDH– and Smokey Robinson–produced tracks such as "Bah-Bah-Bah," written by Brenda Holloway and her sister Patrice, and covers of "Up, Up and Away," "What the World Needs Now Is Love," and "Ode to Billie Joe." Riding on the back of the two hits, the album made it to No. 18 on the album chart and No. 3 on the R&B album chart. If the album didn't reflect any great intensity on the part of Gordy, it did reflect his sense of pique and vindictiveness, as the cover's montage of the Supremes in various candid photographs included none of Florence Ballard—marking the first stage of what would become a general "de-Ballardization" of Supremes history around the Motown camp.

Gordy would claim that, for the next Supremes single, "[w]e were forced to go back to the can," coming up with the HDH "Forever Came Today," which he said had been "cut a year before." Yet on the 2000 box-set *The Supremes*, Harry Weinger lists the session dates for the song as December 20, 1967, and January 1, 1968. That would indicate HDH were on the job, not on strike. As well, Eddie Holland calls the tune "one of my favorites," which seems to suggest that Gordy— who later used the strike against HDH in years of legal warfare—may have overstated just how crippling their work stoppage was.

Even so, "Forever Came Today" is something of a riddle. Session sheets for the song seem not to have been kept. Weinger specified no studio locale for it, though it has that non-Detroit, "L.A." feel—as well as a very strange coronet-piccolo intro that sounds like a riff from Wagner's "Bridal Chorus." Stranger still, perhaps, is that the lyrics are probably the most optimistic love song Eddie Holland ever penned, sans the usual emotional tug of war—"When you walked into my life / You made my lonely life a paradise," Diana joyfully trilled.

Whatever its origins, it is clear that the backing vocalists were not Wilson and Birdsong but the Andantes. That trio had been called in to spruce up Flo's flat background line on "In and Out of Love," but from "Forever" on, Wilson and Birdsong were Supremes merely for appearance's sake. The reason was simple, and cold: Gordy was now actively trying to bring forth a record that would mark Diana's solo breakout, and of course no other Supremes members could be in its grooves. The beauty of it for Gordy was that even on tracks he determined to be

more appropriately Supremes singles—which was the case with all singles chosen for the next year—no one would know the difference anyway, as the Andantes were that good.

Gordy had a more tactful way of putting it—that Mary and Cindy,
by remarkable coincidence, always seemed to be "unavailable" or, more
preposterously, "out of town" when Supremes sessions went down.
(Amazingly, Ross was always available.) However, never truer than now
was Shelly Berger's observation that the Supremes were for all practical
purposes Diana Ross and two who-cares backup vocalists.

The bummer was that "Forever Came Today" came and went without a ripple after it was released on February 29 with an aptly titled
B-side, "Time Changes Things." The Motown promotion machine
plied its trade, but neither that effort nor even the tune's debut by the
Supremes on the March 24 episode of *The Ed Sullivan Show* could
move it higher than No. 28 on the pop charts and 17 on the R&B.

But while the Supremes' crashing chart fortunes could have been a
problem for HDH as well, they decided to put everything on the line
with Gordy. By no coincidence, they extended their own feelers to
other record companies, one of which, Capitol, assured them they
could run their own subsidy label if they jumped ship. In late spring,
Eddie Holland strode into Gordy's office with an ultimatum. His previous demands for a cut of publishing royalties and stock equity having
been rebuffed, his new—and last—demand was for a $100,000 interest-
free loan for the trio so that they could incorporate the HDH brand
into a business entity, with private office space and the freedom to
bring in their own acts while still working at Motown; if they didn't get
the money and the autonomy, Holland said, they were gone.

The terms of the ultimatum sounded nothing but dangerous to
Gordy. He could imagine his authority being whittled away, and that
he'd be in effect financing an independent label under his own roof
that would someday become a competitor. Trying to put them off without saying no, he launched into the "Berry rap," reminding them again
that he had bankrolled their rise to fame, with the hundreds of thousands of dollars in advances and the millions in writers' royalties that
he'd invested in them. (Pulling out a file, he put the exact figure at
$2,235,155.) They were set for life, many times over. And all that stood
between them now was a measly hundred grand?

After listening to the twenty-minute rap, Eddie stood up. "So I
guess that's a no, then?" he said drily.

Weeks later, HDH were gone, even though they all had contracts
through the end of the decade with Motown. Although Gordy contin-

ued to hope they would come to their senses and get to work, news soon broke that Capitol had announced the formation of Invictus Records, to be operated in Detroit with full autonomy by Holland-Dozier-Holland.

Gordy, so out of touch with his own company as to be stunned that his "three sons" would leave him, was close to full panic mode. Bristling about HDH's departure and the flop of "Forever Came Today," he fished for a quick Supremes song to put out as soon as possible. The HDH shelves were so depleted that he had the girls' cover of "What the World Needs Now Is Love" from *Reflections* readied as a single, but thought the better of it and instead went to Motown's newest writing-producing team—Nick Ashford and Valerie Simpson, a young black duo who had met in a Harlem church choir, sang briefly as an act, then wrote for, among others, Ray Charles, Aretha Franklin, and the Shirelles before being signed by Gordy. With the first of their five Top Ten Marvin Gaye–Tammi Terrell hits, "Ain't No Mountain High Enough," just hitting the charts, they were handed the world's top female act.

The hip young team's stock in trade was funky, soulful wailing, but Gordy told them he wanted a song with an "HDH feel." The result was "Some Things You Never Get Used To," which came out as strained big-band pop with an even more quirky intro of castanets chattering—very much like the intro of the surf-rock "Wipe Out"—and HDH-style lyrics about love that is never found. On the upside, it had a wonderfully wild James Jamerson bass line. But what it didn't have was the signature HDH kick to the solar plexus. And its release on May 21, with "You've Been So Wonderful to Me" on the flip, was an instant misfire.

If Gordy felt personally tarred by "Forever Came Today," "Some Things" was even worse—such a titanic failure that, after just three weeks on the chart and a late-July peak at No. 30, a good many people never heard it or knew it had ever existed. For *that*, at least, he could be thankful.

But what now? The Supremes had flourished as a two-headed monster—the "rock group" hit-makers and the regal, show-tune-crooning night club act. For the time being, at least, their club and hotel gigs were not imperiled by a couple of lackluster singles, nor were their whitebread TV gigs—the latest being a January 1968 shot on the campy *Tarzan*, playing, of all things, three nuns and singing "Michael Row the Boat Ashore" and "The Lord Helps Those Who

Help Themselves." (The episode was the most-watched of the season for the popular series—another "mainstream" notch for Gordy, who threw his weight around on the set, barking orders to the crew and actors.)

However, if the downward trend on the charts continued, it would be ever harder to sustain the heat that came with the status of being one of the world's top acts, who as late as 1967 were voted "most popular music group" in the annual *Playboy* readers' poll—as representative a measure of upscale white tastes as there was—ahead of the Beatles and Peter, Paul & Mary. A lower flame would mean less status, lower appearance fees, and fewer prestige invitations.

And if that happened, could doomsday be far behind?

Flo Ballard Chapman was hardly unhappy at that prospect, mainly because it might make Gordy suicidal. When HDH walked and Motown people were frantic, she was beaming about poetic justice. According to Tony Tucker, "Flo said it served those bitches right," and that Diana Ross and the Supremes—five words she could not say without a scoffing sneer—"couldn't make it without HDH songs behind them." Flo, herself, might help fulfill such a prophecy, if she could make her own hits.

How delicious would *that* be, if Flo Ballard had the last laugh, after all?

With the ABC Records deal done, Flo became transformed from outcast to in-crowd hostess. Her period of "rest" had given way to a fresh round of parties, hosting many in the Motown crowd who came by her home to congratulate her on the deal and wish her well. Some would confide that she had stuck it to Gordy the way they wished they had the balls to do. Indeed, a common refrain was anger about "what they did to you" and that it had been right for her to "quit" as she did. In these ego-massaging commiserations, the Supremes were villains, having "stuck a knife in her back." They, went the theme, would "go down the tubes" without her.

Having rarely heard that sort of encouragement before, Flo would bask in it, and then invariably say the same thing: "You got that right, honey," flouncing about like Auntie Mame in her mink stole, hors d'oeuvres tray in her hands, or filling up everyone's glass, including her own, with fire water.

Not the least reason for the late-coming solidarity from the Motown crowd of performers was that her firing exploded false assumptions that the same could not happen to any one of them. Indeed, it *had* happened, to more than a few others.

ANNETTE BEARD: I knew exactly what Flo was going through, why she was so bitter about the Supremes. I didn't blame her a bit—because I was fired by the Vandellas in 1964 for my "behavior" [she had become pregnant by her boyfriend], which was all bull. And that was devastating to me. I did not leave by choice; I came to the studio one day and was told, "Martha doesn't want you to sing with her anymore."

I mean, here you are, doing something you love and enjoy and then poof, it's gone. And for me it was like Flo having started the Supremes. I was with our group before Martha was. We already had a group. We took *her* in and then she was calling all the shots. And today Martha takes all the credit for the group, it's all her and no one else.

It was pretty much the same with Flo and Diana, but worse. When we first met the Supremes, Flo was the lead singer, and a damn good one. Then she was nothing. Just imagine how much that hurt her. With me, at least, there was some closure because Martha called me out of the blue fifteen years later and asked me to sing with her at a reunion engagement. I was really shocked because I hadn't spoken to Martha in all that time, and it helped ease things. But Flo never got that same kind of call, and then it was too late.

Among the regulars at Flo's soirees were the Temptations, who were so pissed off at Flo's sacking that they fired off a telegram to Mary Wilson, which read: *"Mary, stick with Flo, you might be next—the Tempts."*

(Though in the harsh glare of reality, they did not stick with one of their own, David Ruffin, who was dealt with as had been Flo—with a pink slip, delivered to him in mid-'68 when the group got fed up with his cocaine-fueled absences and egomania. Ruffin proceeded to do what Flo would have loved to—first forcing his way onto the stage at Temptations gigs and then, when he was physically obstructed from doing that, battling Motown in court and coming away with a settlement that allowed him to finish out his contract as a solo act. But while the parallels between Ballard and Ruffin are obvious, he was at least as narcissistic as

Diana Ross, feeding off her elevation to demand that his group be billed "David Ruffin and the Temptations"—yet another inevitable upshot of Gordy's fixation on Ross. Neither did the Tempts stick with Paul Williams, who was cashiered in the early '70s for his alcoholism; less resourceful and quick-witted than Ruffin, he fell into a depression and in 1973 killed himself with a gunshot to the head, just steps from Motown.)

Definitely *not* on Flo's guest list were Diana and Mary. As close to each other as they lived, the strip of Buena Vista between them was a kind of "no-man's land," none of the three ever taking a stroll down the road lest they risk bumping into one another. Even on short runs to nearby stores, they would make the trip in their Cadillacs. Flo, however, couldn't seem to ignore her nemeses across the street and down the block. Tony Tucker tells of Lurlee Ballard and other family members acting as sentries, peering through the curtains for any goings-on involving Ross or Wilson, reporting to Flo things such as "There's a car in that bitch's driveway," or "I just saw that bitch Mary Wilson driving down the street."

Wilson received the Temptations' telegram while the Supremes were in New York for a concert at the Forest Hills tennis stadium—though whether she felt shamed by her lack of support for Flo was left unclear; she noted it in *Dreamgirl* without comment. But she did confess that, with Flo gone, she felt "alone." There was also the unending irony that while she kept her distance from the exiled Ballard, she grew peeved at Cindy Birdsong for being too subservient to Diana as the latter further levitated higher above the Supremes. Birdsong, who after all was getting the free ride of her life, just wanted to quietly fit in. Yet Mary was suddenly demanding that she be a personal courtier to *her*. This, of course, was a suggestion that could have led anyone in the Supremes' entourage to say, "Pot, meet kettle."

Wilson would recall Cindy, with faint praise, as "a great singer, a good buddy—but no ally when it came to standing up to Diana and Berry. . . . [S]he believed that just because Diana was the lead singer she called all the shots in the group."

"She's *not* the boss," Mary would tell her.

"Okay," would come the blank reply.

"Don't just go along with everything she wants."

"Okay."

"There won't be any group if you and I don't stick together."

"Okay."

In the end, though, Cindy would always give in to "Miss Ross"—as timorously as Mary had when she forgot to stick with Flo, and still did in matters of stage dress and song selection; everything, really. At least outwardly, however, she wasn't the classic doormat she once had been. As little more now than a piece of stage furniture, she saw Flo getting a solo contract and had to wonder just *who* had been the "third Supreme." "I'd like to do something like that," she would tell people.

Accordingly, her old gung-ho zeal at being seen if not always heard began to flag, along with her obedience to the Supremes' "image." When the girls filmed the *Tarzan* episode on location in Mexico, Mary allowed herself to be photographed by a *paparazzo* during a break, the nun's habit rolled up on her thighs, cigarette in one hand, beer can in the other. Recently, she had found a "gal pal" to hang around with, a brassy woman from New York, Margie Haber, if for no good reason other than that Haber's loud, supercilious manner got under Diana's skin. That, of course, used to be Flo's only source of pleasure; now, it seemed to be Mary's.

Other, that is, than the leather-lunged British singer Tom Jones, with whom she had begun to carry on after her revolving door of men had brought her flings with Berry's brother Fuller Gordy, British producer David Puttnam, and none other than Brian Holland. Mary went gaga over the wild Welshman with the Brillo hair, her ardor replicating that of Jones's typical audience of "mums," who became famous for chucking their panties onstage at his concerts. Soon Mary had taken to lining her dressing rooms with eight-by-ten glossies of herself and Tom in various romantic embraces—or at least, as Tony Tucker noted, "the ones she could show."

Shelly Berger found himself playing travel agent, arranging for her to sneak off for one-night rendezvous with Jones in London; when the Supremes were on a tour of Europe, she took an overnight side trip to shack up with him in Munich. They were inseparable when the girls toured England in February '68, except when he had to go home to Mrs. Jones. Wilson was a sucker for his "man's man" ways, understating his prowess in *Dreamgirl* with the euphemism that he was "a fine lover."

Yet as intimate as they were, she insisted—improbably—that she didn't know until after they'd started up that he was married, because he didn't wear a ring, and that once she became aware she "felt like a fool . . . betrayed, as if I had been the one cheated on." But when she intended to break it off, "I realized I couldn't. It was too late." Instead, they carried on into the '70s, another long-term "secret" liaison within

the glittery world of "America's sweethearts" that no one was supposed
to know about, but which nearly everyone did.

By contrast, in the late winter of 1968, the Supreme who had been
dumped for conduct unbecoming was married, pregnant, and seemingly on the way to that last laugh.

Flo and Tommy drove back to New York in late March, with Flo tin-
gling with excitement and apprehension. As she would admit later, "the
idea of singing solo was "kind of scary. I've never sung solo except in
school," or sung lead in three years, since "Silent Night" from the Christmas album and "Ain't That Good News" from the Sam Cooke tribute
album. Neither had she spent any real time working on her voice before
she would have to leap into rehearsals for the ABC songs.

Anticipating months of recording, after they checked into the
Pierre Hotel they began looking for an apartment to sublet. And not
just any apartment. She wasn't playing the role of Flo now—she was
playing *Diana*. She and Tommy would ride in a limo, Flo decked out in
a mink jacket, and go from one building to another, sniffing at all the
apartments realtors showed them as inadequate, until they took one on
ultra-chic Sutton Place in the East 50s—a penthouse, no less, with a
baby-grand piano, antique furniture, three maids' rooms, and land-
scaped terraces high above the East River. She then sent for the rest of
her furs and jewelry from Detroit. On the table were bottles of Dom
Perignon and tins of Beluga caviar.

Whatever funds they had from the $15,000 advance and from the
Motown termination, they were going out that twenty-fifth-floor window, fast. For Flo, it wasn't enough that people knew she was in New
York making records; they had to know she was living in a manner be-
fitting *the* solo Supreme. Luxury and decadence were what it was all
about. The work of creating acceptable music seemed, at times, not as
important.

As it happened, all the Supremes, past and present, would be working in New York during the early spring—a time frame that was every
bit as crucial to the Diana Ross and the Supremes brand, as they'd be
doing their first high-end gigs under that banner: another *Ed Sullivan
Show* on March 24 and, ten days later, the kick-off of a two-week run
back at the Copa. At first, Flo was under the impression she and
Tommy would be left guest tickets for the *Sullivan* show; Tommy called

the theater to make sure. Then, on the day of the show, someone called from Sullivan's office and told him there were no seats for them.

Flo watched the show at the penthouse, joyfully ragging on the girls as "pitiful" and yelling at the screen "Mary! Wake up!" as they performed "Forever Came Today"—which she recognized as a song she'd sung on, and thus barked that Motown owed her royalties on it. She even had a copy of the record, and later put it on a Victrola while she sang the background part; in her head, Flo Ballard was *still* a Supreme.

Cee

Which was what the ABC Records people would have wanted her to be in her mind and music. It was really the Supremes that the company wanted on vinyl, even if two-thirds removed. Toward that end, ABC had tapped as her producer, George Kerr, a former member of Little Anthony and the Imperials who later turned to writing and producing—first at Northern Soul and then, briefly, at Motown. In '66, Kerr co-wrote with Sylvia Moy and Michael Valvanor "You Hit Me Where It Hurts Me," but when the Kim Weston single he produced was not released he walked and re-cut it with Alice Clark on the Warner Brothers label. (In the '70s he would produce the O'Jays, the Moments, and Linda Jones.)

Kerr knew what his mission was; the first song he cut with Ballard, "It Doesn't Matter How I Say It (It's What I Say That Matters)," which he wrote, could not have been more transparent. Kerr laid on layers of echo and strings, a funky bass line, and *woo-ooo*-ing backup singers, then had Flo do her best Diana Ross imitation, all high and cute and breathy. The similarity was striking at times, with a sensuousness that—channeling "Buttered Popcorn"—lent a real randiness to the saucy Smokey Robinson–esque lyric: "If I were a candy dish," she purred, "I'd wanna be the one you keep your sweets in, my sweet man."

Still, it *wasn't* Ross, or the Funk Brothers; at best, it was a packet of Motown sweet and low set to a pre-disco dance beat, and it wasted her flair as an earthy R&B singer—something she demonstrated on the B-side, a torchy, emotive cover of the Imperials' "Goin' Out of My Head." But the plain truth was that Florence Ballard, as Berry Gordy knew from the start, wasn't a *lead* singer.

Cee

In general, the timing of the sessions seemed to be cursed. It wasn't enough that Flo had to live with the psychological torture of knowing that the Supremes were only blocks away at the New York Hilton and doing star-studded, high-profile gigs. On April 4, only a couple of weeks into the project, all such seemingly important matters were rendered trivial by a shot fired by a born loser named James Earl Ray in Memphis, leaving Martin Luther King sprawled lifeless outside Room 307 on the balcony of the Lorraine Hotel.

Once more, fires burned throughout low-income, predominantly black neighborhoods, with something like eighty riots that night eventually costing nearly fifty lives. But while Baltimore and Chicago and D.C. were afire, this time Detroit stayed cool. So did New York, where the Supremes were to open at the Copa the very same night until Gordy, who'd flown in, postponed the entire engagement for a month. (On a lesser stage, a Temptations concert in South Carolina went on as scheduled, about the last thing the group wanted to do.) Gordy, who had released the album with King's "I Have a Dream" speech and hosted a King visit to Motown, was asked by his widow, Coretta, to arrange, with Harry Belafonte, a June benefit concert in their hometown of Atlanta, to commence the People's March to Freedom—the campaign on which King was working, a symbolic procession to D.C.

The Supremes would be highly visible in these rites of mourning, though nothing in their art or level of intellectual curiosity suited them to be avatars of the struggle. But this was Gordy's time to prove his commitment to the cause—and as the voices of his brand of black capitalism, the girls had to help him make his statement, even if they were props. This was the case, literally, on April 5 after they'd been hurriedly booked onto *The Tonight Show* to help keep the calm through song, which would be a near–a cappella rendition of the affective "Somewhere," which for several years had featured Diana's spoken sermon about people working together in peace and harmony.

That afternoon, Gordy had taught her a reworked rap memorializing King that he'd written himself, including lines from the "Dream" speech. It was an unforgivably heavy burden to place on her at such short notice, and at the 4:40 P.M. taping of the show, the girls came on in muted black gowns and began a dirge-like rendering of the song. On the break, as Mary and Cindy quietly hummed behind her, Diana was so unnerved that she mangled parts of Gordy's rap, which only made her seem more endearing and human. After the song, she, alone, was called over to sit next to Johnny Carson, whereupon she came close to tears speaking extemporaneously of Dr. King. "He lived and died for one reason," she said, "and I want all of us to be together. . . . I think we should walk together. It's very important because, well, just *because*," to emotional audience applause.

Even under the sad circumstances, Gordy saw it as another virtuoso Ross performance, reportedly remarking afterward that "[w]e should have her say more shit like that." For Diana, though, the experience was heart-wrenching, and she saw it as nothing to crow about. Once the show was over, she all but crumbled into a chair and sobbed uncontrollably. Mary and Cindy, having already changed into street clothes, stood waiting in the corridor, sharing a laugh. Motown lackeys were checking itineraries and trying to get Diana moving, but she sat inert, leaning forward, head in her hands.

Annoyed by the nudging, she woofed, "In a minute!" Then, when it didn't stop, she could only beg, "Why can't I just have a minute?" In that pregnant moment, she wasn't a diva, just a small young woman under far too much pressure—a side of her personality that would emerge periodically, endearingly, only to be banished back into hiding.

That night, Gordy and the girls flew to Atlanta for the funeral. The next day, images of a solemn Diana Ross draped in a mourning shawl appeared in newspapers across the country. Three months later, they were back for the People's March ceremonies, where the Supremes reprised "Somewhere." As headliners of the show (Gordy also brought in Stevie Wonder, the Temptations, and Gladys Knight and the Pips), they were standing beside Gordy when he was presented leather-bound volumes of Dr. King's books by Reverend Ralph Abernathy, King's assistant and the new president of the Southern Christian Leadership Conference. At the start of the march, the Motown contingent got in line, if for only a few well-publicized steps, with the Supremes shoulder to shoulder with Gordy, Belafonte, and Reverend Jesse Jackson.

Flo, of course, was not among the celebrity mourners. Neither did she have the option of being able to postpone her recording sessions. On the morning of April 5, she was in the studio, knocking off songs for her album. Meanwhile, ABC readied her first single. In late April, a two-page ad ran in *Billboard* touting the label's new releases, including "It Doesn't Matter How I Say It (It's What I Say That Matters)"/"Goin' Out of My Head" by "Flo/Florence Ballard." Within weeks it began to trickle into record stores and went out to radio stations with a circum-spect PR release stating only that "Florence has been part of an enter-tainment trio for many years."

The ABC Records people, again, could have cheekily tested the boundaries of the prohibition, by perhaps boasting how "supremely proud" they were to have her. But timidity seemed to pervade every as-pect of the song's promotion, or rather lack of it. Overall, they did lit-tle, as if by doing more they would offend Motown—an amazing lack of spine for a huge corporation. Early on, when they tried to book Flo on promotional appearances, they were warned that the big booking agencies "wouldn't touch" her, because this might jeopardize their lucra-tive deals with Motown.

Gordy's tentacles indeed seemed to be everywhere, allowing Flo to see firsthand why bigger Motown expatriates like Mary Wells and Brenda Holloway had run into the same wall. In Detroit, where ABC hoped for some buzz on the record, most stations never were sent copies of it.

ROBIN SEYMOUR: I don't think I ever saw it at WKNR. I think I would have played it.

I loved Flo, I thought she was a helluva singer. But it's pos-sible some deejays wouldn't have. Look, Barney Ales ran the marketing at Motown, he was a powerful guy. And there was, you know, a lot of Teamsters money at Motown. People in the business would be "contacted" every once in a while if Motown had a gripe about playlists, and they'd do what Motown wanted.

Now, listen, I'm not saying they did that with Flo's records. I don't know that they thought they *had* to, those records weren't anything to be afraid of. And I think the deejays in town rubbed off that—there was no reason to play them, ABC wasn't exactly flooding the stations with the records. Maybe it just wasn't very good.

For Flo, the lack of support was hammered home by ABC's own corporate *president*, a bumptious fellow named Larry Newton. When he was introduced to Ballard, he oddly told her, "You know, Flo, it's not good for an artist to switch recording companies," then name-dropped, as if starry-eyed, that he'd played golf recently with Berry Gordy.

But was Gordy—as Flo came to believe, understandably—blackballing her? It seems more accurate to say that ABC was perfectly content to blackball *itself* in the matter of Ballard's work, either out of respect (fear) for Gordy or because the songs didn't make them *want* to cross Gordy.

Yet even after "It Doesn't Matter" proved a prophetic title, ABC held to its part of the bargain, in releasing a second single, needing a stronger song to carry the album that was being completed with low-grade songs such as weak covers of "Yesterday," "It's Not Unusual," and "The Impossible Dream." Toward that end, a new producer was hired, one with real Motown cred. This was none other than Robert Bateman, who'd "discovered" the Primettes at the Windsor Festival and was at their Motown audition. The long-limbed Bateman, after working for MGM, was now freelancing and immediately accepted the Ballard job, which was to produce four sides.

Bateman chose as the single "Love Ain't Love," written by former Columbia writer-producer Van McCoy, whose mien even then was the kind of lush orchestration that would be fully realized in 1975 with the leviathan hit "The Hustle." For the vocal, Bateman let Flo belt away with throaty, playful lustfulness—"Come on, let me kiss you! Stop wasting time!" she exhorted, being very Flo-like. But she was once more mired in a string-coated dance mix. (A better bet seemed to be the B-side, Bateman's "Forever Faithful" with its HDH-style funk and sax solo.)

With ABC still not doing any booking for her, Tommy tried it himself, enlisting Cholly Atkins to brush up Flo's choreography and Cholly's old partner Honi Coles to use his pull to get her into some clubs—until Coles wrote him in June that the agencies had shied away "because of her former connection with Motown." Chapman did make one late-summer gig, a two-nighter at the Wonder Garden in Atlantic City, a venue no one would confuse with the Copa. Tony Tucker, who came in for the show, remembered it as "a hell-hole bar" crawling with "tacky ladies of the evening and their low pimps." Flo, seven months pregnant and looking it—her doctor had told her she would have twins—seemed to want to be anywhere else. Right up until she went on she didn't know what songs she'd sing—because the band knew how to play only a few songs, none of which Flo had sung before. When the show began, people in the audience were stunned by the sight of a very pregnant woman moving about on a stage, looking obviously distressed.

Flo, bathed in harsh, amateurish lighting that accentuated her size, tried to vamp as the band played on, but she was awful and after the disaster she bawled hysterically. Raging at Tommy for making her do this, she vowed, "I ain't going back out there no more!"

Tommy, with not an ounce of sympathy, yanked her arm sharply and screamed in her face, "Shut up!" telling her she *was* going back out for the next show. She did, with even worse results before a half-empty house.

When they got back to New York, there was no reason to stay. The sessions were done, the new single slated for release. And so they gave up the penthouse, packed up, and began driving back to Detroit, where they could be at home when the new single was released in early October—and of course for the birth of the twins. On the way, they stopped off in Chicago, where Flo had gotten a gig as a warm-up act for a Bill Cosby show at the Auditorium Center.

The first week of October, "Love Ain't Love" came out in a 45 jacket with the title and "Florence 'Flo' Ballard" superimposed on an illustration of a pensive Flo. In the *Detroit Free Press*, a review effused, "You begin to understand why a trio might split—with two lead singers and only one being featured." *Detroit* magazine put her on the cover surrounded by flower-filled vases in her home, the cover line reading "FLORENCE BALLARD: THE NEW LIFE OF AN EX-SUPREME"; inside was a photo of Flo and Tommy in a lovey-dovey pose in front of the house.

But, again, airplay was sporadic. Reminiscent of Berry Gordy and Smokey Robinson handing out early Motown records, Tommy drove around town with boxes of Flo's records in his trunk, leaving copies at the radio stations and record stores, to little avail. Seeing the record was going nowhere, ABC Records, perusing the meager sales of its self-prophesied Flo Ballard washout, decided to cancel the album, which had been tentatively titled . . . *You Don't Have To.* It also declined the option for a second year on her contract. One of its executives commented, disingenuously, that they hadn't gotten the hoped-for "Supreme sound" because Ballard was just "a good ballad singer." There was no mention of the company's near-complete lack of effort on her behalf. (The album, along with four Supremes songs with Flo on lead, was released in 2002 by Spectrum Records as *The Supreme Florence Ballard*.) According to Mary Wilson in *Dreamgirl*, word on the street was that Tommy had also "made outrageous demands" of the company "which weren't appreciated."

For Flo, the second termination within a year was just as big a kick in the teeth as the first, the timing of it especially cruel; when she received the call from New York, she was having contractions and within hours would be on the delivery-room table. Now, mixed with the joy of giving birth on October 13 to twin daughters, named Michelle and Nicole, were bilious rants that she'd been betrayed, misused, and black-balled by the "evil" Berry Gordy.

RAY GIBSON: She was so disgusted that she gave me the tapes of the album—I still have them, too. I took them with me when I moved to California and I've kept them ever since. I don't know if Tommy paid for them or if they just said take 'em, we don't want them. But when there was no album, she couldn't stand looking at those cans. She said, "Raymond, here, if you don't take them I'm just gonna burn 'em." That was how disappointed she was. This was the fruit of her labor for the last year; she believed so much she was on the way to success, and then it all came crashing down.

She said ABC didn't use her right, made her do songs she didn't care for, then everybody was scared of Berry and wouldn't play them. She told me, "Honey, people would have come to see me out of curiosity," but no one even knew about her, no one could see her. And to her it was a big conspiracy against her, orchestrated by Berry.

I listened to those tapes and I liked what she did. On some of them she's amazing. But I just wonder what would have happened if Florence had gone to an R&B label that really wanted to nurture her and not worried about being a pop star and an ex-Supreme. There would have been less pressure to become an instant star. I wish she'd just gone somewhere and sang her heart out and not had that "I'll show you, Berry, I'll show you, Diana" attitude. But who was gonna tell her that—Tommy? Let's get real. Tommy wanted nothing less than her to be a big star, so that he could be a big star, too, in his head.

Leaving themselves precious little room to fail, they left themselves no alternative.

twenty-one

"THIS MUST BE
THE
DIANA ROSS SHOW"

The Supremes themselves seemed to be running uphill that fall of '68, the biggest challenge being to find a song that would propel them back to the top of the chart.

By then, with the Capitol deal done, proving conclusively that HDH weren't going to repent and come back home to Motown, Gordy had filed suit against them for breach of contract, asking $4 million in punitive damages and to enjoin them from working for any other company but his. The injunction was granted, but it was determined, oddly, that because Eddie Holland had never signed a producers' contract with Motown, having kept working with a writers' contract, he was free to go ahead producing records at Invictus Records, despite the song writers' contract Motown had in its files for him. However, Brian Holland and Lamont Dozier, having properly executed producers' contracts with Gordy, were forbidden from doing any work at the new shop. That effectively brought Invictus to a standstill. Now, in serious danger of being checkmated by Gordy right out of the box, HDH countersued Motown on the grounds of, well, *everything*—conspiracy, fraud, deceit, and breach of fiduciary trust—for $22 million.

Moreover, in an action they knew would burn Gordy like battery acid, they asked that Motown, with all its accounts and copyrights, be placed in receivership—a legally veiled way of saying they wanted Berry Gordy removed from the financial management of the company he ruled. It was, to Gordy, not business but strictly personal. "Instead of defending themselves against my lawsuit," he wrote in *To Be Loved*, "they were throwing up a smokescreen with this absurd counterattack, attacking me on everything I stood for in business and as a person."

The numbers were dizzying, to be sure, so much so that Eddie Holland can't quite pull off saying, "I don't think it was so much over money." But when he says it *was* about "a greater creative outlet" that Motown "was not structured for," one can decipher that as code for exactly what Gordy said. The HDH game plan was big—to force Gordy out. Accordingly, in Eddie's colloquialism, it was as if "a little spark start[s] and then the next thing you know, it's a full blaze."

One that would burn for years—for no other reason, Gordy would write, than as "a personal vendetta on Eddie's part." HDH, however, did find a way to get around Brian and Lamont's being enjoined by the court from producing records, by doing so under the dual pseudonym of "Wayne/Dunbar"—not that this fooled anyone within the industry with the possible, ironic exception of master conniver Berry Gordy, who was too preoccupied to know, or to care. Or was it that he didn't mind HDH making more money from new hit records so he could get a better payday when damages would be assessed by the court?

Indeed, HDH were about to get richer; in June 1969, Buddha Records also got into the HDH business, giving them a second designer label, Hot Wax, an extraordinary double play for the trio, who wasted no time getting busy. The first Hot Wax rollout was—what were the odds?—a female trio. This was the Honey Cone, who had two releases that year, "While You're Out Looking for Sugar" and "Girls It Ain't Easy," both with a Motown-style groove more suggestive of the Vandellas and Marvelettes than of the Supremes.

Neither of these were big hits; but then, "Wayne/Dunbar," recording in a converted theater on Grand River Avenue with a core of new musicians and moonlighting Funk Brothers—including James Jamerson's backup, Bob Babbitt, who Eddie Holland says "was as close to James' feeling as anybody we found"—were just getting warmed up.

This was precisely what Gordy was afraid of, HDH doing elsewhere what they could have been doing at Motown. Which is why the uncertainties that fall of 1968 were indeed about more than money. With his reputation and dominion at stake in the coming war with HDH, it was imperative that someone, anyone, reestablish the enormous economic security blanket only the Supremes had proved they could provide.

Cee

And none too soon. Hard on the heels of the failure of "Forever Came Today" came two more flops. For some reason, Gordy released a pair of low-grade Supremes albums in August, both of which were just about dead on arrival. One, consisting of cover songs from the Barbra Streisand movie *Funny Girl*, was rushed out to beat the movie sound-track album but did a fraction of its business; at a pitiful 76,000 copies sold, it was easily the worst-selling Supremes album to date. The other, *Live at London's Talk of the Town*, a wan copy of *At the Copa* with Cindy Birdsong in and Flo Ballard out, was the usual fodder of hit medleys and show tunes—including Ross on full-throated lead on Flo's old show-stopper "People"—recorded on their recent tour of England. But it was only a more respectable failure, coming in at No. 57 (though nearly salvaged by reaching No. 6 on the R&B chart).

These flops convinced Gordy that HDH were right in one respect: He *did* need a "wider creative outlet"—not the semi-autonomous oper-ation HDH fancied but a fresher approach to developing material. Even so, whatever new process was found, it would begin and end with Gordy, with no room for flighty creative types getting in the way with their egos and personal agendas. The cause would be egalitarian—everyone under the thumb of Berry Gordy. He was solidifying all the operations in this way. For example, expunging the A&R department of its HDH traces, he changed its name to the Creative Division, which was headed not by a creative type but by Ralph Seltzer, the lawyer he trusted more than anyone.

Gordy wasn't so foolish as to believe he could do it all himself. This was 1968, not 1961. As well, he saw a choice opportunity to fill two needs at once: coupling a Supremes restoration with a greater role for the boys on the coast. While the important recordings were still going to take place in Studio A, for now he would be building a Motown West complex with another state-of-the-art studio, and he wanted the writers and producers encamped out there to be acclimated to a prime-time role. Thus, starting from scratch on the new Supremes song, he brought to Detroit Frank Wilson as well as R. Dean Taylor, a white Canadian emigré who'd recorded self-written songs for Motown's VIP label and collaborated on the Temptations' "All I Need" and the Four Tops' "I'll Turn to Stone."

When the L.A. boys got in, they were taken not to West Grand Boulevard or a hotel room but to a ballroom in the Pontchartrain Ho-tel, where Gordy had deposited two other white Motown writers, Deke Richards and British native Pam Sawyer, and old hand Hank Cosby, who had helped mold Stevie Wonder's material. As Gordy recalled it, "I told them we'd lock ourselves in until we came out with the right product," and they began right away working around the clock.

Actually, in those skull sessions Gordy played little part, disappearing for hours and coming back asking, "What you got?" The answer, for a day and a half, was: nothing. Gordy then took a seat at the piano and improvised some HDH-style chords, "with a sad, soulful feel," he would recall. That's when Sawyer, a very hip young woman who had previously written in the blue-eyed soul idiom for the Young Rascals, piped up, possibly semi-delirious from exhaustion, that the song be about an illegitimate child—"A love child!" she shouted.

No one thought this was either a remotely sane suggestion or, more important, one remotely appropriate for the princess-bride Supremes— except for the one person everyone assumed would be the first to object. Instead, Gordy stroked at his beard and said, "Love child. That's heavy. I like it."

That, in retrospect, may well have been the precise moment when the Supremes were saved and Motown proved it could get funky. The song that emerged from The Clan—which is what the song writers actually called themselves as a group, with a capital T and C, in a snarky send-up of that other clan, the one spelled with a K—would leave an indelible a marker of when rock got real; like "Eleanor Rigby," it was a prying eye into the soul of hopelessness, but with the extra sensitivity supplied by putting a human face and voice on what only "other people" were.

The lyrics were withering and sure-footed, the daring twist being that the bastard is a girl who sees herself reflected in others' eyes as a "hurt, scorned, rejected love child" and begs off sex with a demanding guy with the plaint "Don't think I don't need you / Don't think I don't wanna please you / But no child of mine will be wearing / The name of shame I been wearing" and "This love we're contemplating / Is worth the pain of waiting / We'll only end up hating the child we may be creating." All the verses, in fact, seemed to be written with a scalpel peeling back flesh: being born in "an old, cold rundown tenement slum," starting school in "a worn torn dress that somebody threw out," being "never quite as good, afraid, ashamed, misunderstood."

This was serious, dangerous stuff—for Gordy, like sticking his hand in a bonfire and hoping it wouldn't come back charred to the bone. While "Reflections" had widened Motown's thematic purview, it was still about love, albeit in ruins. The only other time he would have to consider the danger in a song was with "Cloud Nine," which he instinctively rejected as an obvious drug metaphor until Whitfield cajoled him to go with it. (In 1969, it would win Motown's first Grammy, as "Best R&B Vocal Group Performance.") "Love Child" was an even tougher call for Gordy with its all-too-literal parable of ignominy, but for the fact that he approved its construction—and that, with it, The Clan had hit a grand slam. And, now, it really was Gordy's own love child.

Accordingly, he appointed himself head Clansman and returned to the studio in earnest to work on the track on September 17, 19, and 20. Joining with the arranger Paul Riser, The Clan (the production end being all the writers but Sawyer, plus Gordy) kept the track rooted in the chugging HDH snare-bass-tambourine beat while vaulting into new directions with remarkable precision and cohesion. "Nothing short of miraculous," Alan Slutsky calls the mix of classic Motown, psychedelic soul, and proto-funk, with the low-register riffling guitar licks so ahead of the game that "they could have been used as is on Michael Jackson's *Thriller*."

The wonder is that all this didn't dissolve into mawk and mire. The song seemed almost tempered with strings and vibes swelling only to fall away for the darker lines, holding something back as if with the numbed emotion in Diana's brilliantly haunted lead vocal, then letting loose at the end as she affirms that, no matter, what, "I'll always love *you-ooo-ooo, you-ooo-ooo* . . . ," over fevered backing choruses of "Hold on, just a little bit longer, hold on."

Sadly for Mary and Cindy, Gordy had wanted them to sing backup on the song, as it was created for the Supremes. By now, though, Wilson was nearly as inclined to spite Gordy as Ballard had been, such was her resentment at being downgraded, and informed him she needed a vacation after months of nonstop touring. "Things were changing," she wrote in *Dreamgirl*, "and I felt like I was in limbo. I had no real home and felt that I needed to get away."

The truth was that Wilson, seeing what was coming, was buying a home in L.A. and wanted to keep it from Gordy, who hadn't made his own move yet. Neither was he okay with the vacation idea.

"Mary, you'd better work while you can," he told her, as nasty as ever.

Disappointed in her, but not really needing her, he gave her a last chance, boasting about the new song and how "hot" it was. The suddenly strong-willed Mary wouldn't relent, and off she went to the coast with a side trip to Mexico. Still playing romantic musical chairs, she went with old flame Duke Fakir. That meant Gordy would have to keep Cindy off the record, too, since he needed tightly knitted, practiced harmonies. And so, on what would be the biggest Supremes record in history, Diana Ross would be backed by the anonymous voices of the ubiquitous Andantes: Marlene Barrow, Jackie Hicks, and Gordy's first client at Motown, Louvain Demps.

As always, they would nail the assignment, superbly complementing moods both dark and bright, as Wilson partied in Acapulco and Birdsong sat at home, her one shot to matter as a Supreme dashed, not by Berry Gordy or Diana Ross but by Mary Wilson. Later, perhaps feeling the heat, Wilson would try to pin all the blame on Gordy, saying he had assured her "Love Child" was still being written, fooling her into believing she would do the vocal when she returned; staying on that script, she said that by being cut out of the song, Gordy had "sen[t] Cindy and me a message, namely, that Diana Ross was all they wanted."

Ce

When they would hear an early pressing of "Love Child," HDH did an aural double-take. "I said, 'Is that one of *ours*?'" Eddie Holland recalls. "I give Berry all the credit in the world. That was a *great* record. That's why Berry Gordy is a genius, man. We never thought of him as anything less. He got it all perfect: the melody, the lyrics, everything. He said, 'I'm gonna make a big hit record for the Supremes,' and that's what he did. I'll tell you what, we *wished* we could have made that one. The only question was if he could repeat it, keep it going, the way we did."

That The Clan wouldn't was perhaps unwittingly explained by Ross, who was not so knocked out by "Love Child." Telling why in *Secrets of a Sparrow*, she wrote of a disconnect she had for the post-HDH songs given the Supremes. "[T]hey weren't as wonderful as . . . 'Baby Love' and 'Stop! In the Name of Love' [which] had been written especially for us [rather than for] somebody else's life." For all the acting involved in singing "Love Child," she said, it "was like doing an audio movie." No matter how good on so many levels "Love Child" was, that quality Ross wrote of, the ligature that organically ties song to artist, was not there, though Lord knows Motown tried to create one.

The upshot was that it was Diana herself who asked for—and obediently granted—a change in the group's image to fit the new "self-awareness" motif. The results were on full view—the fullest ever, actually—when they went on the September 29 *Ed Sullivan Show* to break the song and, before millions of viewers, were seen in repose on the "stoop" of a painted facsimile of a ghetto street, Mary dangling a bare and quite nice leg from under a chocolate-brown shorts-suit, Cindy in a brown and white pantsuit, both barefooted, and—most shockingly—Diana looking every bit the street urchin, wearing a close-cropped Afro wig, a baggy yellow sweatshirt, tattered cut-offs, her legs like matchsticks, her feet also bare. Originally, all three Supremes were to appear like this and had rehearsed in matching yellow sweatshirts and cutoffs before it was decided that doing so would make Diana stand out less. If this was her idea of "ghetto chic" she was more than up to playing the part, etching pain in her eyes as she and the girls slowly, desultorily, shuffled their way across the set while lip-synching.

The very un-Supremely image, especially Diana's scrawny, scraggly appearance, was the talk of the pop world the next day—some were shocked, some merely amused by the preciousness of the high-fashion Supremes in their Halloween "ghetto chic" costumes a month early—and the reaction no doubt helped to light a bigger fire under the record, as Diana had cannily foreseen. Released a day later, backed by "Will This Be the Day," within three weeks "Love Child" was all over the radio. Distributors and station managers who might have had reservations about the rawness of the subject matter were swept up in a whirlpool that did the seemingly undoable —during the week of November 30 somehow dislodging the Beatles' "Hey Jude" from the top of the chart after nine weeks, for a two-week run of its own (as well as on the R&B chart), before bowing to Marvin Gaye's "I Heard It Through the Grapevine." It didn't fall out of the Top Forty for fifteen weeks, the longest run by any Supremes record.

Not one to let a good thing pass without milking it dry, Gordy whipped up an obligatory album titled *Love Child* for a December release. Except for the title track and the Ashford-Simpson "Some Things You Never Get Used To," it was mainly a surfeit of filler from the Motown vault, including two more A&S songs, "Keep an Eye" and "You Ain't Livin' Till You're Lovin'," though by far the most memorable today is "Can't Shake It Loose," co-written by George Clinton, making for a one-off marriage made in funk heaven—James Jamerson and the future "Dr. Funkenstein." (A decade later, Clinton would re-cut the song as "Field Maneuvers" with the ultimate funk brothers, Funkadelic.) For the cover of the album, the Supremes re-created the *Sulli-*

van milieu—Diana gazing out of a doorway of a "tenement slum," in the same yellow sweatshirt, while Wilson and Birdsong loitered in an alley, Mary leaning against a brick wall in a leather fringe halter and black pants, a barefooted Cindy in a black shirt, vest, and jeans.

Somehow, the cause survived the radical chic promulgated by people who would never have actually set foot in a ghetto doorway, and so did the Supremes, who, by the time they returned to the Sullivan stage on January 5, 1969, to again sing "Love Child," had removed the ghetto from the chic. Only Diana still had the Afro, with Mary and Cindy back to the usual high-fashion wigs. They all wore tight hot-pink pantsuits and smart high heels and belted out a live, up-tempo version on a mod, criss-crossed ladder set, Mary and Cindy doing a hip-grinding frug, with Mary seeming almost giddy singing the song she'd never recorded.

Even before then, the ghetto shtick was tabled; clearly having been meant for a very short run, it was anathema to the Supremes' cause, the coiffed and manicured one—and to their itinerary. In mid-November they went off on a major European tour, with stops in Scandinavia, Belgium, Ireland, Germany, and England, including two command performances at the London Palladium for the Royal Family—the sweatshirt, fringe, and jeans not part of their wardrobe. Of that jaunt, Wilson would fondly remember playing Stockholm's Bern's Café and seeing Sweden's Princess Christina and her upper-class mates get piss-faced and dance on table tops—along with more intimate moments with Tom Jones in Munich, their favorite tryst rendezvous spot. On this jet-set carousel ride, the "hood" seemed much further than halfway around the planet.

Not that the always contentious British press would let them get away with their quick-change artistry from upper crust to ghetto and back again. As if expecting them to come out wearing dashikis and raising Black Power salutes, several blowhard Brits blistered them with the old "sellout" charge—"Go to Church, Baby!" one of the papers headlined, as if all the "Love Child" imagery couldn't do as much to "sanctify" the Supremes as a good turn in a gospel choir.

However, the Brits were no slouches when it came to rank hypocrisy. Some of the same writers who were offended by the girls' lack of sincerity took to slamming Ross for getting too "political" at the second Palladium show, when, before the assembled likes of Prince Charles, Princess Margaret and Lord Snowden, and the Queen Mother, she did her Martin Luther King soliloquy during the performance of "Somewhere," far more comfortably and vigorously than she had that terrifying night on *The Tonight Show* hours after King's murder. Practically squealing, she cried out, "Free at last! Great God almighty, free at last!" Despite the journalists' claim that such behavior was somehow improper, the Royals had actually gotten to their feet and joined a standing ovation that didn't die down for two minutes.

Still, one defender of the realm mystifyingly wrote in *The Daily Mirror* the next day that the moment was "not the high drama it was intended to be" and drew "the coolest reception of the evening." Another stooge, in *The Guardian*, wrote of the "rather mawkish tribute that seemed inappropriate for the occasion."

Indeed, the Ross who braved the stuffed shirts was at her peak as a crusader on this trip, spouting some highly charged rhetoric. For a time, too, she threatened not to go out on stage at the Palladium at all because the opening act was a thirty-member troupe called The Black and White Minstrels who, incredibly, performed in blackface and white gloves! That this effrontery could have been placed by the promoters on the bill of a Supremes show was yet another example of how little the British really understood of the cause they so wanted to champion. Ross, barely believing what she saw when the troupe went through its Jim Crow–style paces in dress rehearsal, asked, "They're making fun of Negroes, aren't they?"

She was persuaded to bite her tongue and go on, but before leaving jolly old England she was in a snit, tearing into the Minstrels as "disrespectful." Now stoked and uncontainable, when she was asked about where she fit into the "black movement," she quickly corrected, "It's a *people's* movement," and, as she went on, approvingly name-dropped no less than a Black Panther, saying airily that "[w]e should listen to Stokely Carmichael. He has a good philosophy," not filling in exactly what that might be. Then, an encore: "James Brown says something and I agree with it—I'm black and I am *proud* of it!"

But such noble, or naive, babble, like the sartorial and thematic symbolism of "Love Child," was not to become a habit. The last gasp of the Supremes' ghetto fable was, by necessity, the follow-up to "Child," from which every last ounce of profit needed to be wrung. The song, "I'm Livin' in Shame," was really "Love Child: The Sequel," set in a "college town" where she found a "new identity"—of being "born elite, with maids and servants at my feet." Having "married a guy" and "living high," she lied that her mother "died on a weekend trip to Spain" rather than letting "my uptown friends see her" in her "dirty raggedy scarf" and "stockings rolled to her feet"—before word came that "Momma" died, never having seen her grandson and begging to "see me by her side." In her guilt she could only wail, "Momma, I miss you. Won't you forgive me mom for all the wrong I have done."

Apparently out of new ideas, The Clan lifted these suds from the 1959 Lana Turner tear-jerker *Imitation of Life*, even appropriating from the flick the hook "Momma, momma, momma can you hear me?" and fitting the song with another grand-scale production, again with the Andantes as the choir backing up Diana. But cutting it was no easy chore. Wrestling with how to make it believable, Gordy and his underlings needed six sessions over late November and December, constantly re-doing tracks. When it was released on January 6, 1969, with "I'm So Glad I Got Somebody" on the B-side, many wouldn't be able to stifle a chuckle, the biggest from Diana's classic line, "Came a telegram / Momma passed away while making homemade jam." The Supremes' *éclat* nevertheless lifted it to No. 10 in March; but, by then, the ghetto pandering was already history.

In fact, Gordy had veered away from inner-city blues to Hollywood spit 'n' polish. Months before, Shelly Berger's connections to George Schlatter and Ed Friendly came through in a huge way, yielding a critical milestone for his "MoWest" strategy. The two producers, then riding high on the hip slapstick of *Laugh-In*, were able to leverage backing from NBC to produce an hour-long special to air in early December featuring Motown's two big-gun acts, the Supremes and the Temptations. The genesis of the special, as well as the virtual audition for it, had come about when the two groups performed several show-tune duets on *The Ed Sullivan Show* in mid-'68, forging a palpable chemistry between them (though not with David Ruffin, who, because Diana was so worried that he'd outshine her in the battle of lead singers, ordered all the vocals to be done in her key, forcing Ruffin to strain to hit the higher notes).

While the special was being cemented with the NBC brass, Motown went to work, using it as a fulcrum for a wider Supremes-Temptations strategy. As early as May 1968, in fact, sessions had begun for a joint album targeted to precede the airing of the TV show. These sessions—with most of the Temptations' leads now taken by ex-Contour Dennis Edwards, whose gruff, pleading voice was similar to Ruffin's, if not as palatable—continued through the summer. Completed after the TV show had already been recorded, it was released on November 8 as *Diana Ross & the Supremes Join the Temptations,* to an enthusiastic reception.

Tuning up for the TV show, the Supremes and Temptations had played a week together at the Carousel Theater in Framingham, Massachusetts. Then they came to L.A., taping the show on August 23 at the NBC Burbank studios. It was called "TCB"—shorthand for the in-vogue neologism "takin' care of business," forever burned into the pop cultural vernacular by Aretha Franklin in her '67 mega-hit "Respect," when she managed to use both forms, singing, "Take Care of TCB!" Marking Gordy's entree into the Hollywood inner sanctum, the project was produced by Schlatter-Friendly in conjunction with the newly minted Motown Productions, which Gordy put under the supervision of Suzanne DePasse, a stunning 21-year-old from Harlem with long, sweeping brown hair whose only experience in the business was as a promoter for the hip New York disco Cheetah—yet another Gordy "hunch" that many, including Diana, assumed was more about pulchritude than proficiency. (An assumption proven wrong: DePasse is still with the company, in the same job, to this day.)

To the other entertainers, it should have been called "TCMR"—"Takin' Care of Miss Ross." Just those two imperious words—"Miss Ross"—became embedded in most everyone's craw, as they had already for Mary and Cindy. Per Gordy's order, production people could address her only in that way; no such directive was ever applied to the other Supremes or to the Temptations. For the guys, it was all the proof they needed that while they shared the billing, they were not equals. Indeed, though the show was certainly a boon to them, allowing them to break out to a wider audience (especially now that Gordy had shunted them into the same class-act venues as the Supremes), their primary value was to balance off the girls' appeal and keep them "real" for black record-buyers.

Indeed, it struck the Tempts that quality had rubbed off the Supremes in the years since both groups had ridden those rickety buses on the Motortown Revues.

OTIS WILLIAMS: Well, the first thing was that Florence wasn't there, and for me particularly, being so close to Florence and knowing how far she'd fallen and how upset she was by it, it was hard for me to look at them the same. This is nothing against Mary and Cindy, everybody loved them, they were always sweethearts. But to be truthful, to me it wasn't the Supremes without Flo.

Then there was that "Miss Ross" shit. We had a hard time with that. I remember Melvin, who knew Diana from way back. I mean, she used to call *him* "Mr. Franklin"!

And Melvin, he told us, "From now on, call me Mr. Franklin." There was a movie out about that time, *In the Heat of the Night*, with Sidney Poitier. He played Detective [Virgil] Tibbs and his tag line in that was "Call me Mr. Tibbs!" So when someone would say, "Hey, Otis," I'd say, "Call me Mr. Williams." Eddie would say, "Call me Mr. Kendricks."

See, that was the only way we could deal with it, because it was bullshit. We'd known Diana since she was a scared little girl. She'd been our "little sis." We'd stopped her from quittin' the business! Paul and Eddie, man, without them there wouldn't never have been no Supremes! And now even *we* were told to call her Miss Ross! Our reaction would be like, you know, we got your Miss Ross right here. [Laughter]

I think she was still the Diana we knew and loved, still a scared little girl. But she didn't want to *feel* that when she went on stage. She had to believe, for herself, that she was a star, that she could do anything. So that's when she *became* Miss Ross. And, hey, I didn't begrudge her that. Look how far she'd come—she *was* a star, one of the biggest in the world, she did that all by herself. The rest of us, we were just singers. We could live with that, but Diana couldn't. And so when she was in that head, she was like a cat marking all the walls, you know, her territory.

Her "territory" during "TCB" were the sets, the main one being a multi-level, circular Plexiglas platform that looked like a flying saucer in a Truffaut movie, towering above the orchestra on seemingly nothing but air. She also wanted to exclude from her realm Suzanne DePasse, whom she suspected of either having or wanting to have an affair with Gordy, and thus saved her most noxious behavior for her, ordering her around like a go-fer or showily dismissing her from sight. Once, when DePasse approached with something important she said she needed to discuss, Diana barked at her, "Can't you see I'm busy? Come back later!"

"Sorry, Miss Ross," DePasse humbly acquiesced, to Diana's great enjoyment, given that when Berry was around she acted like DePasse's closest chum.

On her part, Mary Wilson felt lower on the stepladder than De-Passe, in Diana and Berry's eyes. In fact, Suzanne's arrival confused her, too. "It was hard enough," she recalled, "that none of us had any input [on] the show." That DePasse did, even if no one knew what it was, "indicated how drastically things at Motown were changing. [She] didn't mind telling us what to do, but she didn't dare cross Diane." As for who was really running the show, however, Wilson said that "seven of us were extras."

The confirmation of that seemed to come when an elaborate song-and-dance number around the bossa nova tune "Mas Que Nada" featuring Wilson, Birdsong, Kendricks, and Otis and Paul Williams was performed live for the audience—but was then cut. "This must be the Diana Ross Show!" a disgusted Paul Williams thundered when he was told, taking for granted that Ross simply wouldn't permit Mary and Cindy to show their stuff independently of her. With bitterness billowing everywhere, Wilson said, the "whole situation was a mess [that] seemed to get worse every day."

Even when Diana tried to act collegial it went wrong. During one break, noticing that someone had brought Kendricks some fast food, she mewed in mock indignation, "How'd *you* rate that?" and gave him, according to Otis Williams, a light, playful slap on the cheek. All around, people stood and stared, thinking it was for real.

But while Kendricks, who'd once had a fling with Ross himself, didn't take it for what it wasn't, and never in his life would have a bad word to say about Ross, Wilson still insists that Diana had "gone too far," providing Mary with one more reason why "[i]t was getting harder and harder for me even to want to be around her"—the same sort of overreaction that seems to be common in much of the Motown literature; J. Randy Taraborrelli, for instance, darkly projects in *Call Her Miss Ross* that Kendricks, who died in 1992, "has never said what happened between the two of them to anger her so," perhaps because nothing did.

For all the static, real and imagined, of the ten days of rehearsing and shooting, "TCB" was a tour de force for both groups, Berry Gordy, and particularly Diana Ross—who was unseen in only a half-dozen of the fifteen numbers crammed into forty-one minutes of airtime, and had her own separate "introduction" in addition to that given the Supremes. There were seven Supremes songs either alone or in medleys; a Supremes medley of contemporary pop songs; a Ross solo on a painful "African Vogue" number in which she wore tribal garb and undulated some kind of native dance; the Ross soliloquy on "Somewhere"; and group duets on several Temptations hits (but not on Supremes' hits), and on "Respect" and "The Impossible Dream." The only time Diana receded, sort of, was to share the lead with Mary on a medley of "Mrs. Robinson" and other pop tunes.

Gordy of course was ecstatic about the results, with good reason; but the legendary Gordy reward system was most selective. Weeks later, Otis Williams would find out that "Berry gave them special gifts for doing such a great job on the show, while we didn't even rate a simple thank-you. We just did our job and picked up the check and that was it."

Still, in the run-up to the broadcast of "TCB," the Tempts profited more handsomely when Motown released a single from the *Join* album, "I'm Gonna Make You Love Me," a cover of a modest 1967 hit by Dee Dee Warwick written and produced by Kenny Gamble, Leon Huff, and Jerry Ross, the first two of whom would shortly establish a sort of "Motown East" with Philadelphia International Records. The song had already been covered in '68 by Madeline Ball, but Frank Wilson and Nick Ashford buffed and fluffed it with an arching string and horn arrangement, an intro lifted from Jimmy Ruffin's "What Becomes of the Broken-Hearted," traded leads by Ross and Kendricks, and solemnly spoken love affirmations by Ross and Otis Williams.

Released on November 21, just as "Love Child" was taking off, it soared to No. 2 pop and R&B in mid-December, coinciding with the buzz generated by "TCB" as one of the most-watched television shows of the year and spawning *another* Supremes-Temptations work, the soundtrack of the TV show. The latter, released the day after the show was aired (with all the numbers minus "Afro Vogue"), one-upped the previous LP by going to the top of the pop and R&B album charts early in 1969.

Ce

Gordy wasn't through squeezing every drop out of the two groups yet, but he could sit back for a delirious moment during the Christmas

holiday and savor that he had a Beatle-impressive *five* records in the Top
Ten—"I Heard It Through the Grapevine," Stevie Wonder's "For Once
in My Life," "Love Child," "I'm Gonna Make You Love Me," and
"Cloud Nine"—with "I'm Livin' in Shame" in the hopper for January
and the "TCB" album nearing the roof. And with "Love Child" the
fifth-biggest-selling record of the year, behind "Hey Jude," "Green
Tambourine," "Love in Blue," and "Mrs. Robinson" (and ahead of, to
name two, "Lady Madonna" and "Hello I Love You").

Gordy as well as the Supremes were on a roll no one could have expected only six months after "Some Things You Never Get Used To."
The girls weren't just back on top—they were hotter than ever, their appeal cutting across the demographic spectrum. With their Hollywood
trappings, it was as if they'd replaced Joey Heatherton as the first-call
whenever a wheezing warhorse needed a "happening" female act. Not
counting *Ed Sullivan*, from late '68 to mid-'69 they made guest shots
on Bing Crosby and Bob Hope TV specials, and hosted *The Hollywood
Palace* (or rather, Ross hosted, with Wilson and Birdsong allowed to say
exactly nothing). As well, Diana guest-starred with Rowan and Martin
and no less than Lucille Ball on a Dinah Shore NBC special produced
by Schlatter-Friendly called "Like Hep!"—during which she was treated
poorly by the aging, choleric Ball, who ordered a servile Diana around
like a servant.

To the survivors of "TCB," that could only have been considered
turnabout being fair play.

twenty-two

THE
LAST
MILE

Mary Wilson had become so disenchanted with Gordy and Ross that early in 1968 she broke protocol and began calling Flo every now and then, just to say hello. In the early spring, when Flo had come home to promote her first ABC record, Mary got the idea to bury the lingering bitterness between Flo and her two arch-enemies. Gordy was about to hold a big pool party at Gordy Manor and Mary, wanting to play good guy, suggested that Flo come with her. "It'll be great," she burbled. Flo, who had a hard enough time swallowing her issues with Mary, reeled at the thought.

"Mary," she said, "you know that's a bad idea. Forget it, will you?"

"C'mon, let's do it. Don't worry about Berry and Diane. All your friends will be there. We'll be with you."

It went against every one of her instincts, but Flo did want to heal old wounds—she had confessed to Tommy that she found it difficult to feel hatred for Diana, that she still "cared for her"—and so she went. Later she told Tony Tucker with relish that when she waltzed into the party, "You could have heard a pin drop in a bunch of goose feathers," such was the shock among the Motown crowd, many of whom had urged her to stick it to Gordy when they partied at her house, but who on Gordy's turf could only stare at her—too scared of Gordy, as Flo would put it, to say word one.

Gordy and Ross must have been more than a bit shocked, too, but neither raised an objection as she walked around in her flower-print summer dress. But they kept a wary eye glued to her all the while from across the pool, and, as Wilson recalled, "There was an undercurrent of tension." Finally, Diana sashayed over and asked how she was.

"Pretty good, you?" Flo answered pleasantly enough.

But then Diana began to act like, well, Diana. Slyly mentioning that she'd heard Flo's record had failed, she asked how her career was going.

"Fine," Flo said, her jaw tensing.

Diana continued making small talk but began walking from Flo to Berry and back again, as if relaying some sort of top-secret information to him, which made Flo's insides grind. Settling onto a stool at the cabana bar, Flo began to tipple more heavily to calm herself, and was fairly loaded when Diana again floated over and said, "Oh, isn't that the same dress you wore five years ago? It's amazing it still fits"—a classic Ross-ism. From anyone else, the comment could conceivably have been complimentary, if meant, say, in the sense that it was "amazing" the then-pregnant-and-showing Flo could fit into one of her dresses from the old days. But because it was said by Diana, it was heard only as a slight about Flo's weight—which, if so, was a truly dim-witted thing to say about a pregnant woman.

When Diana floated away, Flo, about to boil over—something Gordy and Ross wanted to happen—called out to Mary, loudly enough to deafen the music being played on loudspeakers, "If she comes back over here, I'm gonna kick her!" Or at least that's Wilson's version; Tucker says the way Flo told it, it came out this way: "If that black bitch comes over here one more time, I'm gonna kick her black ass!"

As the guests went mute and turned to observe the gathering storm, Mary anticipated the worst. While she perhaps might not have been overly upset that Gordy and Ross had been embarrassed, her priority was getting Flo out of there.

"Flo, I think it's time to go," she said, an instant before Gordy bellowed from across the pool, "Who brought that woman here?" and, "Whoever did better get her out of my house!"

Flo, by now very drunk, may have wanted to fight back, but when she got up off her stool her legs gave way and she half-collapsed, her fall broken by Mary who held her upright and walked her off the property to Mary's car—a drill Wilson had become quite practiced at through the years—and drove her back home.

Flo chewed out Mary for taking her into this latest humiliation—the worst part for her being that Mary again had failed to say a word on her behalf when things got ugly and personal. Despite Wilson's protestations otherwise, and her recent independent streak, Flo believed Mary was conning herself, that she was "just scared to death of Berry Gordy. . . . She's scared for her own financial future because Gordy's drilled it into her head that she can't sing anymore." Even more harshly, she told Tucker, "Mary's just brainwashed" and "just a puppet." If that was so, then Wilson was living with her own humiliation.

All that Wilson would admit to in *Dreamgirl* was that after the pool party fiasco she had "curs[ed] myself for trying to make us all friends again." That, she now knew, would never happen, because "[w]e had all suffered wounds that would not heal."

Cee

So lofty was the status of the Supremes in 1968 that after the Martin Luther King rites of mourning and tribute Gordy decided to inject the girls into the national political discourse. Though he had backed Bobby Kennedy for the Democratic nomination, after yet another national trauma when Kennedy was gunned down in the kitchen of the Ambassador Hotel on June 6 after winning the California primary, Gordy felt it was his duty to endorse Vice-President Hubert Humphrey. That meant the Supremes had to as well, whether they cared to or not.

On July 23, a month before Humphrey would claim the nomination as police ran wild clubbing anti-war demonstrators in the streets of Chicago, Gordy arranged for the girls to publicly endorse Humphrey at a press conference at New York's Waldorf-Astoria. As was the case with all public events of this or any kind, the publicity effects were carefully gauged; here, the Supremes would reap more credibility as mature, politically aware artists.

As popping flashbulbs coated them with streaks of lights, they posed in brightly colored mini-dresses with a beaming Humphrey—who likely didn't know "Baby Love" from "Rub a Dub," but was aware that he needed to shore up his support among black voters—and Diana read a prepared statement written by Gordy saying the group had "thoroughly research[ed] his record and talk[ed] to him for hours and hours."

Buying not a word of this tripe, hardboiled political reporters began bombarding her with questions about issues. Not expecting to answer any questions, Diana didn't know what to say, and seeing her discomfort Humphrey shielded her by babbling that they had "discussed a greater emphasis on urban policy" and that "Miss Ross is very interested in the quality of life in the United States."

"Yes, yes I am," she agreed meekly.

It went on like this, with Humphrey having to intercede after each question and Diana assenting to whatever he said. But after Humphrey admitted they hadn't discussed Vietnam she felt she had to add something. "He said he wants to stop the shooting and talk later," she offered—in truth not a bad answer, in contrast to Nixon's inscrutable "secret peace plan" and the endless Paris "peace talks" that hadn't stopped the shooting. But it was too easy for the press to relegate the whole affair as the "Diana Ross show." Still, on the premise that any attention is good attention, it was a success for Motown, whose denizens could read in the August 2 issue of *Time* that "[l]ast week in Manhattan when Diana Ross & the Supremes endorsed Humphrey, aides called a special press conference to announce the event."

Seeing how humiliated Ross had been, Gordy apologized for putting her into such a vulnerable position. But the Supremes were too valuable to forfeit as a symbolic totem in his political and social grandstanding. When he made the scene in April 1969 at a $1,000-a-plate Beverly Hills fundraiser to pay off Bobby Kennedy's campaign debts, the girls were again beside him.

At least on the matter of the '68 presidential race, the last laugh went to Flo Ballard. During the fall campaign, Tommy Chapman, looking for some way to pitch Flo, thought it would be an effective counterpoint to the Supremes' Humphrey endorsement to offer to Nixon's people the "other" Supreme's endorsement. Nixon may have known even less about rock and roll than Humphrey, but he had done a cameo turn on *Laugh-In*, laboring in vain to sound cool uttering in puzzlement, "Sock it to *me?*" Besides, *any* black support for him was welcome; indeed, on the very short list of black celebrities who backed him, Flo was not far down from Sammy Davis Jr. and Lionel Hampton.

And she was not forgotten. At the inauguration on January 20, 1969, it had to be a moment of delirium for Flo Ballard that she was standing where the Supremes would have been had they chosen right in the campaign: up on the stage singing for a well-heeled, powerful, and white crowd—a Berry Gordy kind of crowd.

After the inauguration, Flo and Tommy realized that they'd spent most of the money they had been able to get from Leonard Baun, who as treasurer of their Talent Management company had vowed to toe the line against profligate spending, for their own good. Now, having blown thousands of dollars of their "allowance" and the $15,000 ABC advance on the Manhattan penthouse, gigs like the unfortunate Atlantic City horror show, travel, and the gowns Flo wore at the inauguration, they dropped in on Baun's office for what they thought would be a routine request for funds; they were, after all, president and vice-president of the company.

Baun first tried to dissuade them, saying the money was tied up in high-interest accounts and investments that would cost them large penalties for withdrawals. When they persisted, he seemed to forget that line and instead turned to berating them for wasteful, irresponsible spending. Then he insisted he'd had to spend money trying to help Flo's career, such as the $5,548 that went to Lou Zito when he promised to get her bookings. Then, with real *chutzpah*, Baun criticized them for signing with ABC, because it didn't have the "right concept" for her. To their utter disbelief, he said Flo should have *stayed at Motown*! Gordy, he ventured, "had the right personnel to handle her," confessing that he "didn't know [that] at the beginning."

Flo knew there was more to it than regrets about past deals. Baun was clearly blaming her and Tommy for a reason, which soon followed when he flat-out told them that all their money was gone—or would be when the IRS was finished dunning her for her back taxes and the financial attorneys he'd hired had been paid. The tax issue, of course, had been the great Damoclean sword hanging over her head, given that Baun was unable to obtain the earnings statements from Motown that would have allowed him to blunt a huge tab. Not only was every penny in the company account scrutinized by the IRS, said Baun, but she owed hundreds of thousands more. Insisting that he was working on reducing the debt, he asked them to leave it to him because if Flo wasn't careful she could go to prison for years for tax evasion.

The Chapmans felt numb, nearly unable to move or speak. That this was the first they'd heard about any such consequences made them suspicious that Baun was handing them a line of bull. But that would mean Baun had stolen their money, and they didn't want to believe it; more critically, the idea of jail scared them to death. Seeing them waver, Baun suddenly remembered that he did have the $5,000 for the gowns she'd never been given, in a separate cash account, and said he would withdraw it for her. With that, they agreed to stick with Baun and not press the money issue.

By April, however, not having seen the five grand, they went back to Baun. Flo told him she didn't want to hear any more bull and to hand over to them all of the company's financial records, bankbooks, withdrawal receipts, and copies of the Motown agreements, which Flo had not read in full. Baun produced some of these, but said he didn't have them all, that other attorneys working on the tax case had taken them. Flo had had enough of Baun. What with two children to feed and clothe, a mortgage, car payments, and bills as far as the eye could see, she had recently taken to borrowing from friends to get by, and Tommy had returned to driving (though not for Motown, contrary to what he said Gordy had promised). Desperate as she was, she could think clearly enough to figure that Leonard Baun had swindled her. Right there on the spot she fired him as her manager and as treasurer of Talent Management.

For Baun, this would not bring about a marked life change. If she was right about him, he'd abandoned his responsibility to her long ago, having cleaned her out and left her with a mountain of debt—but he had little to worry about in the way of amercement since for decades victimized artists had recovered about as little from finagling managers as from exploitive record companies, and for the same reason: onerous contracts.

That didn't stop Flo from trying. Aided by her brother Willie, she began a full-on crusade to make Baun pay. Over the course of months, then years, she would tell her tale of woe to anyone who might help, the police, prosecutors, the Michigan State Bar Association, the state attorney general, even the FBI and black political figures like Congressman John Conyers and Julian Bond. But the outcome was similar to the blanket resistance she faced getting her records played: No one wanted to listen. Neither did lawyers want to represent her on a contingency basis, asking instead for money up front. One who did come aboard requested documents from Baun, was rebuffed, and quit. Her own bank, the Commonwealth, refused to let her examine records pertaining to the account or to the Motown settlement, which only Baun had access to. To get those she'd need a subpoena, but how could she obtain one with no lawyer?

Ballard's plight found its way into the press in mid-'69. Only a few months before, her story was still being played not as paradise lost but as one merely in pause. In a February *Ebony* article, "FORMER SUPREME TALKS—A LITTLE," Flo, tiptoeing along the Motown line, explained her departure from the group with "Oh, I was just tired of traveling so much and wanted to settle down"—the same line, the story noted, that she "has used for 18 months. . . . Nobody has been able to get beyond 'that answer.'" Hardly seeming to be suffering, she was photographed happily holding the twins as she stood beside Tommy, wearing an "at-home gown" with "ranch mink sleeves" and at ease in her home with its "feel of Oriental splendor, crystal chandeliers [and] a large round shell-topped table suspended from the ceiling by a brass chain."

At the time, both of Flo's records had been, she admitted, "flops, just plain flops," but the ABC deal still wasn't dead and she vowed to "hit the road hard. . . . My husband has lots of things lined up for me." After all, she reasoned, the Supremes had endured many "flops" before finding success. Tommy chirped in, "Flo's in for some really big things . . . college dates, TV, everything."

As for the suggestion that "Motown gave her a fantastic sum of money to relinquish all claims," she laughed, saying that she was "far from being a millionaire," but that she and Gordy were "very cordial to each other . . . he's a very nice man." Lying that she didn't know about the name change to feature Ross until after she "decided to quit," she denied there'd been any "fights" with Diana, merely "arguments and things, just like sisters," and, "They're doing their thing and Flo Ballard is going to do hers."

Now, in early summer, no "really big things" were happening and she was in debt up to her eyeballs: Because Baun hadn't paid any of her back taxes, the IRS put liens on her house and car as collateral as she began to make restitution herself, the money coming partly from Tommy's job and whatever else the Ballard family could bring in. But most of it was from selling off her jewelry and designer clothing.

By the end of the decade she'd helped define, visitors to the house would find her tramping around in old, torn housecoats and dust-trap slippers in drafty, nearly completely empty rooms, dressing the twins in secondhand-store rags. The basement nightclub was now a dark, deserted catacomb. She did, however, seem to have enough to keep the liquor cabinets filled.

She also was making noises about going public with Berry Gordy's "dirty laundry," though it's unclear what she could have had on him beyond the Ross affair and the Mob rumors, both of which everyone already knew about; most likely she meant the details of her firing, since she'd begun talking of writing a "tell-all" book, which surely would have made Gordy look bad but could do little lasting damage since the Supremes were about to be recast anyway with Ross's impending exit. With all those thoughts swimming in her head, the last thing she seemed to want was to sing.

In early July 1969, the *Detroit Free Press*, following up its own optimistic take on Ballard the year before, ran a story titled "FORMER SUPREME SUFFERS LONG FALL FROM STARDOM." It morosely told of Ballard being "flat broke" and "deserted by her husband," and claimed that an offer had come to Baun for Flo to record again and that the Chapmans turned it down. Whether any of it beyond her being broke was accurate—Tommy's regular desertions of Flo, for instance, had become something of a joke to her; so soon would he come crawling back that she'd tell her family, "Just leave the door open for him"—or lie after lie planted by Baun to make her look bad, Flo's pride was hurt. Scrounging up enough cash to hire a lawyer, she and Tommy filed a defamation lawsuit against the paper asking for $10 million in damages and an apology.

That was just another delusion. Not only would they get nowhere with the suit, but by the time they dropped it in October 1970—the same month that Flo would make her legal move against Motown—she wouldn't be able to argue that she wasn't in an even worse way.

While Flo was trying to keep afloat in Detroit, the Supremes had found some California grass. Carrying out Gordy's westward-ho plans—which were accelerated when Gordy Manor, in spite of its many alarms, was burglarized and ransacked, with expensive pieces of furniture and Persian rugs ruined, leaving Gordy to rant, "I've had it with Detroit!" though he had already given up on it—Ross and Wilson had, like him, moved into homes in the Hollywood Hills. Gordy's, naturally, took opulence to burlesque excess, with an impressive estate bought from comedian Tommy Smothers that came complete with a stable grounds and even a moat around the property. Mary's was a spectacular spired, glass-paneled ranch with a kidney-shaped pool out back. Diana found a mansion just down the hill from Gordy's, and while it was being refurbished she took a rented home nearby. Cindy, meanwhile, made do in an apartment in Hollywood, living there with her boyfriend and future husband, a dental salesman named Charles Hewlett, while awaiting the closing on a house in Benedict Canyon next door to Diahann Carroll.

Diana and Mary left their families to continue living in their homes on Buena Vista, and Gordy kept Gordy Manor as a place to hang his hat during what could now only be described as business trips back to Detroit—which was how the Supremes' trips back to Motown could be described as well, for sessions in Studio A deemed to be worthy of a single release, although Wilson and Birdsong were left off of those trips so that Diana could lay down her vocals with the Andantes on the backing track.

However, Hitsville sessions began to wither after Gordy gave the go-ahead to erect the MoWest complex in a modern, two-story brick office complex with an atrium on the roof at 6464 Sunset Boulevard. A new Studio A was built to Gordy's demanding acoustic specifications on the first floor by his West Coast engineer, Guy Costa, nephew of the famous producer and arranger Don Costa; a second studio, to be used mainly for overdubbing and mixing, was erected on the second floor. Musicians who'd worked in the original Studio A would come into the new one and do a double-take, seeing bits and pieces they knew had been taken from the old shop.

One of the more recent session players, guitarist Dennis Coffey, whose fuzzy feedback licks were heard most notably on the Temptations' psychedelic funk records, recalled: "I saw a drum baffle, a sound separator, and a familiar microphone or two sitting in a corner, and I wondered why Motown had moved all that stuff to L.A. It felt really strange seeing it here, two thousand miles from home in sunny California, where almost everything else was brand new and unfamiliar."

Plainly, Gordy was not going to leave the future of Motown to chance; he had seen enough proof of a blessed voodoo while making music in the Hitsville snakepit to leave behind the tools of the magic. It was the beginning of what would become a wholesale dismantling of 2648 West Grand Boulevard.

And yet most of what the Supremes recorded in L.A. were slapdash albums meant to cash in on the group's still-strong brand name and move as much product as possible, with or without a major hit—a commodity that would become rarer after "I'm Livin' in Shame." This was not exactly how Gordy wanted it, but he was comforted by the fact that albums were far more market-friendly in 1969 than in 1964. It also didn't hurt that the providential teaming of his two biggest acts kept spilling forth ready-made albums—two more of which would come out in the fall, including the soundtrack of the second Supremes-Temptations TV special.

Not incidental to the sudden reliance on albums was the dearth of solid single material, the inevitable result of The Clan's dismantlement—thus answering Eddie Holland's question about whether they could create a continuum of hits. After "I'm Livin' in Shame," Gordy decided to shuffle them to other projects. With arguably the most important Clansman (other than himself), Deke Richards, he formed a new coterie, airily dubbed The Corporation, whose priority was to develop material for the exciting new pubescent group he'd recently signed to Motown—the Jackson 5.

They had been "discovered" not by Diana Ross but by the Motown group Bobby Taylor and the Vancouvers—who had been signed to Motown after Mary Wilson and Flo Ballard saw them perform in '65 when the Supremes were in Vancouver. Seeing the kiddie act at Chicago's Regal Theater, Bobby Taylor (whose guitar player and main songwriting partner in the group was Tommy Chong, of future Cheech and Chong fame) raved about them to Suzanne DePasse, who, in turn, auditioned them. Gordy was so knocked out that he immediately put the Jackson brothers on a fast track.

Having proved his point by propping the Supremes up—way up— without the help of HDH, Gordy had no reason to divert valuable assembly-line manpower to a model about to be redesigned without its most popular feature. In truth, through most of 1969 there was no real urgency about fitting the group with another chart-topper. Because word of Ross's imminent departure had been leaked to death in the media, even absent an official announcement from Motown the girls' schedule of appearances was construed by fans as a kind of farewell tour, a victory lap that could easily get by on "Love Child," nostalgic medleys of their hits, and vacuous show tunes.

They were, to be sure, certified. With Ross and Wilson now a ripe 25, showbiz veterans, even cultural icons, they and Gordy could savor a status that he would have considered a calumny in 1961—middle of the road. And so entrenched that within a new rock idiom—oldies but goodies—their legacy was already intact, even if they never had another hit. Dissecting this baby boomer–fed phenomenon, the March 22, 1968, issue of *Time*, in an article titled "Tapping the Roots," reported that "[r]adio stations, courting the lucrative advertising market of 18-to-34-year-olds who grew up on rock 'n' roll, [are] carefully balanc[ing] their play list of new releases with selected classics of the genre (examples: the Platters' "The Great Pretender," Chuck Berry's "Roll Over Beethoven," the Everly Brothers' "Bye Bye Love"). 'For the young married adult,' explains one radio executive, 'the so-called middle-of-the-road music is no longer Tony Bennett but Elvis Presley, no longer the Andrews Sisters but the Supremes.'"

The girls did cut a mass of songs during the year, but nothing was deemed remotely close to a decent single; some of these tracks found their way onto two albums of new material that were released in '69, the first being the May issue of *Let the Sunshine In*—appending late-model Motown pop-funk like Smokey Robinson's "The Composer" and the Gordy-Cosby "No Matter What Sign You Are" to covers like the Gamble-Huff "Hey Western Union Man," the Bacharach-David "Let the Music Play," and Sly Stone's "Everyday People." What didn't make the cut was bagged, most permanently, never to see the light even in latter-day compilations and box-sets. To at least keep the Supremes' presence on the charts, Gordy cherry-picked tracks from their albums. The first new release of the year, on February 20, was "I'll Try Something New," a Smokey Robinson tune produced by Frank Wilson and Deke Richards for *Diana Ross & the Supremes Join the Temptations*, a perfectly charming ballad reminiscent of the Tempts' "You're My Everything," with a tropical xylophone-conga intro and a diaphanous, building string arrangement.

Next was the March 27 release of "The Composer," another Smokey song produced by Robinson as a sweet, dainty piece with funky guitars and pealing strings, though a better title for it might have been "You Put a Song in My Heart," from one of the verses. Neither single, however, made much of a mark, with "Something New" going to No. 25 and "The Composer" to No. 27. Gordy then made it a less than triumphant trifecta by putting out on May 9 "No Matter What Sign You Are" from *Let the Sunshine In*. This hash of pop, rock, funk, and new-age pretension—with an electric sitar playing an opening blues lick—had Diana and the Andantes yowling about love, the zodiac, and "good vibrations," Diana with a harder, sort of Joplin edge. Perhaps this was the reason it didn't fly, stalling at No. 31. (Neither did it keep deejays from flipping it to play the B-side, "The Young Folks," moving that song—later to be covered by the Jackson 5—to No. 69.)

Whereas in past years three straight bombs like that would have driven Gordy onto a ledge, after selling 12 million Supremes records and seeing eleven No. 1 hits he could have described his attitude in terms of the title of his quickly forgotten song—no matter. By now, his plans for Diana were a given, as he'd made no attempt to stifle the growing speculation about her going solo; nor did he have any real objection to the media's tendency, of late, to make the other two Supremes magically vanish.

An example of this prestidigitation was a *TV Guide* puff piece titled, simply but saying it all, "DIANA." It ran the week of the "TCB" special but said almost nothing about anyone else—in fact, its subtitle was a mortal diss of the Temptations: "Her soul music will be heard in a special this week." Three pages were filled with details of Diana's life and ruminations, in tidbits such as "I'd like to have my own television show. But it's very hard for a Negro. I think we have to work twice as hard to get that. I mean, if there were three white girls who had as many hit records as we do, they would probably have their own show by now," and, "I would also like to get involved with the business end of the recording industry, producing records and so forth."

Though it was the "so forth" that might have scared some people, Gordy had to be thrilled about the story's contention that Diana "does not exist apart from Motown," which it said "has a '1984' hold on her waking hours." Diana, meanwhile, was quoted as saying—with "a cheerful indifference," according to writer Digby Diehl—"Why should I interfere with the way he runs my affairs? He's certainly been doing everything right."

Cee

The manipulations to build a Ross groundswell continued all through 1969. In the spring, Gordy cannily welded the nascent fortunes of the Jackson 5 to her stardom by trying to create a bogus narrative that she was not just the boys' guardian angel but their *guardian*, especially to 10-year-old Michael Jackson, who carried the group with a youthful exuberance in his voice and on-stage dance moves that left audiences breathless. Gordy saw a future for the kid that would retrace Stevie Wonder's footprints to fame, eventually outshining and discarding his four brothers. In this respect, he was the perfect "student" of Diana Ross. Indeed, Gordy had wanted to name the group "Michael Jackson and the Jackson 5," until the exacting family patriarch, Joe Jackson, ruled that out, not wanting one son elevated above the rest.

That Diana had never heard of them before they came to Motown was a detail soon to be expunged by a massive and meticulous PR campaign at the core of which was Diana Ross as much as the group itself. In the early spring, after Gordy introduced her to little Michael, she hosted a party for the Jackson 5 at the Daisy Club in Beverly Hills, attended by 300 invited guests, many from the media (and, as last-minute-afterthought invitees, Mary Wilson and Cindy Birdsong, who were sent telegrams by Ross asking them to come and "listen to this fabulous new Motown group." Years later, Wilson was still affronted; reprinting the telegram in the photo section of *Dreamgirl*, she provided as a caption: "How's this for impersonal?") When asked by reporters about his relationship with Ross, Michael finessed his words just as Motown had prepared him to do; not exactly lying but not quite telling the truth, he said with a weariness that was comical given his tender years that he had "just about given up hope. I thought I was going to be an old man before being discovered, but along came Diana Ross to save my career."

Only by a careful parsing of his words could one not infer that he was saying Ross had "discovered" him. As Gordy would recall, approvingly, that was when "people started saying Diana had discovered the group. That didn't hurt, either."

Diana herself was careful not to make the claim, not outright. But she was more than willing to play along with the charade. When the Supremes played the L.A. Forum on August 16, Gordy made sure to install the Jackson 5 as the warm-up act, so that their first major gig could be "introduced" by Diana. Throughout the summer, as well, he had arranged for Michael to live in Diana's house to further the prevarication of Ross mentoring him (the truth was that she was hardly ever there, practically living with Gordy up the hill). The Jacksons' debut single, "I Want You Back," was ready to roll out in mid-October—coincidentally, just as the Supremes had been booked to host *The Hollywood Palace* on October 18, with the proviso that the Jackson 5 also be on the show, their first national TV appearance.

Two months later, their debut album, produced by Bobby Taylor, would be released with the enough-already title *Diana Ross Presents the Jackson 5*, in the liner notes for which Diana wrote with a loony irony, "Honesty has always been a very special word for me," before relating that the mayor of the boys' hometown of Gary, Indiana, had "brought them to my attention." Again, this detail may not have been factually untrue; but because it implied that Ross became aware of them before they were discovered by Bobby Taylor and the Vancouvers, it was anything but honest.

Neither did it hurt Gordy's schema for Diana that she was now growing a little too comfortable in the role of the temperamental diva. Because each of the other Supremes, Florence included, had sometimes brought a Yorkshire terrier on the road with them, Diana literally one-upped them by starting to tote two dogs, both Malteses, beginning in early 1969. Irresponsibly, she would let them roam unleashed in hotels and theaters. Then, during the second night of a two-week engagement at New Jersey's Latin Casino in June, the dogs ate some rat poison backstage. When the girls came offstage before what was to be their encore, Diana saw the dogs vomiting violently and, as Mary recalled, "let out a blood-curdling scream." She then flew into a furor, alternately screeching to get the dogs help and castigating the theater staff for putting poison out and poor Joe Shaffner for not looking after the dogs—evidently, that being one of his assigned tasks—though she was to blame for letting them roam.

Eschewing the encore, she demanded an ambulance, which came and took the dogs to a hospital, although one had died in Diana's arms and the other was comatose. She then made for her dressing room, saying she was going to the hospital, braying at everyone in her way. Gordy, who was with the girls on the trip, could only watch limply and follow her like just another Maltese into her room. There, one of the club owners, Dave Dushoff, pleaded with her to go back out on stage, claiming that if she didn't he'd have to refund the 400 people in the audience for their tickets and meal and bar tabs. "We had a very famous singer here recently," he went on, "and his *mother* died and he still did the show. It's only your dogs, come on."

Eyes bulging like blown bubbles, she sputtered, "*Only* my dogs! I'm canceling this show—and we're going to sue this club! And we'll never be back here again!"

Once, seemingly ages ago, Gordy would likely have pulled rank and ordered her back out. Now, acting as a foot page, he timidly echoed her, telling Dushoff, "Miss Ross has to leave. She is very upset."

The next morning, with Diana still upset over the dogs' deaths, he agreed to the unthinkably unprofessional move of canceling the rest of the engagement. "You guys can go wherever you want," he said disinterestedly to Mary and Cindy, who as usual weren't asked for an opinion. "I'm taking Diana back to L.A. with me." In so doing, he forfeited the $55,000 fee they would have been paid—still a rather chintzy payout considering their status—and all but begged for a lawsuit by the club (which was promptly filed, and settled years later). Ross, indeed, would never play a return engagement at the Latin Casino, by mutual consent.

But while Gordy was worried about bad publicity, telling everyone in the Supremes' retinue to keep the incident quiet, of course it leaked within hours. In Earl Wilson's column that same day was an item that read, "Diana Ross of the Supremes was left broken hearted by the loss of two dogs, believed to be poisoned, and left the act at the Camden Latin

Casino and flew home"—and a nice big picture of her with the caption "Diana—She flew home."

In the burgeoning mythology of Miss Diana Ross, every little bit helped.

Cee

If only as a launching pad for Diana, only one more big hit was required at this point, which was to be the Supremes' swan song. While that search began in earnest in mid-year, as the farewell tour moved apace, plans were made for Ross's exit, her last performances scheduled for their year-end, three-week run in Las Vegas at the Frontier Hotel. Even as the girls were walking their last mile—in May at the Empire Room of the Waldorf-Astoria, in June at the Center Barron Amphitheater in D.C., in July at the Copa and the Westbury Music Fair in New York and the Carousel Theater in Framingham, Massachusetts—the wheels of the transition were turning.

In the early spring, Gordy had yet to inform Mary and Cindy what he planned for them. He kept them hangin' on as the Supremes toured, knowing, as Birdsong once said, that "it was going to be the end of something, but we didn't know exactly of *what*"—whether just Ross's involvement or the group itself. But then Gordy himself didn't know what direction he would take them. He could opt not to replace Diana and have Wilson and Birdsong go solo and allow the Supremes to "go out on top" with their legacy complete and pristine. Or he could promote the long-aggrieved Wilson to lead singer, which was a logical progression. There was even some (brief) debate about bringing Flo back, which would appease the fans and trade an outgoing Supreme for a reinstated one.

SHELLY BERGER: It was all risk management, to the extreme, because one wrong move and the Supremes would lose all credibility as an ongoing act. We had constant meetings, tearing our hair out in frustration. Mike Roshkind kept on saying, "Let's just think of it as a two-for-one split," meaning, like a stock split, that we'd have two brand-new acts with the Supremes' imprint. Mr. Gordy would say, "But what if they both fail? Then what? We have a two-for-nothing."

We just knew we had to have the ducks all in order, and fast. The first thing we needed to do was find a replacement for

Diana we and the public would feel comfortable with, and see how it worked. Mary just wasn't a good enough singer to carry the Supremes forward, but she was a valuable asset. A Supremes without her wouldn't work. So we assured her we were continuing the group and she was quite happy about that, as was Cindy.

We had to find a voice and a presence ideally like Diana but not an imitation, something with an identifiable difference but strong, not just a backup singer moved out front. And it looked for all the world like that was going to be [Motown singer] Syreeta Wright. She was a gorgeous girl. Everybody loved her, she was family [Wright would marry Stevie Wonder in 1970], she had a Minnie Riperton–like octave range. We all thought, "Perfect!"

Then Mr. Gordy and I were in Miami Beach on business. We were in the hotel bar and suddenly this huge man comes to our table and introduces himself and it's Ernie Terrell, the boxer [and former husband of Tammi Terrell, who'd been pounded and humiliated by Muhammad Ali in a February '67 heavyweight title bout, when after refusing to call him by his adopted name Ali taunted him throughout the fight, "What's my name, Uncle Tom?"]. And Mr. Gordy, being a former boxer, invited him to sit with us, and Ernie started talking about this singing group he had, Ernie Terrell and the Knockouts, in which his sister Jean sang lead. They had a show that night in the lounge at the Fountainbleu Hotel, and he said to come and watch because Jean would blow us away. And we did, and we *were* blown away. Jean Terrell was fabulous.

Mr. Gordy and I looked at each other at once, thinking the same thing. "She's gotta be the replacement," I said first. He said, "I think you're right."

The Mississippi-born, Chicago-raised Terrell, then 24, was signed in late May to Motown with caution as an individual act so it could first be seen if she was right for the Supremes. At the time, Wright seemed already to have earned the job after cutting a track called "The Beginning of the End," which was remixed with a Ross vocal lead and used as the B-side for "The Composer," with Wright adding a backing vocal. Now it was Terrell's turn, though Gordy did have some misgivings about her looks—even with an engaging smile and warm demeanor, Jean seemed almost plain by comparison to Mary and Cindy.

Not that there wasn't an upside to that for those glamorous two: It was unlikely they'd feel overly eclipsed again by the lead singer.

Indeed, being spectacularly unspectacular was the clincher for Terrell, her cool exterior seeming to keep under control her tendency to emote gospel-style flourishes. She presented a certain "sound"—a bit darker and smokier than Diana's—without potential complications, whereas Syreeta Wright's model-looks and vocal pyrotechnics might well make the holdover Supremes feel inadequate. Not that they were ever asked for any input on the matter. In fact, Mary and Cindy met Terrell for the first time only when she came to the studio in June to begin cutting possible Supremes tracks produced by Gordy and Frank Wilson.

The "new" Supremes were recorded with a far greater sense of equality. The backing vocals were turned up in volume and at times sung along with Terrell's lead for a natural cohesion—and Terrell was told to turn down the gospel into a relaxed, sensuous pop-soul, like Diana's but without the hyper-dramatic excursions that characterized the HDH days. In the same way, putting together new on-stage routines for them, Cholly Atkins and other choreographers concocted more intricate movements integrating all three women in weaving patterns rather than having the head singer off to the side on her own, *a la* Ross. Often, songs would begin on stage with Mary and Cindy in front of Jean, a conscious nod to their seniority and group unanimity that had formerly been shunted aside.

For Mary, who hadn't seen Diana in the studio for many months— even when she did do backing tracks, Ross laid down her lead vocals at separate sessions—and Cindy, who barely had seen her at all, it was a genuinely refreshing experience, and for a good reason: It harked back to precisely what the Supremes were at the very beginning. A team. If only they could have been free of the divisive Ross vibe. Instead, they led a bizarre double life—by day, alloying with Terrell on new songs and routines, by night doing the old songs and routines as retainers for Ross, who was just as eager to be rid of them. Even Birdsong, with the free ride she'd been getting, was chafing, recalling later that "[i]t was rough getting onstage with Diana and having to project happiness when everyone was so unhappy."

The forced smiles masked the frigid distance they kept from her off-stage. Wilson, in fact, said she and Birdsong "never once talked [to Ross] about her leaving. . . . Diane and I never said two words to each other about it. Like everyone else in the world, I read about in the papers."

Not long ago, Mary had told Flo she was making herself crazy about Diana and to just go with the Flo. Now, she had come to see why Flo had been driven to drink and distraction. She realized that, as with Flo, the friction wasn't caused by a need for her ego so much as by her psychological reaction to Diana using the lead role to social-climb. She felt no such reaction to Terrell, not needing to sing out front to feel useful—and was actually enjoying not singing lead more now than when she *did* sing it on the rare occasions when Ross was around, as in a new feature of the stage act that had her doing a solo rendition of "Can't Take My Eyes off You" (which she got to perform on *The Hollywood Palace* episode that introduced the Jackson 5).

Part of her resignation was that, with all of Gordy's slurs about her voice, "[m]y confidence was shot." Had the lead been offered, she said, "I am sure I would have declined." In this respect, at least, she was different from Flo. As Mary saw it, "I doubted I could have sung lead well enough."

Flo was never able to admit that.

Not only were the Jackson 5 ready to roll out in the fall of '69, so were Versions 2.0 of Diana Ross and of the Supremes. For Diana, the star treatment in the press was nearly over the top. Proof that there was no bigger media darling on the planet required only a glance at the cover of the September *Look*. It presented just a single image—Diana Ross striking a sexy psychedelic "Aquarius" pose against a black backdrop, shown from the waist up wearing a bikini top and rainbow-hued body paint, a skinny right arm raised at a 45-degree angle, mascara-lined eyes in a hard stare, lips caught between a smile and a pout. The image, diverting all attention from cover lines about the Mafia and an essay by historian William L. Shirer, was eye candy for the article titled "THE SUPREME SUPREME," the lead paragraph of which referred to "Diana Ross and her two Supremes."

She was now the paragon of with-it womanhood, socially and self-aware—"[M]aybe I *am* some sort of symbol for the black girl . . . because I respect myself [and] I just help other black girls respect themselves, too"—but beyond the limits of race and gender, with Hollywood and Broadway on the horizon. Gordy—"Motown's tough multimillionaire head"—laid it on thick: Ross, he said, in addition to whatever else, "was the best athlete I've ever seen [and] she could be the first lady astronaut." Diana herself, though, came off as an enviably down-to-earth womanchild, dispensing baubles like "I want to be a strong woman and a good woman for a man, whatever man I choose—and if he chooses me."

The author of the valentine, Jack Hamilton, called the Supremes a "lacquered fantasy." But for Mary and Cindy, there was no fantasy, or even a promise of one for the new edition of the group, only the workmanlike chore of keeping the "new" Supremes a viable act. Most of their debut album was already in the can, awaiting only the single still to be chosen as their breakout song. But that song, and the group's first round of appearances, would not be considered until Gordy could find that last, enduring valedictory single for the "old" Supremes, as just this sort of hit was needed to boost Diana's solo career.

His problem, though, was that the radically altered record-buying market seemed genuinely uninterested in them, based on the flagging sales since "Love Child"—no shock given Gordy's own indifference in releasing Supremes material throughout most of the year, almost all of which seemed intended to empty his inventory of Supremes product, a far different mindset than demanding "No. 1 hits only." The albums, too, reeked of staleness. Two more Supremes-Temptations albums arrived in the fall. The first, *Together*—another cumulation of covers including those of old songs by Marvin Gaye and Stevie Wonder, the Band's rock classic-to-be "The Weight," Sly and the Family Stone's "Sing a Simple Song," and Frankie Valli's "Can't Take My Eyes off You" (with Mary Wilson's solo)—was a long fall from *Join* and *TCB*; released in September, it lumbered in at No. 28 pop, 6 R&B. One other track, "Why (Must We Fall in Love)" was released only in the U.K. and made the Top Forty there.

Next came the soundtrack of the Supremes and Temptations' TV sequel, "G.I.T. on Broadway." The acronym this time stood for "gettin' it together," something that the show, broadcast on November 12, 1969, did anything but, weighed down as it was by having the two best pop-soul acts in the world perform antiseptic medleys of show tunes—with unwittingly hilarious selections from *Fiddler on the Roof*—and a few unfunny comedy sketches. (One, "The Student Mountie," required the Supremes to wear Indian headdresses, buffalo skins, and moccasins; and the Tempts, Mounted Police uniforms.) The real task, it seemed, had less to do with the songs than with trying not to die of embarrassment. The memory still makes Otis Williams shudder: "Sure it was embarrassing. But again, you did what they wanted, picked up the check and hoped no one ever mentioned it again." A laugh. "So I really appreciate you askin' about it, man."

The soundtrack, out in early November under the name *On Broadway*, somehow got to 38 on the pop charts and to 4 on the R&B charts. And for the Supremes' next single, Gordy could only put out, on August 21, fodder from *Together*, "The Weight"—actually a surprisingly effective cover of the Robbie Robertson parable of unknowingly making a compact with the devil, produced by Frank Wilson in a jazzy, up-tempo style with a lively lead vocal by Eddie Kendricks. But, backed with another album cut, "For Better or Worse," it stalled at No. 46, the worst-charting Supremes single in five years.

Cee

Worse, by the end of September no song had yet been found that could properly close the book on Diana Ross and the Supremes, causing delay for the long-awaited announcement that Ross was leaving—and Gordy and Diana's relationship to fray. With the deadline looming for Motown to be able to get a song out and up the charts in time for the finale at the Frontier Hotel, there arose the horrifying possibility that the curtain-dropping might be postponed until there *was* a hit. Frayed after the hours she had spent rehearsing prodigiously staged numbers with Gil Askey designed for the solo act, Diana whined to Gordy, "When can I get out?"

After listening day after day to possible Supremes songs, he was coming close to losing it, at one point foaming that he wanted Diana "out of this group" but that "we got to have a hit or she ain't goin' nowhere!" (Gordy and Ross blew right past these dicey hours in their respective memoirs, as if the path to Ross's solo career was smooth sailing.) However, when people speak of Berry Gordy being blessed with the luck of timing and the timing of luck, it's because of the kind of thing that happened next.

With no choice but to dip into the pool of recordings Diana had made for use as a solo, he settled on a cover track of a flop record Johnny Bristol had made during his early singing days as part of the duo Johnny and Jackey for Harvey Fuqua's Tri-Phi label in 1961— "Someday We'll Be Together," co-written by Bristol, Fuqua, and his partner Jackey Beavers. The track had been cut for Junior Walker and the All-Stars as a follow-up to the Bristol's "What Does It Take (To Win Your Love)," an enormous summer hit that year, already adding back-

ground vocals by Motown singers and by sisters Maxine and Julia Waters. Before the lead could be cut by Walker, Gordy redirected it to
Ross, who laid down the vocals at a June session.

The track was anything but subtle, Bristol having coated it with
layers and layers of strings that buoyed rather pedestrian lyrics about regret and yearning. "Long time ago, my, my sweet thing / I made a big
mistake, honey," it went, continuing, "Ever since that day / Now, now
all I wanna do is cry, cry, cry." There was no happy ending, only, well,
yearning—"Wanna say, wanna say, wanna say / Someday we'll be together
/ Yes we will, yes we will."

The problem was that, all this schmaltz notwithstanding, Diana's
vocal was borderline sleep-inducing. This caused Bristol so much concern that he opened his microphone in the booth and took to melodi-
cally prodding Diana, exclaiming, "You tell it!" and "Oh yes, baby!" as
the song went on. His exhortations bled into her microphone and were
recorded on the track. Even the Funk Brothers couldn't do much with
it as the mix was overwhelmed with strings. In toto, Allan Slutsky says,
the song, though "quite competent," is "not exactly a barn burner of
a groove."

Gordy in fact regarded the record as not entirely finished, mainly
because of Diana's mordant vocal, which had some Motown executives
wondering if the "someday" would be taken to mean that Diana was
dreaming of a lovers' reunion in the hereafter, when both lovers were
dead. Was it a rock and roll death song, like "Teen Angel" or "Tell
Laura I Love Her"? Was it a suicide death wish? But Gordy was down
to the nub, and heard something that worked. With no time to fiddle
with tracks, Bristol's ad-libbed asides stayed on. Thus, the last Supremes
single was a two-time hand-me-down from 1961 with background vocals from a Junior Walker session.

It was a strange brew, for sure.

It was also, as it turned out, the best song that conceivably could
have served the purpose.

Charmed as Gordy was, the song was heard only, and by huge
numbers, as a dreamy insistence codifying that the Supremes would "be
together" forever—not as an end at all because the end never would
come for their music. All the "clans" in the world working day and
night could not have come up with anything that inspired, and perfect.

The rest was gravy; released as Motown single 1156 on October 14,
1969, it caught the wind from day one, seeming to reconstruct the
Supremes' *au courant* sizzle whenever it was heard. It was in the Top

Forty the week of November 15, crashing into the No. 1 spot six weeks later, the week of December 27—just as it was displaced from the top rung on the R&B chart after two weeks—when the Supremes were well into the Frontier engagement; though moved out after a week by "Raindrops Keep Fallin' on My Head," it would not leave the Top Forty for fifteen weeks—matching the run of "Love Child" and becoming the best-selling Supremes single ever.

(Repeat caveat: With Motown records veiled in secrecy, even with Gordy long out of the company, few know how many it and other Supremes' records sold. An educated guess is that "Someday" has sold around a million and a half copies to this day, and over a million in its day, as did "Where Did Our Love Go," "You Can't Hurry Love," "Love Child," and "I'm Gonna Make You Love Me." Several others—"Baby Love," "Stop! In the Name of Love," "Come See About Me," "You Keep Me Hanging On," and "Reflections"—may well have done a million to date.

Had Gordy ever opened his account books to the RIAA, Ross, Wilson, and Ballard would have earned as many as nine [Birdsong two] platinum records, all of which, plus perhaps four or five more, would have gone gold. Similar guesswork math applies to Marvin Gaye, Stevie Wonder, and Michael Jackson, whose sales figures were confirmed only after 1977.)

"Someday" was a lightning strike that moved all of Gordy's plans forward. The official announcement of Ross's impending exit came in November. It also allowed him to use it as the anchor for the final Supremes studio album, *Cream of the Crop*. Released on December 3 with a mélange of B-sides and other middling Motown fodder such as the Syreeta Wright–originated "The Beginning of the End," and covers of the Beatles' "Hey Jude" and Dylan's "Blowin' in the Wind," *Cream* soured at No. 33 pop (though it did reach 3 R&B). But now Gordy had cause to put out two other albums to exploit all the publicity and sentimentality of the end of the line for the Supremes; one was the mandatory *Greatest Hits Volume 3*, released just fifteen days later (going to No. 31 pop, 5 R&B), while the other, *Farewell*, would be a live double-album of the final show at the Frontier (actually pieces recorded from the last three shows) produced by Deke Richards and issued as a two-LP deluxe edition box-set—one of the first of its kind—in April

1970 (46 pop, 31 R&B). (It was reissued as a two-compact-disc box-set titled *Captured Live on Stage* in 1992.)

That hectic and profitable December, the Supremes were booked on the 21st to do *The Ed Sullivan Show* for the twentieth and last time with Ross. And if Diana, Mary, and Cindy had to get it together again and force some good vibrations, for Cindy it was a relief just to be there, or anywhere.

Though Gordy had turned his back on "rough" Detroit—and endlessly cursed the rampant crime there, which had recently included an unsolved crime (someone came into 2648 West Grand Boulevard and fired off a gun, fortunately hitting no one but leading a secretary to quit in fear)—the only time that any of the Supremes was the victim of a crime was in the "safe haven" of the Hollywood Hills when on the night of December 2 Birdsong opened the door to the apartment she shared with Charles Hewlett and one of his friends and a man she later described as crazed and white came out of the dark and held a butcher knife to her neck. Forcing her to tie the hands of Hewlett and his friend with rope, the guy dragged her by the hair into the garage, shoving her into the passenger seat of her own car before getting behind the wheel and taking off on a joyride along the Long Beach Freeway.

After thirty harrowing minutes, she bravely reached for the knife, cutting her hands in the process, then in a "Mannix"-like stunt jumped out of the speeding car. She could have been killed on contact but, though bloodied, she was, miraculously, not seriously hurt, coming to a stop in a ditch by the road. She then got up and ran into the road, frantically waving and screaming at oncoming cars for someone to stop and help her—which also could have gotten her killed. By another miracle, a California Highway Patrol car just then came along and picked her up, taking her to Long Beach Hospital.

The story broke the next morning on the news, with cops calling it an attempted kidnapping. Hearing of it, Gordy was scared witless, exposing as it did how easily the safety of his priceless commodities could be compromised. Already on edge since the summertime Tate-LaBianca murders, carried out by a crazed pack of hippies who turned out to be the Manson "family," Gordy hired private security to guard his home. Apparently, the girls were encouraged to do the same, at their own expense.

To some around Motown, the whole thing seemed a bit incredible, and there were whispers about it maybe being a publicity stunt. Others spouted wild rumors that Hewlett, whom no one at the company really knew, could have been working with bad guys to set up Cindy for a ransom, even though an ex-con high on drugs and booze was arrested a day after the crime in Las Vegas, still in Cindy's car, and admitted he had done it in an amateurish kidnap-and-ransom attempt. He was eventually sent to prison for kidnapping, armed robbery, and felonious reckless driving, with Cindy testifying at the trial.

None the worse for wear after a short hospital stay during which Diana and Mary rushed to her bedside, Cindy joined them for the trip to New York and their final *Ed Sullivan Show* together. Those who hadn't heard the announcement of Diana's departure on the news learned of it that night from a stone-faced, tuxedo-clad Sullivan, who prefaced the girls' performance by intoning, with the emotion of a turtle, "As you know, Diana Ross is continuing her career as a single star. And now, in their last appearance together, here is Diana and the Supremes singing their current number one record, 'Someday We'll Be Together.'"

As he spoke, the instrumental track of the song began playing—there was no way the Sullivan orchestra could have done justice to the string arrangement—and the girls were seen behind him in the camera angle focusing on Sullivan from stage right, striding onto a set with three columns lit with different color lights. Wearing long, robe-like gold lamé and chiffon gowns with flouncy dolman sleeves and chandelier-sized earrings dangling below chin level, they formed a triangular position, Diana in front; then, as Sullivan finished his intro—without a word about Wilson and Birdsong carrying on the Supremes—the camera switched to a straight-on angle when they began to sing what for the vast majority of Americans would be their final song together.

As such, the performance immediately was heavy on the heart. Diana holding a hand-held microphone, sang in just the right subdued vocal shade of the recording, while Mary and Cindy, who had to again learn a song they hadn't recorded, stood on either side smoothly hitting the extreme high notes of the chorus with sad smiles on their faces.

But, perfect as they were, there seemed to be a chilled air on the set. None of them expressed, or even acted like they had, any real emotion. A small gesture of such, bogus or not—a touching of hands, for example, or a group hug—would have put an unforgettable period on the sentence. Instead, with Mary and Cindy stepping back several feet behind Diana as they finished, they stood basking in the applause, not looking at each other. When Sullivan then called over Diana—and only Diana—for a brief good-luck wish (still not meeting her expectations for what should be a proper greeting, even after all this time), Mary and Cindy, out of camera range as it left them to follow Diana, cast each other a glance and trailed off stage.

When Diana made her way backstage into the retinue of dozens of Motown hangers-on, the temperature was no warmer.

"They were not all hugging together," said Tony Tucker. "Nobody was wishing farewell. . . . You could see that Diana could not be bothered with Mary and Cindy. She was concentrating on herself."

Wilson, still unmelted years later, would explain her lack of feeling with a diffident shrug: "I felt like I'd said goodbye already."

The wall of separation between the two factions, which struck Tucker as "tragic," made a sham of the fantasy of that last record. Indeed, for anyone who was around the Supremes' crumbling universe, at that moment "someday" could only seem very, very far off.

Cee

Florence Ballard had a secret.

Even though she was in dire straits, Flo had begged and borrowed enough money to make sure she would be a part of the Supremes' requiem. As the Frontier engagement approached and it became clear that everyone who was anyone at Motown was expected to be there for the January 14 grand finale, Flo couldn't think of a reason in the world why she shouldn't be among them. Of course, that Gordy and Ross could have come up with at least a thousand reasons why she *shouldn't* only made her more determined to, as she told friends, go there and "shake 'em up."

According to Delcina Wilson, another companion of Mary's who had hung around them as a kind of unofficial photographer and later became a confidante of Ballard's, after Flo made up her mind to crash the party in Vegas she bought tickets for the January 14 show for her and Tommy through a travel agent as part of a package that included first-class fare and a suite at the Frontier. She had a faux Bill Blass gown made by a local seamstress, bought a new fashionable wig, and was ready to go. She was even talking about holding forth with the press, saying things about Berry and Diana that would let the air out of the phony gaiety of the festivities.

There were people around Motown who would have paid good money just to see Berry's and Diana's faces if Flo was there that night. Might she even pull a David Ruffin and clamber up on the stage to sing with the Supremes? Would the audience believe it was a planned part of the program—the only appearance ever of all four Supremes—and cheer themselves hoarse? And if any of this happened, would Berry's and Diana's heads explode in stereo?

In the end, alas, none of these delectable figments, which no doubt were in Flo's mind all along—particularly the notion of stealing Diana's thunder as divine payback for having stolen hers—were not to be, evidently because Tommy Chapman chose the time just before they were to make the trip to confirm the suspicions of many around her. After Flo gave him several thousand dollars to pick up her gown, her wig, her furs from storage, and the plane tickets, he didn't come back for four days.

Tellingly, Flo had no worries that he had been hurt; it was just another of Tommy's routine disappearing acts. She seemed far more upset that without the money she had no way to get to Vegas. When she called Delcina to tell her, she said she thought about taking a Greyhound bus all the way there.

"Don't you dare," the photographer told her, and offered to wire her $2,000.

"Forget it," Flo said, her spirits again in the dumps. "It wasn't meant to be."

Delcina still held out hope. She'd kept Flo's secret from Mary, so it would be a "surprise," but now only Mary could have arranged for Flo to be there so she explained the situation to her.

Thinking Mary would surely help out her old friend and begin making calls to get Flo to Vegas, she instead had little reaction. Having grown tired of playing the good soldier to bring the Supremes together only to see Flo always ruin it, Mary couldn't be bothered.

"Well, perhaps everything worked out for the best" was all she said.

The final show went on without complications. At the midnight performance in the Music Hall of the Frontier Hotel—making the date of the finale technically January 15—the joint was packed. In a house with 1,000 seats, nearly twice that many were allowed in. And everybody was there: Smokey, Marvin, all the Gordys, the girls' mothers, other family members. So was the press, en masse, and the photographers were everywhere. Scattered along the linen-covered tables were celebrities: Johnny Carson, Steve Allen, Jayne Meadows, Dick Clark,

Lou Rawls, Bill Russell. The tension and anticipation made it seem almost as if they were awaiting the bell at a championship fight.

Backstage, Diana felt it the most, her face tight and dour as she stood nervously chain-smoking, flicking the butts to the ground around her expensive high-heel shoes. Mary and Cindy, who were raising toasts to each other with glasses of champagne in the dressing room, felt it as well, though Mary downplayed the whole thing as contrived solely to benefit Diana. Once the house lights dimmed and Gil Askey raised his arm to strike up the band one last time for Diana Ross and the Supremes, there was exactly no doubt about Mary's assumption. For Ross and Gordy, this night wasn't about the Supremes' finale; it was in every way Diana Ross's solo debut.

With the band playing, Gordy approached Diana and kissed her for luck, telling her, "This is your night. You're a star, baby."

Just before going on, Wilson would recall, "Diane and I just looked at each other in silence. There were no 'good-byes' or 'good-lucks,' not even a hug. We could have done those things, but we both knew it would have been a farce."

All three of them were radiant in their floor-length Bob Mackie gowns made of black velvet and gold braided inlays, pearls laid around their necks, and Gibson girl–style wigs with attached falls, Diana's with her now-trademark peek-a-boo spit-curl dangling over her right eye. But this was Diana Ross's spotlight, and no one else would be permitted within it unless at her whim.

The atmosphere was crackling when they took their positions, and they fed off it with an electric performance. They began with the "TCB" theme and went into medleys of four of their older hits and then two show tunes, an "I am so blessed" Ross monologue, "Love Is Here and Now You're Gone," "I'm Gonna Make You Love Me," an "I am so blessed" Mary Wilson monologue and her solo on "Can't Take My Eyes off You," a bit of banter between Ross and Wilson, and "Reflections."

That first third of the show pretty much took care of the Supremes. The rest was a self-indulgent exercise by "Miss Ross," except for when she was metaphorically on her knees for Berry Gordy—her solos on "May Man" and "Didn't We," chosen as her personal "thank you's," no doubt once and for all put to bed the "just good friends" story as she sang to him in the aisle a few feet from where he sat at the head Motown table, her face streaked in tears. Some in the house dabbed at their own tears, although at least a few stifled a derisive giggle at the overbaked mawk, which continued with two more songs dedicated to him,

"Big Spender"—which some past, forsaken Motown acts might have enjoyed a good chuckle at—and "Falling in Love with Love."

With all the emotion spent, the night had already become exhausting. But Diana was only getting warmed up for more extended bathos. When the girls broke into "Aquarius/Let the Sunshine In," few knew what they were in for. After the "Aquarius" part was done and the repetitive choruses had begun, Ross was again bounding off the stage into the aisles, clapping and grooving as Mary and Cindy remained fixed on the stage cooing "Let the sunshine, let the sunshine in" over and over. Looking for familiar faces, Diana began to stick her microphone under their noses so that they could chime in; if they hesitated, she implored, "Come on, ya gotta sing!"

Among her victims were Smokey and Claudette Robinson (with the latter thinking it was just a little late for Diana to show her a little love, eight years after showing her husband a lot of it), Marvin and Anna Gaye, and Esther and Gwen Gordy—Diana squealing that she, too, was "a part of the Gordy family. I'm a sister!" Judging from their restrained look, none of the Gordy sisters seemed overly comfortable with that notion. By the time the likes of Steve Allen and Dick Clark got to sing off-key, Wilson recalled, "[w]e had sung the chorus about fifty times," and now more than a few were so numbed that they just wanted to make it stop.

"One more time!" Diana shouted, bringing the sun out and shining for another few choruses.

Most in the house absolutely loved it, all of it. If some were exhausted, far more were exhilarated by this Motown hootenanny. The mood then, on a dime, became subdued and somber when the Supremes trilled "The Impossible Dream," followed by the big cathartic wrecking ball of a closing number, what else but "Someday We'll Be Together." With not a dry eye in the joint, on stage or in the hall, the girls aced it, leaving 2,000 people limp and drained. Even jaded, battle-fatigued Supremes' insiders could not fail to be moved, and emotionally stripped to the bone.

Not so, however, for the most jaded; as Mary and Cindy remembered it, they had just pulled off the world's most lavish con.

"It was all acting," Birdsong once was quoted, "the smiles, the tears, all of it. Just acting."

As for Wilson, she would write in *Dreamgirl* that there was just no place for reality on that night of fables: "[T]he reporters [later] wrote about how I clowned around and 'teased Diana Ross, much like a sister

would, toying with the spotlight—a demonstration of the girls' closeness.' That the world still believed we were the best of friends seemed
the perfect ending."

Then there was the "Supreme Supreme" herself, who, even while
spouting self-deluded rot about who did dirt to whom during the life
span of the group, told some essential truths.

"A quiet sadness filled me as I realized that I was leaving," she would
say, "not only because I wanted to but because I had to. They had hurt
me very badly, beyond repair. We weren't a group anymore."

At the conclusion of the show, Diana called to the stage Jean Terrell,
acting like doing so was her decision. "I think she should be here right
now," she told the audience. As the new Supreme came into view, some
catty types in the crowd could be heard insulting her gown, a black
polyester crepe facsimile of the obscenely expensive Mackie frocks worn
by the others. Later, after the huzzahs had died down and the crowd
had filed out, there would be private parties, endless champagne toasts,
and the unveiling of a gigantic cake inscribed "Someday We'll Be
Together."

At that moment, no one wanted to look back, only ahead, even
though the only story that would matter was their past, the grainy history of how three girls unified by the deprivations of the ghetto became
three cultural icons and as mature women headed off into three completely different directions: toward unequaled fame and fortune, toward a life without end as an ex-Supreme, and toward a life that ended
much too soon.

Diana Ross, Mary Wilson, and Florence Ballard, and surely Cindy
Birdsong, could not have fully understood why it happened that way,
or why what they were leaving behind was so much bigger than them,
something that would take decades to quantify—although Diana
seemed to have a glimmer in telling *Look* that "[p]eople will always
think when they see three Negro girls, three black faces, that they're the
Supremes. It's a beautiful image to keep. There we are, fixed in time,
forever and ever."

The only thing that really mattered—*to them*—wasn't the metrics
or metaphysics of "Someday We'll Be Together." It was that, on *that*
day, it was over. And to that, they could say hallelujah and amen.

WHERE DID OUR LOVE GO?

That the Supremes' brand name chugged on unabated with its most famous member exchanged for a lead singer who had the nerve to wear polyester in Las Vegas was, Shelly Berger believes, something on the order of sorcery. "When has any other super group been split like that at the height of their fame and not only retained their cache but made new fans? They carried on about as long as they had with Diana." His conclusion: "Only Motown could have done that kind of thing. We did it with the Temptations, too, after David Ruffin."

In 1970, only Motown had the power and the creative timber to change the swiftest river currents and long-held industry assumptions. The mom-and-pop operation run by Mom and Pops Gordy's ne'er-do-well son, stoked by their $800 loan he had to get on his knees for, was a strict paradigm of capitalism and black entrepreneurship. In '69, when only death could have pried Gordy's Motown stock from him, those shares alone were worth $5 million. (Even when he would finally let a few shares go, giving 236 to Esther Edwards in 1972 and 235 to Smokey Robinson in '74, he still retained 4,494 of the company's 4,995 shares.) Since Motown was organized under the IRS code as a subchapter S company, as Motown historian Peter Benjaminson noted before Gordy sold out, "Motown's money is Gordy's money. If the company spends money, it comes out of Gordy's pocket. If it makes money, it goes into Gordy's pocket."

He never would offer Motown shares to the public, causing some executives, who expected to be able to purchase stock, to quit in disgust. Gordy, said Benjaminson, "wanted his wealth nearby and touchable [and] wanted it as soon as it was earned, not at the end of the fiscal year. [That's why] he invested a lot of money in houses." Accountants told him they could lower the company's tax bill but it would take time to know what deductions were accepted; he always said no, telling them to pay at the maximum rate, just so "he could be sure what remained was his." Accordingly, distributors and bookers always knew his money was good, and plentiful. And so even if his resources weren't shared generously, or even fairly, with his stars, they had a cachet, too.

For example, Version 2.0 of the Supremes. By rights, the act had no real claim to mass acceptance. Anything that the Supremes had done was as a unit led by Diana Ross. At least as far as the public cared, they had the same lineup until Ross left—more casual fans wouldn't know that Flo Ballard wasn't still there, or alive for that matter, until years later. But now, very noticeably, Ross was the missing one. Worse, Gordy had left a bitter postscript on that triumphant night at the Frontier. Hours after the show, he couldn't stop fretting about Jean Terrell. It could have been the insults lobbed at her from the house, her appearance, the fact that she was as headstrong at times as Diana, refusing to follow his advice. But where Diana was *Diana*, Jean was just plain Jean. Unable to sleep, he called Mary's room, waking her up.

"I don't like Jean," he barked when she picked up. "I want to replace her with Syreeta."

Mary wasn't so groggy that she didn't think he was completely crazy. The first post-Ross single, "Up the Ladder to the Roof," was only days away from release. The PR campaign was about to gear up.

"You can't do that!" she protested. "We just made the announcement, for Christ's sake."

He insisted that Wright was a better singer, more electric, more seductive—more like Diana.

That alone must have jolted Wilson fully awake. "No way," she said. "Cindy and I want Jean in the group so you can just forget it, Berry."

Even in his crowning moment, Gordy could not leave well enough alone. But while he could have gotten his way with a simple directive, he could tell this wasn't the old Wilson, the footstool he'd tromped on for years. Now the mouse that roared, she might have quit in retort, and then what? Gordy had never respected Mary; recently he'd had a run-in with her and told people, "That's a stupid woman. A *stupid woman*." But now she had him beat. Frustrated, he acted like a 10-year-old.

"Fine, then I wash my hands of the whole goddamn group!" he sputtered, then scowled about how ungrateful "these women are," meaning either the two holdover Supremes who now had the nerve to buck him or the entire gender.

The second-edition (third, technically) Supremes felt his wrath, too. Working on a shoestring budget, at least by Supremes norms, Terrell, Wilson, and Birdsong had to recycle their old gowns, with Mary the only one who could squeeze into Diana's and Jean wearing Mary's. VIP suites were now regular guest rooms. Those teeming retinues of hangers-on were whittled down to one assistant per Supreme, with no traveling hair and makeup stylists, no valets, and no Berry Gordy.

And yet the Motown machine saved Gordy from his own pettiness. Having appointed Frank Wilson to write and produce their first series of recordings, "Up the Ladder to the Roof" came out of the trough as a quite serviceable pop-soul ballad with cool funky guitar licks and dreamy vocals—and, in a roundabout irony, a lyric that was actually about love in the hereafter but heard simply as love on a rooftop.

When it hit No. 10 on the pop charts and 5 on the R&B charts in March 1970, Gordy could pretend to be ecstatic—as in *To Be Loved*, when he shamelessly told of the Supremes' seamless chain of successes—while putting next to nothing behind them. Fortunately, they still had a reservoir of important venues to play, like the Copa and the hotels in Miami Beach and Vegas casinos, and could count on the occasional *Ed Sullivan Show* invitation. And for two years they continued to produce hits, one more in the Top Ten, "Stoned Love" (No. 3) and five in the Top Twenty—"Everybody's Got the Right to Love"; the duet with the Four Tops, "River Deep-Mountain High"; "Nathan Jones" (the previous two also going Top Ten R&B); "Happy (Is a Bumpy Road)"; and "Floy Joy"—plus a Top Forty entry, "Precious Little Things," with Terrell and Wilson as co-leads. There was also a profusion of albums—eight in the first two years—and though only their debut LP, *Right On*, reached as high as No. 25, all charted well on the R&B chart.

In fact, critics registered a fair amount of shock that the Supremes weren't merely a crass commercial confection of mannequins attempting to approximate the same old formula but, rather, an admirably adapted one; reviews called their sound a satisfying return to Motown's R&B roots—"blacker" and truer to the soul genre than the Ross band, though no one was silly enough to say they were better. Overall, the verdict on the "new Supremes" was that they were distinct, pleasant, soulful, sometimes sharply honed, sometimes a bit bland. These sorts of restrained raves were personally gratifying for Wilson after standing up to Gordy. Late in the Supremes' original run, she'd come to believe the material had grown too predictable, too "plastic." Years later, she would say she always thought the Supremes could have "done more" than they were permitted to; now, she was proving it. And even if Gordy had washed his hands of the group, he had no intention of keeping his hands off the money they were making for him.

$$Cee$$

Diana Ross, meanwhile, should have been doing it all, considering the eddies of money appropriated to her solo act—which cost around $100,000 to stage with all the costume and scenery changes—and the $70,000-a-week price tag she commanded for her top appearances. Yet for a time Gordy was mortified that the Supremes were more bankable than his queen. Almost as if there was a backlash against Ross turning her back on the Supremes, the fans were cool to her. When ticket sales lagged for her Las Vegas debut at the Frontier in May 1970, Gordy filled the house only after a promotion handing out fifty-dollar bills torn in half to passersby on the Strip, with the promise that they could collect the other half by attending the show.

By the summer, however, her shows were reliably sold out and she had arrived as a diva to be contended with. In the August 1 *Time*, a piece called "Baby, Baby, Where Did Diana Go?" fawned, "Diana . . . is still all static electricity. She leaps in and out of an assortment of costumes, dances from time to time with two smiling male partners, and makes her way through a repertory of tunes borrowed from the likes of the Beatles, Tony Bennett, Peggy Lee. She even sings a medley of old Supremes hits, but she seems to get through them very quickly."

Mandatorily, it went on, "She owns a Rolls-Royce (a gift from the thrice-wed Gordy) and a new home in Beverly Hills. 'I have clothes for every mood,' she boasts. Her collection ranges from dungarees and bathing suits to 'very classy suits for traveling or teas.' Her aim, naturally, is to be an actress. Doris Day advised her that it was not necessary to study acting, and Diana says, 'If Jim Brown can do it, I can do it—whatever he's doing.'" Noting that Diana wanted to put bitter life experiences into her acting, the article slyly noted that "[h]er biggest trauma so far came last year in New Jersey, when someone poisoned her pet dogs."

Her early records—written and produced, for the most part, by Ashford and Simpson as lushly orchestrated sugary-coated pop—were literally hit and miss. The first single, "Reach Out and Touch (Somebody's Hand)," got to only No. 20, while the second, a cover of "Ain't No Mountain High Enough," was an enormous No. 1 pop and R&B smash. The next, "Remember Me," hit No. 16, but five more tanked until 1973 when "Touch Me in the Morning" went to the top, the last big hit she'd have for another two years. So, too, with her albums, the first real winner among the first four being the 1972 soundtrack from her movie debut as the ill-fated Billie Holiday in the wildly profitable *Lady Sings the Blues*, which went No. 1 pop, 2 R&B.

That film, instantly creating the new star team of Ross and Billy Dee Williams, cost Gordy $3.5 million to produce and made ten times as much. Diana, who hadn't heard of Billie Holiday, got so into the part that she won raves for a brilliantly harrowing portrayal—and one that has worn so well that it prompted a remarkable flip-flop in *Time*: Back then it brutally panned her, saying, "It is eerie to watch and listen to Miss Ross, the princess of plastic soul, work her way through such songs as Strange Fruit and God Bless the Child. She has the phrasing, and the Holiday intonation. What she doesn't have is the passion. Her Billie Holiday is like one of those Audio-Animatronic robots at Disneyland—a perfect facsimile of life until you get close and hear the gears whirling," yet in 2000, in naming the movie one of the twenty-five best films on race, lauded her for "bring[ing] a burnished sexiness" to the role.

Clearly, Diana was now almost exclusively Gordy's meal ticket. Warming up for the movie, in '71 he had produced a Ross ABC-TV special. He not only financed *Lady Sings the Blues*; as its executive producer he ruled by fiat and by nepotism: Suzanne DePasse and, bizarrely, his one-and-off bedmate Chris Clark co-write the script, and Gil Askey composed the score, each one winning Oscar nominations with Ross as vocalist. By now his half-million-dollar home just seemed so common, and so he sold it and bought Red Skelton's palatial Bel-Air estate called the Vistas, near Hugh Hefner's Playboy Mansion. Foreshadowing Michael Jackson's Neverland ranch, Gordy's playground included a menagerie with peacocks, rheas, llamas, and rare birds and fish, as well as several tennis courts.

Rarely, if ever, now did Gordy even pass a thought of his hometown. By the end of '72, with almost all the Motown recording work being done at MoWest and the big acts like the Temptations, Marvin Gaye,

Stevie Wonder, and the Jackson 5 living in L.A., he closed down the hoary shop at 2648 West Grand Boulevard, leaving many of the Funk Brothers to either come out to L.A. on their own dime or wither with the rest of Detroit. Some came, like James Jamerson, but they were no longer indispensable to Gordy's less stringent musical purposes and even Jamerson would be cast aside for younger, cheaper, and less weathered musicians.

The remaining Detroit-bound artists generally didn't receive invitations to relocate. One, Martha Reeves, bitterly recounts that "[t]hey didn't even have the courtesy to tell me [of the closing]. . . . I had recorded million-selling records, had headlined prestigious nightclubs, and became an international star [yet] Motown treated me like a poor stepchild. Free-floating without a direction or a safety net, I felt lost in the shuffle." Yet Motown still would not let Reeves out of her contract until she had repaid $200,000 in "advances."

In L.A., meanwhile, the center of Gordy's universe began to feel adrift, too. Approaching 30 and needing stability, Diana Ross grew tired of Gordy stringing her along, paying no mind to her desire for marriage and children and displaying ugly fits of jealousy—such as when she had a brief, fiery fling with football-player-turned-actor Tim Brown—while never curtailing his endless philandering with Chris Clark and God knows who else. Finally, she gave him a marry-me-or-else ultimatum. When he brushed her aside, the "else" turned out to be a shocking, out-of-left-field marriage when she ran off to Las Vegas on January 10, 1971, to wed 45-year-old Robert Silberstein, a Hollywood music manager whose main client was Chaka Khan, only days after she'd met him, or so she said, in a clothing store while shopping for Berry.

In very un-Ross-like fashion, there was no high-society wedding, no Easter parade of ritzy gowns, no orgy of photographers' flashbulbs; only one guest was present, Suzanne DePasse, as a witness, and she was sworn not to tell Gordy. He found out, after the fact, from his ex-wife and business partner from the early days of Motown, Raynoma Liles. The tensions having eased between the two, with Liles's bootlegging ways in New York now nearly forgotten, he had recently gotten Raynoma to accompany Ross on road trips he couldn't make, as a personal assistant. Though she detested Ross, she agreed, and two days after marrying Silberstein, Diana asked her to break the news to Gordy.

Knowing Gordy as she did, and Diana, she thought it would be the best news he had ever heard.

"Congratulations, Berry," she said.

When she told him, she recalled him saying, "Great, that's absolutely great!" Said Liles: "He sounded as if he was throwing streamers around his office." As Liles tells it, "For a long while, the public sentiment was, 'poor Berry Gordy—getting the shaft by hard-hearted Diana.' [But] Berry told me later that Diana's wedding day was the happiest day of his life. He said that she'd almost forced his hand, until at the last minute he'd realized, 'I can't marry this woman. This woman is as selfish as I am. I'm going to have to be kissing her ass all the time. I need somebody to kiss *my* ass.'" She concluded: "Berry revered the star but basically didn't like the woman," which seems a drastic oversimplification of their complex relationship.

By way of balance, Jim Brown has a completely opposite take: that when Gordy found out about the marriage he reacted like he'd been "punched in the gut." Said Brown: "Berry Gordy's deepest sense of loss did not come from losing Motown. It came from losing Diana Ross."

Gordy, either putting up a brave front to hide his pain or too happy to feel any, told the media Diana's marriage was for the best because he could now concentrate on her career without the added personal complications. Decades later, in a 1994 TV interview with Barbara Walters, he had refined his take on the situation even more: "Diana and I are the same kind of people. She wanted what I wanted. And we saw it up there, we set out to get it and we vowed never to let our personal relationship affect it. I loved her but wasn't selfish enough to want to marry her and take her out of what I knew she had to have. She had to have that stardom up there." Diana, for her part, played it as a semi-declaration of personal independence, saying Gordy was "in charge of my career, but not the director of my life."

Whatever the motivations and ensuing feelings, however, little actually changed between them except that they no longer shared a mattress. He still would attend many of her big appearances, and for Diana his being there always unleashed old emotions. Brown recalled that whenever Gordy was in the audience and Diana sung "Someday We'll Be Together," she would tear up, and "I knew she was crying for Berry." Once, seeing them in the quiet of Diana's dressing room, "I could see the deepness of their love. So I left."

What no one, except the Silbersteins and Gordy, knew for many years was that Diana and Berry would be joined forever in a very tangible way. In the spring of '71 Ross announced she was pregnant, and in the summer she gave birth to a daughter, Rhonda Ross Silberstein, the first of three children she had by Silberstein, or so it was believed. The truth was that Gordy was the real father, the account payable from a night of passion at Christmastime before Ross decided to marry Silberstein several weeks later—and obviously the reason why Diana had put the marry-me-or-else gun to his head, having found out she was pregnant, the product of "one for the road," as Gordy called the night. Whether she told him that he was the father then or after Rhonda was born is unclear, but for years when he would visit Diana's house he consciously pretended to be the girl's "Uncle BB." Rhonda, who had Diana's big round eyes and a wide, thick nose like his, was also light-skinned, making it plausible that her father was white, though hardly preventing rumors from flying through the years about why she had Berry Gordy's nose.

Judging by Gordy's chilled, conscienceless account of the episode, he apparently saw nothing amiss about Diana and him lying to their "love child" about who her real dad was for purely appearances' sake, so that she would have a father around and Diana could go on hushing up a romance that everyone under the sun now knew about. But at least he said something about it. Ross, by contrast, has kept the subject at a great remove, saying that such an intensely private matter is no one's concern but her family's; she even refuses to admit that Rhonda *is* Gordy's child—in *Secrets of a Sparrow*, the only reference to Rhonda is brief and noncommittal, as simply one of her three children with Silberstein.

It was left to Raynoma Liles to confirm the long years of rumors, revealing in her 1990 tell-all *Berry, Me and Motown: The Untold Story* that Diana told Rhonda the truth when she was 17. Gordy then copped to it four years afterward in *To Be Loved*, though he said the revelatory moment came when Rhonda was 12. At the time Rhonda was beginning a career in acting, and Gordy let her have a bit part in one of the later movies he produced, sans Diana, the 1985 martial arts potboiler *The Last Dragon*. One day, Diana came onto the set with Rhonda, pulled him aside, and whispered in his ear, "She knows."

"What did she say?" he wanted to know.

Diana said Rhonda had been "shocked" but that "she handled it like the champion she is," while admitting that the girl's reaction was so neutral she didn't know if Rhonda "was sad or happy" about finding out. As Liles pointed out, "Rhonda had grown up the daughter of a white man—and had to rethink her identity upon finding out her father was a black man, and one with whom she'd casually shaken hands over a hundred times." And yet Gordy had little more to say of the gut-wrenching experience himself beyond semi-perfunctorily noting that Rhonda was "watching me as I had watched her for years, looking for similarities. Every now and then I saw what I thought was a smile of her recognition of some of me in her. We didn't talk about it as such, but I believe that day resolved some questions she may have asked herself over the years."

In fact, Rhonda came to master the art of spinning the drama in an innocuous feel-good manner. In 1994, she would tell the *New York Post* of Gordy, "I've known him forever as a friend of the family. But we always did have a special relationship—even before I knew he was my dad."

Cee

The long years of lies about Ross and Gordy's "love child" were only one myth perpetuated by Diana. Everyone who knew her became convinced early on that her marriage to Robert Silberstein was nothing more than a business arrangement with fringe benefits that would protect her from the scandal of living as an unwed mother. In fact, Silberstein was actually put on her payroll, for reasons never explained. But one possible reason may be that the handsome manager looked good on her arm. Says Liles: "I found Bob to be a warm, soft-spoken guy, and it was sad later on to hear Diana say that the only way she could tolerate him was as an escort."

Most telling was that Gordy didn't recede in her life; rather, he was, Liles recalled, "sort of a third party to the marriage, accompanying the two of them everywhere." If the marriage was a sham, it was no more so than the notion that Diana Ross and Berry Gordy were no longer dependent on each other. The truth was, they may have been more so.

Cee

The Ross public façade as an ambassador of conventional morality and family-values entertainment wasn't damaged, though, and it kept delivering. But she and Gordy had to be patient, as it seemed she had to trade several records that stiffed for one that didn't, like her '73 No. 1 smash "Touch Me in the Morning"—written and produced by a new

Motown recruit, Michael Masser, who had to put up with Ross deni-
grating the song as not good enough for her—and its Oscar-nominated
LP of the same name. When Gordy then tried pairing her with the red-
hot but difficult Marvin Gaye, it nearly died aborning after Gaye refused to stop smoking pot around the again-pregnant Ross.

"Man, don't smoke no weed," Gordy told him. "Diana's gonna
have a baby. You don't want drugs around the baby."

"Fuck Diana Ross," he said, saying stoned what so many around
Motown had wanted to say for so long. "I'm gonna smoke this weed or
I don't sing."

As a result of the discord, it was decided that the only way to get
the project done was for them to cut their vocals separately, at separate
studios, never seeing each other. Thus, all those dreamy love songs on
their two ensuing Top Ten singles and Top Thirty album were sung by
two people who detested each other—something that seemed to be the
overarching rule now at Motown.

It took until 1976 to hit the top again with the Oscar-nominated
theme from Gordy's second vanity movie project for her, "Mahogany
(Do You Know Where You're Going To)"—the only saving grace from
what was a $3.75 million bomb when Gordy fired the original director
and took over the job himself, ensuring a classic of unwitting comedy
that the Ross–Billy Dee Williams chemistry couldn't bail out. It was
Gordy, though, who took most of the hits, with *Time*'s review skewering him for "squandering one of America's most natural resources: Diana Ross."

That year would bring Ross a Tony Award for a one-woman Broadway musical that was taped for a TV special. It also brought another
No. 1 single—a cover of the Sylvester disco hit "Love Hangover," produced by Hal Davis—and the Top Five "I'm Coming Out," a sly wink
at the drag-queen life written and produced by Chic's Nile Rodgers and
Bernard Edwards after seeing drag queens dressed like Diana, who was
increasingly being embraced by gay fans. But now that she and Gordy
were psychologically worn out by each other and barely able to speak
without acrimony, Ross did something she never thought she would:
entertain offers from other record companies.

Ced

Still enmeshed in their morass of lawsuits with Gordy, HDH were
nonetheless able to get Invictus and Hot Wax Records off the ground

after the turn of the decade. Following early success with Honey Cone, their sessions in the old converted theater on Grand River Avenue helped maintain the pulse of the Detroit music scene that had grown faint when Motown transplanted itself to the coast. Many of the town's musicians, including sundry Funk Brothers who had to go scrounging up work for the first time in years, were down with Holland, Dozier, and Holland when they hit their first stride of the decade with a four-some that—what were the odds?—sounded remarkably like the Four Tops: namely, the Chairmen of the Board, whose lead singer Norman "General" Johnson was a near-replicate of Levi Stubbs. Their debut Invictus release, "Give Me Just a Little More Time," stormed to No. 3 in 1970. The same year, HDH would deliver Freda Payne's "Band of Gold," also a No. 3, and hit the top with Honey Cone's "Want Ads." For a while, it seemed as if their magic touch just might make Invictus/Hot Wax another Motown.

The problem for HDH was that Gordy was in a far better position to wait out the lawsuit battle, his lawyer fees absorbed into the Motown fiduciary structure. For HDH, spending hundreds of thousands of dollars in an endless and fruitless court war bled their resources dry, threatening not just their new company but the trio's excessively lavish lifestyle. In 1972, with everyone fatigued by the constant hearings and depositions, HDH approached Gordy with an offer to settle, on terms favorable to him. After all the overheated rhetoric and invective about servitude on one side and a vendetta on the other, in the end the whole *meshugas* was reduced to exactly what Eddie Holland had sworn it wouldn't be about: mere dollars. The terms of the settlement were sealed by mutual consent; reportedly something like $200,000 went to Motown for the breach of contract—which by the time it was paid wasn't even a symbolic victory for Gordy, who had ultimately proven he could get along quite well without his old mates and had moved far beyond the grind of Supremes and Four Tops ditties. "The only financial winners," Gordy would say, "were the lawyers."

For HDH, the early glow of Invictus/Hot Wax began to flicker as musical tastes changed, execrably, from the stripped-down soul and pop-funk of the early '70s to the syncopated miasma of disco, leaving HDH to have to keep up with the work of younger, lesser producers. As with other restless writers like the McFadden-Whitehead team at Gamble and Huff's Philadelphia International Records, Brian Holland and Lamont Dozier wanted some spotlight time, teaming as an act to record middling records like "Why Can't We Be Lovers," "Don't Leave

Me Starvin' for Your Love," and "Slippin' Away." Dozier then quit to record solo for ABC and, later, had a couple of mild hits like "Fish Ain't Biting" and "Let Me Start Tonight" before moving on to Warner Brothers and Columbia. Between long periods of seclusion and living in Europe, he produced Aretha Franklin's 1977 LP *Sweet Passion* and wrote songs for Eric Clapton, Simply Red, Alison Moyet, and Phil Collins (including the No. 1 hit "Two Hearts" from the 1988 movie *Buster*), and recorded again in the '90s for Atlantic.

Having left Invictus/Hot Wax to wither, Dozier and the Holland brothers were kept estranged by the bitterness between them until the onset of *The First Wives Club* Broadway musical score in 2008. On their own, meanwhile, the Hollands tried to make a go of it, replacing Dozier with writer-producer Harold Beaty, but in 1975 they folded the shop. They then formed HDH Records and Productions (Dozier played no part; the acronym had been copyrighted as an intellectual property) and began producing on a freelance basis, with one of their clients none other than Motown Records, a development explained by Berry Gordy this way: "Disagreement or not, the fact was that these guys helped me make history. I did not want war to be our legacy."

Not that their legacy wasn't already preserved. In 2000, *Time* defined it thusly: "You can . . . marvel at the ways in which [HDH] managed to make the boundaries of their two commercially dictated themes—(a) I don't deserve you, please come back; and (b) you don't deserve me, I'm not coming back—seem limitless." The Hollands worked with Michael Jackson on some of his early singles; then, with a perfect symmetry, Gordy would assign them to a group they knew a little about, albeit in a previous lifetime for them and the group—the Supremes.

Their return to Motown, however, was not a return to old formulae. In fact, little about it seemed like a homecoming to them. Working in L.A. under less stringent standards and with Gordy nowhere in sight, says Eddie Holland, "[i]t was a different crowd, a different vibe. There was no family feel to it anymore. It was nice getting back with Mary but it was really just a job. They were doing their material and we tried to mold it. But we'd all moved beyond where we were in the '60s. All that was over, man."

The Supremes had pushed on, with decreasing success and a freely swinging revolving door. In 1972, Cindy Birdsong became pregnant and took a leave from the group, replaced by Linda Laurence, who'd sung backup for Stevie Wonder. The bonus of which was getting Wonder to produce their '73 single "Bad Weather," though it reached only No. 87. Now, with contracts having expired and no one at Motown in a hurry to extend them, the girls' only work for months was outside the studio, in concert venues. Then Terrell, who had fronted the last Top Twenty hit they would ever have, "This Is the Story" in '72, had a run-in with a domineering Mary—she having executed a role reversal in the transition, taking over the Diana Ross I'm-the-boss attitude.

"I'm the original Supreme, I started the group," Mary told her, pulling rank and stretching the truth.

"Well, you're not the lead singer," Jean retorted, now in the "Flo" role. "So I'm not listening to you. Maybe you've been here too long." It was precisely the kind of lip that made Gordy turn on her. Soon after, Terrell split. So, too, had manager Shelly Berger. It might have been a good time to fold the group once and for all. But Wilson doggedly kept it going.

Stardom had become a narcotic for Mary; it appeared to be all that kept her going. Even her romantic life, such as it was, seemed to rub off the group. In '74, after engaging in yet more meaningless flings with famous men as disparate as Flip Wilson and Steve McQueen, she was romanced by a Dominican businessman with a huge Afro, Pedro Ferrer, a big-talking nobody about whom it was said that only one person could tolerate him. Since that person, of course, was Mary Wilson, Ferrrer began to assume a larger role with the Supremes—"assume" being the operative word. In a sense, in fact, Ferrer became Mary's version of Tommy Chapman. After she married him in the chapel of the Riviera Hotel in Las Vegas in mid-'74, she made him the group's manager, and though all the decisions were ultimately hers, it mortified the other girls that she would actually take cues from a guy with no expertise in music or managing.

"Oh yeah," smirks Shelly Berger, "that was a clever move."

Once contracts were extended, Mary made herself co-lead singer with Scherrie Payne, sister of "Band of Gold's" Freda Payne, in yet another Supremes incarnation. Linda Laurence had left as well, and Birdsong agreed to return, though she would exit soon after—one of Pedro Ferrer's suggestions—for another faux Supreme, Susaye Greene, who had sung with Laurence while backing up Stevie Wonder. Still a viable entity, even if one needed a scorecard to keep up with the changing personnel, these Supremes could in no way be compared with the old Supremes. Instead, they were accepted for what they were by the mid-'70s: a tame disco-era act with a marketable name. On the strength of an earlier song that had become a dance club favorite, "He's My Man," in 1975 they recorded five more singles and three albums in that mold. But they were on borrowed time now.

A state of being that another original Supreme, the forgotten one, could relate to.

Cee

It had been six years since Flo Ballard found an attorney to represent her, a rather unstable character named Gerald Dent, whom Flo said she liked because "[h]e wasn't scared of Gordy," though given future events Gordy might have done well to be scared of him. In 1970, he not only sued Leonard Baun but filed an $8.5 million civil lawsuit against the Motown Recording Company claiming that Ballard had been "secretly, subversively and maliciously" fired and that it had concealed money she was owed.

In the interim, however, Dent seemed to crack up. He was indicted for obstruction of justice in another case, after telling a witness to hide out in Canada. Going through some heavy personal problems, he then nearly killed himself with an overdose of pills. Finally, on April 2, 1973, while pleading a different case in court, he whipped out a gun he'd smuggled into the courthouse and fired a shot at an opposing witness. As spectators dove under benches, and the judge under his, the court officer opened fire, killing Dent. Shortly after Dent's bizarre, disturbing death, the lawsuit against Motown, going forward under another attorney, was thrown out of Circuit Court, the judge ruling that Ballard hadn't proven any illegal or malicious intent or financial shenanigans that would mitigate the termination agreements. She could rescind the agreement and move to renegotiate the terms, but only if she repaid Motown the $160,000 she'd been given by the agreement—an option that was comically moot given her economic state and cosmically off the wall in the legal sense, it being a mystery how a binding agreement can be made unbinding for the right price. The judge did say that Flo could press on in a lower court with her mental and emotional claims. But as far as money went, she was out of luck.

Later that year, Flo gave birth to her third daughter, Lisa Chapman, and was scraping by on Tommy's sporadic paychecks. Then came the cruelest blow of all. Because she had been unable to satisfy the IRS judgment, and subsequently unable even to pay the mortgage, the bank holding the mortgage foreclosed on the house on Buena Vista Boulevard.

When word got around, some of her friends, knowing how much she loved the house and what it meant to her that her children have a nice home to grown up in, worried themselves sick that if anything would kill her, this was it.

Flo, swallowing her pride, appealed to Gordy, Ross, and Wilson for help. Maxine Ballard Jenkins remembered Flo reaching Gordy by telephone one day. "Berry," she said, "I need money. My kids got to eat." Maxine didn't know what Gordy said but recalled that "the phone came crashing down" in anger and frustration. The same happened when she tried reaching Diana and Mary, "only to have them hang up on her," said Jenkins, leaving Flo to scream into the dead phone line, "Those black bitches!"

RAY GIBSON: It was just so sad, everything was just so fucked up. I was with Florence the day that Baun told her she was broke. That was after he had told her he'd invested some of her money in an apartment building and we went to see it and there was nothing but a vacant lot. I had begged Florence not to leave the Supremes and she'd said to me, "Raymond, I got all this money and now I'm gonna go spend it." And she did. She had all these "friends" who helped her spend it, then she was broke and they didn't want to know her anymore. And Tommy . . . the thing with Tommy was, I don't think he stole money from her but he sure as hell helped her spend a whole lot of it. I'd moved to L.A. in '73 and I hadn't seen her for a while and then she called and said, "Raymond, you need to come home. I need to see you. You need to help me get my head together." She was lost and confused. Tommy, he was gone. She didn't know what to do. I did what I could. I didn't have much but I sent money for the kids, so she could at least go buy them some food.

At some point, though, she had some kind of rapprochement with Ross. When Diana came to Detroit that year she invited Flo to her second daughter's birthday party at Gordy Manor—not coincidentally, he wasn't on the trip. She and Diana also had chatted on the phone after the release of *Mahogany*. Thereafter Diana, who couldn't conceive that

Flo might lose her home because of a few thousand dollars in missed mortgage payments, agreed to either lend Flo money or just pay off the arrears herself, even though Ross would tell the *Chicago Tribune Magazine* a few months later that Flo "didn't want my help."

Here is where it gets a bit murky. According to Wilson in *Dreamgirl*, someone she identified only as "another recording artist" agreed to lend Flo $700, for what purpose she didn't say; but after Flo was asked to sign an agreement that had several blank pages attached, she "wisely" refused to sign them. That "recording artist" may have been Ross, although $700 seems a bit light for the back mortgage payments Flo owed. It may well have been someone else, since Ray Gibson remembers hearing that Diana tried to send money but backed off because of Tommy Chapman's meddling.

"Diana would only do it if an agreement could be worked out— but Tommy wanted her to send the check to him, which she wouldn't do. Diana is smarter than that. She never would have given Tommy that check. She knew better. We all knew better."

In *Call Her Miss Ross*, J. Randy Taraborrelli contends the opposite, that Chapman was suspicious of Ross's motives—"[H]e thought she had ulterior motives for wanting to save the home"—and thus wanted her check made out to him instead of to the bank, which prompted Diana to call off the deal. In an endnote Taraborrelli wrote: "Ross has never discussed [the payment] but there are many Motown executives who recall this transaction and a copy of the voided check exists in Motown's accounting files." And what of Mary Wilson? In *Dreamgirl* Wilson took pains to explain why she hadn't reached for her checkbook to aid Flo: "Word of Flo's financial plight didn't reach me until she had lost the house. She never asked for help"—a rationalization at best and willful blindness at worst, similar to Diana's unlikely plaint to the *Chicago Tribune Magazine* that Flo hadn't wanted her help (to which she added, "She got to be a pain in the ass and I said, 'Oh, forget it!'"). Indeed, at the time, Mary was trying hard to keep up with Diana Ross in self-absorption; as a result she spent like a drunken sailor, buying among other decadent items a white stretch Mercedes Benz and a classic Silver Cloud Rolls-Royce.

When Tony Tucker brought up Flo's predicament to Mary around that time, she could hardly be bothered. "I can't go around trying to save Flo," she said, adding that Flo had "spent her money, she mismanaged it. So what should I do about it?" Another time: "I have my own problems. I can't start feeling sorry now for Flo."

Flo, sensitive and intuitive as she was, didn't pull any punches about what had happened to the souls of her ex-Supreme mates. Of Ross, she told Tucker, "It's a sickness, honey, simply a sickness; she thinks it's all about her."

She concluded: "That whole Supremes thing is a total sickness."

Cee

Thus did Flo lose her house, and among her other problems—ones that didn't include what color Rolls-Royce to buy—was the dangerous ground she was on with the increasingly violent Tommy Chapman.

Maxine Jenkins recalled that when she made a routine visit to a neighborhood doctor Flo also saw, she spied Flo one time in the waiting room, wearing sunglasses, shaking and crying. Maxine asked her what was wrong and Flo lifted the glasses to show two black eyes and deep red bruises on her face, put there, she said, by Tommy.

Chapman's physical abuse of Flo had been suspected for some time, with Flo always cutting him slack, making excuses, even blaming herself for provoking him. But now he was also shirking his duties as a father and not bringing in any income. A frustrated Flo, who indeed would go right back at Tommy when she was angry, would call Maxine and say, "That black motherfucker didn't bring me any money for my kids!"

With the house gone, Tommy took the car and drove off into the night. This time, Flo didn't keep the porch light on for when he'd return. Sick of being battered and abandoned, she filed for a separation and, with her mother and Maxine, moved into a rundown, $150-a-month apartment on the dumpy west side of town. Shutting off the outside world, she ate her way to over 200 pounds. To feed the kids, she applied for aid from the city's Aid to Dependent Children program and received $135 biweekly.

Shaken and saddened by seeing Flo lose her house and descend into poverty, Mae Atkins, her neighbor on Buena Vista, who with her husband, Cholly, had once rented Flo's basement as a dance studio, anonymously called a reporter at the *Detroit Free Press* and related Flo's story in the hope that someone would come to her aid. When the paper ran the story, many Supremes fans were shocked that she had hit skid row.

Many fans had indeed forgotten her, either assuming she was contentedly raising a family in splendor and leisure or never realizing she'd ever left the group. Few knew of her lawsuit against Motown. Now,

here she was, overweight, abandoned by her husband, and on welfare—
"livin' in shame," indeed. The implication was that Motown had to
be plenty cruel to fire her, pay her off in peanuts, then let her—a
Supreme—go to pot. Because Flo had always played along with the
myth of leaving the group amicably to "get some rest," the truth hurt.
"I didn't leave," she said. "I was told to leave." That story line would
continue to follow Diana Ross and Berry Gordy for many years, with
future implications that would bedevil Ross.

Numerous well-wishers sent her letters and cards. Some came with
checks. A few offered jobs, which she didn't take. The Temptations' Eddie Kendricks dropped by her new place, knocked on the door, and
when Flo's sister answered, stuck a hundred-dollar bill in her hand
and told her, "Here, give this to Flo."

The heartbreaking story was picked up by newspapers across the
country; the *Washington Post* sent two reporters to Detroit to write their
own article. Flo was buoyed by the attention, and was ready with a
juicy quote. "I dislike him very much," she said of Gordy, "since I
trusted him very much and I also had a lot of respect for him at the
time and I put my faith in this man, but the money was never there! I
dislike him *very* much." Interviewed by a Detroit radio station, she
said, "I spend my life trying to come out of this nightmare. I [have] had
mental anguish and a whole lot of mental problems," adding, "I am
feeling a little better. I want to do something. I haven't made the decision what." She mentioned getting a "call from New York to record"
but admitted that she wasn't nearly ready for anything like that—"Not
yet. When I get over these problems."

That summer of 1975, Mary Wilson persuaded Flo to visit her in L.A.
for a few days, and sent her a ticket. Once there, she even accepted
Mary's invitation to come up on stage to take a bow at a Supremes concert at the Magic Mountain amusement park. She happily basked in
the ovation and posed for pictures with her successor Cindy Birdsong.
But whenever Mary would say that Flo should get back to singing, that
it would be beneficial for her head, Flo lost her spark, saying, "I can't,
Mary. I just can't." Despite the momentary peaks of the trip, Mary said
that during her stay Flo "was the saddest person I had ever seen."

Flo went home, feeling no better. But then there came some
long-overdue good news: Leonard Baun, who had been disbarred for

misconduct in a different case, agreed to settle Flo's lawsuit for $50,000. When the money appeared, so did Tommy Chapman. And incredibly, she took him back. The Chapman family moved into a small red-brick cottage on Shaftsbury Street in northwest Detroit, half the size of their Buena Vista digs but to Flo a real home again. Tommy was earning money driving and as a road manager for a local singing group. Flo bought a new Cadillac Seville. All seemed well. Flo even took a huge step—singing again, and better than she thought she could, at a benefit concert at the Ford Auditorium where she performed "I Am Woman" and, as an encore, to the delight of the audience, "Come See About Me."

But looks can be deceiving. Not able to rally herself, she would sink back into ennui and despair, seeing her future as a bleak one. Her drinking, as always, only made her more unstable. Often her mother or sisters would have to pry the kids from her instead of letting them get into the car. They'd then look after them as Flo would ignore their pleas not to drive and cruise the roads for hours. When she was home, she would sit on her bed, sucking down glass after glass of vodka and listening to old Supremes records on the Victrola as if she was trying to somehow relive the high of the glory days and crying over the loss of it all. She would drift off to sleep playing "Where Did Our Love Go" over and over.

Living so long in so much pain, mental and physical, she was weak and in a fragile state of mind. She'd been mugged on the street a number of times, making her paranoid. Then, that winter, she slipped on an icy sidewalk outside a supermarket and broke her ankle. She told people she'd sued the owners and gotten a nice settlement. But the injury laid her up. With a cast on her foot and inactive, she gained even more weight, putting a strain on her heart. She also was prescribed pain killers, which she may have abused and dangerously combined with alcohol.

By the new year, she had plainly lost her mind. To whoever would listen, she would spin conspiracy theories in which Motown villains had plotted against her; they'd spiked her drinks so she'd be woozy and miss rehearsals and look bad, they'd brainwashed her, they'd "controlled my mind." She swore she had more money than people thought, that Berry Gordy had so feared her revealing all this, as well as the bad publicity about her being on welfare with her kids, that he'd secretly paid her under the table. The supermarket suit, she said, was made up to explain the additional money. Yet she had allowed the bad publicity to come to light and was still threatening to write a book revealing Gordy's "dirty laundry" and to "implicate" Diana and Mary in his nefarious plots.

If there was one refuge that brought her calm, it wasn't the new house but the old one she'd had to abandon. Refusing to let go, she'd return there night after night, let herself into the dark and shuttered house, light a candle and go from room to room checking each and making notes about how she'd decorate it when she'd come back there to live. Sometimes she'd awaken the kids, dress and put them in the back of the Cadillac, and drive them there, where she'd put on a show. Making a grand entrance out the door, she'd stand on the "stage" of the front porch, sing songs as the kids sat on the freezing ground, take her bows, then drive home.

At these moments, she was *Flo the Supreme* again. Tony Tucker remembered that when she was *Flo* and someone showed her pity, such as when someone remarked that her friends should stick by her, she'd go ballistic. "I don't need no motherfuckin'-body to stick by me!" she scowled. "I'm Flo Ballard! I'm a Supreme! Get out of the way, I got a show to do!"

For all the delusions, though, Flo actually did get some offers to sing again, and she was seemingly getting used to the idea, mentioning that "big" women were "in," like Aretha and Roberta Flack; and her time was now. Suddenly she was dieting, rehearsing her singing in a new basement studio she'd built. Her doctor had diagnosed her with hypertension and she was taking medication for it, though she didn't realize that the other pills she kept taking elevated her blood pressure all over again.

It was all too much for her heart. In early February 1976, she had a phone conversation with Mae Atkins, during which she slurred her words and sounded drunk. "I don't feel well," she complained. "I have a pain in my chest." Mae told her to get to a hospital, but Flo shrugged it off. Then, going back to the apartment to visit Lurlee and Maxine, she kept drinking ice water, saying that "I'm hot inside. I can't get rid of this hot feeling." Flo always was a hypochondriac so it didn't seem cause for alarm.

Two weeks later, at around 3 A.M. on the morning of February 21, Flo called Lurlee and said she couldn't sleep, that she was having trouble breathing. "Mama," she said, "if anything happens to me, I want you to keep the children." Lurlee told her she was talking crazy and to go back to bed. Tommy was out working overnight, so she was alone in her room, but her labored breathing so worried her daughter Nicole, now 8, that she called Lurlee, who told her the same thing she had Flo, that there was no cause to worry.

At around 10, Tommy came home, opened the bedroom door, and in horror saw Flo lying on the cold floor in her bedclothes, unable to move her lower body. She could only croak in a hoarse whisper, "I can't move my legs." Tommy and the kids lifted her onto a sofa and he called for an ambulance. Taken to Mount Carmel Mercy Hospital, she still had no feeling in her legs and was put in a bed in the emergency ward for observation. She was on her back for the entire day. The doctors did tests but had little to say as family members drifted in and out. When Maxine got to her bedside, Flo was clearly worried. "I got to be able to take care of my kids," she struggled to say.

Maxine would later say that as she looked at her sister, she knew that Flo was taking her last breaths. But when Flo made it into the night, the family went home, saying they'd be back the next morning. Before they could, early on the morning of the 22nd, a blood clot formed in Flo's coronary artery. At around 9 A.M., her heart finally gave up. Flo Ballard was pronounced dead. She was 32 years old.

The death of "Blondie" Ballard caused great and genuine sadness at Motown. When someone phoned Mary to tell her, she stood helpless, phone in hand, repeating, "I knew it . . . I knew it. . . . " She and Ross made immediate plans to fly to Detroit for the funeral. Gordy didn't, but he did insist upon paying for the funeral, which was treated by Motown as a chance to purge, or at least gauze over, old guilts by spending a lot of money on a woman Gordy had recently hung up on when she asked for a few bucks. And if this became an exemplar of how well Motown took care of its own at the same time that it could publicize itself and some of its top acts, well, as Gordy would put it, "That didn't hurt either."

The service at the Reverend C. L. Franklin's New Bethel Church on February 24 was planned as meticulously as a Supremes concert in Las Vegas. Flowers were everywhere, with big wreaths and floral arrangements wrapped in banners identifying Motown acts, and one reading just "MOTOWN," which while meant to articulate the personal tribute of each act and the company in general seemed more like those old *Billboard* ads with Motown artists in bubbles. Some had messages, such as "I LOVE YOU . . . DIANA" and "GOODBYE BLONDIE," which was from Gordy but didn't have his name on it, possibly because he knew how Ballard fans now felt about him. Curiously—or perhaps not—there was no wreath with Mary Wilson's name.

The widower Chapman, hit hard by Flo's death, seemed a little out of his mind as well, telling people he was in charge, having "allowed" Gordy to pay for the funeral and that he had ordered him to "do the right thing" for Flo. And he did in fact overrule the planners' intention to dress Flo in the open coffin in a Supremes gown; instead, she was put in a knee-length powder-blue robe—although through it one could see the black and blue leg bruises that he'd inflicted.

It would be perhaps the biggest funeral ever seen in Detroit, which surely would have elicited one of Flo's sassy one-liners since so few had wanted to know her in her declining years. On that day, the church was stuffed with 2,500 people, many of whom came with cameras to capture the arrival of the VIPs. Maxine Jenkins called it all a "circus" and a "showcase for celebrities," and outside there were twice as many people behind flimsy police barricades and the crowds would lurch forward when each limousine pulled up, forcing cops to drag people away and clear the way into church, with each celebrity cheered as if at a concert.

When Diana emerged from her limo in a dignified black suit, cheers mixed with boos and catcalls—"Hope you're happy now, Diana, *you* did this to Flo!" rang out one loud voice, framing a narrative that would haunt her from now on. Regally ignoring the abuse, shielded by two bodyguards, she was ushered inside and, as planned, right past the other celebrities and guests waiting in line to be seated.

"It was strange," recalls Ray Gibson, who came in from L.A. "All of us came through the side door. Mary, Stevie Wonder, the Four Tops. But Diana came in from the top of the stairs in the back. She made her grand entrance as only Diana can. But did she have to do it on Florence's day? Couldn't she let Florence have the spotlight just this once?"

The word "upstage" was used a lot about Ross that day, and for years later when people spoke of the funeral. Taken straight to the front pew next to Chapman and the Ballard daughters, she could be heard screaming in grief and appeared faint in the hot and stifling church, prompting others to fan her. Mary, in a mirrored and jeweled skull cap she'd worn on her last album cover, and a veil, boa, and fur coat, was seated a symbolic three rows behind her. According to *Call Her Miss Ross*, Lurlee Ballard "eye[d] Diana Ross suspiciously at her left"—but while many in the house did eye Ross in that manner, it would have been quite a feat for Lurlee, who wasn't there. "Flo's mama didn't go to the funeral," says Gibson. "The doctors told her not to, it would've been too much for her. In fact, they had to take me out of there. It was so emotional for me that I was making a terrible mess of myself."

Because many in the audience continued hooting and hollering, C. L. Franklin admonished them to hush up out of respect for the dead as he gave the eulogy, saying it was "Flo's homecoming." All the while, chants of "We want Diana!" could be heard from outside. Then came a crash as a car window was shattered, unnerving everyone. When the eulogy was over, many were eager to leave before the mob could surge inside. But Diana rose and came forward. Picking up a microphone, she called Mary up. Wilson, sobbing in her seat and not expecting to have to say anything, haltingly joined her standing next to the coffin, "furious," she would later say, "that I was being dragged into this."

Diana intoned, "I believe nothing disappears, and Flo will always be with us," then handed the mike to Mary, saying, "Here Mary." Not knowing what to say, she uttered, "I loved her very much," and touched Flo's cheek.

The service ended with the organist playing and a choir singing "Someday We'll Be Together," which might have fit the occasion except for the fact that Flo and Mary had not sung on the record. Flo's casket was carried out to a hearse, the Four Tops and Marv Johnson among the pallbearers. The flower arrangements were tossed into the crowd like meat into a pool of sharks, to keep it at bay; but within minutes the flowers had been stripped bare, leaving only the wire and Styrofoam frames lying twisted in the gutter.

The burial was at Detroit's Memorial Park cemetery, away from the mobs and the media. Only around a dozen mourners had made their way there when the coffin was lowered into the ground. Diana, having done her part, was nowhere to be seen, something close to an *infamia* to Mary.

"We were the only two people who had shared Flo's greatest moments," she would write. "For that reason alone, Diane should have been there."

Mary threw a flower on the coffin as it went down.

The February 27 coroner's report determined the cause of death as "coronary artery thrombosis [blood clot] which totally occluded the right coronary artery [causing] cardiac arrest." There were only trace amounts of alcohol or drugs in her blood, and the leg numbness she had suffered was called an "emotional" and "hysterical" reaction, not a physical symptom. Meaning that nothing else killed Flo Ballard but the cumulative damage to her heart. Those like Lurlee who would take to saying Flo had died of a broken heart were perhaps half-right; in truth, she had lived with a broken heart, for too long.

Berry Gordy's generosity stopped at the grave site. All that the Ballard family could afford as a headstone was a flat metal plaque on the plot embroidered with flowers and engraved "Florence Glenda Chapman, wife and mother," with dates of birth and death separated by two musical notes. (When Lurlee died five years later, her grave would be marked only with a concrete cement marker, without any name on it.)

Diana set up a small trust fund of a few thousand dollars for each of Flo's daughters, specifying Lurlee and not Tommy Chapman as the guardian. Rather than be grateful for the gift, Tommy became enraged at the slight, and when Lurlee petitioned for and won custody of the girls, he blamed Ross for turning the judge against him. But when Lurlee died in 1982, he didn't demand the children be with him and they would be passed from one Ballard relative to another until they were adults.

Always the operator, Tommy did have one asset left, the "hot" manuscript Flo had been working on about her life, which he now tried pitching to publishers, only to sell it for $10,000 to Motown— not to publish but to *prevent* it from being published. By the '80s, however, he was broke and, like Flo near the end, frothing at the mouth, cursing Gordy for conspiring to destroy Flo. "Motown killed my wife," he was fond of saying, and the funeral and the Ross trust fund were "just publicity."

In a very weird contention, Tony Tucker in *All That Glittered* claimed that Mary had agreed to interview Chapman in the mid-'80s to get "the whole story" about Flo for *Dreamgirl*, but all Tucker seemed to know was that Tommy had moved "down South" and that just before Wilson was to allegedly have met with him, Chapman was killed. "Somebody shot him in the head in a pool hall" was the story, setting in motion a new offshoot to the conspiracy theories in which Chapman had been "silenced" after Gordy learned of the meeting.

What really happened, of course, was far more mundane. Chapman was working in Baton Rouge, Louisiana, as a city bus driver with a route in the area of the LSU campus. Occasionally he'd come back to Detroit to visit his daughters, and once in a while he sent them some money. City police records of the time do not include the violent murder of anyone named Thomas Chapman, and his boss at the bus company said Chapman died of a heart attack. What's more, the Tucker tale—with its very shaky premise that Wilson, who despised Chapman, would have had anything to do with him for her book—falls apart in light of the fact that Chapman apparently was still alive when *Dreamgirl* was published.

Cee

For the two surviving Supremes, life continued to be good but was by no means untouched by tragedy and personal problems.

Mary, inexorably, moved in the mid-'70s toward folding the faux Supremes, but not before they and two-thirds of HDH could dually execute a symbolic closure with Motown. In 1976, with almost no fanfare or even notice, Brian and Eddie Holland produced the group's *High Energy* album. Released on April Fool's Day, just weeks after Florence Ballard's death, the work yielded the single "I'm Gonna Let My Heart Do the Walking," a disco number derivative of the Three Degrees; fronted by Payne and Greene, it went to No. 40 on the pop charts and No. 25 on the R&B charts—the girls' final Top Forty hit—while the album performed respectably (42 on the pop charts, 24 on R&B). Fittingly, the Hollands then produced what would be the Supremes' final studio album, the soggy *Mary, Scherrie & Susaye*; released in October, it consisted of more disco rhythms and violin-smothered ballads. None of its three singles rose higher than No. 85, while the album failed to chart at all.

Mary soon pulled the plug. Although Payne and Greene wanted to continue with a new member, Motown saw no sustainable upside, and since Gordy owned the name of the Supremes, it was over. With a tiny fraction of the bathos of the Frontier farewell to Ross, the Supremes' final concert came in June 1977 at London's Drury Lane Theater. There were no songs sung to Berry Gordy, no toasts, no big cake, and almost no tears.

Wilson was given a farewell gift of her own by Motown, an eponymous solo album, from which came a single, "Red Hot," that reached No. 95 on the R&B charts and 85 on *Billboard*'s new dance-music charts in late '79.

Ross's star, of course, kept shining brightly, even though her overall record of achievement would play out in starts and stops. After hitting No. 1 on the charts for the last time at Motown with her 1981 duet with Lionel Richie, "Endless Love," and a last movie role done for Gordy, the costly megaton bomb *The Wiz* (an "urban" re-telling of *The Wizard of Oz* wherein 11-year-old Dorothy becomes a Harlem school-teacher), she jumped for a then-record $20 million contract with RCA. But the returns were only so-so. None of her twenty singles through '88 reached higher than the first, "Why Do Fools Fall in Love," which hit No. 4, though she did ring up a platinum and two gold albums. Her last RCA album, *Red Hot Rhythm and Blues*, tanked at No. 73— sending her back to a dramatically downsized Motown in 1989.

Music had clearly become a secondary concern to Gordy in the mid-1970s, far behind the rush and Hollywood high-society requisite of making movies, despite the diminishing returns that had begun with only his second project, *Mahogany*, and the beating he took with *The Wiz*, a high crime reviewed by *Time* as a "lyrical lemon."

As for the inspiration that made Motown—music—Gordy's last serious attention came in the early '70s when he said to hell with caution and formed the Black Forum label for racially/politically uncompromising, spoken-word albums, including Dr. Martin Luther King's *Why I Oppose the War in Vietnam*, Stokely Carmichael's *Free Huey*, and Amiri Baraka's *Black Spirits*. He also put out some of the era's most visceral protest records with Edwin Starr's raspy imprecation "War" and Marvin Gaye's trilogy of plaintive social mourning (though Gordy originally resisted releasing "What's Going On"). Paying Stevie Wonder a then-record $13 million to re-sign with Motown in 1971, he was rewarded with Wonder's epochal and hugely successful synthesizer-laden pop-funk works like *Songs in the Key of Life* and *Innervisions*. He also created the expressly *white*, rock-oriented Rare Earth label, striking gold with R. Dean Taylor's "Indiana Wants Me." However, Motown was clearly atrophying by mid-decade, its roster of 100 acts in the late '60s pared to half that. Gordy started to lose his biggest artists—first the Jackson 5, who bailed to CBS Records' Epic label. Gaye would leave for Columbia. And, in the biggest kick to the head, in 1980, Diana Ross's defection to RCA.

Motown lost more than its soul; with the exception of Stevie Wonder, it lost its family. For the self-congratulatory "Motown 25: Yesterday, Today, Forever" TV special on May 16, 1983, Ross, Gaye, and Michael Jackson (who'd electrify the nation by Moonwalking to "Billie

Jean") performed as a favor to Gordy. But the show would go on, not only without some seminal Motown acts, like the Marvelettes and Contours, but with some rather odd choices to perform classic Motown tunes: Linda Ronstadt, who at least had hit covers of "Ooo Baby, Baby" and "Tracks of My Tears," and—to the astonishment of everyone— British "new wave" singer Adam Ant, who murdered "Where Did Our Love Go."

Diana, on her part, would only grudgingly do a turn with the Supremes, calling out Wilson and Birdsong from the wings and doing a drive-by rendition of "Someday We'll Be Together"—or rather half of it before she suddenly shoved Mary out of her way, to an audible gasp from the audience. Evidently Motown people had suspected something like that could happen, because in a flash Smokey Robinson rushed onto the stage, on what Wilson would later call "a rescue mission," cueing all the acts to get out there pronto and execute a feel-good ending, sung not to "Someday" but to the song Diana neatly switched to, "Reach Out and Touch (Somebody's Hand)." Mary, foregoing the shove, got into the mood, yelling into a microphone, "Berry, come on down!"

Hearing it, Diana, in pro-wrestling fashion, forced Mary's hand down, pushing the microphone from her mouth, and yelling into her own the same instruction. When Gordy arrived, Ross waylaid him, letting go of him only momentarily, and giving his ass little pinches. Upon reaching Wilson, he jested, "You finally learned how to sing, huh?" Ross then closed the show by climbing onto a platform above the rest of the cast before scampering back down to the very center of the stage for media pictures of the group.

It was classic "bad Diana," and while her abuse of Wilson was carefully excised from the tape when the show ran, it left Wilson feeling "hurt and angry. What a terrible way to end an evening, a career, a friendship." Ross had, she wrote in her memoir, "done many things to hurt, humiliate and upset me," though she hastened to addend, "strangely enough, I still love her and am proud of her."

"Motown 25" also provided one of the saddest footnotes to Motown history. None of the Funk Brothers were recognized and James Jamerson, who had virtually created the Motown "sound" with his ungodly bass licks, asked for a ticket and was refused. Dissipated by time and alcohol, he had suffered a mortal blow recently when his Sunburst Fender Precision bass—the only electric bass he'd used on hundreds of Motown sessions—was stolen from his home. He hadn't played a date in years, and on the rare occasions he spoke of his past he would say only that he'd "done all that Motown shit." Nearly broke, he bought a ticket to the show and watched from the balcony, unknown, as the songs he made immortal were given tribute. A few weeks later, on August 2, 1983, he died at 45 of cirrhosis of the liver, heart failure, and pneumonia, and was not given his due until 2000, when he was inducted into the Rock and Roll Hall of Fame.

"Motown 25" can be thought of as Berry Gordy's last rites. Only five years later, with Motown in disarray and coughing red ink, he unloaded it to the L.A. entertainment conglomerate MCA for $61 million, conceding that if he didn't sell, Motown would fold and he'd be damned if he was going to wind up like his boyhood hero Joe Louis—"just another nigger who made it to the top and died broke," crowing in *To Be Loved* about his rise "[f]rom eight hundred dollars to sixty-one million. I had done it. I had won the poker hand." For him it was the good life now: days spent mainly at the country clubs of Bel-Air, a glass of Cristal or a nine-iron in his hand, or at the Playboy Mansion with fellow big-shots David Geffen and Quincy Jones. Shortly after the sale he married a third time, to Grace Easton, but typically, the marriage began to disintegrate almost immediately after the nuptials—another propitious bit of timing for the cash-out, as would be his 1993 sale of Jobete Publishing to EMI for $132 million.

For Motown, life wouldn't be so good. Aside from Suzanne DePasse's multi-award-winning TV miniseries about the Jackson 5 and the Temptations, MCA was said to treat Motown "like a Third World country." In 1993, $24 million in the red, Motown was sold to PolyGram, subsequently wending a serpentine path via Seagram to a home in the Universal Music Group. And while things took a turn for the better there, with young acts like Brian McKnight, Erykah Badu, Mya, and Yummy Bingham helping to turn its first profit in a decade, for Motown there will never be a real renaissance, only a higher (or lower) bottom line. With Gordy in his 80s and far removed from any imperative except *la dolce vita*, Motown—like its top-selling act of all time—can only be appreciated in the past tense.

Diana Ross—hailed by MCA executives as "the queen returning home"—was given stock in MCA that carried over to PolyGram and Universal, but has failed to register a single Top Forty pop hit since 1981, compiling only scattered lightweight R&B hits such as "Workin'

Overtime" in '89 and her '91 duet with hip-hop star Al B. Sure, "No Matter What You Do." Her 2007 "I Love You" world tour was a financial and critical success. But her albums sold more poorly than any she'd recorded in the last twenty years.

Not that Diana Ross needs record sales to keep her diva status intact. Now fabled is her 1983 free concert in New York's Central Park (on the outskirts of which she has long kept an apartment), when after a downpour rousted her from the stage in mid-show she returned the following day to complete it; today, a playground in the park is named for her. Neither is she hurting for money. In her mid-60s, she has a net worth of an estimated $150 million. The only thing she lacks is a husband. In 1985, having careened from actor Ryan O'Neal to—comically— tongue-flicking, blood-gurgling KISS rocker Gene Simmons, she married multimillionaire Norwegian shipping magnate Arne Naess Jr., had two sons, and began living a lifestyle so crazily excessive that even Naess would complain of her profligate spending, which included $25,000 a week on private jets, $20,000 a month to rent private homes, and $50,000 a month on clothing. They separated in 1999 and a year later divorced in the Dominican Republic.

Ross became a running joke in the tabloids. In October 1999, while being searched by a female airport security officer, she slapped her and was arrested and released with a warning. Three years later, she had a hitch in Malibu's Promises drug and alcohol rehabilitation center "to clear up some personal issues." Then a year after, she was busted for "extreme DUI" in Tucson, Arizona. During a breath test, it was reported, she fell down laughing while trying to stand on one leg and count to ten. Her blood-alcohol level was 0.20 percent, more than twice the limit, but drew only a misdemeanor charge and a slap on the wrist.

In 1996, her younger brother Arthur ("T-Boy") Ross and his wife were found suffocated to death in their Michigan home. Two men were charged with murder, and according to cops the crime was drug-related.

Eight years later, on February 2, 2004, Arne Naess Jr. fell to his death while climbing in the mountains near Cape Town, South Africa.

Mary Wilson kept herself busy through the years, plying her faded fame to keep singing in nightclubs while raising three children by Pedro Ferrer, whom she divorced in 1981 after absorbing numerous beatings that she revealed in *Supreme Faith: Someday We'll Be Together*. She made a few recordings for Atlantic and Boardwalk Records and played regular gigs in Las Vegas and Reno. In the early 1990s she cut her first album in twelve years, *Walk the Line* for CEO Records, releasing the singles "One Night with You" and "Walk the Line." However, when she got the idea to tour with two other singers in a show called "The Supremes Show with Mary Wilson," Motown slapped a suit on her; like Flo, she couldn't use the name after leaving Motown. Though she fought it, she lost. (Ironically, Motown couldn't stop interlopers from using the name, leading Wilson to lobby for laws against such copycat groups, noting that "[t]here are like five or six Supremes" out there.)

Wilson and Ross have not shared the same stage since the unsightly "Motown 25" proceedings. The closest thing to a Supremes reunion in the last three decades was a "Motown 45" TV special on April 4, 2004, at which Wilson and Birdsong sang a Supremes medley with Kelly Rowland of Destiny's Child.

In 1994, Wilson was driving with her son Raphael on a California highway when she fell asleep at the wheel of her Jeep Cherokee. The car hit the center divider, severely injuring Wilson and killing her son. While recovering, she claimed Ross had been there for her and that the two of them had ended their "feud." Wilson then moved from L.A. to New York to start a new life, getting a liberal arts degree from New York University and acting in some off-Broadway plays. She starred in the national touring company of Duke Ellington's *Sophisticated Ladies* in 2001 and in *The Vagina Monologues* at the Detroit Opera House in 2003.

In July 2006, she underwent an emergency angioplasty after suffering sharp chest pains. In short order, she was back on the road again and during the same year moved to Las Vegas. In late 2008 she was reportedly in the studio with Brian and Eddie Holland—who themselves had done little since the '70s (other than issuing bonds in 1998 worth $30 million backed by future royalties of their old songs)—recording songs adapted from her personal diaries.

Wilson endures not just as a Supremes echo but, fairly or not, as the antithesis of Diana Ross, through her own smart planning. *Dreamgirl*'s slams at Ross all but guaranteed a best-seller that extended the cleft between Ross and the "other" Supremes dating back to the '60s. But if that was a wise business decision, the notion of Wilson playing living martyr to Ross's designing woman may not be entirely accurate, or fair. Wilson, for example, conveniently omitted from her memoirs that when she was in financial trouble in the early '80s, Diana loaned her a substantial amount of money.

Indeed, chapter and verse can be written about Ross's generosity—witness the trust fund for Flo Ballard's children, a gesture not matched by Wilson. Another example comes from Janie Bradford, the former Motown receptionist and co-writer of "Money." In the early '80s, down on her luck, she and Freddie Gorman—who wrote the Supremes' first songs—co-wrote a song called "'I Am Me.'"

"I had this song," she recalls, "and one day I left a message for Diana, not expecting her to return it; I hadn't spoken with Diana in years. But then my daughter picked up and squealed, 'Mom, it's Diana Ross!' I said to myself, look, I'm going through hell, I'm gonna tell her the truth. And I did. I said, 'Diana, if there's any way you can record this song of mine, please do it because I need the money.' And she cut it and put it on the back of 'Muscles'! That was a huge hit. So you can imagine the royalties that came in, and still do. That's Diana Ross."

Jack Ashford, the tambourine master of the Funk Brothers, has a similar story:

> I was on the bus with the Supremes on a tour of England, and being one of the downtrodden musicians, I was in the back, on the hump. Berry and the girls were up front. And it was cold on that bus. And Diana came walking back, saw me shivering under a blanket, and asked, "You wanna share that blanket?" I'm trying to act cool but inside I'm like, "Yeah, yeah, come on!" Earl Van Dyke, he's looking at me and Diana under the blanket and he goes, "Watch out, Jack, it's a long way from England to Detroit!" So anyway, we got to Manchester and Diana and I were on a boat and I was saying I was broke, which was just the fact, we'd all blown our expense money like the first day. I said, "Diana, got any money?" And she pulls out of her purse a St. Christopher medal and gives it to me. She says, "It's my grandmother's, but take it, maybe it's worth some money."
>
> You know something? I still got that medal. I would've never sold it. That was the kindest thing anyone ever did for me—and it was Diana Ross who did it!

In *Secrets of a Sparrow*, anecdotes like this go unmentioned. But Ross does make a case that it was actually she who was victimized by the Supremes, who she says "treated me very badly" and went "against me with a vengeance. They had blamed me, acted as if everything were my fault"; after being "tormented, treated as if I were invisible, talked about behind my back, I tried to perform and pretend all was well. [But] when they stopped talking to me, it was too much to ignore."

The problem is that few ever believed such a thing—and never will after the debacle of the Supremes' 2000 Reunion Tour, which, as *Time* reported, was "STOPPED IN THE NAME OF INDIFFERENCE," leaving Ross as the foil for having tried to make herself five times more valuable than Wilson, fifteen times more than Cindy Birdsong. And allowing Wilson to wallow in the martyr role again, declaring, "I am very hurt and disappointed. Never in my wildest dreams did I think I wouldn't be part of a reunion. It was very devastating."

Diana, in turn, was compelled to crack back, "In my heart, I know that it would be very hard for me to be with her on stage."

Cut to Wilson: "People walk up to me and say, 'I just want to give you a hug and say, 'Thank you for standing up to her.'"

Back to Ross: "I think if we offered her the moon, she will not be happy."

And so on, and on. The feud, back on, apparently will never end. And without the music they left, we might hate them both for it.

Concludes Shelly Berger:

Listen, when you go down the road with those two, sometimes you want to scream. I love them both, dearly, and both of 'em fired me! All the bullshit goes with the territory, and they both have their own territory.

I happen to have my own story about Diana. On our first trip to Europe, we went to Germany, and people would kid me because I'm a Jew, they'd call me, "Herr Berger," and ask, in a German accent, "You have relatives in this country?" But Diana was genuinely worried about me because there was a lot of anti-Semitism over there. And at the Frankfurt Airport, an attendant told me there was a call for me in a private room so I went inside. When I came out, there was Diana Ross, standing all alone in the middle of the terminal. Talk about a shocking sight. The Supremes were *always* with people, the managers, the valets, they were never alone, especially Diana. I said, "What are you doing here?" She said, "I was waiting for you. I thought someone was gonna try and take you away." She'd slipped away from everyone just because she was worried about me. I can only assume she was ready to fight the entire German army the way she was ready to fight those rednecks in that bar.

So when people talk to me about Diana Ross, I remember her standing there like that, 90 pounds dripping wet, ready to go to war to protect me.

I'll only say this: Diana can be very tough. She's very demanding—of herself. She knows how to push better than anyone else, for better and for worse. That's why we're talking about her. That's why we're talking about *them*.

Ross could be more artful than to look back on the Supremes, as she does, with only grudging enchantment—calling those times a "positive" experience, because "I decided to make it that way, and so it was."

But when she allows that it was an "amazing time," on *that* point there can be peace. The chorus can take the cue, draw breath deeply and wail for the congregation:

And so it was, brothers and sisters. And so it was.

Bibliography

Books

Ballard, Maxine "Precious." *The True Story of Florence Ballard*. Precious4max, Inc., 2007.

Benjaminson, Peter. *The Story of Motown*. Grove Press, 1979.

Clemente, John. *Girl Groups: Fabulous Females That Rocked the World*. Krause Publications, 2000.

Coffey, Dennis. *Guitars, Bars, and Motown Superstars*. University of Michigan Press, 2004.

Early, Gerald Lyn. *One Nation Under a Groove: Motown and American Culture*. University of Michigan Press, 2004.

George, Nelson. *Where Did Our Love Go? The Rise and Fall of the Motown Sound*. St Martin's Press, 1986.

Goldsmith, Olivia. *First Wives Club*. Pocket, 1996.

Gordy, Berry. *To Be Loved: The Music, the Magic, the Memories of Motown: An Autobiography*. Warner Books, 1994.

Hirshey, Gerri. *Nowhere to Run: The Story of Soul Music*. Da Capo Press, 1994.

Liles, Raynoma. *Berry, Me and Motown: The Untold Story*. Contemporary Books, 1990.

Posner, Gerald L. *Motown: Music, Money, Sex, and Power*. Random House Trade Paperbacks, 2005.

Reeves, Martha. *Dancing in the Street: Confessions of a Motown Diva*. Hyperion Books, 1995.

Ritz, David. *Divided Soul: The Life of Marvin Gaye*. Da Capo Press, 2003.

Robinson, Smokey. *Smokey: Inside My Life*. McGraw-Hill, 1989.

Ross, Diana. *Secrets of a Sparrow*. Villard, 1993.

Singleton, Raynoma Gordy. *Berry, Me and Motown*. McGraw-Hill Contemporary, 1991.

Slutsky, Allan. *Standing in the Shadows of Motown: The Life and Music of Legendary Bassist James Jamerson*. Hal Leonard Corporation, 1989.

Smith, Suzanne E. *Dancing in the Street: Motown and the Cultural Politics of Detroit*. Harvard University Press, 2001.

Taraborrelli, J. Randy. *Call Her Miss Ross: The Unauthorized Biography of Diana Ross*. Pan Books, 1991.

Taylor, Harold Keith. *The Motown Music Machine*. Jadmeg Music Publishing, 2004.

Taylor, Marc. *The Original Marvelettes: Motown's Mystery Girl Group*. Aloiv Publishing Co., 2004.

Turner, Tony. *All That Glittered: My Life with the Supremes*. Penguin Group, 1991.

Waller, Don. *The Motown Story*. Gale Cengage, 1985.

Williams, Otis, and Patricia Romanowski. *Temptations*. G. P. Putnam's Sons, 1988.

Wilson, Mary. *Dreamgirl: My Life as a Supreme*. St. Martin's Press, 1986.

Wilson, Randall. *Forever Faithful! A Study of Florence Ballard and the Supremes*. Renaissance Sound Publications, 1999.

Newspaper and Magazine Articles

Detroit Magazine, "Motown Is Really Big," Van Gordon Sauter, 3/21/65.

Time, "The Sound of the Sixties," Ray Kennedy and A.T. Baker, 5/21/65.

The Toledo Blade, "Hitsville U.S.A.," Ray Oviatt, 8/22/65.

Billboard, "An Act for All Ages," Aaron Steinfeld, 8/7/65.

Variety, "Supremes Swing at Philharmonic," 9/15/65.

Chicago Daily News, "The Motown Sound," Michaela Williams, 9/25/65.

Detroit Magazine, "The Supremes in Eight Easy Lessons," Mort Persky, 1/30/66.

Time, "The Girls from Motown," 3/4/66.

Chicago Tribune, "Supremes: 11 Frantic Hours," Nancy Moss, 3/20/66.

Look, "The Supremes: From Real Rags to Real Riches," 5/3/66.

Billboard, "Motown Expansion in High Gear with Broadway, TV, Movies," Eliot Tiegel, 6/11/66.

Sepia Magazine, "Supremes and Hitsville U.S.A.," 8/66.

New York Times Magazine, "The Big, Happy Beating Heart of the Detroit Sound," Richard B. Lingeman, 9/27/66.

Detroit Magazine, "Supremes Starring on Behalf of Our Torch Drive," George Walker, 7/30/65.

Time, "Democracy in the Foxhole," 5/26/67.

Time, "Homemade Bomb" (film review), 5/26/67.

Time, "Heavyweight Featherweight," 9/8/67.

Cosmopolitan, "The Supremes: They Make You Believe," Rona Jaffe, 9/67.

Detroit Free Press, "Supremes' Flo Ballard: It's Said She's Leaving," Lorraine Alterman, 9/1/67.

Fortune, "The Motown Sound of Money," Stanley H. Brown, 9/1/67.

Time, "Tapping the Roots," 3/22/68.

TV Guide, "Diana," Digby Diehl, 12/7/68.

Ebony, "Former Supreme Talks a Little," 2/69.

Detroit Free Press, "A Talk with Berry Gordy," Bob Talbert and Lee Winfrey, 3/23/69.

Philadelphia Bulletin, "Diana Ross Walks Out," William Forsythe, 6/1/69.
New York Post, "Diana Ross Sings the Blues for Her Dogs," Earl Wilson, 6/9/69.
Look, "The Supreme Supreme," Jack Hamilton, 9/23/69.
Time, "Situation Report," 4/6/70.
Time, "Baby, Baby, Where Did Diana Go?" 8/1/70.
Michigan Chronicle, "Super Sacrifice for Ballard," 11/14/70.
Time, "Lady Sings the Blues Review," 11/6/72.
Time, "Stopped in the Name of Indifference," 7/24/00.
Billboard, Archives, 1964–1970.

SINGLES

Label and Catalogue Number	Title (Writing Credits)[a]	Release Date	Highest Chart Position (R&B[b])
	THE PRIMETTES		
1960			
LuPine LR120	"Tears of Sorrow" (R. Morrison) "Pretty Baby" (R. Morrison)	3/11	
	THE SUPREMES		
1961			
Tamla 54038 (also issued as Motown 1008)	"I Want a Guy" (F. Gorman, B. Holland, B. Gordy)/"Never Again" (B. Gordy)	3/9	
Tamla 54045	"Buttered Popcorn" (B. Gordy, B. Ales) "Who's Lovin' You" (S. Robinson)	7/21	
1961			
Motown 1027	"Your Heart Belongs to Me" (S. Robinson) "(He's) Seventeen" (R. Liles, M. Johnsson)	5/8	95
Motown 1034	"Let Me Go the Right Way" (B. Gordy) "Time Changes Things" (B. Holland, J. Bradford, L. Dozier)	11/5	90 (26)
MTS-1	Motor Town Special Promo for first Motortown Revue; includes the Supremes talking over "Let Me Go the Right Way"		
1963			
Motown 1040	"My Heart Can't Take It No More" (C. Paul)/"You Bring Back Memories" (S. Robinson)	2/2	129

[a]All songs in the Diana Ross era written by Holland-Dozier-Holland unless otherwise noted.

[b]Chart positions for single releases per *Billboard*'s Hot 100 and Bubbling Under the Top 100 charts; for albums, per *Billboard*'s Hot Albums charts. From 1963 to 1965 there was no *Billboard* R&B chart; positions for those years per the Cashbox R&B chart.

SINGLES

Label and Catalogue Number	Title (Writing Credits)	Release Date	Highest Chart Position (R&B)
1963 (continued)			
Motown 1044	"A Breath Taking, First Sight Soul Shaking, One Night Love Making, Next Day Heart Breaking Guy" (S. Robinson)/"Rock and Roll Banjo Band" (C. Paul, B. Gordy)		
Motown 1044 (replaced previous)	"A Breath Taking Guy" "Rock and Roll Band"	6/12	75
Motown 1051	"When the Lovelight Starts Shining Through His Eyes"/"Standing at the Crossroads of Love"	10/31	23 (2)
1964			
Motown 1054	"Run, Run, Run" "I'm Giving You Your Freedom"	2/7	93 (22)
Motown 1060	"Where Did Our Love Go" "He Means the World to Me"	6/17	1 (1)
Motown 1066	"Baby Love" "Ask Any Girl"	9/17	1 (1)
Motown 1068	"Come See About Me" "Always in My Heart"	10/27	1 (3)
Hitsville U.S.A DM 097311	"Greetings to the Tamla Motown Appreciation Society" (promo for first Motortown European tour)		
1965			
Motown 1074	"Stop! In the Name of Love" "I'm in Love Again"	2/8	1 (2)
Motown 1075	"Back in My Arms Again" "Whisper You Love Me Boy"	4/15	1 (1)
Motown 1079	Supremes' Interview/"The Only Time I'm Happy" (Special Premium 45)		
Motown 1080	"Nothing But Heartaches" "He Holds His Own"	7/16	11(6)
Motown 1083	"I Hear a Symphony" "Who Could Ever Doubt My Love"	10/6	1 (2)
EEOC Sl4m 3114	"Things Are Changing" (promo for The Equal Employment Opportunity Commission; written and produced by Phil Spector)		

SINGLES

Label and Catalogue Number	Title (Writing Credits)	Release Date	Highest Chart Position (R&B)
1965 (continued)			
Motown 1085	"Children's Christmas Song" (H. Fuqua, (I. Freeman)/"Twinkle, Twinkle, Little Me" (R. Miller, W. O'Malley)	11/18	7[c]
Motown 1089	"My World Is Empty Without You" "Everything Is Good About You" (J. Dean, E. Holland)	12/29	5 (10)
1966			
American Int. Pictures	"Dr. Goldfoot and the Bikini Machine" (G. Hemric, J. Styner) (single-sided 45 used to promote the film)		
Motown L-294m05	"I Wanna Mother You, Smother You with Love" (as "Christine Schumacher with the Supremes," winner of "Record a Record with the Supremes" Contest)		
Motown 1094	"Love Is Like an Itching in My Heart"/"He's All I Got" (Holland-Dozier-Holland, J. Dean)	4/8	9 (7)
Motown 1097	"You Can't Hurry Love" "Put Yourself in My Place"	7/25	1 (1)
Motown 1101	"You Keep Me Hangin' On" "Remove This Doubt"	10/12	1 (1)
1967			
Motown 1103	"Love Is Here and Now You're Gone" "There's No Stopping Us Now"	1/11	1 (1)
Colgems Music Corp	"The Happening" (promo 45 for the film)		
Motown 1107	"The Happening"/"All I Know About You"	3/20	1 (12)
PDMN 0375 FHLL	"We Couldn't Make It Without You" (one-sided acetate made for Berry Gordy)		
City of Detroit M 1900 7568e1	"Detroit Is Happening" (altered version of "The Happening")		
Topps/Motown 1,2,3,15,16	1."Baby Love"; 2."Stop! In the Name of Love"; 3. "Where Did Our Love Go"; 15. "Come See About Me"; 16. "My World Is Empty Without You" (special promotion of cardboard records)		

---

[c] *Billboard*'s Hot 100 Holiday chart

SINGLES

Label and Catalogue Number	Title (Writing Credits)	Release Date	Highest Chart Position (R&B)

DIANA ROSS AND THE SUPREMES

1967

Motown 1111	"Reflections" "Going Down for the Third Time"	7/24	2 (4)
Motown 1116	"In and Out of Love" "Guess I'll Always Love You"	10/28	9 (16)

1968

Motown 1122	"Forever Came Today" "Time Changes Things" (B. Holland, J. Bradford, L. Dozier)	2/24	28 (17)
Motown 1125	"What the World Needs Now" (B. Bacharach, H. David)/"Your Kiss of Fire" (Fuqua/R. Gordy) (unreleased)		
Motown 1126	"Some Things You Never Get Used To" (Ashford, Simpson)/"You've Been So Wonderful to Me" (A. Gordy, A. Gaye, G. Gordy, A. Story)	5/21	30 (43)
Motown 1135	"Love Child" (H. Cosby, F. Wilson, P. Sawyer, D. Richards, R. Taylor) "Will This Be the Day" (B. Verdi, S. Robinson, P. Moore)	9/30	1 (2)
Motown 1137	"I'm Gonna Make You Love Me" (K. Gamble, L. Huff, J. Ross)/"A Place in the Sun" (B. Wells, R. Miller, C. Paul) (with the Temptations)	11/21	2 (2)
Motown 1139	"I'm Livin' in Shame" (H. Cosby, P. Sawyer, F. Wilson, R. Taylor, B. Gordy)/"I'm So Glad I Got Somebody" (L. Brown, G. Gordy, A. Story, A. Gaye)	1/6	10 (8)
Motown 1142	"I'll Try Something New" (S. Robinson) "The Way You Do the Things You Do" (S. Robinson, B. Rodgers) (with the Temptations)	2/20	25 (8)

1969

Motown 1146	"The Composer" (S. Robinson) "The Beginning of the End" (D. Lussier, D. Dean, R. Taylor)	3/27	27 (21)

SINGLES

Label and Catalogue Number	Title (Writing Credits)	Release Date	Highest Chart Position (R&B)

1969 (continued)

Motown 1148	"No Matter What Sign You Are" (H. Cosby, B. Gordy)/"The Young Folks" (A. Story, G. Gordy)	5/9	31 (17)
Motown 1153	"The Weight" (R. Robertson)/"For Better or Worse" (P. Sawyer, J. Hinton)	8/29	46 (33)
Motown 1156	"Someday We'll Be Together" (J. Bristol, H. Fuqua, R. Beavers) "He's My Sunny Boy" (S. Robinson)	10/14	1 (1)

ALBUMS

Label and Catalogue Number	Title-Track Listings	Release Date	Highest Chart Position (R&B)

Note: There have been literally dozens of Supremes' albums since 1970, with at least one or two released nearly every year, including several in 2008. These albums—emanating not only from Motown but also from many independent labels that have leasing arrangements with Motown, such as Time-Life, Hip-O Select, Rhino, and Madacy—include compilations, retrospective packages, anthologies, "Masters" collections, re-releases, never-before-released material (e.g., *There's a Place for Us*), imports, rarities, box-sets (the gold standard being the 2000 five-CD *The Supremes*, with the bonus performance disk omitted in subsequent issues), original masters, re-masters, studio out-takes, and live concert videos, and can be found in vinyl, CD, and DVD (e.g., *Live in Amsterdam*) formats; there are also a number of bootleg albums available. It may well be impossible to know exactly how many of these albums exist; even Motown may have lost track of all the repackaged material it has released of its '60s songs through the years, and the Supremes likely are the most regurgitated act in the history of recorded music. The major Motown acts, as well, appear on an indeterminate number of Motown anthologies (e.g., *The Motown Story* and the *Motown Chartbusters* series) and on DVDs such as the *Ed Sullivan Rock 'n' Roll Classics* series. For as comprehensive as possible a listing of the Supremes' '60s and post-'60s albums, singles, and EPs, both originals and reissues, and of their availability, any dedicated Supremes aficionado or collector is urged to visit the Discogs website at http://www .discogs.com/artist/Supremes,+The or http://rateyourmusic.com/artist/the_ supremes.

THE SUPREMES

1964

| Motown 606 | *Meet the Supremes* "Your Heart Belongs to Me"/"Who's Lovin' You"/ "Baby Don't Go"/"Buttered Popcorn"/ "I Want a Guy"/"Let Me Go the Right Way" | 12/9 | |

ALBUMS

Label and Catalogue Number	Title-Track Listings	Release Date	Highest Chart Position (R&B)

1964 (continued)

Motown 606 (continued):
"You Bring Back Memories"/"Time Changes Things"/"Play a Sad Song"/"Never Again"/"(He's) Seventeen"

Motown 621	*Where Did Our Love Go* "Where Did Our Love Go"/"Run Run Run"/"Baby Love"/"When the Love Light Starts Shining Through His Eyes"/"Come See About Me"/"Long Gone Lover"/"I'm Giving You Your Freedom"/"A Breath Taking Guy"/"He Means the World to Me"/"Standing at the Crossroads of Love"/"Your Kiss of Fire"/"Ask Any Girl"	8/31	2 (1)
Motown 623	*A Bit of Liverpool* "How Do You Do It"/"World Without Love"/"House of the Rising Sun"/"A Hard Day's Night"/"Because"/"You've Really Got a Hold on Me"/"You Can't Do That"/"Do You Love Me"/"Can't Buy Me Love"/"I Want to Hold Your Hand"/"Bits and Pieces"	10/16	21 (5)
Motown 625	*The Supremes Sing Country and Western and Pop* "Funny How Time Slips Away"/"My Heart Can't Take It No More"/"It Makes No Difference Now"/"You Didn't Care/"Tears in Vain"/"Tumbling Tumbleweeds"/"Lazy Bones"/"You Need Me"/ "Baby Doll"/"Sunset"/"(The Man with the) Rock and Roll Banjo Band"	2/22	
Motown 626	*The Supremes Recorded Live!* (unreleased)		
Motown 629	*We Remember Sam Cooke* Tracks: "You Send Me"/"Nothing Can Change This Love"/"Cupid"/"Chain Gang"/"Bring It on Home to Me"/"Only Sixteen"/"Havin' a Party"/"Shake"/"Wonderful World"/"A Change Is Gonna Come"/"(Ain't That) Good News"	4/12	75 (5)
Motown 627	*More Hits by the Supremes* Tracks: "Ask Any Girl"/"Nothing But Heartaches"/"Mother Dear"/"Stop! In the Name of Love"/"Honey Boy"/"Back in My Arms Again"/"Whisper You Love Me Boy"/"The Only Time I'm Happy"/"He Holds His Own"/"Who Could Ever Doubt My Love"/"(I'm So Glad) Heartaches Don't Last Always"/"I'm in Love Again"	7/23	1 (6)

ALBUMS

Label and Catalogue Number	Title-Track Listings	Release Date	Highest Chart Position (R&B)

1964 (continued)

Motown 628   *There's a Place for Us* (unreleased)

Motown 635   *Tribute to the Girls* (unreleased)

Motown 636   *The Supremes at the Copa* Tracks: Opening Introduction/"Put on a Happy Face"/"I Am Woman"/"Baby Love"/"Stop! In the Name of Love"/"The Boy from Ipanema"/"Make Someone Happy"/"Come See About Me"/"Rock-a-Bye Your Baby with a Dixie Melody"/"Queen of the House"/ "Group Introduction"/"Somewhere"/"Back in My Arms Again"/"Sam Cooke Medley"/ "You're Nobody 'Til Somebody Loves You"   11/1   11 (6)

Motown 638   *Merry Christmas, The Supremes* Tracks: "White Christmas"/"Silver Bells"/"Born of Mary"/"Children's Christmas Song"/"The Little Drummer Boy"/"My Christmas Tree"/ "Rudolph the Red-Nosed Reindeer"/"Santa Claus Is Coming to Town"/"My Favorite Things"/ "Twinkle Twinkle Little Me"/"Little Bright Star"/ "Joy to the World"   11/1   6[d]

1966

Motown 643   *I Hear a Symphony* Tracks: "Stranger in Paradise"/"Yesterday"/"I Hear a Symphony"/"Unchained Melody"/"With a Song in My Heart"/"Without a Song"/"My World Is Empty Without You"/"A Lover's Concerto"/"Any Girl in Love (Knows What I'm Going Through)"/"Wonderful Wonderful"/"Everything Is Good About You"/ "He's All I Got"   2/18   8 (1)

Motown 648   *Pure Gold* (Unreleased)

Motown 649   *Supremes A Go-Go* Tracks: "Love Is Like an Itching in My Heart"/"This Old Heart of Mine (Is Weak for You)"/"You Can't Hurry Love"/"Shake Me Wake Me (When It's Over)"/"Baby I Need Your Loving"/"These Boots Are Made for Walking"/"I Can't Help Myself"/"Get Ready"/"Put Yourself in My Place"/"Money (That's What I Want)"/"Come and Get These Memories"/"Hang On Sloopy"   8/25   1 (1)

----

[d] *Billboard*'s Hot 100 Holiday chart

ALBUMS

Label and Catalogue Number	Title-Track Listings	Release Date	Highest Chart Position (R&B)

1967 (continued)

Motown 650	*The Supremes Sing Holland-Dozier-Holland* Tracks: "You Keep Me Hangin' On"/"You're Gone (But Always in My Heart)"/"Love Is Here and Now You're Gone"/"I Wanna Mother You, Smother You with Love"/"I Guess I'll Always Love You"/"I'll Turn to Stone"/"It's the Same Old Song"/"Going Down for the Third Time"/"Love Is in Our Hearts"/"Remove This Doubt/"There's No Stopping Us Now"/"Love Is Like a Heat Wave"	1/23	6 (1)
Motown 656	*Supremes and the Motown Sound* (unreleased)		
Motown 659	· *The Supremes Sing Rodgers and Hart* (Originally planned as a double album; songs recorded but not released appear on the *Supremes 25th Anniversary Album*, Motown 5381ML3.) Tracks: "The Lady Is a Tramp"/"Mountain Greenery"/"This Can't Be Love"/"Where or When"/"Lover"/"My Funny Valentine"/"My Romance"/"My Heart Stood Still"/"Falling in Love with Love"/"Thou Swell"/"Dancing on the Ceiling"/"Blue Moon"	5/22	20 (3)

DIANA ROSS AND THE SUPREMES

1967

Motown 663	*Diana Ross and the Supremes Greatest Hits, Volumes 1 & 2* (2-LP set) Tracks: Disc 1: "When the Lovelight Starts Shining Through His Eyes"/"Where Did Our Love Go"/"Ask Any Girl"/"Baby Love"/"Run Run Run"/"Stop! In the Name of Love"/"Back in My Arms Again"/"Come See About Me"/"Nothing But Heartaches"/"Everything Is Good About You"; Disc 2: "I Hear a Symphony"/"Love Is Here and Now You're Gone"/"My World Is Empty Without You"/"Whisper You Love Me Boy"/"The Happening"/"You Keep Me Hangin' On"/"You Can't Hurry Love"/"Standing at the Crossroads of Love"/"Love Is Like an Itching in My Heart"/"There's No Stopping Us Now" (Reissued as two separate albums in 1986: *Greatest Hits* and *Greatest Hits Volume 2.*)	8/29	1 (1)
Motown 656	*The Supremes and the Motown Sound* (unreleased)		

ALBUMS

Label and Catalogue Number	Title-Track Listings	Release Date	Highest Chart Position (R&B)
1968			
Motown 665	*Reflections* Tracks: "I'm Gonna Make It (I Will Wait for You)"/"Forever Came Today"/"I Can't Make It Alone"/"In and Out of Love"/"Bah-Bah-Bah"/"What the World Needs Now Is Love"/"Up Up and Away"/"Love (Makes Me Do Foolish Things)"/"Then"/"Misery Makes Its Home in My Heart"/"Ode to Billie Joe"	3/25	18 (3)
Motown 676	*Live at London's Talk of the Town* Tracks: Medley: "With a Song in My Heart"–"Stranger in Paradise"–"Wonderful Wonderful"–"Without a Song"/Medley: "Stop! in the Name of Love"–Come See About Me"–"My World Is Empty Without You"–"Baby Love"/"Love Is Here and Now You're Gone"/"More"/"You Keep Me Hangin' On"/Medley: "Michelle"–"Yesterday"/"In and Out of Love"/Medley: "The Lady Is a Tramp"–"Let's Get Away from It All"/"The Happening"/Medley: "Thoroughly Modern Millie"–"Second Hand Rose"–"Mama"/"Reflections"/"You're Nobody Till Somebody Loves You"	8/26	57 (6)
Motown 672	Tracks: "Funny Girl"/"If a Girl Isn't Pretty"/"I Am Woman"/"The Music That Makes Me Dance"/"Don't Rain on My Parade"/"People"/"Cornet Man"/"His Love Makes Me Beautiful"/"Sadie Sadie"/"I'm the Greatest Star"	8/26	150
Motown 642	*In Loving Memory* (Memorial album to Loucye Gordy Wakefield) Various Artists. Includes "He"	9/68	
Motown 679	*Diana Ross & the Supremes Join the Temptations* Tracks: "Try It Baby"/"I Second That Emotion"/"Ain't No Mountain High Enough"/"I'm Gonna Make You Love Me"/"This Guy's in Love With You"/"Funky Broadway"/"I'll Try Something New"/"A Place in the Sun"/"Sweet Inspiration"/"Then"/"The Impossible Dream"	11/8	2 (1)

ALBUMS

Label and Catalogue Number	Title-Track Listings	Release Date	Highest Chart Position (R&B)

1968 (continued)

Motown 670 — *Love Child* Tracks: "Love Child"/"Keep an Eye"/"How Long Has That Evening Train Been Gone"/"Does Your Mama Know About Me"/"Honey Bee (Keep on Stinging Me)"/ "Some Things You Never Get Used To"/"He's My Sunny Boy"/"You've Been So Wonderful to Me"/"You Ain't Livin' Till You're Lovin'"/ "(Don't Break These) Chains of Love"/"I'll Set You Free"/"Can't Shake It Loose" — 11/13 — 14 (3)

Motown 681 — *Merry Christmas from Motown* Various Artists. Includes "Santa Claus Is Comin' to Town"; "My Christmas Tree"; "Silver Bells" by Diana Ross and the Supremes — 12/68

Motown 682 — *T.C.B.* (Original Soundtrack) Diana Ross and the Supremes and the Temptations. Tracks: "T.C.B"/"Stop! In the Name of Love"/ Introduction of Diana Ross & Supremes/ "You Keep Me Hangin' On"/Introduction of the Temptations/"Get Ready"/Introduction of Diana Ross/"The Way You Do the Things You Do"/Medley: "A Taste of Honey"–"Eleanor Rigby"–"Do You Know the Way to San Jose"– "Mrs. Robinson"/"Respect"/"Somewhere"/ "Ain't Too Proud to Beg"/Introduction of the Temptations/"Hello Young Lovers"/"For Once in My Life"/"(I Know) I'm Losing You"/ Medley: "With a Song in My Heart"–"Without a Song"/Medley: "Come See About Me"–"My World Is Empty Without You"–"Baby Love"/ "I Hear a Symphony"/"The Impossible Dream" — 12/2 — 1 (1)

1969

Motown 689 — *Let the Sunshine In* Tracks: "The Composer"/"Everyday People"/"No Matter What Sign You Are"/"Hey Western Union Man"/"What Becomes of the Broken Hearted"/"I'm Livin' in Shame"/"Aquarius"/ "Let the Sunshine In"/"Let the Music Play"/ "With a Child's Heart"/"(And You'll Discover Love)"/"Will This Be the Day"/"Somebody (Like You Around)" — 5/26 — 24 (7)

Motown 692 — *Together* Diana Ross and the Supremes and the Temptations. Tracks: "Stubborn Kind of Fellow"/"I'll Be Doggone"/"The Weight"/"Ain't Nothing Like the Real Thing"/ — 9/23 — 28 (6)

ALBUMS

Label and Catalogue Number	Title-Track Listings	Release Date	Highest Chart Position (R&B)

1969 (continued)

"Uptight (Everything's Alright)"/
"Sing a Simple Song"/"My Guy–My Girl"/
"For Better or Worse"/"Can't Take My Eyes
off You"/"Why (Must We Fall in Love)"

Motown 694	*Cream of the Crop* Tracks: "Someday We'll Be Together"/"Can't You See It's Me"/"You Gave Me Love"/"Hey Jude"/"The Young Folks"/"Shadows of Society"/"Loving You Is Better Than Ever"/"When It's to the Top (Still I Won't Stop Giving You Love)"/"Till Johnny Comes"/"Blowin' in the Wind"/ "The Beginning of the End"	11/3	33 (3)
Motown 699	*On Broadway* (Original T.V. Soundtrack: "G.I.T. on Broadway") Diana Ross and the Supremes & the Temptations Tracks: "G.I.T. on Broadway"/Broadway Medley/"Malteds Over Manhattan"/Leading Lady Medley/ "Fiddler on the Roof" Medley/"Student Mountie"/"Rhythm of Life"/Finale: "Let the Sunshine In"-"Funky Broadway"-"G.I.T. on Broadway" (reprise)	11/7	38 (4)
Motown 702	*Diana Ross and the Supremes' Greatest Hits, Volume 3* Tracks: "Reflections"/"Love Is Here and Now You're Gone"/"Someday We'll Be Together"/"Love Child"/"Some Things You Never Get Used To"/"Forever Came Today"/"In and Out of Love"/"The Happening"/"I'm Livin' in Shame"/"No Matter What Sign You Are"/"The Composer"	12/18	31 (5)
Motown 703	*Motown at the Hollywood Palace* Various Artists. Includes: Medley: "Where Do I Go"- "Good Morning Starshine"; "Someday We'll Be Together"-Diana Ross & the Supremes/ "Can't Take My Eyes off You"-Diana Ross & the Supremes featuring Mary Wilson/"I'm Gonna Make You Love Me"; "For Once in My Life"-Stevie Wonder & Diana Ross	3/70	105
Motown 708	*Farewell* Diana Ross & Supremes (2-LP set) Diana Ross's last performance with the Supremes, recorded in Las Vegas on January 14, 1970. Originally released in a box-set with a 16-page booklet.		

ALBUMS

Label and Catalogue Number	Title-Track Listings	Release Date	Highest Chart Position (R&B)

1969 (continued)

Tracks: "T.C.B."/Medley: "Stop! In the Name of Love"–"Come See About Me"–"My World Is Empty Without You"–"Baby Love"/Medley: "The Lady Is a Tramp"–"Let's Get Away from It All"/"Love Is Here and Now You're Gone"/ "I'm Gonna Make You Love Me"/"Reflections"/ "My Man"/"Didn't We"/"It's All Right with Me"/ "Big Spender"/Falling in Love with Love"/ "Love Child"/"Aquarius"/"Let the Sunshine In"/"The Impossible Dream"/"Someday We'll Be Together"

SINGLES

Label and Catalogue Number	Title (Writing Credits)	Release Date	Highest Chart Position (R&B)

THE SUPREMES (1970s)

1970

Motown 1162	"Up the Ladder to the Roof" "Bill, When Are You Coming Home"	2/16	10 (5)
Motown 1167	"Everybody's Got the Right to Love" "But I Love You More"	4/10	21 (11)
Motown 1172	"Stoned Love" "Shine on Me"	10/15	7 (1)
Motown 1173	"River Deep–Mountain High" "Together We Can Make Such Sweet Music"	11/5	14 (7)

1971

Motown 1181	"You Gotta Have Love in Your Heart" "I'm Glad About It"	5/11	55 (41)
Motown 1182	"Nathan Jones" "Happy (Is a Bumpy Road)"	4/15	16 (8)
Motown 1190	"Touch" "It's So Hard for Me to Say Goodbye"	9/7	71

SINGLES

Label and Catalogue Number	Title (Writing Credits)	Release Date	Highest Chart Position (R&B)
1972			
Motown 1195	"Floy Joy" "This Is the Story"	1/15	16 (5)
Motown 1200	"Automatically Sunshine" "Precious Little Things"	4/11	37 (21)
Motown 1206	"Your Wonderful, Sweet Sweet Love" "The Wisdom of Time"	7/11	59 (22)
Motown 1213	"I Guess I'll Miss the Man" "Over and Over"	9/15	85
1973			
Motown 1225	"Bad Weather" "Oh Be My Love"	3/22	87 (74)
1975			
Motown 1357	"He's My Man" "Give Out but Don't Give Up"	6/12	(69)
Motown 1374	"Where Do I Go from Here" "Give Out but Don't Give Up"	9/5	(93)
1976			
Motown 1391	"I'm Gonna Let My Heart Do the Walking" "Early Morning Love"	3/16	40 (25)
Motown 1407	"You're My Driving Wheel" "You're What's Missing in My Life"	9/30	85 (50)
1977			
Motown 1415	"Let Yourself Go" "You Are the Heart of Me"	1/25	(83)

ALBUMS

Label and Catalogue Number	Title (Writing Credits)	Release Date	Highest Chart Position (R&B)
1970			
Motown 705	*Right On*	4/26	25 (4)
Motown 717	*The Magnificent 7* Supremes & Four Tops	9/1	113
Motown 720	*New Ways but Love Stays*	10/7	68 (12)
1971			
Motown 736	*The Return of the Magnificent 7* Supremes & Four Tops 154	8/10	

ALBUMS

Label and Catalogue Number	Title (Writing Credits)	Release Date	Highest Chart Position (R&B)
1971			
Motown 737	*Touch*	6/15	85 (6)
Motown 745	*Dynamite* Supremes & Four Tops	12/3	160 (21)
1972			
Motown 746	*Promises Kept* (unreleased)		
Motown 751	*Floy Joy*	5/17	54 (12)
Motown 756	*The Supremes* Produced and Arranged by Jimmy Webb	11/8	129 (27)
1975			
Motown 828S1	*The Supremes*	5/12	152 (25)
1976			
Motown 863S1	*High Energy*	4/1	42 (24)
Motown 873S1	*Mary, Scherrie & Susaye*	10/10	